# Preface

CW01500307

Lawrence Bragg, the centenary of whose birth we celebrate this year, has been described as one of the most successful scientists of all time: indeed the claim is made afresh, and justified, in this volume. He was a man of many talents, admired, revered and loved by those who have had the privilege of knowing him.

Editing the reminiscences collected here has been a pleasure; and we take this opportunity of thanking all the contributors for responding to our requests with enthusiasm and in such evocative terms. Selecting the papers of W.L.B.'s to be reproduced here was not an easy task. We are, however, reasonably confident that our choice properly reflects the scientific insights and achievements as well as several other aspects of the multifacetted character of the youngest–ever winner of the Nobel Prize.

John M. Thomas
*Royal Institution of Great Britain*
Sir David C. Phillips
*Advisory Board to the Scientific Councils*

# List of Contributors and Addresses

**Professor T.E. Allibone, CBE, FRS**
Emeritus Professor of Electrical Engineering, University of Leeds,
and formerly Chief Scientist, Central Electricity Generating Board

**Dr U.W. Arndt, FRS**
Laboratory of Molecular Biology, MRC, Cambridge

**Mr Stephen Bragg (Elder Son)**
Formerly Vice-Chancellor of Brunel University

**Professor S. Chandresekhar, FRS**
Raman Research Institute, Bangalore, India

**Mr W.A. Coates, MBE**
Formerly Senior Experimental Officer, Royal Institution

**Professor W. Cochran, FRS**
Emeritus Professor of Natural Philosophy, Edinburgh University

**Professor F.C.H. Crick, FRS (Nobel Laureate)**
Distinguished Research Professor, The Salk Institute, California, USA

**Professor J.D. Dunitz, FRS**
Formerly Professor of Chemical Crystallography, Swiss Federal
Institute of Technology, Zurich, Switzerland

**Professor A. Guinier**
Emeritus Professor of Physics, Université Paris–Sud, France

**Professor Dorothy Hodgkin, OM, FRS (Nobel Laureate)**
Emeritus Professor, University of Oxford

**Professor H.E. Huxley, FRS**
Director, Rosenthal Basic Medical Sciences Center, Brandeis
University of Massachusetts, USA

**Sir John C. Kendrew, CBE, FRS (Nobel Laureate)**
Formerly President of St John's College, Oxford, and Director
General of the European Molecular Biology Laboratory

**Professor R. King, FRS**
Honorary Professor of Physics, Royal Institution

**Sir Aaron Klug, FRS (Nobel Laureate)**
Director, Laboratory of Molecular Biology, MRC, Cambridge

*Selections and Reflections*

# The Legacy of Sir Lawrence Bragg

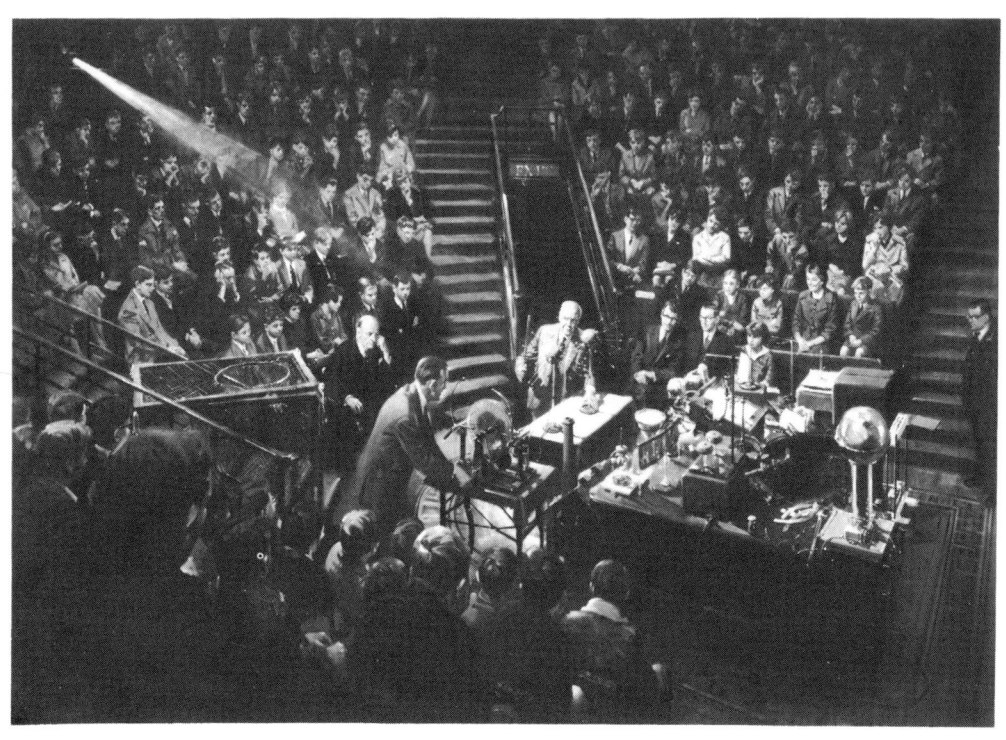

*Sir Lawrence Bragg lecturing to a young audience at the Royal Institution*

*Selections and Reflections:*

# The Legacy of Sir Lawrence Bragg

*edited by*

## John M. Thomas, FRS

## Sir David Phillips, KBE, FRS

*Production editor*

## Sara T. Nash, BSc

**British Library Cataloguing in Publication Data**
Royal Institution of Great Britain
1.Science - Periodicals
I. Title      II.  Thomas, John M.


**ISBN 0-905927-43-5**

Published by Science Reviews Ltd,
40 The Fairway,
Northwood, Middlesex HA6 3DY, UK

Printed in Great Britain by Whitstable Press, Whitstable, Kent

# Contents

**Professor H.S. Lipson, FRS**
Emeritus Professor of Physics, UMIST, Manchester

**Dr W.M. Lomer**
Formerly Director of Culham Laboratory, UK Atomic Energy Authority

**Mr S. Bruce Morris**
Formerly Maintenance and Workshop Manager, Royal Institution

**Sir Nevill Mott, FRS (Nobel Laureate)**
Formerly Cavendish Professor of Physics, University of Cambridge

**Professor L.C. Pauling, For. Mem. RS (Double Nobel Laureate)**
Research Professor of Linus Pauling Institute of Science and Technology, California, USA

**Professor Max Perutz, OM, FRS (Nobel Laureate)**
Formerly Director of Laboratory of Molecular Biology, MRC, Cambridge

**Sir David Phillips, KBE, FRS**
Chairman, Advisory Board for the Research Councils, London

**Sir Brian Pippard, FRS**
Formerly Cavendish Professor of Physics, University of Cambridge

**Professor The Lord Porter, OM, PRS (Nobel Laureate)**
President of the the Royal Society and former Director, Royal Institution

**Professor Charles Taylor**
Emeritus Professor, Royal Institution and University College Cardiff

**Professor J.M. Thomas, FRS**
Director, Royal Institution

**Mrs Patience Thomson (Daughter)**
Headmistress of Fairley House School, London

**Lord Todd, OM, PRS (Nobel Laureate)**
Formerly Master of Christ's college and Head of Department of Organic and Inorganic chemistry, University of Cambridge

**Professor R.L. Wain, CBE, FRS**
Emeritus Professor of Agricultural Chemistry, Westfield College, University of London

**Professor J.D. Watson, For. Mem. RS (Nobel Laureate)**
Director, Cold Spring Harbor laboratory, New York, USA

J C Kendrew.

W L Bragg
Oct 1964

*John Kendrew as portrayed by Sir Lawrence Bragg (drawing courtesy of Sir John C. Kendrew)*

Reprinted from
*Biographical Memoirs of Fellows of the Royal Society,* Volume 25, November 1979

# WILLIAM LAWRENCE BRAGG

## 31 March 1890 — 1 July 1971

### Elected F.R.S. 1921

### By Sir David Phillips, Sec.R.S.

WALKING along the Backs in Cambridge one day in the autumn of 1912 William Lawrence Bragg had an idea that led immediately to a dramatic advance in physics and has since transformed chemistry, mineralogy, metallurgy and, most recently, biology. He realized that the observations of X-ray diffraction by a crystal, which had been reported by von Laue and his associates earlier in that year, can be interpreted very simply as arising from reflexion of the X-rays by planes of atoms in the crystal and hence that the X-ray observations provide evidence from which the arrangement of atoms in the crystal may be determined. A few weeks of intensive work on simple inorganic compounds were enough to demonstrate the correctness of these ideas but the development of the method, at first in association with his father and later as the leader or guiding influence of a host of workers, was the labour of a lifetime. When he died on 1 July 1971, X-ray crystallography had revealed the arrangement of atoms in matter of all kinds from the simplest of salts to the macromolecules of the living cell. The story of his life is very largely the story of that achievement and the circumstances that led to his unique part in it.

### FAMILY BACKGROUND

The Bragg family (*a*)\* had its roots in Cumberland where the men farmed or went to sea. In the 1820s one of them, John Bragg, married a Workington girl, Lucy Brown, who had settled near Belfast and they had four children, William, Robert John, James Brown and Mary McCleary. When William the eldest was twelve, in about 1840, his father was lost at sea between Cumberland and Belfast. Some time later the family moved to Birkenhead where William was apprenticed to a chemist, James went into an office and, in 1846, Robert John went to sea as an indentured apprentice in the *Nereides* of Workington, 530 tons. Robert completed his apprenticeship in October 1851 and soon afterwards sailed again for India in the *Nereides*, now as second mate. The outward voyage to Calcutta was uneventful but the return had barely begun, with Robert now chief mate, when the ship was wrecked in the Hoogli River. Only Robert, four crew members and the pilot were saved.

---

\* The labels (*a*) etc. refer to the General References and (*A*) etc. and (1) etc. to the two lists (books and papers respectively) in the Bibliography.

After this disaster he went back to sea again but only until the late 1850s when he bought Stoneraise Place, near Wigton in Cumberland, and settled down to farm there in the parish of Westward within sight of the Solway Firth. In 1861, he married Mary, daughter of the Vicar, the Rev. Robert Wood and his wife Ruth (Hayton). Mary, who was 28, was remembered as a gracious figure with a natural bent for mathematics. On 2 July 1862, when Robert Bragg was returning from a visit to London to see the Great Exhibition of that year, their eldest son, William Henry, was born. Two more sons, John and James, came later.

There are few records of W. H. Bragg's early childhood, but he remembered his mother teaching him to read and then, at the age of five, going to the Westward village school. But in 1869, when he was only seven, his mother died at the early age of 36. It was Uncle William, long accustomed to thinking of himself as head of the family and now established as a chemist in Market Harborough, who came to the rescue. He had just helped to re-establish the old Grammar School in Market Harborough, and the young W. H. Bragg was promptly moved there, to live with his grandmother and uncles (James ran the grocer's shop next door).

Summer holidays were spent in Cumberland and in 1875, at his father's insistence, W. H. Bragg was sent to school at King William's College in the Isle of Man. In 1889 he was awarded an exhibition at Trinity College, Cambridge, but he stayed at school a further year before going up for the long-vacation term in July 1881. At about the same time his father retired to Ramsey, in the Isle of Man, and Market Harborough, not so far from Cambridge and dominated by Uncle William, was clearly the young man's home.

At Cambridge W.H.B.* read mathematics and in 1884 he graduated third in the class with first class honours, Third Wrangler. The following year, encouraged by J. J. Thomson, he applied for the position of Professor of Mathematics and Physics in the University of South Australia. The electors were Horace Lamb (the retiring Professor), J. J. Thomson and the Agent General, Sir Arthur Blyth, but before deciding to send out so young a man they consulted the Government Astronomer of South Australia, Charles Todd, who happened to be in London at the time. He had no objection and the 23-year-old Third Wrangler was appointed to start as soon as possible.

Up to this time W.H.B. had done very little physics, but the electors assumed that he could learn enough as he went along. On the six week voyage to Australia he read *Electricity and magnetism* by Deschanel but on arrival in Adelaide he found that the physics classes were small and elementary and was well able to keep ahead of them. One of the principal difficulties was a shortage of apparatus so he went to work with a firm of instrument makers in the town and helped to equip the laboratories himself. His head mechanic, Rogers, was a key figure who worked with him throughout his period in Australia, initially making apparatus for classes and later the apparatus designed by W.H.B. for his researches.

---

* From this point it is convenient to distinguish W. H. Bragg from his son, the subject of this memoir, by referring to him as W.H.B.

On the day after his arrival in Adelaide W.H.B. went for supper with the Todd family. Charles Todd, born in England in 1826, and his wife Alice, had been in Australia since 1855 when he was sent out from Greenwich as Government Astronomer with the particular task of installing an electric telegraph system in South Australia. Alice, who came from a Cambridge family named Bell, was 19 and already pregnant when they arrived in Adelaide, a town which had been founded only 19 years earlier by Charles Sturt and William Light and named after the Consort of William IV. By 1872, after years of surveying the bush, the overland telegraph line from Adelaide to Port Darwin in the north was completed and direct communication with Europe by the submarine cable from Darwin was made possible. The final connection was made near an oasis in central Australia, known since as Alice Springs after the Astronomer's wife. Postmaster General and Superintendent of Telegraphs, South Australia, Todd was elected F.R.S. in 1889 and appointed K.C.M.G. in 1893.

The Todds lived at the Observatory in West Terrace, Adelaide, a spacious house surrounded by paddocks and the buildings housing the offices, the transit telescope and other equipment. With six children, Elizabeth, Charles, Headley, Maude, Gwendoline and Lorna, they were at the centre of Adelaide society and they soon made the young professor a regular member of their lively circle. A happy working relationship between the two scientists was quickly established and a closer connection followed. On 1 June 1889, W.H.B. and Gwendoline Todd were married. She was just on 19, lively, sociable, without much formal education but a gifted artist who had been a star pupil at the Design School. They set up house, with a cook and a housemaid not easily managed by the young wife, in Lefevre Terrace, North Adelaide and on 31 March 1890 their elder son, William Lawrence, was born. A second son, Robert Charles, was born a year later and a daughter, Gwendolen Mary, in 1907.

ADELAIDE, 1890–1909

W. L. Bragg's earliest memories (*b*) went back to the period following the birth of his brother, Bob, when his mother was convalescing after a difficult delivery. He remembered the pleasures of listening to her stories when she was still in bed but also the indignities of being wheeled out in the pram together with his baby brother and of wearing the blue tunics with red belts and straw hats favoured by his artistic parent. Quite early a nursemaid named Charlotte Schlegel was recruited who stayed with the family for nearly 30 years. She came from the part of Denmark that was lost to Prussia in the war of 1867 which she remembered. Having a fierce and repressive temperament she sternly discouraged any games in which the participants could conceivably get dirty. Writing years after Bragg noted sadly 'I do not think my brother Bob was much affected by her—even as a child he had considerable calm self-confidence —but I was very impressionable and unsure of myself and I am certain that Charlotte was very much the wrong person for me'. Even so there was clearly plenty of fun in the backyards and tree house in Lefevre Street with Eric Gill, later well known as an artist, who lived nearby, the principal playmate.

Even more memorable were the regular Sunday visits to the Observatory, a veritable paradise for small boys with its rambling construction and exciting out-buildings. In the storerooms treasures of all kinds—souvenirs of the Todd's journeys, discarded scientific equipment, old letters and so on—provided the basis for endless play and later for the design and construction of electrical gadgets.

Holidays were spent at the seaside, either on the shore of the Gulf of St Vincent, a horse-tram ride away, or at Port Elliott on the ocean coast. Here the Bragg and Todd families combined to take a large part of a boarding house. Gwendoline Bragg sketched and coached W.H.B. also, so that in time their styles were said to be indistinguishable. W.H.B. also played games of all sorts but Bragg remembered best his happy relationship with his Aunt Lorna, then still in her teens, who 'looked after me, invented games for me, read Grimm's Fairy Tales to me and altogether constituted herself my guardian'.

Bragg started school when he was five, attending a convent school, to which he walked, on the far side of North Adelaide. Then there was a setback. Riding his tricycle one afternoon, he was overturned by his brother and shattered his left elbow. The damage was so serious that the doctor thought nothing could be done but allow the joint to set rigid. But the family intervened. Uncle Charlie (Todd) was himself a doctor and devised an heroic treatment. Every few days Bragg was anaesthetized so that his arm could be flexed to prevent stiffening while a new joint was formed. The treatment worked but he was left with a slightly short and crooked left arm and, 40 years later, in Manchester, had to have an operation to relieve pressure on a nerve that was giving rise to paralysis in his left hand.

This incident involved Bragg in his first encounter with X-rays. While working hard to develop his subjects at the University, W.H.B. took a keen interest in all the latest developments in science as news of them reached him from the other side of the world. In 1895 the greatest excitement was created by Röntgen's discovery of X-rays and W.H.B. eagerly set out to repeat the experiments in Adelaide. The apparatus was ready just in time for examination of Bragg's elbow. The scene was described later by Stanley Addison, W.H.B.'s laboratory assistant (a). 'In the area below the laboratory proper the Professor had set up a primitive X-ray apparatus based on the discovery which Dr Röntgen of Würzburg, Germany, had announced to the world a few weeks earlier. Although Professor Bragg's machine [had been] hurriedly brought into being, [it] nevertheless worked, despite its crudity, and was put into motion. Fascinated, the Doctor watched as the big induction coil buzzed loudly, electric sparks crackled and the vacuum tube emitted a weird green glow. Later on there appeared on the screen an X-ray photograph which distinctly showed the extent and location of the injury to the boy's arm. This was the first recorded surgical use of the Röntgen Ray, as it was then called, in Australia'. But W.H.B.'s son remembered (b): 'I was scared stiff by the fizzing sparks and smell of ozone and could only be persuaded to submit to the exposure after my much calmer small brother Bob had his radiograph taken to set me an example.'

An account of Röntgen's experiments, with demonstrations, was one of the university extension lectures W.H.B. gave at that time (1896) as he developed his skills and reputation as a popular lecturer. Another of his major interests was the school system in South Australia since he recognized early on that the quality of his students at the university depended in large part on how well they had been taught at school. He gave an address on this subject at the University Commemoration in 1888 and in 1897 the interest led to a momentous decision. He would take a year's leave—it was 12 years after his appointment—and study the educational system in England. But the major inducement, no doubt, was the opportunity this would provide of seeing the uncles again and introducing his family to them.

The family was divided for the journey. W.H.B. and his wife went ahead to make a tour of Egypt and Italy while the two boys followed with Charlotte and Aunt Lizzie, who was now married to a Cambridge solicitor, Charles Squires, and had been visiting her parents. The two parties were reunited at Marseilles and went on together to Market Harborough. Here the boys stayed most of the time while their father visited schools, enquired into the educational system and renewed his acquaintance with leading scientists. But they also visited W.H.B.'s cousins, William Addison and Fanny (now Kemp-Smith) and their families and they stayed in Cambridge near to the Squires family, so that Bragg and his brother Bob got to know their English cousins. And they saw the sights of London. Among many vivid memories Bragg remembered that his father started a series of bed-time stories during these holidays: 'they were always the same—about the properties of atoms'. He also remembered reading a large volume on the voyages of Captain Cook.

On returning to Adelaide the family stayed at first at the Observatory—saddened no doubt by the death of Grandmother Todd during their absence—while a new house was being built for them. It was called Catherwood House, after Uncle William's house in Market Harborough, and looked out across the park lands towards the race-course. It had a large garden in which Bragg had a plot of his own and began his life-long interest in gardening. He also went to a new school, a preparatory school named Queen's on the far side of North Adelaide, which was reached by horse-tram—with a walk at each end of the journey. The headmaster named Hood did not believe in sparing the rod and kept a supply of canes ready to discourage spelling mistakes and other misdemeanours. Looking back, Bragg decided 'I was a misfit at school, being so very immature in some ways and so precocious in others'. He remembered (b) being in the same room as a very senior class doing Euclid. 'From what I overheard I realized what it was all about. Somehow Hood must have caught on to what was happening for he pulled me, a very small boy, out of my class and made me explain the theorems to the large boys while he crowed with delight.'

When about 11 years old, he was sent to St Peter's College, the leading Church of England School in South Australia. There were between 300 and 400 day-boys and some 70 boarders under a headmaster named Girdlestone whose main distinction was a passion for good English. Bragg took English language and literature, French, Latin, Greek, scripture, mathematics and chemistry, all to an equal level. The only available subjects that he did not take were German and physics—and he always regretted learning no German. His closest friend was Bob Chapman, son of the Professor of Applied Mathematics at the University, and together they revelled in mathematics, with their fathers' help and encouragement. But again there were difficulties which Bragg attributed later to his being always in a class of older boys and too proud to play with those of his own age and stature. But 'it was a kindly school, because the boys treated me as an amusing freak instead of the teasing and bullying which might so easily have been my lot'. He was in the sixth form at 14 and at 15 his father decided that he should leave and enter the university.

This was in 1905 and the previous year had been a turning point for W.H.B. Throughout his career in Adelaide he had maintained a lively interest in the latest scientific developments and had struggled to repeat the key experiments as they were reported by the leading research workers of the day and to explain them to the interested public. His latest efforts in this direction had been particularly fruitful. In the years following his return from England he had collaborated closely with his father-in-law in emulating Marconi's experiments on wireless telegraphy which had achieved a dramatic success in 1896–97 and must have been much discussed during the visit to Europe. Together they set up a transmitter in the grounds of the Observatory and a receiving station seven miles away at Henley Beach. The successful outcome, described in a popular lecture in 1899, aroused great interest in the isolated community of South Australia and the scientists were local heroes. Bragg remembered this as his first real contact with practical science: 'Bob and I took a great interest in these experiments, especially because it meant a picnic on Sunday afternoons, when my grandfather and father drove to Henley Beach with us in the official Post Office Wagonette to see the signals coming in.' But this was not really original research and W.H.B. had no experience of that until 1904 when he was 41 years old and had been professor for 17 years.

On 7 January 1904 he was to give the Presidential address to the mathematics–physics section of the Australian Association for the Advancement of Science meeting in Dunedin, New Zealand. This was not his first lecture as President of the Section, he had been President at the Hobart meeting in 1892, but now he was to speak on Rutherford's home ground and, stimulated perhaps by the lively interest of his son, he chose to talk on 'Some recent advances in the theory of the ionization of gases'. Reading the published work of Rutherford, Mme Curie and others, he had noticed that the absorption of $\alpha$- and $\beta$-rays had been assumed to be analogous to the exponential decrease in the intensity of a wave traversing an absorbing medium and that this had led to some absurd conclusions. At the same time Mme Curie had described experiments which implied that all of the $\alpha$- particles emitted by radium travelled about the same distance into the surrounding air. W.H.B. realized that the $\alpha$-particles must behave 'like bullets fired into a block of wood' and that they must pass through the air atoms that they meet, losing some of their energy with each encounter. He concluded:

'It cannot be correct to say that the amount of the radiation which penetrates a distance $x$ is proportional to the expression $\exp(-ax)$: it must rather be proper to say that (1) the number of $\alpha$-particles penetrating a given distance does not alter much with distance until a certain critical value is passed, when there is a rapid fall; (2) the energy of the $\alpha$-particles penetrating a given distance gradually decreases as the distance is increased and dies out at the same critical value. These statements are the expression of what we should expect if ionization, consuming energy, were alone responsible for absorption of the radiation.'

On his return to Adelaide he obtained some radium, through the generosity of a Mr Barr-Smith, and with the assistance of R. Kleeman set out to test his ideas. They were brilliantly confirmed—$\alpha$-particles of 'four different ranges were shot out from the radium preparation'—and he was able to write to E. Rutherford and J. J. Thomson with the news. Papers describing the results were published in the *Philosophical Magazine* on 8 December 1904. In them he described the absorption of $\beta$-rays with characteristic imagery: 'the general effect will be that of a stream whose borders become ill-defined, which weakens as it goes, and is surrounded by a haze of scattered electrons. At a certain distance from the source all definition is gone and the force of the stream is spent.'

Rutherford replied promptly and generously and thereafter kept closely in touch through the regular exchange of long letters. Proposed by Lamb, with the support of Rutherford and J. J. Thomson, W. H. Bragg was elected F.R.S. on 2 May 1907.

This sudden flowering of his father's research coincided with Bragg's career as an undergraduate at Adelaide University. He read mathematics with subsidiary courses in chemistry and physics, graduating with first class honours in mathematics in 1908 at the age of 18. Most of his tuition was from his father—he even had a desk in his father's office—and from Chapman, the Professor of Applied Mathematics. At his father's suggestion he also took a course in English and was particularly pleased at winning the University prize for the best English essay 'from under the noses of the professionals'. Through it all there were detailed discussions of the latest researches with W.H.B. trying out his ideas and his papers on his son.

The most important of these ideas was broached one day just as they were boarding the horse-tram for the Observatory (*b*). W.H.B. had turned to the consideration of $\gamma$- and X-rays and, building on his earlier studies of the ionizing properties of $\alpha$- and $\beta$-rays, he questioned the commonly held view, proposed by G. G. Stokes, that X-rays are formless pulses of electromagnetic radiation caused by the electrons in the X-ray tube hitting the anticathode. Instead, arguing from the similarities between X- and $\gamma$-rays, he suggested that many of the properties of these rays are easier to explain if the rays are supposed to consist mainly of neutral pairs of material particles (*d*). In a paper 'On the properties and natures of various electric radiations' published in 1907, he compared the known properties of the various rays ($\alpha$-, $\beta$-, X- and $\gamma$-rays and ultraviolet light) and discussed 'the possibility that $\gamma$- and X-rays may be of a material nature'. He noted that earlier corpuscular theories of $\gamma$- and X-rays had been discounted because 'it was always felt that the difficulty of accounting for the great penetration of these radiations was insuperable' and he argued that this difficulty 'was quite exaggerated and even imaginary' since neutral pairs, consisting perhaps of one α or positive particle [the charge of an α particle was not yet known] and one β or negative particle' would be expected to have weak ionizing power and hence great penetration. On the other hand, if X-rays were electromagnetic pulses which spread as they travelled why did they not ionize most of the atoms as they passed through a gas, instead of the relatively few actually observed, and how could a spreading pulse concentrate enough energy on an atom to ionize it.

But many physicists at this time believed that X-rays had been shown un-equivocally to be electromagnetic pulses by the experiment of C. G. Barkla. These experiments were inspired by J. J. Thomson's theory of X-ray scattering which showed that X-rays, regarded as unpolarized electromagnetic waves, should be scattered through an angle $\theta$ with intensity proportional to $(1 + \cos^2 \theta)$. In single-scattering and double-scattering experiments Barkla showed that the scattering of relatively soft X-rays is consistent with this formula and that the X-rays can be polarized. Naturally a controversy developed, with Barkla the chief proponent of the ether-pulse theory. It was conducted mainly in *Nature* and the *Philosophical Magazine* and it stimulated both W.H.B. and Barkla to engage in further experiments that were concentrated initially on more detailed studies of the angular distribution of secondary X- and γ-radiation. W.H.B. emphasized the asymmetric scattering and emission of γ-rays (with higher in-tensity at $\theta = 0°$ than at 180°) which he claimed was consistent with the neutral pair theory and 'fatal to the ether-pulse theory of the γ-rays'. Barkla in reply claimed close agreement between his X-ray experiments and the predictions of the electromagnetic pulse theory but had to admit some difficulty with the harder X-rays and γ-rays: 'My argument has not been concerned with γ rays but with the type of radiation with which I am experimentally most familiar—X rays of ordinary penetrating power.'

In retrospect it is easy to see the connection between the properties of X- and γ-rays that concerned W.H.B. and the quantum properties of light but W.H.B. had not read Einstein's paper on the photoelectric effect and neither he nor Barkla saw the connection. But both made important new discoveries whose true significance was recognized later. Thus Barkla and C. A. Sadler found that secondary X-rays in general consist of two distinct types: (1) the ordinary Thomson-scattered X-rays; and (2) entirely new homogeneous X-rays, the hardness of which is *characteristic* of the emitting element. W.H.B. and J.P.V. Madsen found that γ-rays excite β-rays of the same velocity from a number of different scatterers and they proved that the velocity of the β-rays depends only on the hardness of the primary γ-rays.

Bragg followed the arguments closely, acting as a sounding board for his father's ideas: he remembered living 'in an inspiring scientific atmosphere'. Then, in 1908 at the height of the debate W.H.B. accepted the Chair of Physics at Leeds University. They left in the *Waratah* in January 1909 and arrived in Plymouth in March. The *Waratah* was lost with all hands on her next voyage.

It was more than 50 years before Bragg saw Australia again but his memory of it remained vivid. He remembered particularly the long summer holidays, in the hills or by the sea to escape the heat in the city; collecting shells on the coastal reefs (including a new *Sepia* that was called in his honour *Sepia Braggi*, Verco); galloping bareback along the sands and into the sea: and learning from his mother, together with the rest of the family, how to draw and paint. England under snow in March 1909 must have seemed very different.

## CAMBRIDGE, 1909–14

The family were left in lodgings in Plymouth while W.H.B. and his wife went into Leeds to report for duty and find a house. Initially they rented a furnished house and through the spring and early summer lived rather miserably there, surrounded by the unfamiliar grime of an industrial city. Bragg afterwards regretted not having done something more constructive in this period but eventually, following his father's example, he went up to Trinity College, Cambridge, for the long-vacation term. His brother Bob went to Oundle School, before following him to Trinity in 1912.

Bragg began by reading mathematics at Cambridge. His tutor was the Rev. E. W. Barnes, afterwards well known as a radical Bishop of Birmingham, and he attended lectures by A. N. Whitehead, G. H. Hardy and Professor A. R. Forsyth and was coached by R. A. Herman, all of Trinity. Having been unable to take the Scholarship Examination before going up he sat it in the spring of 1910—while in bed suffering from a serious attack of pneumonia—and was awarded a major scholarship in mathematics, the Master of the College commenting on the brilliant imagination shown in his essays. In the Part I examinations he gained first class honours in mathematics, and then, strongly urged by his father, he transferred to physics for Part II of the degree course. C. T. R. Wilson, who ran the practical class at that time and lectured on optics, made the strongest impression and left him with a love of physical optics which never deserted him. But he also remembered dull lectures from Searle on heat, stimulating fireworks from J. J. Thomson (who staunchly favoured the wave-theory of X-rays) and the excitement of J. H. Jeans's lectures on statistical mechanics and the emerging quantum theory. One of his letters home (*b*) recounts in detail Jeans's discussion of the black-body radiation of a cavity, showing that the observed energy distribution cannot be derived from Maxwell's equations but without mentioning Planck's quantum hypothesis of 1900. He wrote 'I got an awful lot from a Dane who had seen me asking Jeans questions, and after the lecture came up to me and talked over the whole thing. He was awfully sound on it, and most interesting, his name was Böhr or something that sounds like it.' Bohr soon went on to Rutherford in Manchester but he remained one of Bragg's friends for life.

Bragg sat the final examination in Part II Physics in 1911, gaining first class honours, and he spent his third year mainly doing 'a crude research into the velocity of ions in various gases, suggested by J. J. Thomson' (*c*). It was not an

encouraging experience since, contrary to popular belief, the facilities for research in the Cavendish at that time were extremely primitive. The large number
of research workers attracted there by J. J. Thomson's reputation quite over-
whelmed the meagre resources. Bragg remembered for example: 'that there was
only one foot bellows between the forty of us for our glass blowing which we had
to carry out for ourselves, and it was very hard to get hold of it. I managed to
sneak it once from the room of a young lady researcher when she was temporarily
absent, and passing her room somewhat later I saw her bowed over her desk in
floods of tears. I did not give the foot pump back' (226).

But life in Cambridge, or more particularly in Trinity, had proved to be rewarding and provided compensations. A. L. Goodhart remembered dining
regularly in Trinity with Bragg, E. D. Adrian, F. W. Aston and G. P. Thomson,
probably during 1913, and listening fascinated to the chaffing of the scientists:
Braggs were good at experiments, Thomsons were not!

The beginnings in 1909 were not so happy, perhaps not surprisingly for a
young man away from home for the first time, but Bragg's colonial background
led to a rewarding activity. On 6 November 1909, following the example of one
of his Squires cousins, he enlisted as a Trooper in King Edward's Horse. This
Cambridge unit of the Special Reserve had been called originally 'The King's
Colonials' and was composed of men who had come from, or had some close
connection with, the colonies. They were mounted infantry and trained in the
tactics developed during the Boer War, concentrating on marksmanship, riding
and the care of horses. Joined by his brother in 1912, Bragg trained during the
year and at summer camps for four years until his discharge in November 1913.
The company seems to have produced no close friends but it must have helped
in the first experience of a new culture to have this link with the old.

It was College life that provided the closest friends. Chief among these was
Cecil Hopkinson who came from a family of engineers and was the youngest
brother of Bertram Hopkinson the Professor of Engineering in Cambridge at
that time. Hopkinson introduced Bragg to skiing, sailing, shooting and climbing
and 'dragged him into adventures which he thoroughly enjoyed once he was
launched into them'. Sailing remained a particular pleasure, though an early
cruise off the south coast of Ireland gave rise to another dangerous bout of
pneumonia. The only available hospital was the infirmary of Skibbereen Work-
house, where Bragg was looked after by nuns and spent much time in long con-
versations with the local schoolmaster, Jeremy O'Regan, who remained a life-
long friend. He went to convalesce with the Townshends at Castle Townshend, a
summer resort of hunting people. This and other adventures cemented his friendship with Cecil Hopkinson whom he regarded as a major formative influence.

At Trinity Bragg also became close friends with a group of contemporaries
who shared his interest in intellectual exploration. They formed a discussion
group, not only sitting up late discussing the world in the universal manner of
undergraduates but also reading formal papers to each other on a wide variety of
of subjects. H. Townsend was a mathematician, C. S. S. Higham a historian,
H. W. St C. Tisdall a classicist and B. S. Gossling a physicist. Bragg remembered

giving a joint paper with Townsend on Minkowski's interpretation of relativity and he remembered also a paper by Gossling on the theory of crystal structures with particular emphasis on the latest ideas of Pope and Barlow. This was Bragg's first introduction to crystallography and to the work of W. J. Pope, Professor of Chemistry in the University, 1908–39, which were soon to be of critical importance.

Throughout this undergraduate period, while enjoying new friendships and experiences, Bragg remained closely in touch with his family as they settled down in Leeds. After the initial shock, his mother had come to terms with the industrial north. Securely established in 'Rosehurst', a commodious stone home in Grosvenor Road, and with a cottage near Bolton Abbey in Wharfedale for weekends and holidays, she entered wholeheartedly into the social life of Leeds and its surroundings. According to her son, she was gregarious by nature and clever at making people enjoy themselves and these qualities found full expression in a ceaseless round of visiting, entertaining and welfare work.

For W.H.B. the move to Leeds had been less successful. Reproaching himself for his wife's initial unhappiness and engaged in organizing a large department and giving more formal lectures and courses than those he had given in Adelaide, he found little time or inspiration for new research. The controversy with Barkla was still unresolved, however, and W.H.B. continued to think and to write about the nature of the X- and γ-rays. Early in 1910 he began a correspondence with A. Sommerfeld of Munich (*d*). The occasion was the publication of papers by Sommerfeld and by J. Stark of Aachen in which they advocated rival views of the origin and nature of X-rays. Stark, apparently the first to be stimulated by Einstein, had proposed that X-ray quanta are produced when a beam of electrons collides with electrons in a metal plate and he described the individual collisions on the assumption that momentum is conserved, using the quantum value for that of the X-ray. Sommerfeld, a strong advocate of the view that X-rays are classical electromagnetic radiation, challenged Stark's theory, claiming that the experimental evidence, including the asymmetric emission of the X-rays, could be explained on the pulse theory. W.H.B.s letter to Sommerfeld (7 February 1910) admitted the difficulty he had in accounting for the polarization of X-rays with his neutral-pair theory but emphasized his belief that the difficulties that arise from the spreading of waves are even greater. Sommerfeld's reply conceded the 'weakness of his position regarding the production of the secondary rays' but claimed that 'concerning the emission of the primary rays, we are by contrast on familiar ground'. A year later Sommerfeld sent W.H.B. a reprint of the article in which he showed that if an electron moving at nearly the speed of light is brought to rest in a distance of atomic dimensions nearly all of the resultant radiation (Bremsstrahlung) is emitted into a narrow region between two concentric cones around the direction of motion of the electron. Thus, according to Sommerfeld, the radiation has 'the character of a projectile and in its energy localization is no longer appreciably different from a corpuscular radiation' (*f*). W.H.B. replied immediately (17 May 1911) 'Your hollow cone is most interesting and the ring structure of the γ-ray. But this does not meet the real difficulty to my mind. How do you propose to get the energy back again from this everspreading ring to a single electron? In other words, how are you going to account for the production of a β-ray by a γ-ray?' But he went on: 'I am very far from averse to the reconcilement of a corpuscular and a wave theory: I think that some day it must come. But at present it seems to me that it is right to think of the X- or the γ-ray as a self contained quantum which does not alter in form or any other way as it moves along. . . . My chief point is that it does not spread: and it seems that spreading is the inevitable accompaniment of the electromagnetic theory.' Finally he drew attention to C. T. R. Wilson's recently published 'pictures of the fog formed instantly after the passage of ionizing rays through a gas' noting that: 'there is no visible general fog due to the direct action of the X-rays: nor is there any corresponding effect in the γ-ray picture. All that is seen is the track of the [secondary] β-ray like a fine hair right across the chamber.'

Despite these difficulties, Sommerfeld believed at this time that only a demonstration of the diffraction of X-rays was needed to exclude every corpuscular theory of X-rays and early in 1912 he thought he had found such evidence in the diffuse broadening of the image of a wedge-shaped slit illuminated by X-rays. But he had also appointed a young assistant, Walter Friedrich, to investigate whether polarization and directional emission could be found for characteristic radiation. Meanwhile, W.H.B. had been confronted by further evidence that his neutral-pair theory was inadequate to account for all the properties of X-rays: Otto Stuhlmann and R. D. Klee discovered independently that ultraviolet light ejects β-rays asymmetrically from a thin metal plate. Thus a relationship had been established between X-rays and light, an accepted electromagnetic radiation, using the very phenomenon that he had used most often in support of his own theory. Nevertheless, while accepting more and more openly that something new was needed to embrace both the corpuscular and wave concepts, he continued to argue the case for a corpuscular theory, sustained by Whiddington's observations, clearly consistent with such a theory, that X-rays cannot excite the characteristic rays of any substance unless they have themselves been excited by cathode rays of energy exceeding a certain limit. In his book *Studies in radioactivity*' which was published in 1912, he wrote: 'it still seems to me that the neutral pair theory correctly pictures the chief processes of the X-ray, which the old form of the spreading pulse, even the modified Thomson's pulse, are unable to do. But I should now add that we ought to search for a possible scheme of greater comprehensiveness, under which the light wave and the corpuscular X-ray may appear as the extreme presentments of some general effect'.

It was another ten years before A. Compton showed that X-rays are scattered by matter in two ways: for the soft X-rays studied by Barkla, Thomson scattering predominates; for γ-rays and hard X-rays the asymmetric Compton scattering is the more important. And it was longer still before it was accepted that both radiation and matter have particle-like and wave-like properties. Meanwhile, the balance of the argument was pushed dramatically to the side of the wave theory as the result of experiments conducted by W. Friedrich and P. Knipping at the suggestion of Max von Laue in Sommerfeld's Institute for Theoretical Physics in Munich.

These experiments and the ideas underlying them have often been described. (Ewald (*e*), who played a major part in the story, and Forman (*f*) give most detail in somewhat contradictory efforts to recapture the scientific climate of the time.) In brief, Ewald had worked out the theory governing the interaction of electromagnetic radiation with a simple orthorhombic lattice of dipoles and he sought to discuss his results with Laue. Without going deeply into the theory, Laue was struck by the possibility that a crystal irradiated with X-rays might give diffraction effects, if X-rays were indeed electromagnetic radiation. He therefore persuaded Friedrich and Knipping to try an experiment. Friedrich and Knipping first irradiated a copper sulphate crystal and subsequently zinc sulphide (ZnS) and various other crystals of cubic symmetry and observed that the X-rays were scattered by the crystals in discrete directions close to the direction of the incident X-ray beam. The pattern of spots made by the scattered X-rays on a photographic plate depended upon the orientation of the crystal and upon its symmetry so that, for example, cubic crystals irradiated along a four-fold axis gave a characteristic four-fold pattern of spots, though the intensities and absolute positions of the spots varied from substance to substance.

An account of these experiments, with an introduction by Laue on the theory of diffraction by a three-dimensional lattice, was presented at a meeting of the Bavarian Academy on 8 June 1912 followed on 6 July 1912 by Laue's attempt to explain in detail the effects observed with ZnS (*e*).

Unfortunately, after his faultless derivation of the basic conditions for diffraction from a three-dimensional lattice, Laue went wrong in his consideration of the experimental results with ZnS. First, in order to estimate the size of the unit cell of the ZnS crystal structure (which was, of course, unknown at the time and which he needed to derive the wavelengths of the X-rays) Laue assumed that ZnS has a primitive cubic structure with one ZnS molecule per unit cell whereas in fact, as we shall see, the structure is face-centred cubic with four ZnS molecules per cell. Secondly, and more disastrously, he was preoccupied with the idea that the observed effects were associated with characteristic X-rays arising in the crystal. Consequently he sought to explain the results in terms of a limited number of X-ray wavelengths and showed that, *if the conditions for diffraction need be fulfilled only approximately*, the observed spots could be explained in terms of only five different wavelengths. He noticed that some additional spots should be expected to appear, but nevertheless he was strongly persuaded by his success in explaining the observed spots that the phenomenon could be explained by diffraction and hence that it established the wave nature of X-rays.

The papers of Laue and his colleagues appeared in late August 1912 and aroused intense interest, but the conclusions were not immediately accepted, even by convinced advocates of the wave theory. Thus Barkla, writing to Rutherford on 29 October 1912, remarked 'I have had a copy of Laue's paper for some little time and certainly am sceptical of any interference interpretation of the results. A number of features do not point that way . . . this in no way affects my absolute confidence of the truth of the wave theory of X-rays' (*f*). The confusion and the lack of understanding of Laue's theory is well illustrated by the fact that Laue himself, in March 1913 (*e*), was arguing that the effects could not be due to the interaction of a crystal with a continuous range of X-ray wavelengths since this would lead (by analogy with the properties of a simple diffraction grating) to the photographic plate being blackened everywhere. If he had followed up his initial discussion with Ewald, who shortly showed his mastery of the theory, this story would have been different.

Bragg and his father were of course deeply interested in this new evidence on the nature of X-rays and they had the details in time to discuss them during the family holiday, which was spent in 1912 as guests of Leeds friends at Cloughton on the Yorkshire coast. Naturally the first thought was to explain the results in terms of corpuscles and on returning to Leeds Bragg set up an experiment to test whether the spots on the photographs might be due to neutral particles shooting down the avenues between rows of atoms in the crystal structure. The same idea had occurred to Stark (1912) in Aachen and it led to the first mention of Bragg in a published paper. In a letter to *Nature*, written on 18 October 1912, W.H.B. (*g*) noted 'a fact which my son pointed out to me, *viz.* that all the directions of the secondary pencils in this position of the crystal are "avenues" between the crystal atoms'.

Back in Cambridge, Bragg continued to think about Laue's papers and here several bits of knowledge came together to provide the answer. First he remembered that J. J. Thomson had lectured on Stokes's theory of X-rays as very short pulses of electromagnetic radiation, picturing an electron moving with its associated lines of force and X-rays as the whip crack which would run along these lines when the motion of the electron is arrested suddenly at the anti-cathode of the X-ray tube. Next he recalled C. T. R. Wilson's lectures on the nature of white light which had shown (following Schuster)* that white light could be regarded either as a combination of light of all wavelengths, each wavelength being diffracted at the appropriate angle by a diffraction grating, or as a succession of formless pulses which the lines of the grating converted into a train of waves. Then, drawing on the ideas about crystal lattices that his friend Gossling had described at one of their discussion meetings and remembering that the Laue spots became increasingly elliptical as the photographic plate was moved further from the crystal, he had the idea that the formless X-ray pulses could be regarded as reflected by sheets of atoms in the crystals. The pulses reflected from successive equidistant sheets then would form a wave train, just as in Wilson's treatment of the diffraction grating. Since the path difference between the waves of the reflected train is $2d \sin \theta$, where $\theta$ is the glancing angle at which the radiation falls on the planes and $d$ is their spacing, it followed immediately that the wavelengths ($\lambda$) of the different orders of reflexion

---

* In the preface to the second edition of his textbook (*h*), Schuster notes 'the treatment of white light and of interference problems has been made more consistent—and I hope clearer—by introducing the theory of impulses at an earlier stage'.

would be given by

$$n\lambda = 2d \sin \theta,$$

where $n$ is an integer.

The critical test was to see whether these ideas explained the observations from ZnS, including the absence of some spots predicted by Laue's analysis. Here Bragg inverted the argument and used the fact that the X-ray pulses can be regarded as equivalent to a 'white-light' spectrum extending over a characteristic range of wavelengths and with maximum energy at a certain wavelength. The intensities of the Laue spots ought, therefore, to fall in a regular series depending upon which part of the spectrum was responsible for each of them. Examination showed that this did not work.

At this juncture Gossling's talk on crystal structures again came to the rescue since his discussion of Pope's ideas ($i$) had embraced not only the simple cubic lattice but also the face-centred lattice. Remembering this Bragg tried to explain the ZnS pattern on the assumption that the structure is face-centred cubic and everything fell into place. Thus he showed that the Laue pictures were made by a continuous range of X-ray wavelengths, a kind of 'white' radiation, and that X-ray diffraction could be used to get information about the crystal structure. This was the start of the X-ray analysis of crystals.

The work was described (1) at a meeting of the Cambridge Philosophical Society on 11 November 1912 and briefly reported in *Nature* of 5 December, though not before W.H.B. ($j$) had remarked in another letter (28 November) 'my son has given a theory which makes it possible to calculate the positions of the spots for all dispositions of crystal and photographic plate'.

The paper, which appeared in January 1913, was called 'The diffraction of short electromagnetic waves by a crystal' because Bragg was still unwilling to relinquish his father's views that the X-rays were particles; he thought they might possibly be particles accompanied by waves. W.H.B., however, did not cling to his ideas but, noting that 'the problem then becomes, it seems to me, not to decide between two theories of X-rays but to find one theory which possesses the capacities of both' ($j$) he went on vigorously to exploit the new possibilities. At this stage they began to lead in two directions, towards the analysis of crystal structures and studies of the nature of X-rays.

Naturally enough, Pope was very pleased at the support for his theories provided by this work on ZnS and he suggested to Bragg that studies of the alkali halides NaCl, KCl, KBr and KI might be even more rewarding, presenting him with suitable crystals. 'The Laue pictures which they gave were simpler than those of zinc blende and led to a complete solution of their structure. These were the first crystals to be analysed by X-rays' (G). But before these results of Bragg's individual work were published (5) there had been other developments.

During the discussion following the presentation of Bragg's epoch-making first paper (1) C. T. R. Wilson suggested to Bragg that crystals with very distinct cleavage planes such as mica might show strong specular reflection of the X-rays. Bragg tried the experiment and well remembered J. J. Thomson's excitement on seeing the still-wet photographic plate with a mirror reflection of X-rays on it (G). This observation was published in *Nature* on 12 December (2) in a letter dated 8 December, the first of Bragg's papers actually to appear in print; and it aroused great interest, not least on the part of W.H.B. who saw at once the possibility of using the effect to study the nature of reflected X-rays by methods with which he was long familiar. On 23 January 1913 (*k*), in a letter dated 17 January, W.H.B. reported in seven lines his success in measuring the ionization produced by X-rays reflected from mica. This urgency illustrates the high excitement of the time and the competitiveness: the following week Moseley and Darwin (*l*), in a letter dated 21 January, published a rather more detailed record of similar experiments in which they acknowledged the stimulus of Bragg's original observation of reflection (2) even though they seem to have had similar ideas independently (*m*).

The apparatus used by W.H.B. in this experiment was rapidly developed in Leeds into the X-ray spectrometer and with this instrument he examined in detail the reflection of X-rays from a number of crystal faces, including those of rock salt. This provided the next great discovery. 'In addition to the "white" X-irradiation of all wavelengths which Bragg had called the X-ray pulses, W.H.B. found that each metal used in the X-ray tube as source of radiation gave a characteristic X-ray spectrum of definite wavelengths, just as elements give spectra in the optical region.' This work was presented at the Royal Society on 7 April 1913 in a joint paper (4). Bragg later (*M*) disclaimed having played more than a general part in the design of the spectrometer or in its use, though his knowledge of the crystals that were studied and which he had been analysing in Cambridge must have been important. Such was the start of X-ray spectroscopy. Moseley and Darwin in similar experiments had missed the characteristic spectra, apparently through the use of too-fine collimating slits, but prompted by details communicated privately by W.H.B. they went on immediately to improve the measurements, discover the fine structure of the spectra and start the classical survey which led Moseley to establish the atomic numbers of the elements.

The development of the X-ray spectrometer by W.H.B. and Jenkinson, his instrument maker in Leeds, highlighted the inadequacies of the Cavendish Laboratory where Bragg had great difficulty in getting on with his experiments. Years later he remembered (*M*) 'When I achieved the first X-ray reflections I worked the Rumkorff coil too hard in my excitement and burnt out the platinum contact. Lincoln, the mechanic, was very annoyed as a contact cost ten shillings [a week's wages at the time], and refused to provide me with another for a month. I could never have exploited my ideas about X-ray diffraction under such conditions'. Furthermore, the X-ray spectrometer promised a far more powerful way of analysing crystal structures than the laborious and indirect method of the Laue photograph. Accordingly it was at this stage, in the early summer of 1913, that Bragg and his father began to work together during the vacations in Leeds. But the Cambridge picture was not entirely black. Pope was always helpful and, although the Professor of Mineralogy had given strict orders that no minerals should ever leave the collections, Bragg got his specimens from Hutchinson, who was then a lecturer and later became Professor (155), and he was able to take them to Leeds with him.

The next papers were published at about the same time in a somewhat strange order. In the first of them W.H.B. (*n*) derived the wavelengths of various radiations and correlated them with Barkla's characterististic radiations, making use of the structure of rock salt which had been worked out by his son, but not yet published. This paper was followed immediately by Bragg's detailed account (5) of NaCl and related structures in a paper described by Ewald (*e*) as 'the great break-through to actual crystal structure determination and to the absolute measurement of X-ray wavelengths'. The analysis depended mainly on Laue photographs taken in Cambridge, supported by some measurements with the spectrometer, and led to a conclusion that was to disturb chemists for many years that 'in sodium chloride the sodium atom has six neighbouring chlorine atoms equally close with which it might pair off to form a molecule of NaCl'.

Finally, in this group of consecutive papers, came a paper jointly by Bragg and his father (7) on the structure of the diamond. Bragg later (234) attributed the credit for this analysis mainly to W.H.B., who succeeded with the spectrometer where he had himself failed with Laue photographs, but as Ewald (*e*) points out, this paper again employed all of the arguments developed in the preceding paper. Ewald goes on to note: 'Diamond was the first example of a structure in which the effective scattering centres did not coincide with the points of a single (Bravais type) lattice. Whereas in the structures of rock salt, zinc blende and fluorite the absence of molecules in the accepted sense created an element of bewilderment, the beautiful confirmation of the tetravalency of carbon on purely optical principles made this structure and the method by which it was obtained immediately acceptable to physicists and chemists alike'.

The summer of 1913 in Leeds was described by Bragg (*G*) in glowing terms. 'The X-ray spectrometer opened up a new world. It proved to be a far more powerful method of analysing crystal structure than the Laue photographs which I had used. One could examine the various faces of a crystal in succession, and by noting the angles at which and the intensity with which they reflected the X-rays, one could deduce the way in which the atoms were arranged in sheets parallel to these faces. The intersections of these sheets pinned down the positions of the atoms in space. . . . It was like discovering an alluvial gold field with nuggets lying around waiting to be picked up. . . . It was a glorious time when we worked far into every night with new worlds unfolding before us in the silent laboratory.'

During this period W.H.B. was more interested in X-rays than he was in crystals and he left the crystal structures to Bragg whose next great paper (10) described a refined analysis of NaCl, using spectrometer measurements of the reflected intensities and went on to describe the structures of zinc blende (ZnS), fluorspar ($CaF_2$), iron pyrites ($FeS_2$) and calcite ($CaCO_3$). This paper represents further remarkable progress, in particular showing how the intensities of the reflexion must be measured and evaluated in a complete structure analysis and in demonstrating the possibility of solving structures in which atomic positions are not fixed by the symmetry but have to be found by a detailed analysis of the X-ray intensities. Iron pyrites and calcite were the first structures involving undefined atomic parameters—one in each structure.

Apart from the structure of copper (11) these were the last to be completed for publication before the outbreak of war in August 1914 brought this period to an end. But even before that happened there were signs of difficulty in the unique working relationship between father and son. As the importance of the work was recognized W.H.B., the established scientist, naturally was consulted or asked to talk about it and, however hard he tried, he did not quite avoid leaving the impression that his was the guiding part: what was no more than fair looked like parental generosity. Thus W.H.B. gave his son credit, though without mentioning him by name, in the earliest *Nature* letters (*g*, *j*) but they were still W.H.B.'s letters and Bragg's first papers came later and were over-shadowed by the first joint paper.

Then in 1913 W.H.B. described the work at the annual meeting of the British Association and was invited to the Second Solvay Conference on Physics, 27–31 October 1913. The subject was 'The structure of matter' and Laue, Pope and Barlow were there as well as W.H.B., each of them relying on Bragg's work for major parts of their presentations. They all acknowledged the importance of his contribution and the members of the Conference, including Sommerfeld, Laue, Einstein, Lorentz and Rutherford, sent him a postcard congratulating him on 'advancing the course of natural science'. But there is no doubt that a cloud remained that overshadowed his future relations with W.H.B. and was remembered 60 years later with pain mixed with gratitude for his father's part in making possible the rapid development of the work.

It was in the discussion of the Solvay Conference that Bragg, who was known to family and friends as Willy, was first referred to as W. Lawrence Bragg, to distinguish him more clearly from W.H.B.; and he used this style in his subsequent publications.

Back in Cambridge during 1914 Bragg struggled to extend his methods of analysis to more complex crystals. By this time he had a spectrometer of his father's design but work remained difficult at the Cavendish ('They keep the wretched liquid-air machines going most of the day, which makes the leaf jump all over the shop') and he did not find it easy to get on with writing the book that he and W.H.B. had planned. In a typically undated letter he wrote: 'I find it impossible to do my experiments and write the book at the same time, the book requires one to be absolutely on the spot. I nearly faint when I think of the article for the Jahrbuch. All this kind of thing does make ones brain boil so. Its a curse this continual writing'. But he kept up and extended his contacts with classical crystallographers. Barlow wrote frequently and in March Bragg spent a weekend with W. J. Sollas, the Professor of Mineralogy in Oxford, during which he had a 'great' talk with Barker and visited Moseley who was then near the end of experiments on X-ray spectroscopy that established the idea of atomic number.

In the summer of 1914 Bragg was elected to a lectureship and Fellowship at Trinity College and he occupied a set of rooms there with his close friend Cecil Hopkinson. His brother Bob was also in Trinity, in his second year as an undergraduate, and he had his first research student, E. V. Appleton. At this stage he was working on aragonite, a structure involving several undefined parameters, and writing to his father on 19 July 1914 he said: 'I have been writing up the aragonite but am a bit puzzled about the structure. I would really like to do a little more work on it. I wish I could go over it with you, I don't know quite how infallible I am.' As a postcript he added: 'Could you tell me about our programme in Germany? Where is the meeting and when?' There was no meeting: on 24 August 1914 he was commissioned as a 2nd Lieutenant in the Leicestershire Royal Horse Artillery.

### WORLD WAR I, 1914–18

On the strength of his service with King Edward's Horse and knowledge of mathematics, Bragg was posted to a Territorial battery of the Leicestershire R.H.A. and spent the first year of the war training at Diss in Norfolk. Describing this experience he wrote (*L*) 'I was very much out of my element as my knowledge of horses was not at all extensive, and my fellow officers and men were Leicestershire hunting enthusiasts'. But he managed and wrote daily letters home describing his new life and yearning to continue his research. Meanwhile, despite the war, recognition of the importance of the new crystallography was growing. In February 1915 'X-rays and crystal structure' (*A*), describing the results obtained so far, was published with a preface in which W.H.B. tried hard to put the record straight: 'I am anxious to make one point clear, viz. that my son is responsible for the "reflection" idea which has made it possible to advance, as well as for much the greater portion of the work of unravelling crystal structure to which the advance has led.' In May the Barnard Medal of Columbia University was awarded to them both jointly. Throughout the early part of 1915 there was much family discussion about W.H.B.'s move to University College London, and all the time there were exchanges about crystal structures.

Then in August 1915 everything changed. The French Army had been experimenting with a method of locating enemy guns from the sound of their firing and the War Office decided that the British Army should follow suit. Bragg was selected to do the work helped by H. Robinson, a member of Rutherford's staff in Manchester, and they left for France at the beginning of September.

Bragg has described the general principle of sound-ranging (*L*) as follows: 'A series of listening posts or microphones are situated in known positions along a base behind the front line. The time differences between the arrival of the report at the posts are measured. Suppose the sound to reach post 1 at time $T_1$, post 2 at time $T_2$ and so forth. Then if one draws a circle on the map around post 2 with radius $V(T_2 - T_1)$, where $V$ is the velocity of sound, and similar circles for the other posts, a great circle which passes through post 1 and touches the other circles represents the form of the report wave, with the gun at its centre.'

The chief requirements for an effective system were to identify the sound due to a particular gun and to record the time intervals precisely. After a study of the French equipment in the front line in the Vosges, Bragg chose the recording equipment developed by Lucien Bull of the Institut Marey in Paris. This was the most elegant and accurate of the recorders but it was complex and required photographic development of a cine film on which the displacements of galvonometer wires were recorded (*L*). The more difficult problem was to find a microphone that distinguished between the report of the gun and the shock wave associated with the shell and this was not solved until late in 1916. Bragg (240) has described how the solution was found. 'We were living in tarred felt huts in bitterly cold weather at the time and we noticed that whereas the shell wave was a deafening crack, the faint gun wave blew jets of very cold air through the readily available holes in the sides of our hut. Now I had in my unit a certain corporal Tucker, who in peace time was a lecturer at Imperial College and who had made experiments on the cooling of heated fine platinum wires by currents of air. The joint brainwave came to us, I think mainly to him, that we could use this effect. We sent to England for a supply of the thin wire. We scrounged some ammunition boxes, bored a hole in each, and stretched the wire across the hole. We incorporated this in one arm of a Wheatstone Bridge, with a sufficient current to heat it to a dull red. . . . The idea was that the high-pitched noises which were so troublesome would have such rapid fluctuations that they would hardly displace the shell of warm air around the wire, whereas the low-pitched gun wave would blow a blast of air through the hole, sweep the warm air away, cool the wire, and so reduce its resistance, upset the bridge, and make the galvanometer record a current.'

The Tucker microphone worked 'like a charm' and this and other developments (*L*), all devised at the Front, made sound ranging a powerful and trusted method.

In the meantime, however, Bragg's personal life was deeply affected during the autumn of 1915 by the death of his brother Bob at Gallipoli, where Moseley was also killed, and by the eventually fatal wounding of his friend Cecil Hopkinson. News of a different kind, the award of the 1915 Nobel Prize for Physics to Bragg and his father, came when he was setting up the first sound-ranging station near the front line south of Ypres. He wrote home on 17 November: 'Just got Dad's letter and yours with the cheery news in it.' The village curé with whom he was billeted produced a bottle of Lachryma Christi.

From the beginning of 1917 to the end of the war Bragg supervised the successful application of sound ranging and a great expansion of the number of units. Many young scientists, including Andrade, were involved. In the process Bragg was awarded the O.B.E. and M.C., was mentioned in dispatches three times, and rose to the rank of Major. This service also brought him new friends. One of them was Harold Hemming, who was in charge of a complementary operation, flash-spotting, and another of lasting importance was R. W. James (232). Bragg and James had been in the same Part II class at Cambridge, where G. R. Crowe, then a precocious lab. boy who had recognized James's more conventional ability, had predicted that: 'Mr. James would get a first and Mr. Bragg might get a first.' James had subsequently had an adventurous time on Shackleton's expedition to the Antarctic and then, returning home, he joined Bragg's unit near Ypres. Later when Bragg moved to G.H.Q., James helped him set up a school for sound rangers where they worked together a great deal and no doubt discussed the future development of crystallography.

As the war drew to an end, their thoughts turned towards jobs and letters home were full of the possibilities. Thus, Bragg wrote to W.H.B. on 21 October 1918: 'I got your letter yesterday about the G.E.C. work. I had never contemplated anything else than a University career . . . training men in the University to take up applied science afterwards.' In December he wrote about James, who was thinking of applying for the Professorship in Cape Town: 'I know that I would feel absolutely happy and confident in taking on any University Chair, such as Leeds even, with a fellow like James to back me up.' But in January 1919, this was followed by 'I am just a bit doubtful of my powers of tackling the Birmingham University job right now as I know so little physics. I've had no experience in lecturing.'

After appropriate celebrations of the end of the war (Major Bragg and Captain G. P. Thomson made their first appearances at the Royal Society Dining Club on 30 November 1918) Bragg returned to Cambridge early in 1919 to take up his duties at Trinity College and demonstrate in G. F. C. Searle's (193) practical class at the Cavendish laboratory. With his brother, Hopkinson and Tisdall all dead it must have been a sad return but he found Cambridge a lively place with the social life dominated by young demobilized officers—Blackett amongst them. He had just enough time to fall in love with Alice Hopkinson, Cecil's first cousin who was then reading History at Newnham College, before accepting the Langworthy Professorship of Physics at Manchester, in succession to Rutherford.

## MANCHESTER, 1919–37

At this time the Vice-Chancellor of Manchester University was Sir Henry Miers, F.R.S., who had previously been Professor of Mineralogy in Oxford (1895–1908). In Manchester the University had created a special Chair of Crystallography for him and he was deeply interested in the development of the subject that had been made possible by Bragg's work. His influence in the appointment is clear. Lecturing on 'the old and the new mineralogy' (*o*) he had said: 'In my opinion, the importance of the study of crystals has now become so great, not only for the identification of substances by crystal measurements but also on account of the new knowledge which modern crystal study is contributing to problems belonging to different sciences, that there is a real need for a department of pure crystallographic research, one in which such studies can be carried out quite independently of elementary teaching or of immediate applications, and without being tied to mineralogy. I venture to hope that it will not be long before some such department is founded either in connection with one of our Universities or elsewhere.' Through Bragg's appointment and the support and encouragement he gave to him Miers was able to realize much of this dream. He also became a firm family friend, godfather to Bragg's younger son David (1926), and his diary records many contacts.

Despite Miers's support, Bragg's early days in Manchester were not easy. Most of the other professors were relatively old—Horace Lamb the Professor of Mathematics had preceded W.H.B. in Adelaide—and they were used to dealing with Rutherford who had made the Physics Department world-famous. Bragg took over at a difficult moment. During the war most of the staff had been away on war work and the teaching had been continued mainly by E. J. Evans and N. Tunstall. When Bragg joined the Department in the autumn of 1919 he brought with him R. W. James and E. C. S. Dickson. H. Robinson (with D. C. H. Florance) had returned a little earlier so that he had at the beginning a nucleus of sound-rangers to support him. He lived with another, a classics lecturer named Drew, in an establishment arranged by his mother with his formidable old nanny, Charlotte, as housekeeper.

The first priority was to organize the teaching and Bragg at the age of 29 was very conscious that he had had essentially no previous experience that was relevant to the elementary teaching—even as an undergraduate. The beginnings were disastrous. Many of the undergraduates were returning ex-servicemen and they had no mercy on the novices. Tunstall remembered that there were 'rowdy, boisterous goings on in the lecture room particularly when medicos were being lectured to. One could hear this not only on the same floor but in the laboratory under the large lecture theatre and there was visible evidence in the fact that panels of the benches were kicked into matchwood during the lecture periods taken by Bragg, James and Dickson'. In one dramatic episode a student set off a firework under the reading desk and Bragg boxed his ears. To make matters worse anonymous letters began to arrive, addressed to the Vice-Chancellor and others, in which Bragg and his young colleagues were accused of incompetence with evidence quoted that was clearly based on a detailed knowledge of events in the department. Bragg was brought close to the edge of breakdown but recovered when the letters began to attack his father and Rutherford and when his research began to flourish again. But he was deeply scarred and it took a year or two for him to gain confident control. Miers gave what support he could and noted laconically in his diary at the end of 1924: 'there was a plague of anonymous letters at the University against certain members of the Professorial staff. But these ceased with the disappearance of one of the Junior staff to another post (with his wife).'

Research had a more promising beginning and in the autumn of 1919 Bragg was writing optimistically, but somewhat guardedly, to his father: 'My own apparatus is nearly set and James and I are eager to get going. I have one or two ideas I am anxious to try right away,' The heart of the apparatus was the X-ray spectrometer made by Jenkinson but it was used initially with a 'very inadequate gas X-ray bulb with a palladium target' (*p*). It wasn't until the following year, when the General Electric Company at Schenectady gave them a Coolidge tube, that rapid progress became possible. In the meantime Bragg returned to the study of zinc oxide that he had begun in 1914 (15) and this work, which included comparisons with related structures, combined with reconsideration of the pre-war analyses in terms of the new ideas about atomic structure and chemical bonding that had emerged during the war led him to the idea that interatomic distances in ionic compounds obey an additive law as if ions had characteristic sizes. He assigned sizes to the common ions and showed that the sums of their radii agreed quite closely with measured interatomic distances (16, 23). This important idea provided the subject for his first Friday Evening Discourse at the Royal Institution, on 28 May 1920, but unfortunately in working it out he had been too ambitious in attempting to embrace the sizes of individual atoms in compound ions (such as $CO_3^{2-}$) and in simple ions (such as $Cl^-$) in the same system. Accordingly, as he was fond of saying later, his scheme was inside out; all the negative ions were too small and the positive ions too large, though the sums of their radii were correct. J. A. Wasastjerna and V. M. Goldschmidt soon corrected Bragg's values (38) and the idea of atomic radii has played an important part in crystal structure analysis ever since.

Established for the first time in his own laboratory Bragg also had to consider the relationship between his own and his father's research programme. W.H.B. was now at University College London with a growing research group and Bragg continued the letter quoted above: 'I have been wondering what you were intending to go on with. I do hope you will never keep from doing any bit of work, Dad, because you think that may be the line I am going on. . . . If we did happen to do the same thing its all to the family credit, isn't it? and I am sure I would never be the loser if people weren't quite sure which of us did a piece of work.' This philosophy was to prove difficult to live by, and they arrived later at a tacit agreement to work on different aspects of the subject, but at this stage he went on: 'I wish you would go on with some of those experiments on the temperature coefficient of the strength of reflection, you did get such interesting results on the ones you started and I don't think anyone else has done that. I have had one or two brain-waves which I am keen to develop but I want to work at ordinary temperatures and get good numerical results.'

This foreshadowed the research programme in which Bragg, James and Bosanquet (18–20, 24) set themselves the task of making X-ray analysis a quantitative science (240). James (1962) has described how they set themselves to make 'a series of measurements of the absolute intensity of reflexion of X-rays from rocksalt, a crystal whose structure was definitely known, with no uncertain parameters'. The idea was, firstly, to test the applicability of the formulae governing X-ray reflexion which had been derived by C. G. Darwin in 1914. Secondly, they hoped to measure the atomic scattering factors, the ratio of the X-ray amplitude scattered by an atom to that scattered by a simple classical electron under the same conditions, since this would provide evidence of the distribution of electrons in the atoms and fundamental data that would be needed in the analysis of more complex crystal structures. The experimental work was very demanding but they succeeded in showing that the rock-salt crystals reflected X-rays very nearly according to Darwin's formula for an imperfect crystal—a 'mosaic' crystal in Ewald's graphic description—according to which the reflected X-ray intensity is proportional to the square of the structure amplitude ($F$, the effective number of electrons in the unit cell contributing to that reflexion). Furthermore, they were able to derive experimental atomic scattering factors for sodium and chlorine which were 'in fair agreement with what was to be expected from what was known at the time of the electron distribution in those atoms.'

It turned out later that the choice of rock-salt had been fortunate, since the crystals conformed closely to the mosaic model, but the work did much to establish the methods needed for the quantitative analysis of crystal structures. Bragg's unique contribution here was to see the value of making experimental measurements of the absolute intensities of the X-ray reflexions which showed directly the effective number of electrons contributing to each reflexion. The work on rock-salt also stimulated work on the theoretical derivation of the atomic scattering factors that were needed to calculate the intensities of reflexions corresponding to any model structure for comparison with the observed values. In 1925, D. R. Hartree, who was then at Cambridge but soon afterwards became a close colleague as Professor of Applied Mathematics in Manchester, calculated promising atomic scattering factors ( $f$-curves) based on the Bohr-orbit model of the atom and, stimulated by the need for better $f$-curves in crystal-structure analysis, he went on to devise the method of the self-consistent field. Recognizing the importance of this work at any early stage, Bragg (33) laid down the criterion that has guided all subsequent structure analysts: 'The structure which leads to the best agreement between observed and calculated values [of the X-ray intensities] is chosen as the closest approximation to the truth.'

The painstaking work of measuring individual X-ray reflexions in detail and studying their dependence upon temperature and crystal perfection was not Bragg's forte. In later years, comparing himself with his father he said that W.H.B. was the better physicist: 'His points always lay on smooth curves; mine didn't,' So from 1922 onwards he left this side of the work to James and concentrated on the analysis of structures.

In the meantime, however, there had been happy domestic changes. Bragg was elected F.R.S. on 12 May 1921 and among the letters of congratulation was one from Alice Hopkinson, then in the final year of the History Tripos, whom he had not seen since leaving Cambridge. They were married in December and moved into a house in Didsbury. Bragg had misgivings about bringing a lively 22-year-old wife to grimy Manchester and introducing her to the sober society of middle-aged professors but she had, after all, been brought up in Manchester, where her father had been a much-loved physician, and she knew the place well and was able to help her rather reserved husband in his developing contacts with the city as well as the university, while he introduced her to the wider scientific world in which he was becoming a leading figure. Earlier in 1921 Bragg (but not W.H.B.) attended the Third Solvay Conference on Physics, the subject was 'Atoms and electrons', and in the autumn of 1922 he had the pleasure of taking his young wife with him to Sweden where he delivered his Nobel lecture

(25) and they established friendly relations with Arrhenius, Westgren and other Swedish scientists. Then, in the summer of 1924 when their first child was a few months old, they made the first of many visits to North America where Bragg lectured at Ann Arbor and they attended the meeting of the British Association in Toronto. In all respects it was an eventful and fruitful marriage which remained a romance to the end. After Stephen Lawrence, born in 1923, there were three other children, David William born in 1926, Margaret Alice in 1931 and Patience Mary in 1935.

Bragg's contacts outside the university had begun early in his career in Manchester. Miers's diary for April 1920 notes that he discussed cotton industry research with the science professors and visited the Tootal Broadhurst Mill. At this time the leading figure in that firm was Kenneth Lee who was a friend of the Hopkinsons and became a close friend of the Braggs and godfather to their daughter Patience. Bragg (243) has described the contact that this friendship gave him with the work of Dr R. S. Willows at the Shirley Institute which certainly coloured his views of scientific research in industry. Important contacts with other firms, especially Metropolitan-Vickers, came later but another Manchester activity must be mentioned here. Bragg's first lecture to the Manchester Literary and Philosophical Society, on 'Sound ranging', was given soon after his arrival in the city (14) and, thereafter, he lectured regularly to the Society. He was President in 1927–28 (49) and Dalton Medallist in 1942.

In 1924 Bragg turned again to the study of aragonite which he had begun in Cambridge just before the war. This analysis required the determination of nine variable parameters and was much the most complex yet attempted (28). The solution depended upon careful absolute measurements of the X-ray intensities made with the spectrometer and Coolidge tube and, for the first time, Bragg discussed the symmetry of the crystals in terms of formal space-group theory.

Miers was deeply interested in this work and his influence, both direct and through his publications, can be discerned in Bragg's next achievement. Having a consuming interest in how best to use physical observations of all kinds to establish the arrangement of atoms in crystals, he turned briefly to the inverse problem of deriving the physical properties of crystals from their atomic structures. He showed that the refractive indices of calcite and aragonite could, with simple assumptions, be calculated essentially from the arrangement of carbonate ions in them (29) and in a second paper (30) he made some progress in generalizing the result and showing how consideration of the refractive indices may help in the analysis of crystal structures. This work aroused considerable attention and Bragg interested Sydney Chapman in it. Chapman had been a contemporary at Cambridge, though not a close friend, and had succeeded Lamb as Professor of Mathematics. In taking a further step they were prompted, perhaps, by a letter from W.H.B. (12 iii 22) discussing the structure of ruby, in which he noted the question 'of why the rhomb takes the particular shape it does', and they showed how the rhombohedral angle of crystals of the calcite type can be predicted quite precisely (31). But Bragg then left this field to

Chapman, who moved away from Manchester shortly afterwards. Although neglected for some time these were important early stages in crystal physics.

The study of aragonite also underlined a problem that struck at the heart of Bragg's quantitative method of structure analysis: the intensities of the reflexions appeared to be more nearly proportional to the structure amplitudes than to their squares (28), as W.H.B. had also observed in his work on diamond and on calcite. This was a consequence of the state of perfection of the crystals, as the theories of Darwin and Ewald had shown, but the mosaic model had worked so well for rock-salt that the theory of 'perfect' crystals was temporarily overlooked. Ewald was aware of the problem, however, and he wrote to W.H.B. about experimental measurements for comparison with his theory. W.H.B.'s response was to send some data but also to write an illuminating letter to Bragg (21 i 25) in which he reported Ewald's suggestion that new measurements on iron pyrites would be useful, and continued: 'I feel this is your province entirely and am thinking of writing to tell him so.' Later in the same letter W.H.B. promised to send an organic paper but in a discussion of mercuric chloride remarks: 'This also is your line rather than mine,' By this time, then, a division of work between W.H.B., who had moved to the Royal Institution in 1923, and Bragg seems to have been understood between them: W.H.B. worked on organic structures (and silica) while Bragg concentrated on inorganic compounds and the physics of crystals and diffraction.

The result of Ewald's interest was a study conference that he organized at Holzhausen in Bavaria in 1925 which was attended by the leading exponents of theory and experiment, including Bragg, James and Darwin. Bragg used to tell how they put forward their champion, Darwin, to present his theories of crystal reflexion only to find that he had forgotten how to derive them. However, the result of the meeting (43) was a much clearer understanding of the role of crystal perfection in determining the intensities of X-ray reflexions and this led, in turn, to increased confidence and success in the quantitative analysis of crystal structures.

From 1925 Bragg concentrated on an intensive programme of research into the structures of silicate minerals. The initial objective was to develop a technique for the analysis of crystals in which the atomic positions were defined by a large number of parameters and the silicates provided excellent material for this purpose owing to their complexity and the ease with which well-formed natural crystals could be obtained (67). The main source of supply was still Hutchinson in Cambridge. The first of these structures to be described were the olivines (40) and this success was soon followed by the analysis of beryl, $Be_3Al_2Si_6O_{18}$ by Bragg in collaboration with J. West (42), who played a large part in the silicate analyses and the training of those who worked on them. This was a remarkable study in a number of ways. The high symmetry of the crystals, which they described by means of the recently published diagrams of Astbury and Yardley, made the analysis very straightforward: Bragg later (59) noted that 'when West and I had determined the space group, I remember well that we found all the atomic positions in about a quarter of an hour, and all subsequent work only altered our first estimates slightly'. This also depended, of course, on their developing knowledge of atomic sizes, which Bragg had discussed again at the Solvay Conference on Chemistry in April 1925 (45), and the expectation that these structures would be defined mainly by the close packing of the oxygen atoms with the other, smaller, atoms tucked in between them (240). Careful measurements were made of absolute intensities and, referring to the earlier difficulties over crystal perfection, they noted that 'accurate allowance for extinction appears to be the key to the analysis of complex structures'. Finally, for the first time in this paper Bragg and West reported their use of a Fourier synthesis of an electron density distribution. Based upon WHB's Bakerian lecture of 1915 and subsequent work by Duane, Compton, Havighurst and others, this synthesis was in only one dimension but it pointed the way ahead and Bragg clearly saw what would follow: 'The Duane method cannot be applied until the signs of the coefficient $F$ (in the Fourier series) are fixed by preliminary analysis, for the observed intensities only give the squares of these quantities. Probably the most convenient procedure will be to combine the trial-and-error method of assuming structures and calculating the spectra to be expected from them, with the Fourier-analysis method, the latter being used to make the final adjustments of atomic position and to indicate the accuracy of the results.'

A discussion of one-dimensional Fourier syntheses as used by various workers, including J. M. Cork in his studies of isomorphous replacement in the alums which were carried out during a visit to Manchester in 1926–27, formed a large part of Bragg's contribution to the 5th Solvay Physics Conference on 'Electrons and photons' in October 1927 (54).

Over the next few years the structures of many silicates were determined by the standard method, of which Bragg and West (55) gave a definitive account in one of his favourite papers, entitled 'A technique for the X-ray examination of crystal structures with many parameters'. Many means 20 or 30. In addition to Bragg himself and West, the workers most involved were W. H. Taylor, a research student who was appointed to a lectureship in 1928, and two of the many visitors from abroad, W. Zachariasen (1927–29) and B. E. Warren (1929).

Bragg introduced Warren to crystal-structure analysis during a visit to M.I.T., where he spent a term lecturing in the spring of 1928. Before leaving Manchester he had begun a study of diopside, $Ca\,Mg(SiO_3)_2$, and had encouraged West to make a much more complete set of intensity measurements for this mineral than had been achieved in any previous study. This was made possible by the crystals, provided by Hutchinson (by this time professor in Cambridge), which had been cut perpendicular to the principal axes and permitted the measurement of complete zones of reflexions. Bragg took these data to M.I.T. with him and worked there with Warren on the analysis of the structure which proved to be of key importance (56). Throughout his work on the silicates there was doubt about the extent to which the oxygen atoms were associated more closely with the silicon than with the other atoms, but it was clear in diopside that tetrahedral $SiO_4$ units were joined by their corners to form long chains running through the structure. Systematic analysis of the other structures showed that the essential properties of the various types of silicates were largely determined by the $SiO_4$ tetrahedra which could join together sharing corners or edges, but not faces, to form three-dimensional structures, plates or chains.

The classification of silicate structures on this basis was initiated by Machatschki (236), a visitor in 1928–29, and it was elaborated by Bragg in his review of the whole programme in 1930 (67). Even at this stage, however, Bragg was reluctant to recognize the importance of $SiO_4$ units as complex ions and preferred to consider the individual atoms separately—as had been found appropriate in rocksalt. He was still deeply attached to the views expressed in his Royal Institution Discourse on 20 May 1927 when he had said (48): 'Some of the very earliest structures which were analysed caused us to revise our ideas of what was meant by the "molecule" of the chemist. In sodium chloride there appear to be no molecules of NaCl. The equality in numbers of Na and Cl atoms is arrived at by a chess-board pattern of these atoms; it is a result of geometry and not of a pairing-off of the atoms. This is, of course, not universally true, for this absence of the molecule in solids is in general only found in inorganic compounds. It would appear, however, that the silicates are of this non-molecular type and that in seeking to assign formulae to them, and to the hypothetical acids of silicon on which they are based, it should be borne in mind that they are really extended patterns. The relative numbers of their constituent atoms are characteristic of the extended pattern, and essentially a result of their solid state, so that it is doubtful whether a grouping of the atoms into molecules has in this case a meaning.'*

In contrast with this view, Linus Pauling (r), who was a visitor in 1929–30, had proposed a method of describing the structures in terms of $SiO_4$ and other polyhedral units and he went on to propound a set of principles governing the assembly of ionic compounds which depended heavily on the evidence accumulated in Manchester, as Bragg rather sadly remarked (67), and subsumed the less-well-developed rules that had been evolved there (James (e)).

Nevertheless, no subsequent analysis can diminish Bragg's achievement in guiding the studies of these complex mineral structures to a fruitful conclusion. His was clearly the guiding hand and his colleagues of those days have written of the excitement of working with him as more and more complex arrangements of atoms yielded to their attack. Silicate chemistry was shown to be inherently a chemistry of the solid state, intelligible only in terms of the three-dimensional structures, and Bragg never tired of using the story of its explanation to illustrate his conviction that the analysis of increasingly complicated structures can lead to the discovery of unimagined new principles.

After 1930 Bragg left further research on mineral structures to others, though he remained closely interested and spent the spring of 1934 at Cornell University

---

* It was the reporting of this Discourse that provoked H. E. Armstrong's well-known letter to *Nature* (q), which included the sentence: 'It were time that chemists took charge of chemistry once more and protected neophytes against the worship of false gods: at least taught them to ask for something more than chess-board evidence.' In his later years, Bragg enjoyed showing a slide of this letter in his lectures—usually a little out of context.

delivering the Baker lectures and writing *The atomic structure of minerals* (E). He was more concerned with crystal physics and the physical methods of structure analysis and he had, by this time, already defined the method that was to dominate crystal-structure determination for the next 20 years. This was another benefit from the work on diopside. Given the complete two-dimensional data that had been measured for the structure analysis he was able to explore the possibility of using Fourier series in two dimensions to calculate the electron density projected on the three faces of the unit cell (60). This was possible because, following the procedure outlined in the paper on beryl (42), the phases (or in this case the signs) of the Fourier coefficients could be calculated from the model of the structure proposed by himself and Warren (56); that is to say, the crystallographic phase problem, which arises because only the structure amplitudes and not their phases are given directly by X-ray observations, was already solved. Unlike most professors, he did not ask someone else to do the calculations for him. Armed only with a slide rule and mathematical tables, he did them himself and so produced the first two-dimensional electron-density projections. The results were very pretty and, although they did not lead to much new structural information since the positioning of the atoms in the original structure analysis had been closely correct, they did show the possibility of identifying atoms (or ions) from their electron counts and they suggested the method of the future. In discussing the results, Bragg posed the question whether the phases could be derived without knowing the complete structure: would partial information do ? Investigation showed that the answer could be yes. In the projection on (010), for example, the Ca and Mg atoms overlap giving the equivalent of an atom of atomic number 32. Furthermore, this 'atom' always gives its maximum contribution whereas the other atoms, although they total 74 electrons, tend to cancel out. Consequently only one reflexion differs in phase from that given by the Ca/Mg alone. Bragg was, therefore, able to point the way ahead more precisely than before: 'a preliminary analysis of the crystal which gives approximate positions of the heavy atoms suffixes to fix the signs of the coefficients $F$. The Fourier series may thus be formed and the positions of all the atoms accurately read off on the projections.' In a further paper with West (65) the defects of the image that arise from errors and terminations of the series were defined and possible remedies discussed.

Subsequently, Bragg was sorry not to have published his work on Fourier syntheses jointly with his father, since it derived directly from W.H.B.'s Bakerian lecture and the two of them had discussed it in detail. He did not use the method himself to determine new structures but he encouraged members of his Laboratory to explore it further. In 1929 Zachariasen used two-dimensional projections in his refined determination of the structure of sodium chlorate, in which the oxygen positions were read from the maps; in 1930 West studied potassium dihydrogen phosphate in the same way (incidentally demonstrating the presence of regular $PO_4$ tetrahedra); and in 1932 Parker and Whitehouse re-examined iron pyrites. Characteristically Bragg was content to be thanked for his advice and help at the ends of their papers. He had demonstrated the potential of the method and left it to others to develop in detail: it has been an essential feature of X-ray crystallography ever since.

However, he did not leave it without trying to impress upon others the physical basis of the new method. He began to lecture on X-ray optics (58) and he had the idea of showing directly that the production of an X-ray image was an optical process. Remembering again C. T. R. Wilson's lectures on optics, he knew that a microscope image could be regarded as the superposition of individual waves (or fringes) and that Fourier synthesis was merely a way of adding these waves mathematically instead of experimentally through a lens. He therefore tried to see whether he could produce an image of diopside by superposing fringes on a piece of photographic paper.

Again he carried out the painstaking business himself, with the help of his laboratory superintendent, William Kay. His fringes were the out-of-focus images of a set of parallel rods: each set had to be given the right spacing, orientation, displacement (phase) and exposure to represent the corresponding Fourier coefficient. In spite of the odds against carrying out all these operations without mistakes for about 25 terms, the results were very convincing (61).

Although this analogue method was not taken up generally, and satisfactory numerical methods were devised instead, it is notable as the first of Bragg's instructive developments of optical methods and as a clear illustration of his over-riding interest in the physics of his subject.

At about the same time the possibility of his returning to Cambridge forced Bragg to consider his hopes for the future, and on 3 June 1929 he wrote to Rutherford (c) as follows:

'I have been thinking very hard about the possible post at Cambridge which you mentioned to me some time ago. . . .

'To come to Cambridge would in itself be delightful and anything which would bring me there has all the attractions of Cambridge to recommend it. Here on the other hand are a few of the "cons". I have got used to the running of a big physics laboratory, and although I often grumble at the administrative work and would like to be freed from much of it, it is very pleasant to have a constant supply of men eager to do research. I have about twenty or twenty five doing research here and do much of my work through them. Then again I take a great interest in the teaching of physics in general and do not want to drop that. I do not want to label myself a crystallographer as against a physicist and think indeed that though my research is concerned with crystals it is the physical side of it which attracts me. I might at any time wish to switch over into a more purely physical line, and want to feel quite free to do that.

'Could you tell me what the post at Cambridge might involve? I realize of course that it is all very much in the air at present. Would it carry with it a laboratory in which I could house a large group of research men? What funds for research would be available? What students would come other than men from abroad coming to research under me on crystal problems? Could I take part in the teaching of physics at the Cavendish?

'I could perhaps explain my views best by describing what would seem to me a very attractive post. This would be an additional chair of experimental physics with especial charge of the physics of the solid state. You talked to me about the future of the Cavendish, and the possibility that in time to come the work might be divided as the ground to be covered in experimental physics is so great. Is there any possibility of this being done in the next year or two and of your devolving part of the responsibility? If I might put it quite frankly, I feel that such a post would offer unlimited scope for one's energy, whereas the subject of crystallography by itself is very limited. The parts of it which are growing and important are really pure physics, and it would best be developed as part of a big Physics School, not as a subject on its own.'

Nothing came of this negotiation and J. D. Bernal, who had moved from W.H.B.'s group at the Royal Institution to Cambridge in 1927, remained in charge of crystallography there. But it served to focus Bragg's views and may have suggested to him that there would be a danger of losing contact with mainstream physics if he concentrated too much on analysing structures. Disappointment at the outcome may also have contributed to the crisis that overtook him in 1930. In addition to the normal strains of his office, which at this time included the planning of a new building, the introduction of a new series of lectures for industrial physicists and writing a book (*C*), other factors also contributed. There was the excitement but also the tension involved in bringing the silicate work to its climax, especially when understanding the results drew him into the unfamiliar, fast-developing and competitive field of chemical bonding; there was the continuing conflict between his simple enjoyment of family life and his obsessive preoccupation with research at critical moments; there was the distant and guarded relationship with his father,* and the recollection of his lack of rapport with his mother, who had died in 1929 after a long illness; and there was the worsening economic situation which was more evident in Manchester than in many other places.

A real chance to move brought matters to a head. He was offered the Professorship of Physics at Imperial College, London, but, after anxious thought and unhelpful discussion with his father, he refused the appointment, largely through strong feelings of loyalty to the university that had given him so much. His friend G. P. Thomson was appointed instead. It was at this point, fearful that he had lost his last opportunity to move his family to more attractive surroundings, that he broke down.

Bragg's colleagues appear to have been largely unaware of the tensions that produced this crisis and, with the staunch support of his family, Bragg recovered his balance quite quickly. In this he was greatly helped by spending the spring of 1931 on leave in Sommerfeld's laboratory in Munich, where he sought to

---

* On 17 November 1926, for example, he wrote to W.H.B.: 'I am too lucky in too many ways to have any reason for feeling low at all. I think we ought to talk more about the lines we are doing and I would like to co-operate in the sense that each of us specialized in some particular line which supplemented the work of the other.'

broaden his command of the latest developments in physics, and by the birth in June 1931 of his third child and first daughter, Margaret Alice.

Back in Manchester at Easter, however, he changed his style of working, involving himself less closely in the day-to-day experiments and analysis, and looked for new and more physical lines of research while encouraging the continuation of mineral-structure studies by Taylor and others. With his reputation renewed by the silicate work, he also became somewhat more involved in general scientific affairs which took him outside the university. In 1931 he was awarded the Hughes Medal of the Royal Society and from 1931 to 1933 he served on its Council. He was elected a member of the Dining Club in 1934. During this period, in the summer of 1932, he and his wife made a trip to Russia, together with R. H. Fowler, Dirac, Gurney and the Kapitzas who arranged the trip. This may have made Manchester seem more attractive but, however that may be, everything brightened up in 1933 when he was able to move his family from Didsbury to Alderley Edge, to a house overlooking the Cheshire plain, within sight of the Welsh hills and with a beautiful garden. At the same time research became exciting again and Bragg faced the world with renewed vigour. In 1934 he not only spent a term lecturing at Cornell, he also made his first contribution to broadcasting by giving a course of six lectures on 'Light' and, at the end of the year, delivered the Royal Institution's Christmas lectures to a juvenile auditory on the subject of 'Electricity' (*D*).

Bragg's new research subject was a development of one of his established interests. A short excursion into electron diffraction (76, 79) did not promise much but his attention was attracted by another of Pauling's papers, this time on 'Rotational motions of molecules in crystals', and he made the new idea, that there is a much greater freedom of movement in the solid state than had been suspected, the theme of his lecture at the Centenary Meeting of the British Association in 1931 (77). Although he did not include an account of it in his lecture, this topic was directly related to new work in Manchester that was growing out of the long-standing studies of metals and alloys.

Bragg's first research student in Manchester was A. J. Bradley and, when he had completed his doctorate, Bragg asked him to explore the use of the powder diffraction method, which had been shown by Hull in America and Debye and Scherrer in Switzerland to be valuable in studies of elements and other simple structures. This approach had also been taken up by Westgren in Sweden, whose laboratory had become one of the main centres for the developing study of metals and alloys, so in 1926 Bragg sent Bradley to spend a year with Westgren and Phragmén in Stockholm to learn the trade. This proved extraordinarily successful. Bradley was in his element and was soon solving problems that others had considered impossible. On his return to Manchester he became the leading exponent of powder methods, solving problems of surprising complexity and attaining an accuracy in measurements that has hardly been surpassed in present times (*s*).

Bradley's most outstanding contribution was to determine the structure of $\gamma$-brass, $Cu_5Zn_8$, which has 52 atoms in a cubic unit cell and had defied Westgren and Phragmén whose single crystal Laue and rotation photographs and powder diagrams Bradley used in his analysis. The structure of γ-brass—an otherwise quite useless alloy—played a considerable part in the development of modern solid-state physics: the γ-structure was found to exist because its Brillouin zone is more nearly spherical than those of the simpler body-centred and face-centred structures. Bradley was no theoretician, his genius was to provide the evidence, but Bragg saw the importance of his work and discussed it with a succession of lecturers and visitors in the department whose contributions to the development of the theory are universally recognized. They included N. F. Mott (1929–30), W. Hume-Rothery (1932–33), H. A. Bethe (1933–34) and R. E. Peierls (1933–35). The part that Bragg played in this work is not now fully appreciated; he published no original papers on the subject and he would have been the last to claim that he had made any significant contributions. Nevertheless, his role as a catalyst cannot be denied and it is entirely appropriate that the term 'Bragg reflexion' now occurs naturally in solid-state physics and is used by people who have never carried out any X-ray diffraction work themselves.

During the period 1928–32 Bradley was paid by Metropolitan-Vickers, though he continued to work in the university, and it was natural, therefore, for Charles Sykes to consult him when he encountered a problem with iron-aluminium alloys at the Company's Research Laboratories in Trafford Park. Sykes was carrying out an industrial investigation into the properties of these alloys and, during the work, he found that their electrical resistivity varied as a function of aluminium content in what appeared to be a completely haphazard manner. Bragg was immediately drawn into the discussions and suggested, as it turned out correctly, that superlattice formation might be the cause of this behaviour. This started a long and fruitful association with Sykes and it stimulated Bragg's interest in order–disorder phenomena.

Bradley investigated the iron–aluminium system and found that the resistivity effects were due to the difference between an ordered structure of the alloy when cooled slowly and a disordered structure when it was cooled rapidly. The former had the lower resistance. Bradley then gave a colloquium in the department at which he described his results and Bragg put forward some general qualitative ideas about the nature of the order–disorder change. This occasion was attended by E. J. Williams, the Lecturer in Mathematical Physics, who was fascinated and overnight drafted a thermodynamic theory of the phenomena which he showed to Bragg the following day. There is no doubt that the detailed theory which developed from this beginning was very largely due to Williams, as Bragg made clear in his Royal Institution Discourse of 17 March 1933 (81), but Bragg took it up enthusiastically and used it as the basis of his Bakerian lecture in June 1934 which was published, most unusually, in their joint names (83). At this stage they discovered that theoretical treatments on similar lines had been published earlier by other workers and they discussed these, and a new approach to the problem by Bethe (who, together with Peierls, had contributed importantly to the discussions in Manchester), in a second paper (86). Williams rounded off the series of papers with an independent publication in which he acknowledged help from Bragg and from Peierls, who subsequently made further developments to Bethe's approach.

Although the Bragg-Williams contribution was not as original as it first seemed, there is no doubt that it attracted great attention and stimulated much further work all over the world. In Manchester experimental studies were continued in the university in collaboration with Sykes at the research laboratory of Metropolitan-Vickers and they were summarized in joint papers in 1937 (96) and 1940 (111, 113, 114). Meanwhile Bragg encouraged Bradley to devote himself to the study of alloy systems in the hope that X-ray methods, which made possible the unequivocal recognition of individual phases, would clarify the interpretation and use of complex phase diagrams. The work developed naturally into a classification of alloy phases in binary, ternary and even quaternary systems but this did not generally fire Bragg's imagination, though he was excited by the work on magnetic alloys (106), and he left this field in the main for Bradley to develop.

Single-crystal structure analysis continued to be an important part of the work in Manchester during the 1930s but Bragg did not involve himself closely in any particular study after the work on β-alumina which was completed in 1930 (75). But he continued to encourage this branch of research and it is interesting to note that he was present at the Washington meeting of the American Physical Society where Patterson presented his first account of the Fourier syntheses formed with the observables $F^2$ as coefficients which are now known universally as Patterson functions. Patterson, who noted (*e*) that 'Bragg [was] in the audience to ask the right questions', had used West's data on $KH_2PO_4$ in his first tests of the method but Bragg told him about the work by C. A. Beevers and H. Lipson at Liverpool on copper sulphate pentahydrate, which they had had solved by Fourier methods but not yet published, and suggested that he might use their data in more detailed tests. Bragg also described the new numerical methods of Beevers and Lipson for summing Fourier series which Patterson then used, together with the copper sulphate data, to calculate the two-dimensional synthesis that illustrates his classic paper (*t*). First Beevers and then Lipson subsequently moved to Manchester where they continued their development of the famous 'strips' and worked on a number of structures, Lipson for the most part with Bradley. Their work on a method for computing Fourier syntheses of electron density from the structure factors probably stimulated Bragg's invention of a graphical method to solve the inverse problem, the calculation of structure factors from atomic positions (90), which was elaborated in a joint paper with Lipson (91).

By the spring of 1937 there must have been an end-of-term feeling in Bragg's Department in Manchester: W. H. Taylor had left in 1934; West (for a professorship in Rangoon) and Peierls in 1935; Williams in 1936; and James (who now realized his earlier ambition to become professor at Cape Town) in April 1937. In May Bragg was invited to succeed Sir Joseph Petavel as Director of the National Physical Laboratory. He accepted and, arranging for Bradley and Lipson to move with him, took up his new duties on 1 November. He was succeeded at Manchester by Blackett.

In his final departmental report at Manchester, Bragg wrote: 'It is with great regret that I leave a department in which I have spent eighteen happy years. I came to it directly after the war, with no previous teaching experience. Manchester University has taught me all I know about the running of a department, and the fascinating and intricate life of a modern university. I shall always remember with gratitude the kindness of my colleagues and the inspiring atmosphere of this University.' He had certainly served it well, not least by making Manchester the centre of his subject. Visitors came from all over the world and they found him a charming and helpful person, with none of the pomposity they might have expected in so eminent a man. Many have remarked upon the personal kindness of Bragg and his wife and their hospitality at Alderley Edge but Sir Charles Sykes may have provided the most illuminating snapshot: 'when we got down to the serious discussion he would adjourn to the billiard room which contained a full-size billiard table. On all my visits to this room, I never saw any balls on the billiard table; it was covered with reprints of papers and, as the argument developed, Bragg would get up from his chair, wander round the table, pick out the appropriate reprint, and we would then examine it in terms of the ideas we were discussing at the table.'

### THE NATIONAL PHYSICAL LABORATORY 1937–38

The National Physical Laboratory was at that time administered by the Department of Scientific and Industrial Research whose Secretary, Sir Frank Smith, was much concerned in Bragg's appointment. W.H.B., who was now President of the Royal Society and had strong views on the importance of applied science, very much approved of the move.

But Bragg found the work disappointing. Although some of the research was flourishing, many things were being done that had long ceased to be useful. In taking Bradley (who was then Royal Society Warren Research Fellow) and Lipson with him he hoped to set an example in research. They worked in the Metallurgy Division, whose Superintendent was C. H. Desch, but most of the short time they were there was spent in writing up for publication work done in Manchester. Bragg's only original paper published from the N.P.L. was a short note with Lipson on high-dispersion X-ray photographs of metals (101). One of his few innovations was to attempt the introduction of a series of lectures from prominent scientists: he found that there was no proper lecture room for them; there had been one but it was so little used that it was converted into an extension of the library. But there were plenty of committees and formal occasions, which he did not enjoy.

Rutherford died on 17 October 1937, before Bragg had left Manchester, and there was immediate speculation about who should succeed him as Cavendish Professor of Experimental Physics in the University of Cambridge. Bragg was clearly a possibility but W.H.B., who was himself ill at ease in Cambridge and opposed the move, wrote advising his son's wife not to be disappointed at not being able to go to the Cavendish having just moved to the N.P.L. Sir Frank Smith, who was an elector to the chair, took a different view and with the rest of the Board (The Vice-Chancellor, H. E. Dean; R. H. Fowler; C. G. Darwin; H. Thirkill; W. J. Pope; W. Wilson; O. W. Richardson; and G. I. Taylor) decided to offer Bragg the appointment which was announced in March 1938. Election to a Professorial Fellowship at Trinity College followed shortly afterwards. There was undoubtedly some consternation, especially among nuclear physicists, but Darwin is reported to have remarked that 'nuclear physics is a passing phase' and *Nature* commented: 'The Cavendish laboratory is now so large that no one man can control it all closely and Bragg's tact and gift of leadership form the best possible assurance of the happy cooperation of its many groups of research workers.' The next 15 years showed that this was closer to the mark than most editorial comments.

CAMBRIDGE DURING WORLD WAR II, 1938–45

Bragg moved to Cambridge with his wife and four children in October 1938 where, at the age of 48, he succeeded Rutherford in a major appointment for the second time. Again it was not easy since many members of the laboratory had hoped that Rutherford would be succeeded by another nuclear physicist and Bragg not only had different interests, his style of management was quite different also. P. I. Dee and N. Feather were the principal nuclear physicists remaining in Cambridge and the other research interests at the Cavendish were the work of the Mond Low-temperature Laboratory under J. D. Cockcroft, the ionospheric research under E. V. Appleton, and the crystallography, which had been directed hitherto by Bernal. During the previous ten years Bernal had inspired a very lively group which had been particularly successful in starting studies of biologically important molecules and macromolecules, but he had been appointed to succeed Blackett at Birkbeck College in the round of musical chairs that followed Bragg's leaving Manchester. Bragg brought Bradley, with Lipson to assist him, from the N.P.L. to succeed Bernal in charge of the Crystallographic Laboratory and, in the next year, he strengthened metal physics by attracting E. Orowan from Birmingham.

Another change was quickly needed. Appleton, who had been Bragg's first student, resigned the Jacksonian chair in order to succeed Sir Frank Smith as Secretary of the D.S.I.R. and Cockcroft was appointed in his place. In this first year Bragg worked closely with Cockcroft, who had played a large part in designing the new Austin wing of the laboratory and was now supervising its construction—on the understanding that it would be used by the Services in the event of war (138). As war grew increasingly probable, however, ideas for reorganization of the laboratory were set on one side and, by September 1939, most of the basic research work was suspended as the members of staff left for war service or turned their attention to related research.

Nevertheless, Bragg's first year back in Cambridge was scientifically fruitful and, in particular, his first weeks there were marked, most significantly as it turned out, by a dramatic revival of his interest in the analysis of more and more complicated crystal structures. M. F. Perutz, who was the only member of

Bernal's group of biological crystallographers left behind in Cambridge, has described what happened (*u*): 'I waited from day to day, hoping for Bragg to come round the Crystallographic Laboratory to find out what was going on there. After about six weeks of this I plucked up courage and called on him in Rutherford's Victorian office in Free School Lane. When I showed him my X-ray pictures of haemoglobin his face lit up. He realized at once the challenge of extending X-ray analysis to the giant molecules of the living cell. Within less than three months he obtained a grant from the Rockefeller Foundation and appointed me his research assistant. Bragg's action saved my scientific career and enabled me to bring my parents to Britain' (as refugees from Hitler's invasions of Austria and Czechoslovakia).

This meeting with Perutz introduced Bragg to the problem that was to be his main research interest for the rest of his career and his first paper related directly to protein-structure analysis followed almost immediately (107). Here he discussed the problems involved in determining complex structures directly from their Patterson functions and, referring to recently published claims that the Patterson of insulin could be interpreted, he pleaded 'for a due sense of proportion'. This note shows him already thinking about proteins but its main interest now is as an introduction to the two letters that followed immediately afterwards from Bernal and J. M. Robertson. In his letter Bernal paid attention to the then uncertain chemical constitution of proteins, a problem ignored by Bragg, and referred to the difficulty of locating a zinc atom with 28 electrons in a molecule with 20 000 electrons. Robertson, however, while agreeing with Bragg's comments about Patterson diagrams, went on to suggest how the structure of insulin might be determined: 'the molecule does, however, contain a few zinc atoms, and if these could be replaced by mercury, as has been suggested, a very profitable study might ensue'. It was to be a long time before essentially this method was used to solve the structure of a protein crystal and, in the meantime, Bragg played a major part in keeping alive the hope that success would be achieved at last despite the scepticism of most crystallographers—including many of those in his own laboratory.

Meanwhile, in a new burst of creativity, there was time for one more advance before the war intervened to stop most of the research. This was a development of Bragg's earlier attempt to devise an optical method for making Fourier syntheses of electron-density maps (61). Now he had the idea of using Young's fringes instead of the out-of-focus images of a set of rods to represent the Fourier components. Each set of fringes could be produced by a pair of holes with the right orientation and spacing. He suddenly realized that he had rediscovered the reciprocal lattice. The holes had to have areas proportional to the structure amplitudes but there was no easy way of simulating the phases. Nevertheless, the method could be used to synthesize the familar (010) projection of diopside for which all but one of the phase angles were zero. Crowe, the precocious lab. boy of his undergraduate days, built the necessary apparatus—Bragg called it the X-ray microscope—and Chapman, the instrument maker of the crystallography section, drilled the plate simulating the reciprocal lattice. Its diffraction pattern showed clearly the arrangement of atoms in the crystal (108). Bragg was delighted with this result and demonstrated it at a Royal Society Conversazione.

Further developments of these ideas continued intermittently during the war and it is convenient to describe them without interruption here. The first (119) in 1942 was a relatively simple extension of the method just described in which a photographic method was used to produce the reciprocal-lattice plate. This took advantage of a photographic process developed by the British Scientific Instrument Research Association, whose director, A. J. Philpot, was a fellow member of war-time committees, and it made possible the synthesis of a Patterson projection of horse haemoglobin from measurements by Perutz. The possibility of synthesizing centrosymmetrical electron-density projections, for which the phase angles are all $0°$ or $180°$, by using half-wave plates of mica was also described. Having obtained images in this way, Bragg next turned his attention to the opposite problem, how to simulate optically the production of a single crystal X-ray diffraction pattern—in two dimensions. His solution to this problem, first demonstrated at a Royal Institution Discourse in 1942 (128, 136), was to make a set of images of the contents of a unit cell by using a multiple pin-hole camera, in which the holes were arranged on the points of the crystal lattice—the so-called 'fly's eye'. Crowe again carried out the work and it was a success which led to practical results: C. W. Bunn used the device in helping to solve the structure for penicillin.

Finally, Bragg realized that the fly's eye was unnecessary: one image of a unit cell would give rise to a continuous diffraction pattern from which the reciprocal lattice picked out the appropriate intensities. In a joint paper with Lipson, he therefore proposed the use of a simple optical diffractometer and illustrated its value in studies of alloys (123).

These optical devices were taken up and further developed by several people, especially by Lipson and his colleagues. They proved very important educationally in emphasizing the Fourier-transform theory that underlies X-ray diffraction phenomena and they have been used intensively in the analysis of electron micrographs of periodic structures.

But in September 1939 Bragg's main preoccupation was to make what contribution he could to the war effort and he took pains to see that his staff and ex-students were efficiently deployed. His problem then was to carry on the teaching of physics in Cambridge, suitably adapted to meet the demands of the war. Queen Mary College and Bedford College, London, were evacuated to Cambridge and their physics classes and teaching staff were combined with those of the Cavendish. The Queen Mary College professor was an old friend and colleague, H. Robinson, and he stayed with the Braggs. Most remarkably, Searle was brought back from retirement and he took charge of the practical classes until the end of the war (193). Much of the teaching was concentrated on short two-year Honours courses with special classes in electronics for potential radar personnel.

In addition to the X-ray optics already described, Bragg continued the metals research with a good deal of emphasis on practical problems as it had been in

Manchester. Unhappily, however, Bradley was not good at the day-to-day running of a laboratory and he went into a sad decline, finally having to give up charge of the Crystallography Group. Lipson took over responsibility for running the section. Apart from the continued work with Bradley and Sykes on alloys and order–disorder phenomena that has already been mentioned (111, 113, 114) Bragg's most important contribution to metals research in this period was the invention of his remarkably useful bubble model of a metal structure (118). Inspired by his discussions about the strength of metals with Orowan, this simple model illuminated the behaviour of domain boundaries in plastic deformation and, developed further after the war, did much to popularize the theory of dislocations (145, 156). It illustrates very well Bragg's uncanny gift for visualizing atomic arrangements and expressing their essence in simple models, and the fact that Feynman, most unusually, quotes one of Bragg's papers (145) verbatim in his *Lectures on physics* clearly expresses his appreciation of the model and of Bragg's gift for exposition.

Bragg played no part in the war research that was conducted in the Cavendish, by Halban, Kowarski and others, but he did contribute to services research of two main kinds. As early as 1937 he was consulted about the equipment and tactics of the Sound Ranging Section in the Army and he continued throughout the war to advise on its development. The centre of research and teaching was on Salisbury Plain and there he renewed contact with World War I friends, including Hemming who had been in charge of the complementary method of flash spotting. This latter method was no longer useful, since gun flashes had been eliminated, but sound ranging was. Bragg found it in much the state in which he had left it in 1918, without even an effective radio communications system though with some not-very-useful accretions (L). Refined under the pressures of war it again proved valuable and, in addition to being employed in essentially the old way in the main land engagements of the war, the same principles were used in plotting the trajectories of the V2 rockets.

Secondly, Bragg was consulted by the Admiralty on the development of Asdic (sonar). This method of underwater detection by the use of sound waves had been developed to some extent during World War I by a research group led by W. H. Bragg at Parkeston Quay (*a*) but it came into use only in the World War II. Bragg regularly visited the Admiralty Research Station at Fairlie on the Clyde for discussions of the problems encountered in the further development and use of the system. Writing about it later he remarked modestly: 'I find it hard to estimate how much I helped. Only the people on the spot could appreciate the practical difficulties and such help as an outsider could give came from a knowledge of the man to consult about this or that special point... Quite apart from direct help, I think the researcher liked talking about their problems to someone who understood and could appreciate their work.' He continued to serve as an advisor on this work for about 15 years.

Bragg also served on committees set up by the Ministry of Supply to keep its scientific activities under review, as Chairman of the General Physics Committee and member of the Metallurgy Committee, and this enabled him to keep the

Ministry closely aware of the work still going on in Cambridge. Other members of these committees included A. V. Hill, Andrade and A. J. Philpot. From the end of 1942 he was also a member of the Advisory Council of the D.S.I.R.

Early in 1941 Appleton asked Bragg to serve a term of six months in Canada as Scientific Liaison Officer between Canada and the U.K., in succession to R. H. Fowler. He sailed to Halifax in March accompanied by C. G. Darwin who was on his way to Washington, D.C., and was attached to the team of scientists working under the leadership of C. J. Mackenzie at the National Research Council Laboratories in Ottawa. Bragg and Mackenzie had met briefly at a sound-ranging course on the Vimy Ridge front in World War I. In Ottawa they collaborated closely and Mackenzie has described Bragg's performance, which was based upon his close relations with the scientific community in Canada and the United States and his standing in the U.K., as that of 'a superb liaison officer for the exchange of secret information and arranging useful and congenial meetings between distinguished allied scientists'. Bragg's report to Appleton on 12 August 1941 advocated the policy of keeping the liaison office small and encouraging experts in each subject to travel backwards and forwards between the two countries that was largely followed. After visits to Vancouver and other centres he flew home in September in a bomber on its way to active service and was succeeded in Ottawa by G. P. Thomson.

A second wartime journey abroad, of a more cultural but possibly equally hazardous nature, took place in 1943 when he visited Sweden at the invitation of the British Council to talk to Anglo-Swedish Societies and re-establish contacts with Swedish scientists. Bragg flew to Stockholm on 16 April and gave some 14 lectures, mainly on his research interests in X-ray optics, proteins, metals and minerals, in six Swedish centres before returning home on 12 May. He met many old friends—Westgren was especially remembered—and his report, which ranged over the availability of scientific journals and the importance of further exchanges, concluded: 'I cannot exaggerate the warmth of my welcome.' With the tide of war changing and thoughts turning more confidently to its end, Bragg clearly made a valuable contribution to Anglo-Swedish relations.

Bragg performed at least one other public function during the war which was of great importance. From October 1939 to September 1943 he served as President of the Institute of Physics and worked hard to maintain the activities of the Institute at as normal a level as possible and to initiate constructive discussions about the likely needs of the postwar world (117). Throughout his time in Manchester he had fostered the activities of the Institute in that area and he had also taken a special interest in the application of X-ray methods to industrial problems (78). At the beginning of his Presidency plans were made to hold a Conference of the Institute on 'X-ray Analysis in Industry' but they were frustrated first by the outbreak of war and then by the events of 1940. It was then decided to publish the papers that had been prepared (116) and a Conference to discuss them was at last held in Cambridge on 10–11 April 1942. The report in *Nature* noted that 'some anxiety was felt by those responsible for the arrangements, lest preoccupation with war work would prevent many from attending, but the decision to proceed was made because the X-ray tool is being widely used for problems directly connected with the war. The large attendance at the Conference (some 280 participated) and the generally expressed appreciation of this opportunity for discussion have shown that this anxiety was unnecessary.' Bragg gave an historical review and mentioned proteins and the 'fine' structure of deformed metal as problems on the threshold of solution.

This meeting was such a success that its members decided to set up an organization under the aegis of the Institute of Physics to arrange similar conferences from time to time. As a result, a discussion meeting on the determination of equilibrium diagrams by X-ray methods was held in September at the Royal Institution, with Bragg in the chair, and a second full conference on X-ray analysis in industry was held in Cambridge on 9–10 April 1943, again with Bragg as chairman. This led to the establishment of the X-ray Analysis Group of the Institute of Physics to arrange meetings and perform other functions connected with X-ray research for a membership drawn from both university departments and industry. The committee of the new group, which met in July 1943, was made up largely of Bragg's associates and he was elected chairman with Lipson as secretary.

The X-ray Analysis Group (XRAG) adopted the pattern of meetings that was set in 1942 and meetings were held regularly in the spring and autumn of each year until the end of the war and, with few exceptions, this has continued to the present time. Bragg remained chairman until April 1947 and was thereafter a vice-chairman until his death.

At the end of the war the XRAG, led by Bragg, played a critical part in the organization of crystallographic research internationally. At the committee meeting held in July 1945, following suggestions by Ewald at the Oxford Meeting a year earlier, there was discussion of the need for a new journal to succeed he then-defunct *Zeitschrift für Kristallographie*. Bragg consulted Wyart, Mauguin, Ewald and others and it was agreed that advantage should be taken of the summer meeting of XRAG in 1946 to hold international discussions of the problem. This XRAG meeting was held with Bragg as chairman on 9–11 July 1946 at the Royal Institution. The subject was 'X-ray analysis during the war years' and it was a memorable occasion which provided the first opportunity after the war for crystallographers of all nationalities to re-establish contacts. In addition to about 250 U.K. participants some 75 visitors from 15 different countries around the world were present, happily including Laue, and many moving accounts were given of research during the hostilities.

On the following two days formal meetings were held at Brown's Hotel of a Provisional International Crystallographic Committee to explore the question of publishing an international journal of crystallography and to consider other questions of crystallographic interest. Bragg opened the meeting which agreed, after much discussion of detail, that a new journal was needed and that it should be called *Structural crystallography*. Bragg then noted that it would be necessary for some organization to assume formal responsibility for the journal and suggested that one possibility would be to form an International Union within the existing framework of Unions, either as a Union of Crystallography or as a Commission of the Union of Physics or of the Union of Chemistry. Unanimous agreement in favour of a separate International Union of Crystallography was quickly reached and Bragg was asked to explore the possibility further.

At this time the General Secretary of the International Council of Scientific Unions was Professor F. J. M. Stratton of Cambridge and Bragg was able quickly to arrange a meeting at which Stratton gave his opinion that a new Union would be acceptable. In this way the International Union of Crystallography was conceived. Bragg was not able to attend its first formal meeting at Cambridge Mass. in 1948 but he was there elected its first President. He also served as a founder member of the Editorial Board of the new journal, which was actually given the fittingly general and international title 'Acta Crystallographica' at the request of the Russians, and he played a large part in raising the money that was needed to launch it.

This account of the International Union has taken the story beyond the end of the war but some brief details of Bragg's personal life in those years remain to be added.

Bragg's knighthood was announced in the New Year Honours list of 1941 and W.H.B. wrote to Lorna Todd in Adelaide on 5 January: 'Isn't that fine ? . . . He will have to be Sir Lawrence: we can't have confusion worse than ever. I am so very glad for his sake. In spite of all care, people mix us up and are apt to give me a first credit on occasions when he should have it: I think he does not worry about that at all now, and will never anyhow have cause to do so now. I think I am more relieved about that than he is' (*a*).

W. H. Bragg died on 12 March 1942, still in his post at the Royal Institution where Bragg had spent part of the day with him. Since 1938, when Bragg was appointed (non-resident) Professor of Natural Philosophy in the Institution in succession to Rutherford, they had met more often and their relationship seems to have grown more easy. Writing about their father 20 years later on the centenary of his birth (223), Bragg and his sister described him in terms which show clearly the qualities that endeared him to so many and reveal to some extent how difficulties arose in family relationships.

From the summer of 1938, Lady Bragg was heavily involved in the work of the Women's Voluntary Service (W.V.S.), initially at the head office in London and subsequently as head of the Service in Cambridge. Bragg took great pride in his wife's work which made her a well-known public figure in Cambridge and led to her election to the Council and, in 1946, to her becoming Mayor. With their four children, the two girls still at school at the end of the war, they had a busy time.

### CAMBRIDGE AFTER THE WAR, 1946–53

Bragg's cogitations during the war about the future need for physicists (117) and the organizations that would be needed to provide them (130) prepared him to meet some of the problems that faced him in Cambridge at the end of 1945. He was clear, at least, that the Cavendish Laboratory would no longer be dominated by any single research group under one dominating figure since he believed that 'the ideal research unit is one of six to twelve scientists and a few assistants, together with one or more first-class mechanics and a workshop in which the general run of apparatus can be constructed'. With this model in mind he waited, for the most part, for people to emerge with ideas that engaged his interest.

But the teaching as well as the research had to be reorganized and in both departments he relied heavily on J. A. Ratcliffe who returned early from his war service and became Bragg's most trusted helper, especially in the handling of University Committees at which Bragg did not excel. Ratcliffe's intervention, 'We think, don't we Professor . . .,' seems to have been heard at awkward moments in more than one meeting. To some extent the changes within the laboratory were forced by the veterans returning from the war whose ideas were very different from the old ones: senior members of staff expected an office, a a secretary and a telephone whereas before the war they had none of these. Bragg met these wishes and, as Ratcliffe recalls, 'modernised the very antiquated notepaper, introduced a departmental secretary to help him run the laboratory and opened up the Austin wing. There was a complete transition to a new style laboratory and the place worked in a completely different way from the old one.' A. B. Pippard, one of his successors as Cavendish Professor, wrote long afterwards in 1972: 'Bragg performed a notably excellent job in decentralizing the work of the Cavendish, and thus effectively breaking away from what would have ultimately become the dead hand of the Rutherford tradition. His decision to give each research section as near as possible autonomy, consistent only with very general central principles and of course financial control, has played a significant part in the subsequent developments. Ever since then, the Cavendish has been notable among Cambridge departments for the democratic way in which it conducts its business. There has been no suspicion, I believe, of essential decisions being taken by the head of the department without consultation.'

The development of autonomous sections was made difficult in 1945 by the need to replace staff and fill vacant positions. A. J. Bradley had suffered a serious breakdown and his appointment in charge of the Crystallography Laboratory could not be renewed. To replace him Bragg appointed W. H. Taylor, his most valued and productive associate and successor in the silicate work, who had been Head of the Physics Department at the Manchester College of Science and Technology where Lipson succeeded him. From the end of the war Cockcroft was expected to resign the Jacksonian Chair in order to direct government research in atomic energy but his new appointment was delayed and it was not until 1947 that O. R. Frisch was appointed in his place to take charge of the of the laboratory's continuing effort in nuclear physics. At the same time there were delays in finding a new Plummer Professor of Mathematical Physics before Hartree, another old Manchester colleague, was appointed. However, in November 1946, Bragg was encouraged by the award of a Royal Medal of the Royal Society.

The rapid build up of work after the war and the new range of interests are illustrated broadly by the Departmental reports (printed in the *University Reporter*) and by the public lectures which Bragg gave about the general work of the laboratory (149). In 1948 the major groups were 'nuclear, radio and low-temperature physics, crystallography, metal physics and mathematical physics, with some minor groupings'. Of these Bragg was, of course, most directly interested in the crystallography and metal physics, with the associated electron microscopy under V. E. Cosslett, but his interest had also been engaged in radio physics, which was directed by J. A. Ratcliffe and embraced M. Ryle's developing radio astronomy. Bragg recognized in this latter work a further application of the principles of physical optics to set alongside X-ray crystallography and he supported it vigorously. After he had left Cambridge in 1953 Ryle wrote to him: 'The fact that you were so enthusiastic about our early work on the sun really made me feel that it was worthwhile. The same enthusiasm has made such a tremendous difference ever since—and it has always been a most happy thing to come to you with some new result.'

Nuclear physics, under Frisch and E. S. Shire, remained the largest group in the laboratory but Bragg wrote of it without the same evident enthusiasm. Noting the heavy investment in equipment and the need for technical officers to run it, he must have recalled his thoughts about research institutes (117): 'The strikingly successful places of this kind are those which may be regarded not as a body of men but as a body of equipment. Such a place has a nucleus of permanent staff and accumulates traditions of technique peculiarly its own, but its main service is as a place open to all for short periods of intense work and its main population a changing one'.

Echoing his earlier letter to Rutherford, Bragg described his own central interests as follows (153): 'The department which we call crystallography would perhaps be better described as the department for discovery of the structure of the solid state. . . . Mainly by X-rays we seek to discover the way the atoms are arranged in crystals and in other forms of solids. The scope of the work is very considerable. At one end we are investigating such substances as minerals and alloys in the inorganic field; other researchers are examining complex organic compounds . . .; finally at the other extreme we have a little group which is financed by the Medical Research Council under the direction of Perutz, which is engaged in a gallant attempt to work out the structure of the highly complex molecules which build up living matter, the proteins. . . .

'This section of the laboratory is closely linked to metal physics under Orowan. His students are particularly studying the mechanical properties of metals and relating them to their structure. The effects of cold work on a metal, recrystallisation, the yield point and plastic flow, brittle fracture, distortion under rolling or drawing and so on, are being investigated as physical phenomena. A satisfactory theory of the strength of a metal has yet to be formed.'

Bragg's contributions to research in the early days after the war were concerned mainly with these problems in metal physics, especially through his further development of the bubble-raft model (145, 156) which he discussed now in terms of dislocations. He also promoted the development of X-ray microbeam methods by Taylor's group, with a view to studying directly the variations in grain size in cold-worked metals, and he encouraged J. N. Kellar and P. B. Hirsch to build a big rotating-anode X-ray tube to produce a high-intensity microbeam. With this instrument they produced encouraging pictures of aluminium but work elsewhere then suggested that electron microscopy might provide a better approach. Happily an essential shift in technique in this direction was possible because of Bragg's earlier encouragement of electron microscopy: in 1946 he recruited Cosslett who had proposed a programme of work on electron microscopy. But in 1948 there was an upset. As the new rotating-anode tube came into operation Bragg's interest was becoming more and more focused on proteins and he stunned the metals group by suggesting that it should be diverted to this work. Taylor helped to preserve a balance and, in the end, both lines flourished (*v*).

Perutz had engaged Bragg's interest in proteins in 1938 and this was maintained throughout the war, although Perutz was prevented by internment and subsequent war work from doing much research until he returned to the Cavendish in January 1944. He was joined in January 1946 by J. C. Kendrew. By early 1947 Bragg was seeking some way of ensuring long-term support for the group and on 21 May 1947, with Keilin's encouragement, he wrote a long letter to Sir Edward Mellanby, the Secretary of the Medical Research Council, asking for help. In this letter Bragg gave an outline of the proposed research and its difficulties and described its promise with reference to his earlier experience: 'We thought it a great triumph to analyse quite simple inorganic salts by X-ray methods in the early days, and a complex organic molecule then seemed almost as far beyond our reach as the proteins might seem now. Yet a patient accumulation of clues, and improved techniques, have made it possible to enter the organic field. If the structure of a few molecules of a new type can be analysed, a rich harvest is then reaped, because the structures of many others will then be clear by analogy. I foresee the same happening in the protein field. . . .'

After discussions at the Athenaeum Club, Mellanby agreed that a case could be made to the M.R.C. and, after further talks and correspondence during the summer of 1947, he wrote to Bragg on 20 October: 'Rather to my surprise, your project for the establishment by the M.R.C. of a Research Unit at the Cavendish Laboratory, on molecular structure of biological systems, was adopted by the Council at the meeting on Friday October 17th, although I had put it forward only for a preliminary run.' Such was the birth of the Medical Research Council's most famous Research Unit, now the M.R.C. Laboratory of Molecular Biology. The original application was for a grant of £2550 rising to £2650 per annum to support Perutz, Kendrew and two research assistants for five years.

The work that kept Bragg's enthusiasm for protein research alight was the attempt by Perutz, which had continued on and off through the war years, to derive structural information directly from the diffraction patterns of haemoglobin crystals and, most especially, from a complete three-dimensional Patterson synthesis of horse haemoglobin. On the assumption that the polypeptide chains were arranged in some kind of regular fold (which alone seemed to offer any hope of solution) Perutz devised a model of haemoglobin in which the molecules were shaped like 'pill-boxes' with the chains folded to give prominent repeat distances of about 5 and 10 Å.

At this stage Bragg became deeply interested and, together with Perutz and Kendrew, turned his attention to the possible forms of the folded polypeptide chain. Various models had already been discussed, especially by Astbury, but Bragg was attracted to the idea propounded by Huggins that the most likely structure was a helix because it placed each amino-acid residue in the same kind of position in the chain. There were various observations to take into account, in particular Astbury's studies of α-keratin indicated a repeat distance of 5.1Å, closely similar to one of the distances observed by Perutz whose data also suggested that the number of amino-acid residues in such a repeat was 3.3. Furthermore, it was regarded as very probable that the chain was held in a folded condition by hydrogen bonds between NH and CO and that these bonds were nearly parallel to the axis of the chain.

With these features to guide them Bragg, Kendrew and Perutz (161) tried various forms of helical chain. They allowed free rotation about all the single bonds in the chain and various symmetries in which there were 2, 3 or 4 amino acid residues per turn of helix but they failed to find any structure that was especially convincing. Sadly they concluded: 'In X-ray analysis in general, when a crystal structure has been successfully analysed and a model of it is built, it presents so neat a solution of the requirements of packing and interplay of atomic forces that it carries conviction as to its essential correctness. In the present case the models to which we have been led have no obvious advantages over their alternatives.'

Pauling and Corey showed within a year by their description of the α-helix that Bragg and his colleagues had missed an important feature of protein structure: lacking the necessary chemical insight, they had not realized that the peptide units would be planar—thus reducing the number of possible bends in the chain to one per residue. They had also adhered too firmly to the apparent keratin repeat distances of 5.1Å (which turned out to arise from a higher level of structure) and they had given insufficient consideration to the possibility of non-integral helices.

Otherwise their four-fold helix, which had planar peptide units and the correct hydrogen-bonding pattern, might have been refined to the α-helix with its 3.6 residues per turn and 5.4Å repeat. But the main shortcoming was clearly in the chemistry and Bragg never forgave himself. Years later he wrote (233): 'I have always regarded this paper as the most ill-planned and abortive in which I have ever been involved.' It was especially aggravating to have asked the right question only to have Pauling provide the answer.

Discouraging though this was, the protein work was continued with increasing intensity and Bragg's influence on the next stage can be seen especially in the use of absolute measurements of the X-ray intensities which derived directly from the Manchester methods (55). Following a lead of Crick's, Bragg and

Perutz showed by careful analysis of projection data that the reflexions were too weak to be consistent with a model in which the polypeptide chains were straight and parallel throughout the molecule and this finding raised the possibility that less regular models would have to be considered (171). Analysis of the changes in absolute intensities when a salt solution was substituted for water as the medium permeating a haemoglobin crystal next revealed the approximate outer shape of the molecule (172), a result that was clarified further by examination of different crystal forms (173, 189). Then, in a fourth paper in 1952, Bragg and Perutz (175) at last succeeded in determining the signs (phases) of some protein reflexions. Using the fact that the cell dimensions of haemoglobin crystals change as their liquid content varies, they were able to plot the variation of the molecular transform along the c*-axis of the crystals. Since the projection on the c*-axis had a centre of symmetry the transform was either positive or negative and passed through zero at intervals along the axis. A key question was to decide the minimum wavelength of these variations and Bragg (176) illuminated the problem with a characteristic example, showing that the transform of any random function, such as the times of arrival of the Cambridge trains at Liverpool Street Station on Sundays between 8 a.m. and midnight, contained a set of loops which change sign only at certain minimum intervals. These intervals were determined by the width of the function, $2 \times 16$ hours for the trains (when a centre of symmetry is added) or 38Å for the haemoglobin molecule. Bragg's principle of minimum wavelength was used to determine the signs of the 00*l* reflexions and hence the electron density of the molecule projected on the c*-axis.

This method of plotting the molecular transform was extended by Perutz and it proved especially valuable in providing a check on the working of the much more powerful method that emerged soon afterwards. Bragg's (233) account of its origin illustrates well his enthusiastic involvement in the work: 'I remember going to Perutz in great excitement one day because I had heard from Professor Roughton that an American worker had succeeded in attracting a mercury complex to haemoglobin in stoichiometric proportions, only to have Perutz tell me very coldly that *he* had given this information to Professor Roughton.' The possibilities opened up by this discovery were explored very quickly and Perutz (*u*) remembered that in July 1953 he was able to show Bragg an X-ray photograph from a haemoglobin crystal which had two atoms of mercury attached to each molecule of haemoglobin. At this moment they both realized that the phase problem was solved, at least in principle, and that the way was at last open to unravelling the structure of proteins by X-ray analysis. The signs of the *h*0*l* reflexions of haemoglobin were quickly determined by Green, Ingram and Perutz and compared with the other evidence (175, 188): 'Everything checked and double-checked perfectly; it was a thrilling time' (231). This work gave directly an image of the haemoglobin structure projected down the *b*-axis of the crystals (190) and although this told very little about the structure of the protein it paved the way for a detailed investigation in three dimensions. But at this stage Bragg left Cambridge for the Royal Institution and continued his collaboration with Perutz and Kendrew at a distance.

The period 1951–53 during which these critical advances were made in the protein work witnessed also the first great triumph of the M.R.C. Unit. Bragg played no direct part in the study of DNA; indeed at one stage he actively discouraged Crick and Watson from working on it in an attempt to avoid competition with the M.R.C. Unit at King's College, London, but Watson (*w*) has given a colourful and irreverent account of his growing appreciation of its importance, his encouragement at a critical stage and his quick comprehension of the result. Watson also noted Bragg's concern that the chemistry underlying the final model should be checked by A. R. Todd, Pope's successor as Professor of Chemistry and the leading expert on the chemistry of nucleic acids. When Todd approved he was more than willing to promote rapid publication. As Watson saw it: 'The solution to the structure was bringing genuine happiness to Bragg. That the result came out of the Cavendish and not Pasadena was obviously a factor. More important was the unexpectedly marvellous nature of the answer, and the fact that the X-ray method he had developed forty years before was at the heart of a profound insight into the nature of life itself.'

In the report for 1952–3, his final year as Cavendish Professor, Bragg described these dramatic advances in work on 'The molecular structure of biological systems' very briefly together with progress in the other sections of the laboratory. By this time there were seven sections to be listed and their relative sizes were indicated by the distribution of research students between them: nuclear physics 30, radio waves 17; low temperature physics 10; crystallography 16; electron microscopy 4; meteorological physics 4; fluid dynamics 4. In addition there were a number of theoretical physicists housed in the laboratory and working with the various experimental groups. The descriptions of research in progress began with nuclear physics, still the largest group, and recorded the decision to instal a linear accelerator and the work that had been done to implement it. But the longest and most obviously enthusiastic section described the work on radio waves which was divided between the physics of the ionosphere under Ratcliffe and radio astonomy under Ryle. On the last topic the report concluded: 'The new knowledge of the Universe which it is yielding is proving to be of intense interest and, as the Cambridge unit under Mr Ryle has already established a leading position, the opportunity to develop this new science should be exploited vigorously.'

The report on crystallography noted particularly that 'The analysis of crystal structure by X-rays is a typical borderline subject' and went on to record the collaboration with chemistry, metallurgy and mineralogy. Bragg's own papers, which included a description of a simple device for calculating structure factors (174), were included in the list of the M.R.C. Unit and it is remarkable that, although he undoubtedly played a significant part in advising and helping the crystallographers, he scrupulously avoided (as did Taylor) sharing the authorship of papers unless he had made a major contribution to the experiments or theoretical developments recorded in them.

At his Farewell Dinner on 18 December 1953 (*v*) Bragg spoke with pride of the resurgence of the laboratory after the war, attributing the success to advances made by one member of the staff after another. Characteristically he emphasized that the atmosphere of 'affairs of state' was not one that he found easy to breathe and he thanked Ratcliffe particularly for his help with these matters and E. H. K. Dibden, whom he had appointed General Secretary of the laboratory in 1948, for his skilled administration.

From Dibden's point of view Bragg was, in fact, a good administrator because he knew what needed doing and believed in delegation. Ratcliffe has provided a more comprehensive summary which embraces this view: 'A Cavendish Professor plays at least four parts. He must be a scientist, run the laboratory, uphold the interests of the department in the University, and act as an Elder Statesman of Science outside. Bragg was pre-eminently the active scientist, and he ran the laboratory extremely well. I do not think he played the part that some others have done in the University itself, and I am not sure that his part as Elder Statesman was quite as large as theirs would have been. I found him extremely helpful and kindly, and above all things a real gentleman in every way. He was quite open and straight-forward and ready to help anyone who had the good of the laboratory at heart. I think there was an extremely good feeling in the laboratory during his time and all liked him.'

### THE ROYAL INSTITUTION, 1953–66

From the time of his appointment to the non-residential Professorship of Natural Philosophy at the Royal Institution in 1938 Bragg had played an increasing part in the affairs of the Royal Institution. At first with his father as Resident Professor and then, after his father's death in March 1942, with Sir Henry Dale (1942–46) and E. K. Rideal (1946–49) as Resident Professors for short periods he lectured regularly in every year except 1941 when he was away in Canada. In this way he remained in touch with the staff after the family connection had been broken and he followed the fortunes of the Institution with close interest as it sought a new role in the difficult post-war period.

When Rideal arrived at the R.I. it was suffering from the inevitable neglect of the wartime period but he established a lively research group, with grants from industry and Government, worked hard at the programme of Friday Evening Discourses and, with his wife's help, struggled to maintain the tradition of weekly dinner parties at a time of shortage and rationing. It seems to have been because of the difficulties associated with this regular entertaining that Rideal suggested unexpectedly in 1949 that E. N. da C. Andrade should take over the Resident Professorship and responsibility for the lectures and entertaining while he remained in charge of the research. When this proved unacceptable to the President, Lord Brabazon, and the Managers, Rideal resigned and Andrade was appointed in his place.

Andrade took up his appointment in January 1950 and began his attempt to refashion the Institution. Unhappily, but perhaps not surprisingly in view of Andrade's temperament and the traditions of the place, this led to trouble. The root of the difficulty was that the Resident Professor, although enjoying the resounding titles of Fullerian Professor of Chemistry, Superintendent of the

House and Director of the Davy–Faraday Research Laboratory, was specifically not the Director of the Royal Institution and much of the responsibility for day-to-day affairs and the staff of the Institution remained with the President, and other honorary officers and the committees of managers and visitors elected by the members. It was widely held at the time that the R.I. had much of the character of a club, though one with scientific objectives, and in Brabazon's opinion the position of Director of a club was unthinkable. Andrade, however, understood that the terms of his appointment gave him powers within the Institution analogous to those of a managing director and this led to friction and discord especially with the honorary secretary, Professor A. O. Rankine. Despite strenuous efforts by many people to find a solution the situation deteriorated rapidly until in March 1952 at a meeting of the members a vote of confidence in Andrade was lost by a substantial majority. Andrade then resigned, though arbitration of his claim for compensation and the litigation that followed were not completed until March 1953.

This unfortunate affair deeply divided the members of the Royal Institution and strong feelings were expressed on both sides. Inevitably Bragg was consulted and, although he tried to stand aside as a servant of the Institution (he was still Professor of Natural Philosophy giving his annual lecture), there was no concealing his concern for the future of the Institution or his disapproval of Andrade's approach. Early in 1950, following the accelerated retirement of W. J. Green who had been the principal lecture assistant in his father's day, he commented in *Nature* 'We shall miss him greatly, for he has come to be a part of the Institution he has served', and later, in a letter to the President, he recalled the difficulties he had encountered when Andrade was in command of one of his Sound-Ranging Sections in France. By mid-1952 he was believed by Sir Henry Dale and other leading figures in the Royal Society to be an advocate, with Brabazon, of a policy to get rid of Andrade and then put the organization of the Institution on a proper basis—a policy that seemed to them grossly unfair and improper on their interpretation of Andrade's letter of appointment. Bragg was faced, therefore, by a difficult and embarrassing decision when the Managers of the Royal Institution in April 1953 offered him the vacant post of Resident Professor. There can be no doubt that he saw it as his duty to revive the fortunes of the Institution but equally he realized that the task was a difficult one and that his motives for intervening at all in the recent troubles would be called into question. Adrian, one of his oldest friends who was now President of the Royal Society and Master of Trinity College, Cambridge, reluctantly acknowledged that he would have to accept the post 'because no-one else would' and he did so, taking up the duties of the Fullerian Professorship immediately and the residential duties on 1 January 1954.

Thus, for the third time Bragg accepted a challenging appointment at a difficult time and against a background of disapproval. But despite the difficulties it was not all gloom. There was a chance to develop a new role for the Institution and, perhaps most important, a chance to continue with the protein research for a few more years just when success seemed imminent and retirement from Cambridge in the normal way, he was already 63, might have deprived him of an active part in it.

From the outset Bragg asserted that his appointment required him to work closely with the Honorary Officers (Brabazon continued as President but the Secretary and Treasurer were new), the Managers, Visitors and members of the Institution and he set out, in the main with their grateful help, to rebuild the reputation of the Institution. His aim above all was to avoid further public discord. Although he knew that the administrative structure would have to be changed he reconciled himself to a patient process of persuasion in order to prepare the ground for his successor and, as it turned out, he was made Director of the R.I. in 1965 when he was about to retire.

In 1953 the immediate problem was financial. The costs of keeping up the premises and running the traditional activities of the R.I. could no longer be covered by the subscriptions of the members and the endowment income and for some years the Institution had been drawing on its reserves. Bragg argued at once that new sources of support would have to be found and that the Institution should seek to provide a public service of some kind, in addition to research, that would justify an appeal for funds. At this time the main activities, apart from research, were the Friday Evening Discourses, occasional Afternoon Lectures on a variety of subjects, and the famous Christmas Lectures adapted to a juvenile auditory. Of these, the Afternoon Lectures no longer attracted large audiences, even though free tickets were issued to undergraduates, and the Discourses were largely reserved for the members and their friends. It was the Christmas Lectures that pointed the way ahead: Bragg offered courses of lectures for London schoolchildren, initially at the sixth form level.

This initiative was based securely on the long experience of the R.I. in presenting science to essentially lay audiences by the lavish use of experimental demonstrations. The idea was to show schoolchildren the experiments they would otherwise only read about, and it received an enthusiastic response from the schools and the Education Authorities. Bragg gave the first course of three lectures on Electricity during the session 1954–55 and it was repeated four times. The lecture theatre holds 500 so that 2000 tickets were issued, but this by no means satisfied demand. Later in the year Bragg gave a further single lecture on 'Famous experimenters in the Royal Institution' for sixth formers that was repeated four times and this eventually set the pattern. The Advisory Committee, which included representative science teachers and members of the Education Authorities, recommended that the demand would best be met by single lectures each repeated four times. They were given usually on the Tuesdays and Wednesdays of consecutive weeks and by 1965 a regular pattern had developed with 20 000 schoolchildren of various ages attending the lectures every year (199, 235).

Armed with this evidence of the Royal Institution's concern for and contribution to the training of future scientists, Bragg turned to Industry and Commerce for support and received a ready response. A new category of Corporate Subscribers was introduced which soon brought in more than the individual members' private subscriptions and allowed the activities both new and old to flourish.

Naturally these activities demanded a great effort from Bragg and the permanent staff of the Institution in developing the contacts with schools and with industry and, especially, in devising and mounting the large number of experimental demonstrations. Here Bragg was supported mainly by Ronald King, who had come to the Institution with Andrade and stayed on as Assistant Director of Research (and later Professor of Metal Physics), Kenneth Vernon the Librarian, and the Lecture Assistant. This important post was held first by Leonard Walden, who left in 1957 to rejoin Andrade, and then by W. A. (Bill) Coates, whom Bragg and King persuaded with some difficulty to leave the research laboratory for this more public role. Together they built up a wide repertoire of demonstrations, exploiting apparatus that had been accumulating in the Institution throughout its existence (208) and drawing on the advice and help of both staff and members. Bragg gave many of the lectures himself and the staff, research workers and office staff alike, would crowd into the gallery to watch him enthral, stimulate and provoke the packed audiences. One week there would be free-hand drawings of highland dances to illustrate the formation of ionic bonds and the next he would be seen lovingly caressing the Paget speech models and beaming with pleasure at every successful 'Ma-Ma'. With a wealth of everyday analogy and a complete avoidance of jargon he inspired a generation of schoolchildren in London and, through the television programmes that followed, the rest of the country.

The public activities of the Institution were also developed in other ways so that throughout his period of office at the R.I. Bragg was engaged continuously with the committees of members and the staff in considering and promoting ideas for new schemes. From 1955 there were 'Research Days' at which teams of workers from various laboratories described their work informally to parties of schoolteachers; television programmes were planned, rehearsed and recorded; films were made; and, towards the end of the period, a new series of lectures to Civil Servants was begun. Bragg's account of this venture (238) brings out well the continuous process of innovation and development in which he was involved with King and others as they sought to create a modern role for the Institution. The general support of industry during this time, the success of a subsequent general appeal, and the continuing vitality of the Institution under his successor are measures of his achievement.

The Friday Evening Discourses were, of course, continued in all their Victorian state accompanied by the traditional entertaining, skilfully managed by Lady Bragg. On each occasion the lecturer was entertained to dinner in the Resident Professor's flat together with a variety of other guests. Bragg attached great importance to this activity and in one of his reports to the Members he wrote: 'The invitations which we send to well known people to meet the lecturer as guests of the Royal Institution have a much greater importance than might perhaps be realized. My wife and I entertain some 120–150 guests in this way during the year. They provide an opportunity to make important people from all walks of life acquainted with the R.I. and its work.' Bragg no doubt enjoyed meeting these people and, for the most part, he also enjoyed listening to the

Discourses which helped him keep abreast of the latest developments in science. He must have listened to some two hundred of these lectures and the experience helped to give final shape to his views on lecturing (239, 250). The lectures were often discussed during the following week in the laboratories and at the daily tea parties for all the staff that helped so much to create a family atmosphere in the Institution. Bragg's favourite criterion for judging the success of a lecture was whether a member of the audience could be expected to remember one idea from it the following morning. More than one failed this test. Bragg also deplored particularly lectures that were read, but he understood too well the difficulties of popularizing science to be over-critical and was always ready to commend a simple explanation or a good experiment.

Two of these Discourses in 1965 gave him particular pleasure. On 7 May, Lady Bragg, who had been a member of the Royal Commission on Marriage and Divorce (1951–55) and was Chairman of the National Marriage Guidance Council, lectured on 'Changing patterns in marriage and divorce'; and on 15 November, Bragg listened with evident pride to the Discourse on 'Oscillations and noise in jet engines' given by his engineer-son Stephen, who was then Chief Scientist at Rolls Royce Ltd and later became Vice-Chancellor of Brunel University.

During this period also Bragg kept up and extended his role as a world figure in science. In 1948 he had been invited to assume the Chairmanship of the Solvay Conferences on Physics and in that year he presided over a discussion of 'Elementary particles'. Conferences followed on 'The solid state' (1951); 'Electrons in metals' (1954); and 'The structure and evolution of the Universe' (1958) until in 1961 he presided over his last conference on the 50th anniversary of the inaugural meeting in 1911. The subject was 'Field theory'—which he confessed to finding 'completely unintelligible'. In 1958 he was the President of the International Science Hall at the Brussels Exhibition (207) and arranged the British contribution to it.

At this time he was also Chairman of the Soirée Committee of the Royal Society. This was one of the few committees that he enjoyed, and he greatly appreciated the contact that it gave him with the growing points of science. In this role he was responsible for organizing the exhibition at the Tercentenary Celebrations of the Society in 1960.

The Davy–Faraday research laboratories are an integral part of the Institution and in Bragg's time they were partly in the basement and partly in the upper floors of the house next door, connected to the main building at the level of the Resident Professor's flat. This intimate arrangement enabled Bragg to visit the laboratories whenever he had a moment to spare or needed relief from the discussion of some tedious difficulty, and he would announce his imminent arrival by a characteristic stamp on the ancient and creaking floor boards.

On his arrival in 1954 there was very little research still in progress. King and a small group were continuing the research in metal physics started with Andrade, and U. W. Arndt was engaged in X-ray studies, partly technical and partly on proteins. Bragg had hoped to persuade Max Perutz or John Kendrew to move with him from Cambridge, but, at this promising moment in their work, they preferred to stay behind. They undertook instead to help Bragg build up protein research at the Royal Institution and they were each given the title of Reader in the Davy–Faraday Research Laboratory. With help and advice from them and from Dorothy Hodgkin and others, a research team was quickly assembled. Helen Scouloudi, who had worked at Birkbeck with Bernal and Carlisle, came first and she was joined in the autumn of 1955 by D. W. Green, who had been a research student with Perutz and had contributed to the critically important development of isomorphous replacement in protein structure analysis, and by A. C. T. North, who had worked on collagen with Randall at King's College. J. D. Dunitz came back from the U.S.A. at the end of the year and D. C. Phillips returned from a post in Canada at the beginning of 1956. This rapid build up was made possible by the support of the Medical Research Council and the Rockefeller Foundation.

Dunitz continued with work on transition-metal compounds until his departure for Zürich in 1957 but the other members of Bragg's research group concentrated on proteins and worked closely for the first few years with their colleagues in Cambridge. Kendrew visited the laboratory nearly every week to keep everyone closely in touch with the rapidly developing work on myoglobin. Bragg was particularly interested in the development of diffractometer methods for measuring the diffraction data needed to produce the first three-dimensional image of a protein molecule (it reminded him of the early days with the X-ray spectrometer) and he sought ways of using such measurements to locate heavy atoms in the isomorphous derivatives that were the key to the analysis. The popular approach was based upon the use of Fourier methods which take into account all of the X-ray reflexions from the native and a derivative crystal at the same time. Bragg realized that determination of the small number of parameters defining a heavy-atom structure is potentially a simple problem, similar to the early analyses of mineral structure (55), and that careful consideration of a few well chosen and carefully measured reflexions might provide the required information. Using data from the studies of myoglobin and oxyhaemoglobin he set to work in characteristic style with pencil and graph paper and devised two new methods which were described in his last research paper (205). Although they have not been generally adopted, computer methods proved too powerful and appealing, they illustrate well Bragg's quick eye for the practical application of basic principles and one of them has proved invaluable in the study of tobacco mosaic virus.

Bragg (233) has given his own account of the period 1956–58 during which Kendrew produced the first image of a protein molecule in three dimensions: 'I remember well the thrill of that time. The collection of the vast body of data needed was shared between the laboratory at Cambridge and the Davy–Faraday Laboratory at the Royal Institution. I made a private test of my own. Kendrew supplied me with sets of data for the $hk0$ and $0kl$ projections, for which general phases had to be determined because they have no symmetry centres. I developed a method for getting the relative positions of the heavy atoms (205) and verified that the phases could be found by drawing vector diagrams, with a very convincing agreement between the results for the different ligands. This investigation played no part in the final analysis. Kendrew fixed the heavy atom positions by a more general and powerful analytical treatment aided by the electronic computer, and the phases for all *hkl* components were systematically determined. My investigation only had a meaning for myself because it showed that the problem had been solved, and that final success was now certain. Kendrew first determined the structure to a resolution of 6 Å. It showed dense rods marking the stretches of α-helix and the flat disc of the haem group. It was a proud day when he brought the model to show it to me.'

In the following two years Phillips, joined by Violet Shore and a team of assistants, continued the collaboration with Kendrew to extend the resolution so that in 1960 a high-resolution image of the myoglobin molecule was obtained in which the detailed atomic arrangement could be seen. During the same period North helped Perutz to produce a low-resolution image of haemoglobin which showed that this large and complex molecule can be regarded roughly as four myoglobin molecules in a tetrahedral arrangement. Bragg was delighted and arranged to take a model of myoglobin with him when, in the autumn of 1960, he went to New Zealand to give the Rutherford Memorial Lecture at the University of Canterbury (219). But his glowing account includes one slightly regretful note: 'The new feature is that the element of guesswork has gone and been replaced by the handling of vast masses of measurements and calculations.'

This engagement in New Zealand gave Bragg a long-looked-for opportunity to take his wife on a visit to Australia where they saw again his favourite Aunt Lorna. It was a great success but there were disappointments: 'I promised my wife I would show her the shells and other fascinating marine life along the shores, where I knew the habitat of all the species, and we arranged to spend a week in a seaside place of my boyhood. Alas, it had all gone except for a few of the hardiest kinds. I suppose the pollution of extending Adelaide must have poisoned the sea for fifty miles along the coast.'

Returning to London, Bragg had the twin pleasures of watching the growing recognition of the Cambridge work and encouraging the development of an independent research programme at the Royal Institution. The most dramatic advances were initiated in 1960 when Roberto Poljak, a visiting research worker, showed that he could prepare promising heavy-atom derivatives of hen egg-white lysozyme. Bragg was immediately interested and encouraged Phillips to join in the work. With the strong support of the Medical Research Council the main resources of the laboratory were put into this study with the result that the the complete structure of this enzyme, the first to be analysed, was ready to be presented to Bragg on his seventy-fifth birthday. He could not have been more delighted and immediately set to work, perched upon a stool in the dusty store room used for model building, making a drawing of the molecular structure for its first publication (*x*). The value of his constant advice, support and encouragement in this work can hardly be overestimated and his evident joy at the result gave the greatest possible pleasure to the people concerned. The work was described at a Royal Society Discussion meeting held at the Royal Institution on 3 February 1966 (245).

There can be little doubt that Bragg's years at the Royal Institution were his happiest despite the shadow of advancing age and illness. Although the Braggs lived most of the time at the Institution they had a family house at Waldringfield in Suffolk where they entertained their growing family—eventually there were ten grandchildren—and enjoyed a country life by the sea with plenty of opportunities for bird watching, gardening, sailing and painting. There too they entertained the members of the laboratory at memorable parties. The Braggs' elder son, Stephen, had married Maureen Roberts in 1951 and had three sons. Their two daughters were married from the Royal Institution, Margaret to Mark Heath a diplomat, and Patience to David Thomson, the son of G.P. and grandson of J.J.: David, their younger son who worked at the Seed Testing Station in Cambridge and was the artist of the family, was married later to Elizabeth Bruno. The Heaths had three children, two boys and a girl, and the Thomsons four, two boys and two girls; and Bragg, who was most at ease with children, spent happy hours entertaining his grandchildren (and any others he encountered) with animal drawings and fairy stories from an apparently inexhaustible store.

At the same time, through his lectures at the Royal Institution and the television series that followed from them, he became a popular lecturer and an admired and recognized public figure. As a University lecturer he had not been a very great success with undergraduates who expected to obtain detailed and complete expositions of important aspects of physics from his lectures whereas he was concerned to identify and explain general principles. In 1927 he had noted 'The air of detachment when one is explaining a general principle and the eager scribbling in notebooks when one comes out with a fact are well known to every lecturer' (49). Throughout his life he sought, in common with his father, to achieve as complete an understanding as possible of every physical phenomenon that he encountered and, although quantum effects presented some difficulty (85), this understanding provided the basis for his popular lectures. What made them unforgettable was his gift of illustration by analogy coupled with an infectious enthusiasm which engaged all but the most sophisticated.

During his time at the Royal Institution also his reputation as a scientist was finally assured. He was certainly aware that the changes he had promoted as Cavendish Professor had attracted criticism from physicists who hardly recognized crystallography, and certainly not molecular biology, as physics. In 1962, when he was critically ill after a serious operation, he heard the news of the Nobel Prizes awarded to Perutz and Kendrew, for their work on proteins, and to Crick, Watson and Wilkins, for their analysis of DNA. This recognition of molecular biology, coupled with exciting developments in the metal physics and radio astronomy which he had promoted, put his standing as Cavendish Professor beyond question.

The 50th anniversary of his Nobel Prize was marked on 15 October 1965 by a splendid party at the Royal Institution, which was attended by the Lord

Chancellor and some twenty British Nobel-Prize winners. Later in the year, with Lady Bragg, he attended the Nobel Prize celebrations in Stockholm and was treated to all the acclaim he had missed 50 years earlier. In his lecture he reviewed his part in the early work, somewhat more bluntly than hitherto, and the subsequent growth of crystal structure analysis (241).

Bragg's retirement from his posts at the Royal Institution was announced in July 1965, to take place on 1 September 1966, but for some time previously he had been concerned to ensure that the members of his research group were found appropriate situations in which to continue their work. In the event, Green moved to Edinburgh where he continued his studies of β-lactoglobulin in the Department of Natural Philosophy, and Phillips, North, Blake, Scouloudi and others who had worked on lysozyme moved to Oxford where they set up a new Laboratory of Molecular Biophysics in the Department of Zoology. With Bragg's strong recommendation, this move to Oxford was supported by the Medical Research Council, but it almost failed at the last stage of the negotiations because of major differences between the salaries which had been paid to senior staff by the M.R.C. and those paid to university lecturers in Oxford. Lecturers in Oxford usually receive additional salaries as Fellows of Colleges but such Fellowships are awarded to meet teaching needs and, at this stage, no College believed that a need had been established for tutorial teaching in molecular biophysics. Nevertheless this suggested a mechanism for saving the situation. Bragg was advised that three Colleges would be prepared to create appropriate Fellowships if a suitable endowment could be found. At this he turned for help to his old friends Sir Kenneth Lee (243) and Harold Hemming and they generously provided the necessary money. In this way Bragg made sure that his last research workers could leave the Royal Institution for attractive new posts when he was succeeded as Resident Professor and Director by Sir George Porter.

In November 1966, when he had at last retired at the age of 76, Bragg was awarded the Copley Medal of the Royal Society. Bernal wrote to him (23 November 1966): 'This is only to congratulate the Society for giving you at last the Copley which you have deserved many times over. It cannot really at this stage mean much to you as you and the whole scientific world know what you have done. Crystal structure may seem now an old story, and it is, but you, its only begetter, are still with us. Three new subjects, mineralogy, metallurgy, and now molecular biology, all first sprang from your head, firmly based on applied optics. You can afford to look back on it all with justified feelings of pride and achievement.' Public recognition of his achievements was confirmed in the New Year Honours list of 1967 when he was made a Companion of Honour.

## RETIREMENT, 1966–71

After his formal retirement, Bragg continued to live in London most of the year and, as Emeritus Professor, he continued to lecture at the Royal Institution. He also lectured elsewhere, wrote a good deal and visited 'his' laboratories, the old one in Cambridge and the new one in Oxford.

During this time he saw his forecast about the study of proteins begin to come true as more and more structures were determined and patterns began to emerge in them. But he also saw and delighted in the application of physical methods and modes of thought to more complex biological problems. Perutz (*y*) has recorded an anecdote that vividly recaptures Bragg's style as a consultant: 'I took him to a young zoologist working on pattern formation in insect cuticles. The zoologist explained how disturbances introduced into these regular patterns pointed to their formation being governed by some kind of gradient. Bragg listened attentively and then exclaimed: "Your disturbed gradient behaves like a stream of sand running downhill and encountering an obstacle." "Good heavens," replied the zoologist, "I had been working on this problem for years before this simple analogy occurred to me and you think of it after twenty minutes." '

This kind of insight into natural phenomena, especially those concerned with optics and three-dimensional relationships, underlay all of Bragg's scientific work and his lecturing and writing about it. Years of discipline had long overcome his early horror of writing and he was able to concentrate immediately on writing anything from a routine circular to a scientific paper. Perutz (*u*) again has described his approach to paper writing: 'He would illustrate his conclusions in a series of neatly drawn sketches, and then write the accompanying paper in a lucid and vivid prose. Some scientists produce such prose as a result of prolonged redrafting and polishing, but Bragg would do it in one evening, all ready to be typed the next day, rather like Mozart writing the overture to "The Marriage of Figaro" in a single night.' Bragg retained this hard-won facility into retirement, and his last book (*M*), which was barely complete when he died, displays all the old vigour and many examples of his ability to summarize a complex problem in a single polished paragraph. Thus, for example, after discussing the wave-particle problem which had so dominated the scientific discussions of his youth, he wrote: 'So the dividing line between the wave or particle nature of matter and radiation is the moment "Now". As this moment steadily advances through time, it coagulates a wavy future into a particle past.'

This book on *The Development of X-ray Analysis* is a history of X-ray crystal-lography and, since it concentrates particularly on the topics which had interested him most, it is almost Bragg's scientific autobiography. He was writing it in 1970 when crystallographers from all over the world met at the Royal Institution at a meeting to celebrate his eightieth birthday. Organized by W. H. Taylor, this 'Bragg Symposium 1970' was entitled 'X-ray analysis—past, present and future' and it gave many of his old friends and associates a chance to remember old triumphs together and to look to the future. Bragg was himself the liveliest participant. He listened attentively to every session and generally led the discussion—much to everyone's delight.

This Symposium illustrated very well Bragg's essential achievement. The sessions were devoted to most important advances in the forefront of mineralogy, metallurgy, chemistry and molecular biology, subjects which had been revolutionized or in some instances even created by his discoveries. But there were few papers on topics that would be universally recognized as physics by a modern audience of scientists. Centred in physics departments, his achievements had transformed understanding of the natural world and the descriptive sciences in terms of atomic arrangements but his revolution had coincided with others, especially in nuclear and quantum physics, which largely took over physics itself. Bragg remained essentially a classical physicist in the great tradition of those who thought in terms of tangible rather than mathematical models. But he had to struggle to be accepted as a physicist at all and his associates suffered from this, until at last many of them were recognized for their contributions to other fields.

Behind his conventional, even military, appearance as an establishment figure, Bragg had an artistic temperament with strong emotions normally kept in check by stern self-control. He reminded Colin Blake of Elgar, somewhat ironically since Bragg had no appreciation of music at all. But he delighted in painting, a skill he had learned from his mother, and many of his associates treasure examples of his country scenes and portraits. Literature was another of his loves —he instituted special courses in the humanities for physics students in Cambridge—and he delighted in referring to characters in the great novels: the 'philanthropoid' Mrs Norris in Mansfield Park was a great favourite. One of his last broadcasts was a personal choice of verse and prose which he presented 'With great pleasure' on 18 October 1970.

But most of all Bragg was a private family man. The draft autobiography that he was working on at the time of his death abounds with happy memories of family holidays, often sailing on the Broads, and adventures with his adored wife and children. Perutz (z) remembered that 'typically one would find him tending his garden, with Lady Bragg, children and grandchildren somewhere in the background, and before getting down to business he would proudly demonstrate his latest roses'. Even there his creativity was for ever bursting out in some new 'venture': only a short time before his death he was enthusiastically promoting a method for supporting tall plants, such as Michaelmas daisies, by letting them grow through sheets of wire netting.

Bragg was certainly one of the great creative scientists yet he often worried about his relative lack of more mundane gifts. Forgetful of names, uneasy on committees, reluctant to face personal problems or angry scenes, he depended a great deal on his wife who sustained him through all the triumphs and difficulties of a long public life. There is no doubt that he found peace at the last and the abiding affection of those that knew him best. He died in hospital near his home at Waldringfield on 1 July 1971.

My first thanks are due to Lady Bragg and to Stephen Bragg for their help in the preparation of this memoir and for their permission to consult and quote from the Bragg Archives at the Royal Institution. The Director of the Institution, Sir George Porter, F.R.S., and the Librarian, Mrs I. M. McCabe, have been most helpful. Mrs A. Caroe, Sir Lawrence Bragg's sister, whose biography of their father has been an invaluable help, has also given aid and counsel without stint and I am deeply indebted to her.

Very many of Bragg's colleagues and students have responded generously to my importunate appeals for help and I am grateful to them for their generous assistance and for allowing me to quote freely from their letters and articles. There are too many to mention all by name but I am particularly indebted to Mr Norman Tunstall for his account of the early days in Manchester, to Mr J. A. Ratcliffe, F.R.S., and to Dr M. F. Perutz, F.R.S. Most especially, however, am I grateful to Professor Henry Lipson, F.R.S. whose prompting, encouragement and help (which included writing his own account of the Manchester, N.P.L. and Cambridge periods) made a vital contribution to the completion of the memoirs.

Finally, I must record my indebtedness to Mrs C. C. F. Blake, whose researches into the details of Bragg's career were invaluable; and to my ex-secretary, Miss Susan Partridge, who made an essential contribution to the literature survey and in many other ways.

GENERAL REFERENCES

(a) Caroe, G. M. 1978 *William Henry Bragg, 1862–1942: Man and Scientist.* Cambridge University Press.
(b) Royal Institution archives.
(c) Royal Society archives.
(d) Stuewer, R. H. 1971 William H. Bragg's corpuscular theory of X-rays and $\gamma$-rays. *Br. J. Hist. Sci.* **5**, 258–281.
(e) Ewald, P. P. and numerous crystallographers 1962 *Fifty years of X-ray diffraction.* Published for The International Union of Crystallography by N. V. A. Oosthock's Uitgeversmaatschappij, Utrecht, The Netherlands.
(f) Forman, P. 1969 The discovery of the diffraction of X-rays by crystals; a critique of the myths. *Arch. Hist. Exact Sci.* **6**, 38–71.
(g) Bragg, W. H. 1912 *Nature, Lond.* **90**, 219.
(h) Schuster, A. 1909 *An introduction to the theory of optics* (2nd ed., revised). London: Edward Arnold.
(i) Pope, W. J. 1908 *A. Rep. Progr. Chem.* pp. 258–279.
(j) Bragg, W. H. 1912 *Nature, Lond.* **90**, 360–361.
(k) Bragg, W. H. 1913 *Nature, Lond.* **90**, 372.
(l) Moseley, H. & Darwin, C. G. 1913 *Nature, Lond.* **90**, 594.
(m) Heilbron, J. L. 1974 *H. J. C. Moseley—the life and letters of an English physicist 1887–1915.* Berkeley, Los Angeles and London: University of California Press.
(n) Bragg, W. H. 1913 *Proc. R. Soc. Lond.* A **89**, 246–248.
(o) Miers, H. A. 1918 *J. chem. Soc.* **113**, 363–386.
(p) James, R. W. 1952 *Trans. R. Soc. S. Afr.* **34**, 1–16.
(q) Armstrong, H. E. 1927 *Nature, Lond.* **120**, 478.
(r) Pauling, L. 1928 in *Sommerfeld Festschrift.* Leipzig: S. Hirgel.
            1929 *J. Am. chem. Soc.* **51**, 1010.
(s) Lipson, H. S. 1973 A. J. Bradley (1899–1972). *Biogr. Mem. Fellows R. Soc. Lond.* **19**, 117–128.
(t) Patterson, A. L. 1935 *Z. Kristallogr. Kristallgeom.* **90**, 517–542.
(u) Perutz, M. F. 1970 *Acta crystallogr.* **A26**, 183–185.
(v) Crowther, J. G. 1974 *The Cavendish Laboratory 1874–1974.* London and Basingstoke: Macmillan.
(w) Watson, J. D. 1968 *The double helix.* London: Weidenfeld & Nicholson.
(x) Blake, C. C. F., Koenig, D. F., Mair, G. A., North, A. C. T., Phillips, D. C. & Sarma, V. R. 1965 *Nature, Lond.* **206**, 757–761.
(y) Perutz, M. F. 1971 *New Sci. & Sci. J.* 8 July 1967.
(z) Perutz, M. F. 1971 *Nature, Lond.* **233**, 74–76.

BIBLIOGRAPHY

*Books*

(*A*)  1915  (With W. H. BRAGG) *X-rays and crystal structure*. London: G. Bell & Sons Ltd. 2nd ed. 1916, 3rd 1918, 4th (revised) 1924, 5th 1925. Translated into Russian (1916 and 1929) and French (1921).

(*B*)  1930  *The structure of silicates*. 69 pages. Leipzig: Akad. Verlag.

(*C*)  1933  *The crystalline state, a general survey*. London: G. Bell & Sons Ltd. Vol. I of *The crystalline state*, eds, W. H. & W. L. Bragg.

(*D*)  1936  *Electricity*. (The Royal Institution Christmas Lectures, 1934.) London: G. Bell & Sons Ltd. and U.S.A.: Macmillan Company. Translated: Swedish, 1937; Polish, 1939; Czech, 1940; Hungarian, 1948; Finnish, 1950; German, 1951; Japanese, 1951; Italian, 1953.

(*E*)  1937  *Atomic structure of minerals*. Ithaca, N.Y.: Cornell University Press and London: Oxford University Press.

(*F*)  1939  (With A. E. VAN ARKEL, U. R. EVANS & N. PARRAVANO) *Chimie Minéral*. Paris: Hermann & Cie.

(*G*)  1943  *History of X-ray analysis*. London: British Council/Longmans. Revised edn 1946; German translation 1947.

(*H*)  1950  (With H. J. EMELEUS) *Post-graduate Lectures* (sponsored by the Oil and Colour Chemists Association). Cambridge: W. Heffer & Sons Ltd.

(*I*)  1965  (With G. F. CLARINGBULL) *Crystal structures of minerals*. London: G. Bell & Sons Ltd. Vol. IV of *The crystalline state*, ed. W. L. Bragg.

(*J*)  1967  *The start of X-ray analysis*. London: Longmans/Penguin. (Chemistry Background Books, The Nuffield Foundation.)

(*K*)  1970  *Ideas and discoveries in physics*. London: Longmans. (Longman Physics Topics for 6th form pupils.) Translated: French, 1974; Dutch 1969.

(*L*)  1971  (With A. H. DAWSON & H. H. HEMMING) *Artillery survey in the First World War*. London: Field Survey Association.

(*M*)  1975  *The Development of X-ray analysis*, (ed. D. C. Phillips & H. Lipson). London: G. Bell & Sons Ltd.

*Editor*

*The crystalline state*. London: G. Bell & Sons Ltd.
  Vol. I (1933) (with W. H. Bragg)
  Vol. II (1948)
  Vol. III (1953)
  Vol. IV (1965)
(with G. PORTER) *The Royal Institution Library of Science*: *Physical Sciences* (being the Friday Evening Discourses in Physical Sciences held at The Royal Institution, 1851–1939). Amsterdam: Elsevier Publishing Co. (1970). (10 volumes and Index.)

*Consultant Editor*

*Contemporary Physics* (1959–64).

*Papers*

(1)  1912  The diffraction of short electromagnetic waves by a crystal (lecture 11 November 1912). *Proc. Camb. phil. Soc.* **17**, 43–57. *Nature, Lond.* **90**, 402.

(2)  The specular reflection of X-rays. *Nature, Lond.* **90**, 410.

(3)  1913  X-rays and crystals. *Sci. Prog.* **7**, 372–389.

(4)  (With W. H. BRAGG) The reflection of X-rays by crystals. *Proc. R. Soc. Lond.* A **88**, 428–438.

(5)  The structure of some crystals as indicated by their diffraction of X-rays. *Proc. R. Soc. Lond.* A **89**, 248–277.

(6)  (With W. H. BRAGG) The structure of the diamond. *Nature, Lond.* **91**, 557.

(7)  (With W. H. BRAGG) The structure of the diamond. *Proc. R. Soc. Lond.* A **89**, 277–291.

(8)  1914  Eine Bemerkung über die Interferenzfiguren hemiedrischer Kristalle. *Phys. Z.* **15**, 77–79.

(9)  X-rays and crystals. *J. Röntgen Soc.* **10**, 70–78.

(10)  1914  The analysis of crystals by the X-ray spectrometer. *Proc. R. Soc. Lond.* A **89**, 468–489.

(11)        The crystalline structure of copper. *Phil. Mag.* (6) **27**, 355–360.

(12)  1915  (With W. H. BRAGG) X-rays and crystal structure. (British Association for the Advancement of Science, Manchester) *Engineering, Lond.* **100**, 305.

(13)        (With W. H. BRAGG) Die Reflexion von Röntgenstrahlen aus Kristallen (translations of papers in *Proc. Roy. Soc.*, etc., subsequently published by Leopold Voss, 1928). *Z. anorg. Chem.* **90**, 153–296.

(14)  1919  Sound ranging. *Manchester Memoirs* **64**, p. v and *Nature, Lond.* **104**, 187.

(15)  1920  The crystalline structure of zinc oxide. *Phil. Mag.* (6) **39**, 647–651.

(16)        The arrangement of atoms in crystals. *Phil. Mag.* (6) **40**, 169–189.

(17)        Crystal structure (R. I. Discourse, 28 May 1920). *Proc. R. Instn Gt Br.* **23**, 190–205 and *Nature, Lond.* **105**, 646–648.

(18)  1921  (With R. W. JAMES & C. H. BOSANQUET) Über die Streuung der Röntgenstrahlen durch die Atome eines Kristalles. *Z. Phys.* **8**, 77–84.

(19)        (With R. W. JAMES & C. H. BOSANQUET) The intensity of reflexion of X-rays by rock-salt. *Phil. Mag.* (6) **41**, 309–337.

(20)        (With R. W. JAMES & C. H. BOSANQUET) The intensity of reflexion of X-rays by rock-salt. II. *Phil. Mag.* (6) **42**, 1–17.

(21)        The arrangement of atoms in crystals. *Nature, Lond.* **106**, 725.

(22)        (With H. BELL) The dimensions of atoms and molecules. *Nature, Lond.* **107**, 107.

(23)        The dimensions of atoms and molecules. *Sci. Prog.* **16**, 45–55.

(24)  1922  (With R. W. JAMES & C. H. BOSANQUET) The distribution of electrons around the nucleus in the sodium and chlorine atoms. *Phil. Mag.* (6) **44**, 433–449.

(25)        The diffraction of X-rays by crystals. (Nobel Lecture, Stockholm, 6 September 1922.) *Les Prix Nobel en 1921–1922*. (Also published in: *Nobel Lectures, Physics 1901–21*. Amsterdam: Elsevier Publishing Co. (1967), pp. 370–382).

(26)        (With R. W. JAMES) The intensity of X-ray reflection. *Nature, Lond.* **110**, 148.

(27)  1923  Sound. *Manchester Memoirs* **67**, p. xii.

(28)  1924  The structure of aragonite. *Proc. R. Soc. Lond.* A **105**, 16–39.

(29)        The refractive indices of calcite and aragonite. *Proc. R. Soc. Lond.* A **105**, 370–386.

(30)        The influence of atomic arrangement on refractive index. *Proc. R. Soc. Lond.* A **106**, 346–368.

(31)        (With S. CHAPMAN) A theoretical calculation of the rhombohedral angle of crystals of the calcite type. *Proc. R. Soc. Lond.* A **106**, 369–377

(32)        Crystal structure. *Manchester Memoirs* **68**, pp. xiii-xiv.

(33)  1925  The interpretation of intensity measurements in X-ray analysis of crystal structure. *Phil. Mag.* (6) **50**, 306–310.

(34)        Inorganic crystals (address delivered 17 September 1924 on the occasion of the Centenary of The Franklin Institute). *J. Franklin Inst.* **199**, 761–772.

(35)        Model gratings to illustrate the diffraction of X-rays by crystals. *Manchester Memoirs* **69**, 35–38.

(36)        Model illustrating the formation of crystals. *Manchester Memoirs* **69**, p. xvi.

(37)        The sizes of atoms. *Manchester Memoirs* **70**, p. viii.

(38)        The crystalline structure of inorganic salts (R.I. Discourse, 1 May 1925). *Proc. R. Instn. Gt. Br.* **24**, 614–620 and *Nature, Lond.* **116**, 249–251.

(39)  1926  (With G. B. BROWN) Die Kristallstruktur von Chrysoberyll ($BeAl_2O_4$). *Z. Kristallogr. Kristallgeom.* **63**, 122–143.

(40)        (With G. B. BROWN) Die Struktur des Olivins. *Z. Kristallogr. Kristallgeom.* **63**, 538–556.

(41)        (With G. B. BROWN) The crystalline structure of Chrysoberyl. *Proc. R. Soc. Lond.* A **110**, 34–63.

(42)        (With J. WEST) The structure of beryl, $Be_3Al_2Si_6O_{18}$. *Proc. R. Soc. Lond.* A **111**, 691–714.

(43)        (With C. G. DARWIN & R. W. JAMES) The intensity of reflexion of X-rays by crystals. *Phil. Mag.* (7) **1**, 897–922.

(44)        Interatomic distances in crystals. *Phil. Mag.* (7) **2**, 258–266.

(45)        X-ray analysis of crystal structures and its relation with chemical constitution. *2ième Cons. Chim. Inst. Intern. Chim. Solvay, 1926*, 44–65.

(46)  1927  The structure of phenacite, $Be_2SiO_4$ *Proc. R. Soc. Lond.* A **113**, 642–657.

(47)   1927   (With J. West) The structure of certain silicates. *Proc. R. Soc. Lond.* A **114**, 450–473.

(48)          The structure of silicates (R.I. Discourse, 20 May 1927). *Proc. R. Instn Gt Br.* **25**, 302–310.

(49)          Some views on the teaching of science (Presidential Address to the Manchester Library and Philosophical Society, 1927–28 Session). *Manchester Memoirs* **71**, 119–123.

(50)          Some recent advances in the physics of the solid state. *Manchester Memoirs* **71**, p. xii.

(51)          Crystallography. *Ann. Rep. Prog. Chem.* **22**, 257–279.

(52)          (With W. H. Bragg) Stereoscopic photographs of crystal models, to illustrate the results of X-ray crystallography. 2 series (1927, 1930). London: Adam Hilger Ltd.

(53)   1928   The diffraction of short electromagnetic waves by a crystal. *Atti Congr. Internazionale dei Fisici* (Como, September 1927 (V)), 171–180.

(54)          L'Intensité de Réflexion des Rayons X. *Inst. Intern. Phys. Solvay. 5ieme Cons. de Physique, 1927*, 1–43.

(55)          (With J. West) A technique for the X-ray examination of crystal structures with many parameters. *Z. Kristallogr. Kristallgeom.* **69**, 118–148.

(56)          (With B. Warren) The structure of diopside, $CaMg(SiO_3)_2$. *Z. Kristallogr. Kristallgeom.* **69**, 168–193.

(57)   1929   (With R. W. James, J. D. Bernal & A. J. Bradley) Crystallography. *Ann. Rep. Prog. Chem.* **25**, 275–302.

(58)          X-ray optics (the 9th Mackenzie Davidson Memorial Lecture). *Br. J. Radiol.* **2**, 65–71.

(59)          Atomic arrangement in the silicates. *Trans. Faraday Soc.* **25**, 291–314.

(60)          The determination of parameters in crystal structures by means of Fourier series. *Proc. R. Soc. Lond.* A **123**, 537–559.

(61)          An optical method of representing the results of X-ray analysis. *Z. Kristallogr. Kristallgeom.* **70**, 475–492.

(62)          An optical method of displaying the results of X-ray examination of crystals. *Manchester Memoirs* **72**, pp. xii–xiii.

(63)          The diffraction of short electromagnetic waves by a crystal. *Scientia* March 1929, pp. 153–162.

(64)          Diffraction of X-rays by two-dimensional crystal lattice. *Nature, Lond.* **124**, 125.

(65)   1930   (With J. West) A note on the representation of crystal structure by Fourier series. *Phil. Mag.* (7) **10**, 823–841.

(66)          (With W. H. Zachariasen) The crystalline structure of phenacite, $Be_2SiO_4$ and willemite, $Zn_2SiO_4$. *Z. Kristallogr. Kristallgeom.* **72**, 518–528.

(67)          The structure of silicates. *Z. Kristallogr. Kristallgeom.* **74**, 237–305.

(68)          (With B. E. Warren) The structure of chrysotile $H_4Mg_3Si_2O_9$. *Z. Kristallogr. Kristallgeom.* **76**, 201–210.

(69)          Die Untersuchung der Atomanordnung mittels Röntgenstrahlen. *Metallwirtschaft* **9**, 461–465.

(70)          Bau der silikate. *Glastech.* (Frankfurt) **8**, 449–453.

(71)          The structure of silicates (lecture to the Mineralogical Society, 18 March 1930). *Nature, Lond.* **125**, 510–511.

(72)          Structure of silicates. *J. Soc. Glass Technol.* **14**, 295–305.

(73)          X-ray optics. *Photogr. J.* **70**, 179–186.

(74)   1931   The architecture of the solid state (the 22nd Kelvin Lecture, 30 April 1931). *J. Instn elect. Engrs* **69**, 1239–1244 and *Nature, Lond.* **128**, 210–212 and 248–250.

(75)          (With C. Gottfried & J. West) The structure of β alumina. *Z. Kristallogr. Kristallgeom.* **77**, 255–274.

(76)          (With F. Kirchner) The action of a crystal as a two-dimensional lattice in diffracting electrons. *Nature, Lond.* **127**, 738–739.

(77)   1932   The structure of molecules: the solid state. In: *Chemistry at the Centenary (1931) Meeting of the British Association for the Advancement of Science*, pp. 255–256. Cambridge: W. Heffer & Sons Ltd.

(78)   1932   The application of X-ray methods to industrial problems. (lecture at the University of Manchester, 11 July 1932), pamphlet, 19 pages.

(79)  1932  (With J. A. DARBYSHIRE) The structure of thin films of certain metallic oxides *Trans. Faraday Soc.* **28**, 522–529.

(80)        Structure of complex ionic compounds (lecture 20 November 1931). *Trans. Oxf. Univ. jr scient. Club.* Fifth series, no. 5, 151–153.

(81)  1933  The structure of alloys (R.I. Discourse, 17 March 1933). *Proc. R. Instn Gt Br.* **27**, 756–784 and *Nature, Lond.* **131**, 749–753.

(82)        Development of Röntgen-ray analysis of crystals (a review). *Usp. fiz. Nauk.* **13**, 195–208.

(83)  1934  (With E. J. WILLIAMS) The effect of thermal agitation on atomic arrangements in alloys. *Proc. R. Soc. Lond.* A **145**, 699–730.

(84)        The exploration of the mineral world by X-rays. (Evening Discourse to B.A., 10 September 1934.) *Rep. a. Meet Br. Ass. Advmt Sci.* **104**, 437–444 and *Nature, Lond.* **134**, 401–404.

(85)        The Physical Sciences (introductory lecture as non-resident Lecturer in Chemistry at Cornell University). *Science, N.Y.* **79**, 237–240.

(86)  1935  (With E. J. WILLIAMS) The effect of thermal agitation on atomic arrangement in alloys—II. *Proc. R. Soc. Lond.* A **151**, 540–566.

(87)        The new crystallography. *Proc. R. Soc. Edinb.* **55**, 62–71.

(88)        Atomic arrangement in metals and alloys (25th May Lecture to the Institute of Metals, 8 May 1935). *J. Inst. Metals* **56**, 275–299.

(89)  1936  L'exploration du monde minéral a l'aide des rayons X. (Conference faite devant la Societé Francaise de Physique, 21 April 1936.) *J. Phys. Radium, Paris* **7**, (série VII) 321–325.

(90)        (With H. Lipson) The employment of contoured graphs of structure-factor in crystal analysis. *Z. Kristallogr. Kristallgeom.* **95**, 323–337.

(91)        Structure-factor graphs for crystal analysis. *Nature, Lond.* **138**, 362–363.

(92)        Anordnung der Atome in den Metallen und Legierungen. *Usp. fiz. Nauk.* **16**, 977–1000.

(93)  1937  Alloys. *Jl R. Soc. Arts* **85**, 431–447.

(94)        (With W. H. BRAGG) The discovery of X-ray diffraction. *Curr. Sci.* **7** (suppl., special number, 'Laue Diagrams'), 9–13.

(95)        Alloys. (Report of lecture to meeting, 2 February 1937.) *Manchester Memoirs* **81**, p. xii.

(96)        (With C. SYKES & A. J. BRADLEY) A study of the order-disorder transformation. *Proc. phys. Soc.* **49**, 96–102 and 108–109.

(97)  1938  The atomic structure of alloys (Watt Anniversary Lecture for 1938). *Pap. Greenock phil. Soc.* 1938.

(98)        A discussion on plastic flow in metals (opening address). *Proc. R. Soc. Lond.* A **168**, 302–303.

(99)        Forty years of crystal physics. In: *Background to modern science* (eds. W. Pagel & J. Needham), pp. 77–92. Cambridge University Press.

(100)       The Physics Department, Manchester University. *J. Univ. Manchester* **1**, 35–41.

(101)       (With H. LIPSON) Structure of metals. *Nature, Lond.* **141**, 367–368.

(102)       General features of atomic structure of silicates: inferences to be drawn from them as to the structure of clay minerals (summary). *Rep. a. Meet. Br. Ass. Advmt Sci.* **108**, 403.

(103)       The structure of alloys (being the 39th Robert Boyle Lecture delivered before the Oxford University Junior Scientific Club, 11 June 1937). O.U.P. 1938 (5 pages).

(104)       The structure of alloys. *Der Feste Körper* (1938), pp. 24–41. Leipzig: Hirzel.

(105)       Röntgenstrahlen in der Industrie. *Indian east. Engr.* **82**, 219.

(106)  1939  Magnets (R.I. Discourse, 5 May 1939). *Proc. R Instn Gt Br.* **30**, 783–787 and *Engineering* **147**, 595–596.

(107)       Patterson diagrams in crystal analysis. *Nature, Lond.* **143**, 73–74.

(108)       A new type of 'X-ray microscope'. *Nature, Lond.* **143**, 678.

(109)       Atomic patterns of metals (Fourth Edward Williams Lecture, Institute of British Foundrymen, 13 June 1939). *Foundry J.* 12–17 June 1939, pp. 25–31; *Fndry Trade J.* **60**, 506–508; *Proc. Instn Br. Foundrym.* **32**, 25–31 and *Engineering* **147**, 788.

(110)  1940  The structure of a cold-worked metal. *Proc. phys. Soc.* **52**, 105–109.

(111) 1940 (With A. J. BRADLEY & C. SYKES) Researches into the structure of alloys. *J. Iron Steel Inst.* **141**, 63P–156P.

(112) The symmetry of patterns (title only) (R.I. Discourse, 3 May 1940). *Proc. R. Instn Gt Br.* **31**, 149.

(113) (With A. J. BRADLEY & C. SYKES) The structure of alloys: X-ray and thermal analysis. *Iron Steel, Lond.* **13**, (no. 9), 305–307.

(114) (With A. J. BRADLEY) Part I—Investigation of equilibrium diagrams and theory of order-disorder transformation. *Iron Steel, Lond.* **13**, (no. 9), 308–310.

(115) 1941 Diffraction of monochromatic X-rays by crystals at high temperatures. *Proc. R. Soc. Lond.* A **179**, 61–64.

(116) X-ray analysis in industry. *J. scient. Instrum.* **18**, 69.

(117) 1942 Physicists after the War (Afternoon Lecture at the R.I., 26 March 1942). *Proc. R. Instn Gt Br.* **32**, 253–271 and *Nature, Lond.* **150**, 75–80 and 374.

(118) A model illustrating intercrystalline boundaries and plastic flow in metals. *J. scient. Instrum.* **19**, 148–150.

(119) The X-ray microscope. *Nature, Lond.* **149**, 470–471.

(120) A theory of the strength of metals (R.I. Discourse, 31 March 1942). *Nature, Lond.* **149**, 511–513.

(121) Index of X-ray diffraction data. *Nature, Lond.* **150**, 738.

(122) 1943 Seeing ever-smaller worlds (R.I. Discourse, 12 March 1943). *Proc. R. Instn Gt Br.* **32**, 475–481 and *Nature, Lond.* **151**, 545–547.

(123) (With H. LIPSON) A simple method of demonstrating diffraction grating effects. *J. scient. Instrum.* **20**, 110–113.

(124) Tensile strength of metals. *Tek. Tid.* 73, 403–407.

(125) (With R. H. PICKARD & A. FINDLAY) The place of scientists in the community. *Chemy Ind.* **62**, 263.

(126) Metals. *Endeavour* **II**, 43–52; *Trans. Can. Inst. Min. Metall.* **46**, 291–304; and *Can. Mach.* **54**, 95–100.

(127) 1944 The mechanical strength of metals. General discussion on radiological testing. (Introductory Contribution.) *Trans. NE. Cst Instn Engrs Shipbldrs* **60**, 299–306.

(128) Lightning calculations with light (R.I. Discourse, 24 March 1944). *Proc. R. Instn Gt Br.* **33**, 107–113 and *Nature Lond.* **154**, 69–72.

(129) The spirit of science. *The Listener* 10 February 1944, p. 147.

(130) Organization and finance of science in universities. *The Political Quarterly* **15**, 330–341.

(131) Mr. F. Lincoln and the Cavendish Laboratory. *Nature, Lond.* **154**, 643.

(132) Metalle. *Metallurgia Electr.* **8**, 20–26.

(133) 1945 Some problems of the metallic state (14th Andrew Laing Lecture). *Trans. NE. Cst Instn Engrs Shipbldrs* **62**, 25–34 and *Iron Steel, Lond.* **18**, 531–535.

(134) Magnetic materials (Lecture to Measurement Section, 18 May 1945). *J. Instn. elect. Engrs* **92**, (Part I, General), 444–451.

(135) X-ray analysis: past, present and future (R.I. Discourse, 11 May 1945). *Proc. R. Instn Gt Br.* **33**, 393–400.

(136) (With A. R. STOKES) X-ray analysis with the aid of the 'fly's eye'. *Nature, Lond.* **156**, 332–333.

(137) La Cohésion des Métaux *Revue Métall, Paris* **42**, 187–193.

(138) 1946 The Austin Wing of the Cavendish Laboratory. *Nature, Lond.* **158**, 326–327.

(139) (With E. B. BOND) The Rutherford Papers in the Library of the Cavendish Laboratory. *Nature, Lond.* **158**, 714.

(140) X-ray analysis in research and practice today (R.I. Discourse, 24 May 1947). *Proc. R. Instn Gt Br.* **33**, 649–661.

(141) X-rays' part in metallurgical research. In: *Science lifts the veil*, pp. 33–37. London: British Council/Longmans, Green & Co.

(142) 1947 The relationship of the university and the technical college (lecture to the Association of Technical Institutions, 28 February 1947). *Association of Technical Institutions*: miscellaneous pamphlets: London (1947). 6 pages.

(143) The conversion factor for kX units to Ångstrom units. *J. scient. Instrum.* **24**, 27; *Phys. Rev.* **72**, 437; and (with E. A. WOOD) *J. Am. chem. Soc.* **69**, 2919.

(144) 1947 Working models of crystals (R.I. Discourse, 9 May 1947). *Proc. R. Instn Gt Br.* **34**, 103–108.

(145)  1947  (With J. F. Nye) A dynamical model of a crystal structure. *Proc. R. Soc. Lond.* A **190**, 474–481 and *Naturwissenschaften* **34**, 328–336.

(146)        Effects associated with stresses on a microscopic scale. In: Proceedings of Symposium on Internal Stresses in Metals and Alloys, 15–16 October 1947. *Inst. of Metals Monograph and Report Series No. 5*, 221–226.

(147)        Recent advances in X-ray analysis. *Paint Technol.* **12**, 421–425.

(148)  1948  Current researches in the Cavendish Laboratory (lecture to the Manchester Association of Engineers, 9 January 1948). Pamphlet, 10 pages.

(149)        Organisation and work of the Cavendish Laboratory (course of 3 lectures given at the R.I., 4, 11, 18 March 1948). *Nature, Lond.* **161,** 627–628.

(150)        The standards of advanced studies and research in science and technology. (Address to the 19th Annual Convention of the Yorkshire Council for Further Education, May 1948.) Pamphlet no. 36, 10 pages.

(151)        Atomic rearrangement in the metallic state. *Festkr. J. Arvid Hedvall* 1948, 75–81.

(152)        Recent advances in the study of the crystalline state. *Science N.Y.* **108**, 455–463 and *Advmt Sci., Lond.* **5**, 165–174.

(153)        The Cavendish Laboratory (19th Autumn Lecture, Institute of Metals, 16 September 1948). *J. Inst. Metals* **75**, 107–114.

(154)        The yield point of a metal. Rep. Bristol Conf. 'Strength of Solids' (1947). *Phys. Soc. Lond.* (1948) 26–29.

(155)  1949  Acceptance of the Roebling Medal of the Mineralogical Society of America. *Am. Miner.* **34**, 238–241.

(156)        (With W. M. Lomer) A dynamical model of a crystal structure. II. *Proc. R. Soc. Lond.* A **196**, 171–181.

(157)        Giant molecules (R.I. Discourse, 27 April 1949). *Proc. R. Instn Gt Br.* **34**, 395–405 and *Nature, Lond.* **164**, 7–10.

(158)        Slip in metals. *Physica* **15**, 83–91.

(159)        The place of technological education in university studies. Conference on the Home Universities (1949). London: Association of Universities of the British Commonwealth, pp. 72–77 (and 24–25, 56–58).

(160)        The strength of metals. *Proc. Camb. phil. Soc.* **45**, 125–130.

(161)  1950  (With J. C. Kendrew & M. F. Perutz) Polypeptide chain configurations in crystalline proteins. *Proc. R. Soc. Lond.* A **203**, 321–357.

(162)        Famous experiments in the Cavendish Laboratory (R.I. Discourse, 12 May 1950). *Proc. R. Instn Gt Br.* **34**, 626–633 and *Nature, Lond.* **166**, 7–9.

(163)        Microscopy by reconstructed wave-fronts. *Nature, Lond.* **166**, 399–400.

(164)        Science and the adventure of living (the Radford Mather Lecture, 25 October 1950 at the R.I.). *The British Association of the Advancement of Science* **7**, 279–284. (Also Norwegian translation, 1952.)

(165)        Riesenmoleküle. *Usp. fiz. Nauk.* **40**, 108.

(166)        Address at Electrical Research Association Annual Lunch, 1950. *E.R.A./R720*, pamphlet, 18 pages.

(167)  1951  (With G. L. Rogers) Elimination of the unwanted image in diffraction microscopy. *Nature, Lond.* **167**, 190–191.

(168)        Crystallographic research in the Cavendish Laboratory (R.I. Discourse, 16 March 1951). *Proc. R. Instn Gt Br.* **35**, 103–113 and *Mitt. naturf. Ges. Bern.* **8**, xi–xiii.

(169)  1952  The atomic patterns of everyday materials (the Keith Lecture, 2 April 1952, Royal Scottish Society of Arts). *Edinb. J. Sci. Technol. photogr. Art*, pp. 47–56.

(170)        The Cavendish Laboratory archives (R.I. Discourse, 28 March 1952). *Proc. R. Instn Gt Br.* **35**, 299–304 and *Nature, Lond.* **169**, 684–686.

(171)        (With E. R. Howells & M. F. Perutz) Arrangement of polypeptide chains in horse methaemoglobin. *Acta crystallogr.* **5**, 136–141.

(172)        (With M. F. Perutz) The external form of the haemoglobin molecule. I. *Acta crystallogr.* **5**, 277–283.

(173)        (With M. F. Perutz) The external form of the haemoglobin molecule. II. *Acta crystallogr.* **5**, 323–328.

(174)        A device for calculating structure factors. *Acta crystallogr.* **5**, 474–475.

(175)  1952  (With M. F. Perutz) The structure of haemoglobin *Proc. R. Soc. Lond.* A **213**, 425–435.

(176) 1952 X-ray analysis of proteins (36th Guthrie Lecture, 12 March 1952). *Proc. phys. Soc.* **65B**, 833–846.

(177) The Cavendish Laboratories of Cambridge University. *Nucleo (Barcelona)* **7**, 447–449.

(178) 1953 The discovery of X-ray diffraction by crystals (R.I. Discourse, 22 May 1953). *Proc. R. Instn Gt Br.* **35**, 552–559.

(179) X-ray analysis of the haemoglobin molecule. (In: A Discussion on the Structure of Proteins.) *Proc. R. Soc. Lond.* B **141**, 67–69.

(180) Budgets of the scientific departments of the University of Cambridge. *Nature, Lond.* **171**, 642–643.

(181) The X-ray analysis of protein molecules (Fison Memorial Lecture, 15 May 1953). *Guy's Hosp. Gaz.* (new ser) **57**, 242–246.

(182) (With A. B. PIPPARD) The form birefringence of macromolecules. *Acta crystallogr.* **6**, 865–867.

(183) The bubble model of a metal structure (lecture delivered in Johannesburg, 18 July 1952). *A. Proc. ass. tech. Socs S. Afr.* (July 1953), pp. 33–44.

(184) A centre of fundamental research. *Physics to-day* **6**, 18–19.

(185) X-ray analysis of protein structure. *Inst. intern. Chim. Solvay, Conseil. Chim.*, 9th Conseil, Brussels, 1953, pp. 100–109.

(186) 1954 X-ray studies of biological molecules (R.I. Discourse, 29 January 1954). *Proc. R. Instn Gt Br.* **35**, 685–696 and *Nature, Lond.* **174**, 55–59.

(187) Models of metal structure (R.I. Discourse, 19 November 1954). *Proc. R. Instn Gt Br.* **35**, 844–852.

(188) (With E. R. HOWELLS) X-ray diffraction by imidazole methaemoglobin. *Acta crystallogr.* **7**, 409–411.

(189) (With E. R. HOWELLS & M. F. PERUTZ) The structure of haemoglobin, II. *Proc. R. Soc. Lond.* A **222**, 33–44.

(190) (With M. F. PERUTZ) The structure of haemoglobin, VI. Fourier projections on the 010 plane. *Proc. R. Soc. Lond.* A **225**, 315–329.

(191) (With M. F. PERUTZ) I. A Fourier projection of haemoglobin on the 010 plane. II. Sign determination by the isomorphous replacement method (abstracts of the meeting of the International Union of Crystallography, 21–28 July 1954). *Acta crystallogr.* **7**, 653–654.

(192) 1955 X-rays and the molecule (Dunn Memorial Lecture to the Newcastle Section of Soc. of Chemical Industry, 11 May 1955). *Chemy Ind.* 1955, pp. 1164–1169.

(193) Obituary Notice: George Frederick Charles Searle. *Physical Society Year Book*, p. 72.

(194) The Royal Institution—maintaining standards of popular exposition. *The Times Educational Supplement* 3 June 1955, p. 597.

(195) 1956 Masters of modern science, No. V: Michael Faraday—Our greatest experimentalist *The Times Educational Supplement* 9 March 1956, p. 302.

(196) The discovery of useful electricity (R.I. Discourse, 9 December 1955). *Proc. R. Instn Gt Br.* **36**, 278–289.

(197) The diffraction of X-rays (34th Silvanus Thompson Memorial Lecture). *Br. J. Radiol.* **29**, 121–126.

(198) Information centre for science teachers. *The Schoolmaster* 6 July 1956.

(199) 1957 Schools Lectures at The Royal Institution: a new venture. *Discovery* **18**, 66–67 (February 1957).

(200) The interference of waves (Trotter–Patterson Memorial Lecture). *Trans. illum. Engng Soc. Lond.* **22**, 175–181.

(201) Experimental demonstrations (R.I. Discourse, 29 March 1957). *Proc. R. Instn. Gt Br.* **36**, 657–664 and *Nature, Lond.* **179**, 1211–1212.

(202) X-ray analysis. *New Scient.* **3**, 19–21 (21 November 1957).

(203) 1822–1957—135 Years of British Achievement: three great men of physics. *The Sunday Times* 14 July 1957, p. 15.

(204) 1958 Gemstones (R.I. Discourse, 31 January 1958) *Proc. R. Instn Gt Br.* **37**, 1–15.

(205) The determination of the coordinates of heavy atoms in protein crystals. *Acta crystallogr.* **11**, 70–75.

(206) 1958 Interpretation of science to the public. *Nature, Lond.* **181**, 807–808.

(207)   1958   An international survey of recent scientific research. *New Scient.* **3**, 16–17 (27 March 1958).
(208)   1959   Treasures in the collections of apparatus at The Royal Institution (R.I. Discourse, 24 October 1958). *Proc. R. Instn Gt Br.* **37**, 259–275 and *Nature, Lond.* **182**, 1541–1543 (1958).
(209)          The diffraction of Röntgen rays by crystals. In: *Beiträge zur Physik und Chemie des 20 Jahrhunderts* (ed. O. R. Frisch, F. A. Paneth, F. Laves & P. Rosbaud), pp. 147–151. Braunschweig: Friedr. Vieweg & Sohn.
(210)          The contribution of the Royal Institution to the teaching of science (Presidential Address to the Science Masters' Association, 30 December 1958). *Sch. Sci. Rev.* **40**, (no. 141), 240–245.
(211)          Talking and writing about science. (Based on an address given on the occasion of the award of the first Waverley Gold Medal by Butterworths Scientific Publications, 15 October 1956.) *I.R.E. Trans.* **EWS-2**, 69–72.
(212)   1960   Atoms and molecules (R.I. Discourse, 20 November 1959). *Proc. R. Instn Gt Br.* **38**, 87–92 and *Contemp. Phys* **I**, 390–393.
(213)          William Henry Bragg. *New Scient.* **7**, 718–720.
(214)          British achievements in X-ray crystallography. *Science N.Y.* **131**, 1870–1874.
(215)          The Schools Lectures at the Royal Institution. *Public Schools Appointments Bureau*, bulletin no. 89, July 1960, pp. 25–27.
(216)          What constitutes life? *The Times* 19 July 1960, p. xiv (special number on The Royal Society Tercentenary).
(217)          The nature of light. *Trans. illum. Engng. Soc. Lond.* **25**, 6–10.
(218)          Achievements in X-ray crystallography. *Proc. K. ned. Akad. Wet.* B. **63**, 210–220.
(219)   1961   The development of X-ray analysis (Rutherford Memorial Lecture, 1960). *Proc. R. Soc. Lond.* A **262**, 145–158.
(220)          The development of X-ray analysis (R.I. Discourse, 3 March 1961). *Proc. R. Instn Gt Br.* **38**, 526–543.
(221)          Memoir of Maurice, Duc de Broglie. *Proc. phys. Soc.* **77**, 1232.
(222)          Adventures of the mind: what is life made of? *The Saturday Evening Post*, 7 October 1961, Vol. **234** (no. 40), pp. 34–35, 54, 62, 64.
(223)   1962   (With Mrs G. M. CAROE) Sir William Bragg, F.R.S. (1862–1942). *Notes Rec. R. Soc. Lond.* **17**, 169–182.
(224)          The analysis of protein molecules by X-rays. (Discourse at the R.I., 26 September 1961, to delegates attending the 9th General Assembly of I.C.S.U.) *ICSU Rev.* **4**, 33–41.
(225)          The growing power of X-ray analysis. In: *Fifty years of X-ray diffraction* (ed. P. P. Ewald), pp. 120–135. N. V. A. Oosthoek's Uitgeversmaatschappij, Utrecht.
(226)          Personal reminiscences. In *Fifty years of X-ray diffraction*, pp. 531–539.
(227)   1963   X-ray analysis of biological moleculs (Presidential Address to the Madras Symposium, 1963). In: *Aspects of protein structure* (ed. G. N. Ramachandran), pp. 1–9. London: Academic Press.
(228)   1964   The start of X-ray analysis. *Chemistry* **40**, 8–13.
(229)          The difference between living and non-living matter (Saha Memorial Lecture). *Sci. Cult.* **30**, 161–167.
(230)          Minerals (R.I. Discourse, 28 February 1964). *Proc. R. Instn Gt Br.* **40**, 64–81.
(231)          Reginald William James (1891–1964) (Obituary). *Acta crystallogr.* **17**, 1615–1616.
(232)   1965   Reginald William James, 1891–1964. *Biogr. Mem. Fellows R. Soc. Lond.* **11**, 115–125.
(233)          First stages in the X-ray analysis of proteins. *Rep. Prog. Phys.* **28**, 1–14.
(234)          The history of X-ray analysis. *Contemp. Phys.* **6**, 161–171 and *Phys. Teach.* **3**, 295–300.
(235)          The Schools Lectures at The Royal Institution. *Science, N.Y.* **150**, 1420–1423.
(236)          Birthday Greeting to F. Machatschki. (Foreword to 70th birthday tribute). *Tschermaks miner. petrogr. Mitt.* **10**, (3rd ser.) p. 3.
(237)          The two cultures. *Overseas* vol 50, no. 504, pp. 3, 5, 9. October 1965 (pub. Royal Overseas League).
(238)   1966   The Royal Institution Lectures in Science for Members of the Administrative Class of the Civil Service. *Contemp. Phys.* **7**, 358–361.
(239)   1966   The art of talking about science. *Science, N.Y.* **154**, 1613–1616.

(240) 1966 Reminiscences of fifty years' research (R.I. Discourse, 11 March 1966). *Proc. R. Instn Gt Br.* **41**, 92–100.

(241) Half a century of X-ray analysis. Nobel Guest Lecture, I (read 1 June 1966). *Ark. Fys.* **40**, 585–603 (published in 1974).

(242) 1967 The art of talking about science. *Marine Technol.* **4**, 258–261.

(243) Sir Kenneth Lee. (Obituary.) *Nature, Lond.* **216**, 945.

(244) The spirit of science (James Scott Lecture). *Proc. R. Soc. Edinb.* A **67**, 303–308.

(245) Introduction to 'A Discussion on the Structure and Function of Lysozyme'. *Proc. R. Soc. Lond.* B **167**, 349.

(246) Reminiscences of fifty years of research (Redding Lecture, Annual General Meeting of the Franklin Institute, 18 January 1967). *J. Franklin Inst.* **284**, 211–228.

(247) William Henry Bragg. *The Encyclopaedia Americana.*

(248) 1968 Professor P. P. Ewald (appreciation on 80th birthday). *Acta crystallogr.* A **24**, 4.

(249) X-ray crystallography. *Scient. Am.* **219** (1), 58–70.

(250) More on the art of talking about science (editorial) *Nucl. Appl. Technol.* **4**, (no. 5), 282–283.

(251) Foreword to *The double helix* by J. D. Watson. New York: Atheneum.

(252) How a secret of life was discovered (article about *The double helix*). *The Times* 6 May 1968, p. 13.

(253) The white-coated worker. *Punch* vol. 255 (no. 6679), 11 September 1968, pp. 352–354.

(254) 1969 The early history of intensity measurements. *Acta crystallogr.* A **25**, 1–3.

(255) The history of X-ray analysis. In: *Sources of physics teaching* pt 3, pp. 74–84. London: Taylor & Francis.

(256) What makes a scientist. (Lecture for Civil Servants, 11 December 1968.) *Proc. R. Instn Gt Br.* **42**, 397–410.

(257) 1972 Dame Kathleen Lonsdale. (Obituary.) *Acta crystallogr.* A **28**, 226.

(Some additional articles and reports of lectures are listed in *William Henry Bragg and William Lawrence Bragg: A Bibliography of their Non-Technical Writings* (1978), Office for History of Science and Technology, University of California, Berkeley.)

*Max Perutz: a study by Sir Lawrence Bragg (drawing courtesy of Sir John C. Kendrew)*

# How Lawrence Bragg Invented X-ray Analysis

## M.F. PERUTZ OM, FRS

Bragg was a scientific father to me. When Professor Thomas invited me to speak on the occasion of the centenary of his birth, I thought that Bragg would have liked me to describe to you some of his great discoveries, and to recall how he made them. They were his invention of X-ray analysis for finding the arrangement of atoms in crystals and his determinations of the atomic structures of the rocks that make up the bulk of the Earth's crust. They revolutionised the foundations of chemistry, mineralogy and metallurgy [1–4].

I first met Bragg in Cambridge in the autumn of 1938 when he had just been appointed Rutherford's successor as Cavendish Professor of Experimental Physics. One day I burst into his room announcing proudly: "I have received an honour that you can't match, I have had a glacier named after me". "I have one that you can't match" retorted Bragg, "I have had a cuttlefish named after me". He then told me that as a boy in Adelaide he had been a keen collector and found a new species which his seniors promptly named *Sepia Braggi*.

Bragg's father studied mathematics at Cambridge and finished 3rd Wrangler. On the strength of that he was appointed professor of mathematics and physics at the recently founded University of Adelaide when he was only 23, never mind that he had learnt no physics. He read Deschanel's *Electricity and Magnetism* on the boat going out and remained in Adelaide until 1909, when he moved back to England to become professor of physics at Leeds [5]. Willie Bragg was born in 1890; aged 15 he entered Adelaide University to read mathematics, and graduated there at 18. Next year he entered Cambridge University to read mathematics and physics. One day he wrote to his father at Leeds: "Dear Dad, I'm so glad you liked the notes on Jeans. I got an awful lot from a Dane who had seen me asking Jeans questions. He was awfully sound, and most interesting, his name was Böhr or something that sounds like it." That was the start of his lifelong friendship with Niels Bohr. Bragg took his Cambridge degree in 1911. He records in his biography: "Then came a time of research in the Cavendish. It was a sad place. There were too many young researchers (about 40) attracted by its reputation, too few ideas for them to work on, too little money, and too little apparatus. We had to made practically everything for ourselves, and even at that the means were meagre. There were a few senior people who had built little kingdoms for themselves with good equipment, but most of us were breaking our hearts trying to make bricks without straw. J.J. Thomson did his best to think of ideas for us all and guide us, but there were too many of us, and he was the only leader of research. C.T.R. Wilson (the inventor of the cloud chamber) liked doing everything on his own, and no other member of the staff was interested in research". (unpublished memoirs)

After a frustrating year he joined his family on the Yorkshire coast for the summer holidays and found his father excited about a paper by Friedrich, Knipping and Laue that had just appeared in Munich. Bragg's father had regarded X-rays as "minute bundles of energy, tiny entities which move like material particles, but with the speed of light". On the other hand, Max von Laue, a theoretical physicist at the University of Munich, believed that they are electromagnetic waves. It occurred to him that the wavelength of X-rays might be of the same order as the distance between atoms in crystals, in which case crystals would act as diffraction gratings for X-rays. This prediction was verified by Friedrich and Knipping by the discovery of X-ray diffraction patterns given off by crystals of copper sulphate, zincblende and other simple compounds (Figure 1) [6]. Bragg's father thought the Germans' X-ray patterns might have been due, not to diffraction, but to neutral particles running down different channels in their crystals. On returning to Cambridge the son continued to mull over von Laue's results and soon convinced himself that they must be due to diffraction. To his father he wrote: "I have just got a lovely series of reflections of the rays in mica plates with only a few minutes' exposure! Huge joy" and he signed himself: "Your affectionate son, W.L. Bragg." Those were formal days. And the father wrote: "My dear Rutherford, my boy has been getting beautiful X-ray reflections from mica sheet just as simple as the reflections of light in a mirror," but in Cambridge the son was teased for having disproved his father's corpuscular theory when he focused X-rays by reflecting them from a bent sheet of mica.

Laue had assumed the atoms in his crystal of zincblende to lie at the corners of a cube; he argued that if these atoms scattered X-rays, the diffracted X-rays would emerge from the crystal in directions where atoms lay an integral number of wavelengths apart, so that their scattering contributions reinforced each other. Laue himself noticed that there was something wrong with this interpretation, because there were many directions where reinforcements of X-rays diffracted by crystals of zincblende should have occurred, but the relevant spots were absent; he tried to explain this by assuming that the X-rays consisted of only five distinct wavelengths that the crystal lattice had picked out [6].

On the 11 November, 1912, only four months after he had first heard of Laue's papers, Bragg read a paper to the Cambridge Philosophical Society with the correct interpretation of the German results [7]. He describes his success as "an interesting example of the way in which apparently unrelated bits of knowledge click together to suggest something new. J.J. Thomson had lectured to us on the pulse theory of X-rays, which explained them as being electromagnetic pulses created by the sudden stopping of electrons. C.T.R. Wilson, in his brilliant way, had talked about the equivalence of a formless pulse and a continuous range of 'white' radiation. Pope and Barlow had a theory of crystal structure, and our little group had an evening

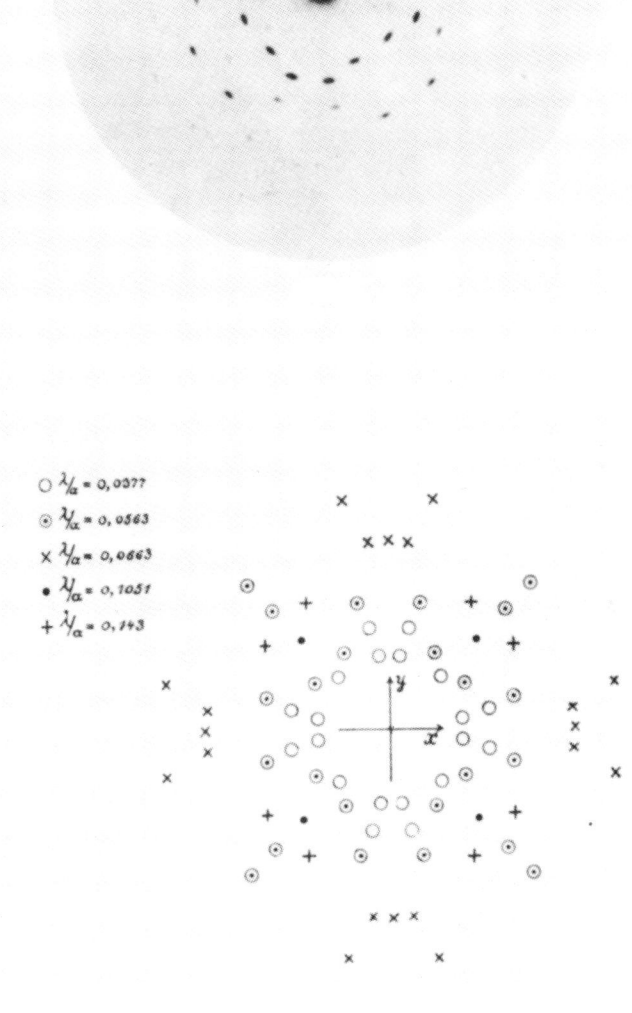

**Figure 1** *Friedrich, Knipping and Laue's X-ray diffraction picture of zincblende, taken with the X-ray beam along one of the cube axes, together with their assignment of the spots to five distinct wavelengths [6].*

meeting when Gossling read a paper on this theory. It was the first time that the idea of a crystal as a regular pattern was brought to my notice. I can remember the exact spot in the Backs where the idea suddenly leapt into my mind that Laue's spots were due to the reflection of X-ray pulses by sheets of atoms in the crystal." (unpublished memoirs).

Bragg noticed that spots which were round when his photographic plate was close to the crystal became elliptical as the plate was moved further away. By a remarkable feat of imaginative insight Bragg realised that such a focusing effect would arise if the X-rays were reflected by successive atomic planes (Figure 2), and he reformulated von Laue's conditions for diffraction into what became known as Bragg's Law, which gives a more direct relationship between the crystal structure and its diffraction pattern ($n\lambda = 2d \sin\theta$). He then noticed something else. The German group had tilted the crystal away from its symmetrical position by 3°. If the X-rays had consisted of five discreet wavelengths as Laue believed, then the spots should have disappeared as the conditions for diffraction for the planes from which these wavelengths were reflected no longer held true. In fact the same spots moved by 6° and changed in intensity. This led Bragg to recognise that sets of parallel lattice selected from a continuous spectrum (or pulse, as he called it) those wavelengths which corresponded to integral multiples of the path difference between reflexions from successive atomic planes, so that each Laue spot was made up of several harmonics of some selected wavelength. Finally, he demonstrated that the presence of spots with certain combinations of indices, and the absence of others in the X-ray diffraction pattern of zincblende could be accounted for by assuming a face-centred rather than a primitive cubic lattice. With that assumption the entire diffraction pattern fell into place (Figure 3) [7].

Why did this 22 year-old student succeed in correctly interpreting the diffraction pattern predicted and discovered by an accomplished theoretician 11 years his senior and two experimental physicists? Bragg himself modestly attributes it to a "concatenation of fortunate circumstances", but his formidable paper soon convinces you that its success owed more to Bragg's astute powers of penetrating through the apparent complexities of physical phenomena to their underlying simplicity.

Bragg's first paper was quickly followed by another, written in collaboration with his father, on their newly developed X-ray spectrometer, and a third, written by himself alone, solving the structure of common salt and showing how the Laue pictures of several simple minerals could be indexed. There follows the structure of diamond, solved, as he relates, largely by his father, and the structures of fluorspar, zincblende, iron pyrites, calcite and dolomite solved by himself alone. Finally, on 16 July, 1914, he communicated a paper on the structure of metallic copper [8–11]. In view of this published record and the fact that for most of the relevant period the father was at Leeds and the son at Cambridge, it seems hardly believable that the scientific public tended to attribute most of the credit for these discoveries to the father, sometimes with the undertone that the son had cashed in on the father's success. The son must have suffered a great deal from these thoughtless and lazy judgments. Lazy, because people could not be bothered to read the literature.

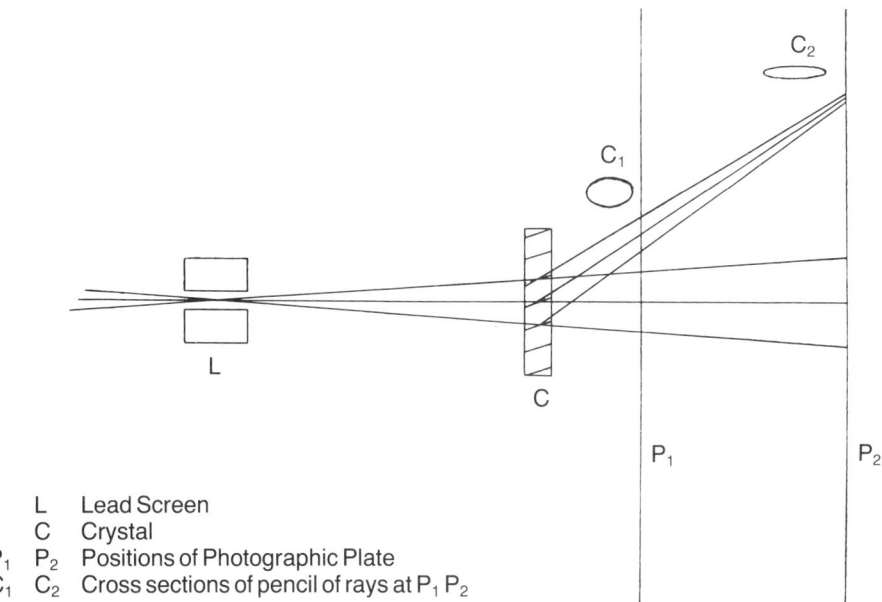

L    Lead Screen
C    Crystal
P₁  P₂  Positions of Photographic Plate
C₁  C₂  Cross sections of pencil of rays at P₁ P₂

**Figure 2** *Change of shape of the X-ray reflexions as the photographic plate was moved away from the crystal. Reflexions that were round when the plate was near the crystal became drawn out in the horizontal direction further away. Bragg pointed out that reflexion by the lattice planes of an incident cone of X-rays of continuously varying wavelength would come to a focus in the vertical direction, but would spread out in the horizontal direction [7].*

Bragg wrote many years later: "Inevitably the results with the spectrometer, especially the solution of the diamond structure, were far more striking and far easier to follow than my elaborate analysis of Laue photographs, and it was my father who announced the new results at the British Association, the Solvay Conference, lectures up and down the country and in America, while I remained at home." Andrade wrote: "It was always a delight to his hearers to note the affection that came into Sir William Bragg's voice when, in lectures, he found occasion to deal with some one or other piece of work which had been carried out by 'my boy'" [12]. But the "boy's" reaction to this patronising was: "My father more than gave me full credit for my part, but I had some heart-aches."

So their great discoveries, which brought them the Nobel Prize for Physics in 1915, are said to have strained relationships between them for the rest of their lives. In his many lectures on the development of X-ray analysis, W.L. Bragg was fond of defining the exact roles played by himself and his father, but he never hinted at those strains until a few days before his death when he wrote to me: "I hope that there are many things your son is tremendously good at which you can't do at all, because that is the best foundation for a father-son relationship".

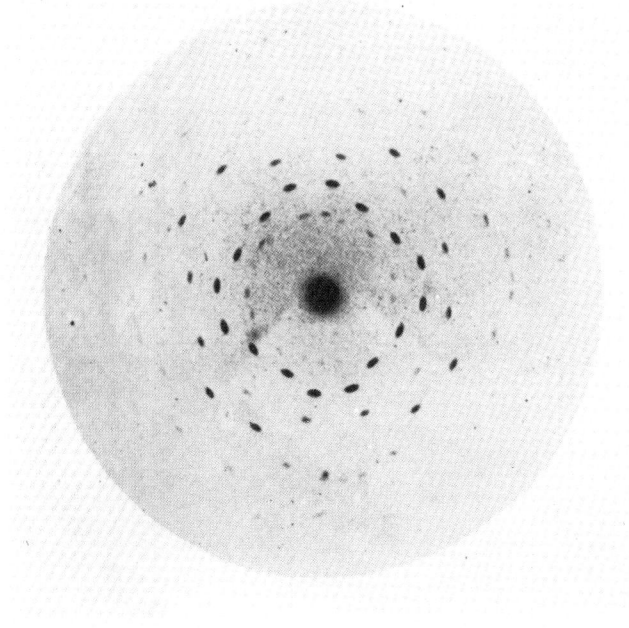

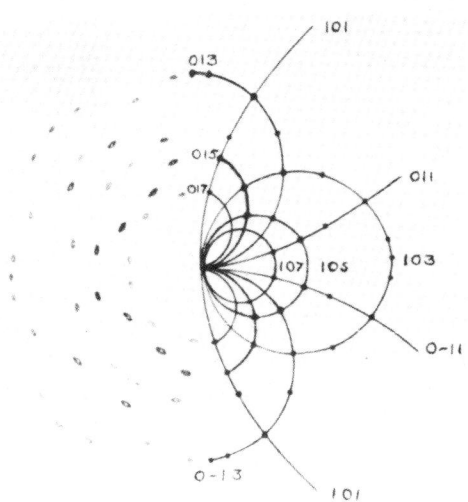

**Figure 3** *W.L. Bragg's re-interpretation of the Germans' X-ray diffraction photograph of zincblende. He indexed the reflexions by assigning a face-centred cubic lattice to zincblende and a continuous spectrum to the X-rays. He showed that the reflexions lie on the intersections of the photographic plate with a series of cones, each cone containing the reflexions from planes parallel to a zone axis [7].*

In most of the earliest structures of elements or simple compounds solved by the Braggs, crystal symmetry had so restricted the choice of atomic arrangements that only very few atomic parameters were left open. For example, the structure of diamond, published in the *Proc. Roy. Soc.* by "Professor W.H. and Mr W.L. Bragg" in 1913, was determined like this. The crystals were cubic. The presence on the Laue photographs of certain spots and the absence of others showed that the atoms of carbon must lie on a face-centred cube. The length of the cube edges could be measured from the angles at which the diffracted rays emerged. This gave the volume of the cube. The volume multiplied by the density of the crystals showed that it contained eight carbon atoms rather than four. Therefore there must be two sets of four carbon atoms, each occupying the corners and face centres of a cube. How far were they shifted relative to each other? This was the only unknown parameter. The Braggs showed that it can be deduced simply from the orders of reflexion that are reinforced and those that are extinguished by interference [9].

The unravelling of the structures of minerals containing several different kinds of atoms presented challenging new problems that could not be solved simply by looking for present and absent reflexions. Bragg described his ingenious new methods for solving such structures in a seminal paper on "A Technique for the X-ray examination of crystal structures with many parameters", published with J. West in the *Zeitschrift für Kristallographie* in 1928, and in the following paper on their application to diopside [13,14].

In the 1920s and 1930s most crystallographers recorded the X-ray diffraction patterns photographically, which told them the *relative* intensities of the X-ray reflexions. They were content with qualitative data, but Bragg, together with R.W. James and C.H. Bosanquet, began his post-war research at Manchester with the introduction of quantitative ones. He used an X-ray spectrometer, the forerunner of today's diffractometer, with which he recorded the *absolute* intensities of the X-ray reflections, *i.e.* the fraction of the incident intensity diffracted by the crystal. This provided him with far more meaningful data for solving structures and testing whether they were correct than those used by most other workers in the field.

Diopside is a silicate mineral that was believed to contain molecules of $CaSiO_3$ and $MgSiO_3$. In 1928 solution of its structure seemed a more formidable undertaking than anything done before, because it involved the determination of 14 independent parameters. Compare this with the 36,000 atomic parameters of the structure of the photochemical reaction centre for which H. Michel, J. Deisenhofer and R. Huber shared the Nobel Prize for Chemistry in 1988.

Diopside crystals are monoclinic with a face-centred unit cell. This is the name given by crystallographers to the smallest volume containing the atomic pattern that repeats itself in all directions. In diopside that unit of pattern consists of four molecules of $CaMg(Si_3)_2$. Crystal symmetry restricts the calcium and magnesium atoms to four alternative positions but does not tell which is the right one; the silicon and oxygen atoms can lie anywhere.

The way to find the silicon atoms may be illustrated by considering the 804 reflexion which is too weak to observe (Figure 4). There is a contribution of +47 from the four Ca and Mg atoms, another of between +44 and –44 from eight silicon atoms, and another of between +41 and –41 from 24 oxygen atoms. The oxygen contribution is unknown within these limits. The silicon atoms cannot be making a positive contribution to F(804), for in that case, even if all the oxygen atoms were making negative contributions, there would be a positive resultant which would be observed. On the other hand, a negative contribution of any amount by silicon is possible. The planes (804) are now drawn and parallel strips are shaded in which atoms making positive contributions might be situated. These areas are forbidden to the silicon atoms. Repetition of this procedure for many reflexions led Bragg to the exclusion of all but four possible positions for the silicons (Figure 5). He then found that in three of them, neighbouring, symmetry-related atoms would be so close together that they would overlap. This left 4 and 4' as the only possible silicon positions. Knowing where the silicons were, Bragg was now able to decide which of the four possible positions for Ca and Mg is the right one. The 1,400 reflexion was so strong that all the atoms had to scatter in phase (Figure 6). If the Ca and Mg atoms were at either B or D they would scatter out of phase with the Si atoms; hence these two positions could be excluded. 406 is equally strong. If the Ca and Mg atoms were at either A or B they would also scatter out of phase with the Si atoms. Hence the only positions not excluded were C which lie on the axes of two-fold symmetry.

That was easy! The difficulty began with finding the positions of the six oxygen atoms, so that the sum of their scattering contribution, together with those from the Ca, Mg and Si atoms, equalled the observed amplitude of each of a hundred reflexions. It was an intricate game of chess where every move made to satisfy agreement with the observed amplitude of one reflexion could spoil the agreement with 10 others. If the calculated amplitude of only a single one of the 100 reflexions came out radically different from the observed amplitude, then your structure was wrong and you had to start all over again. But Bragg got it right (Figure 6).

Was the answer worth such exertion? Or did Bragg just play a sophisticated intellectual game, like some of the people working on artificial intelligence or topology today? In the notes that Bragg left me with his collection of reprints, he wrote: "The analysis of diopside was a turning point in our ideas about silicate structures. I showed that the "$SiO_3$" which appears in the chemical formula does not represent $SiO_3$ acid groups but a string of $SiO_4$ groups joined by shared oxygen atoms. It was a crucial step in showing that silicon always occurs in a tetrahedral group of oxygen atoms."

To appreciate the novelty of Bragg's results you have to put your mind back 70 or 80 years and ask what was the body of knowledge in inorganic chemistry and mineralogy in those days. I looked at textbooks published early in this century and tried to recall the lectures in inorganic chemistry that I attended as an undergraduate in Vienna. In J.R. Partington's textbook of inorganic chemistry published in 1925, 12 years after Bragg had solved the structure of common salt, the question of the atomic arrangement of the sodium and chlorine atoms, their state of ionisation or of the forces that hold the crystal together were never raised. Minerals were described

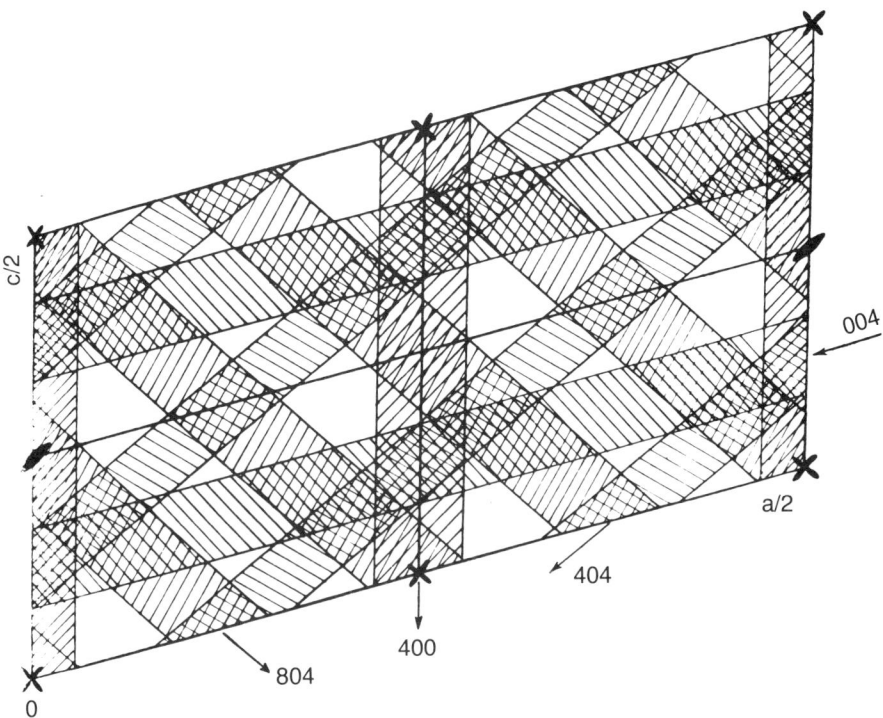

**Figure 4** *Unit cell of diopside projected along the b-axis with shaded areas forbidden to the silicon atoms [14]. The crosses mark centres of symmetry, the black elipse signs two-fold rotation axes.*

by their morphology, and by their optical and chemical properties, but no one asked what heid them together. Many of the chemical formulae given in the textbooks turned out to be mistaken, like that of diopside. Partington's outdated section on silica reminded me of my viva with my professor of Chemistry in Vienna, the formidable Ernst Späth, at the conclusion of my undergraduate courses. A few days beforehand, I heard that he had failed a girl because she could not tell him the different crystalline forms of silica. I quickly memorised them and recited them at the viva to the professor's satisfaction: α-quartz, left or right handed below 575°, β-quartz from 575–800°, tridymite above 800° and crystoballite above 1,470°. Späth purred contentedly and invited me to become his research student. He never wondered what atomic structures underlay these several forms and he must have been unaware that X-ray analysis had shown them to be made up of tetrahedra of $SiO_4$ sharing corners, but stacked in different ways.

Few chemists took much notice of X-ray crystallography's new insights until 1939 when Pauling published *The Nature of the Chemical Bond*, and some ignored them until 1945 when A.F. Wells published his *Structural Inorganic Chemistry*. T.M. Lowry's textbook of inorganic chemistry, published in 1922, was a notable exception. It includes a section on the crystal structures that had been solved and

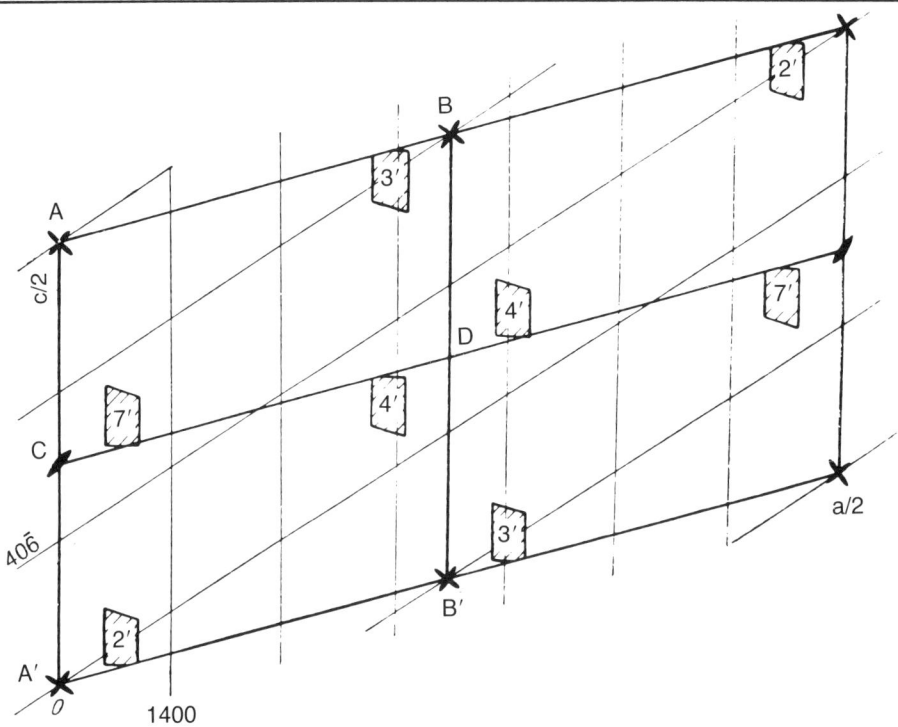

**Figure 5** *Unit cell of diopside showing areas allowed to the silicon atoms. A, B, C and D mark positions of the calcium and magnesium ions allowed by the crystal symmetry. The observed intensities of the 406 and 1,400 reflexions exclude A, B and D [14].*

points out that crystals of common salt do not contain molecules of sodium chloride, but ions of sodium and chlorine.

Bragg and his followers showed that most crystals of inorganic compounds do not contain discrete molecules, but a continuum of alternate positive and negative ions. The positive ones are small and surround themselves with the larger negative ones arranged at the corners of polyhedra so that they are tightly packed and all electric charges are locally compensated. The silicates that form the bulk of the earth's crust are made of $SiO_4$ tetrahedra that are either separate or share corners or edges, and their structures explain each mineral's strength or weakness. Thus Bragg's ingenious and immensely laborious puzzle-solving made people understand for the first time the atomic structure of the ground we stand on, and that surely was worthwhile.

Was there an easier way? When Bragg's father delivered the Bakerian Lecture to the Royal Society in 1915, he suggested that the periodic repeat of atomic patterns in crystals could be represented by Fourier series [15]. "If we know the nature of the periodic variation of the density of the medium we can analyse it by Fourier's method into a series of harmonic terms. The medium may be looked on as

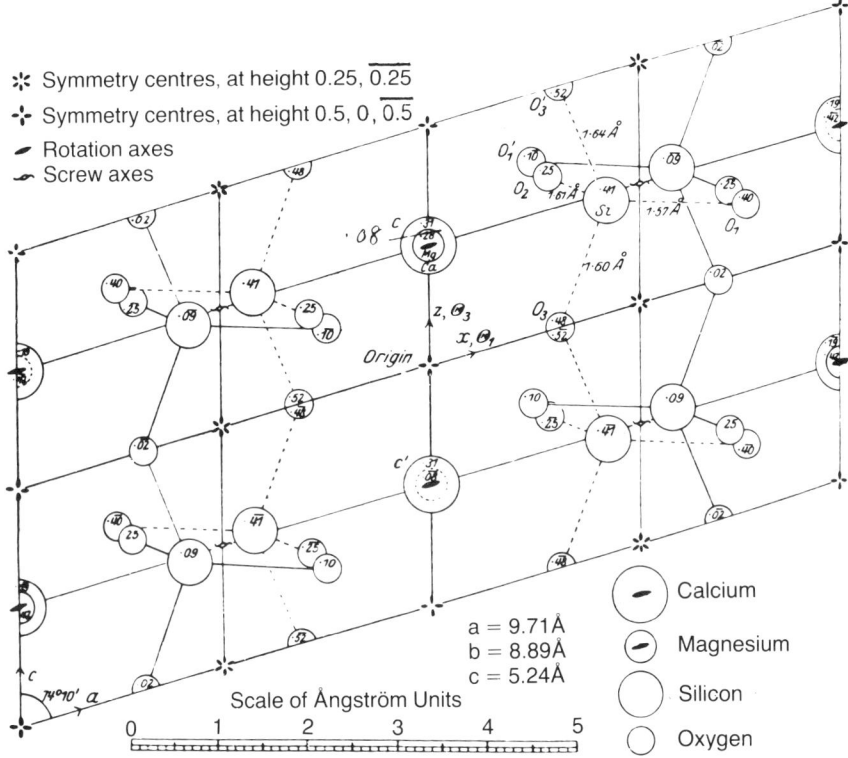

**Figure 6** *Atomic positions of diopside projected along the b- axis. The numbers give the y-coordinates of the atoms [14].*

compounded of a series of harmonic media, each of which will give the medium the power of reflecting at one angle. The series of spectra which we obtain for any given set of crystal planes may be considered as indicating the existence of separate harmonic terms. We may even conceive the possibility of discovering from their relative intensities the actual distribution of the scattering centres, electrons and nucleus, in the atom; but it would be premature to expect too much until all other causes of the variations of intensity have been allowed for, such as the effects of temperature, and the like."

The American physicist R.J. Havighurst later used a triple Fourier series to deduce the electron density distribution in a crystal of sodium chloride along the cube edges and the cube diagonals, using the absolute intensities measured by Bragg, James and Bosanquet [16].

Bragg extended the Fourier series to two dimensions. Each of the shaded stripes of his trial and error work on diopside now became a sinusoidal wave. Symmetry dictated that each wave must have either a crest or a trough at the positions of the magnesium and calcium ions, and it was easy to decide which was right. The sum of all the waves took the form of a map that revealed the positions of the oxygen atoms

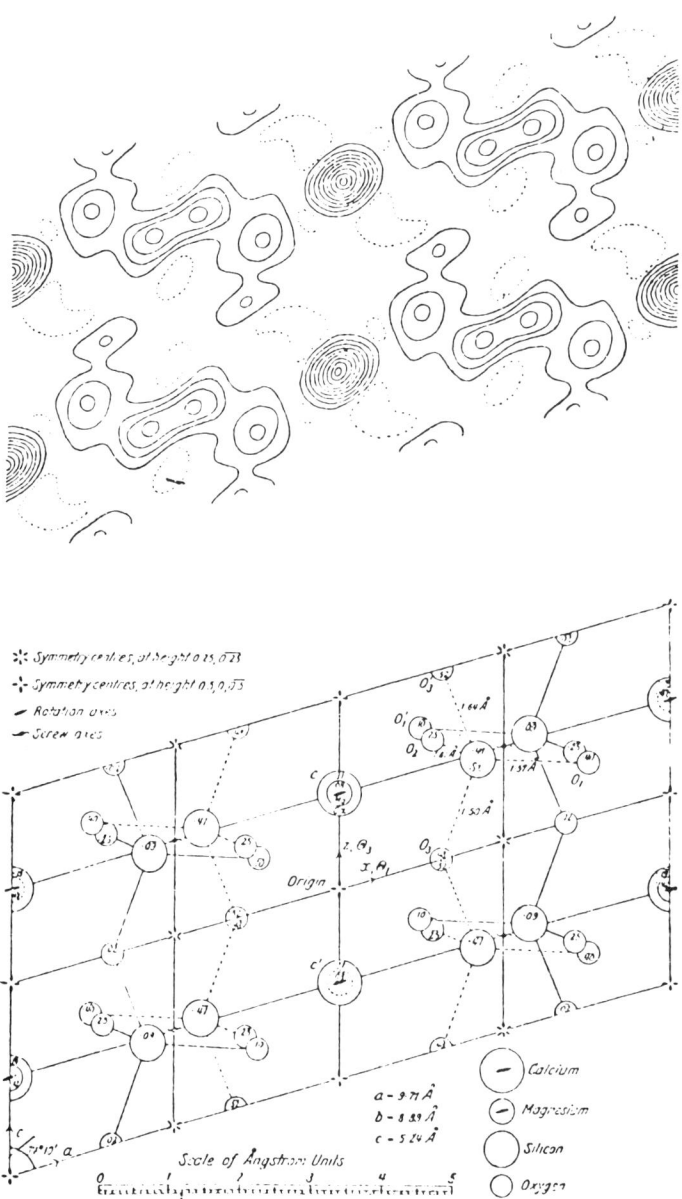

**Figure 7** *Comparison of Fourier map calculated from the known positions of the calcium magnesium and silicon ions alone, and the complete structure solved by trial. The lower peaks in the Fourier map coincide with the oxygens found by trial [17].*

even though these had not been used in deciding whether a crest or trough was to be assigned to any particular wave (Figure 7) [17].

The amount of labour Bragg had to perform to calculate the Fourier projections of diopside on three principal planes was gigantic. For the projection on the *b*-axis alone he had to calculate the value of each of 26 different waves at 288 separate points and then had to sum 7,488 numbers. For the other two projections he had to sum 3,360 and 6,912 numbers respectively, or 17,760 numbers in all. This was the birth of the Fourier projections which were used to solve hundreds of crystal structures for the next 30 years, until the advent of digital computers made it possible to calculate Fourier series in three dimensions.

Bragg's paper on *The Determination of Parameters in Crystal Structures by Means of Fourier Series* is by himself alone. He mentions no collaborators. How did he do all these tedious summations when adding machines had not yet been invented? We shall never know.

Incidentally, reports of continual tension between himself and his father are belied by the final paragraph of that paper [17].

"It is with great pleasure that I acknowledge my indebtedness to my father, Sir William Bragg, for suggestions which materially contributed to the work described in this paper. At the time when I was following up the connection between our usual methods of analysis and the analysis by Fourier series, a connection briefly treated in the paper by Mr West and myself, my father showed me some results which he had obtained by using relative values of the first few terms of two- and three-dimensional Fourier series to indicate the general distribution of scattering matter in certain organic compounds. It was largely as a result of his suggestions that I was encouraged to make all the computations for this two-dimensional series, using the extensive absolute measurements which we had made on certain crystals."

In the notes he left me, Bragg wrote: "This paper should really have been written with my father. He produced a crucial idea about two-dimensional Fourier series; I happened to have all the experimental data which showed how much a series could be used. It was the first paper in which Fourier series were used for parameter determination."

Bragg's application of the Fourier method to diopside required knowledge of the calcium, magnesium and silicon positions to determine whether any particular set of waves had a peak or a trough at the calcium plus magnesium positions. In 1927, Bragg's American postdoctoral student J.M. Cork showed that this ambiguity of sign can be solved by the method of isomorphous replacement with heavy atoms [18]. The alums form an isomorphous series of the general formula $AB(SO_4)_2 \cdot 12H_2O$ where A can be any alkali metal and B can be a trivalent metal such as aluminium. Cork determined the signs of the Fourier terms in a one dimensional series by analysing the changes in intensity that substitution of one metal ion by another brought about in the reflexions from one set of planes. With the solution of the alums Bragg's school laid the foundation for the method of isomorphous replacement that I used 25 years later to solve the structure of haemoglobin.

Peter Medawar wrote that "Every discovery, every enlargement of the understanding, begins as an imaginative understanding of what the truth might be" [19]. Bragg's success in solving structures was based on a remarkable imaginative insight into the workings of natural phenomena, especially those concerned with optics and the properties of matter. According to Karl Popper and Peter Medawar, research consists of the formulation of imaginative hypotheses that are open to falsification by experiment. This is exactly how Bragg went about finding where the atoms lay, but he combined imagination with a phenomenal amount of hard work. Popper and Medawar argue further that no hypothesis can ever be completely proved, but that it can only be disproved experimentally so that it gradually corresponds more and more closely to the truth. However, Bragg's structures are not preliminary approximations subject to revision; any student setting out to redetermine the structures of calcite, quartz or beryl will be disappointed.

T.S. Kuhn argued that science advances by a succession of paradigms [20], but the perusal of old textbooks of chemistry and mineralogy have convinced me that there was no paradigm for the atomic structure of solid matter before 1912. The results of X- ray analysis opened a new world that had not even been imagined before.

When reviewing scientific work I sometimes paraphrase people's papers, but when I tried to paraphrase Bragg's I always found that he had said it much better. As everyone who has heard Bragg here at the Royal Institution will remember, his superb powers of combining simplicity with rigour, his enthusiasm, liveliness and charm and his beautiful demonstrations conspired to make him one of the best lecturers on science that ever lived.

Bragg united C.P. Snow's two cultures because his approach to science was an artistic, imaginative one. He thought visually rather than mathematically, generally in terms of concrete models that could be either static, like his crystal structures, or dynamic, like the interaction between crystals and electromagnetic waves or the order-disorder transitions and mobile dislocations in metals. His artistic gifts surfaced in his delicate sketches and water colours, and in his limpid prose [21].

His scientific output in the 1920s and 1930s was prodigious, yet I am told that he was never rushed and always had time for his family, because his penetrating intellect and powers of concentration made all work easy. Instead of losing himself in a labyrinth of conflicting evidence which he would rarely bother to read, he would think of the best way interatomic forces could be satisfied to give stable structures.

Nowadays, cynics want us to believe that scientists work only for fame and money, but Bragg slaved away at hard problems when he was a Nobel Laureate of comfortable means. He was driven by scientific curiosity. He was not a public figure and he liked to do his work at home rather than in aeroplanes. So often men of genius were hellish to live with, but Bragg was a genial person whose creativity was sustained by a happy home life; typically one would find him tending his garden, with Lady Bragg, children and grandchildren somewhere in the background, and before getting down to crystal structures, he would proudly demonstrate his latest roses.

### References

1 Bragg, W.L. 1933. *The Crystalline State*. G. Bell & Sons, Ltd., London.
2 Bragg, W.L. 1937. *Atomic Structure of Minerals*. Cornell University Press, Ithaca.
3 Sir Lawrence Bragg and Claringbull, G.F. 1965. *Crystal Structure of Minerals*. G. Bell & Sons, Ltd., London.
4 Sir Lawrence Bragg, 1975. *The Development of X-ray Analysis*. G. Bell & Sons, Ltd., London.
5 Caroe, G.M. 1978. *William Henry Bragg 1862–1942: Man and Scientist*. Cambridge University Press, Cambridge.
6 Friedrich, W., Knipping, P. and Laue, M. 1912. *Interferenz- Erscheinungen bei Röntgenstrahlen*, in Sitzungsberichte der Kgl. Bayrischen Akademie der Wissenschaften, pp.303–322.
7 Bragg, W.L. 1913. The diffraction of short electromagnetic waves by a crystal. *Proc. Cambr. Phil. Soc.*, **17**(I), 43–57.
8 Bragg, W.L. 1913. The structure of some crystals as indicated by their diffraction of X-rays. *Proc. Roy. Soc. Lond. A*, **89**, 248–277.
9 Bragg, W.H. and Bragg, W.L. 1913. The structure of diamond. *Proc. Roy. Soc. Lond. A*, **89**, 272–291.
10 Bragg, W.L. 1914. The analysis of crystals by the x-ray spectrometer. *Proc. Roy. Soc. Lond. A*, **90**, 468–489.
11 Bragg, W.L. 1914. The structure of Copper. *Phil. Mag.*, **27**, 355–360.
da C. Andrade, E.N.C. 1943. William Henry Bragg, Obituary. *Notices of Fellows of the Royal Society*, **4**, 277–300.
13 Bragg, W.L. and West, J. 1928. A technique for the X-ray examination of crystal structures with many parameters. *Z. Kristall.*, **69**, 118–148.
14 Bragg, W.L. and Warren, B. 1928. The structure of diopside, $CaMg(SiO_3)_2$. *Z. Kristall.*, **69**, 168–193.
15 Bragg, W.H. 1915. X-rays and crystal structure. *Phil. Trans. Roy. Soc. Lond. A*, **215**, 253–275.
16 Havighurst, R.J. 1927. Electron distribution in the atoms of crystals. Sodium chloride, and lithium, sodium and calcium fluoride. *Phys. Rev.*, **29**, 1.
17 Bragg, W.L. 1929. The determination of parameters in crystal structures by means of Fourier series. *Proc. Roy. Soc. Lond. A.*, **123**, 537–559.
18 Cork, J.M. 1927. The crystal structure of some of the alums. *Phil. Mag.*, **IV**, 688–698.
19 Medawar, B.P. 1979. *Advice to a Young Scientist*. Harper & Row, New York.
20 Kuhn, T.S. 1970. *The Structure of Scientific Revolutions*, University of Chicago Press, Chicago, Illinois.
21 Sir David Phillips, 1979. William Lawrence Bragg, 31 March 1890–1 July 1971. *Biographical Memoirs of Fellows of the Royal Society*, **25**, 75–143.

# My Indebtedness to and my Contacts with Lawrence Bragg

## LINUS PAULING, For. Mem. RS

I regret that I never expressed to Lawrence Bragg my feeling of great personal indebtedness to him. A number of years ago I recognised that my own scientific career has been based on the work that I did in the determination of the structure of crystals by X–ray diffraction, beginning in 1922, and that I was accordingly indebted to Lawrence Bragg for having discovered the Bragg equation, a few years earlier, and applied it in the determination of a few simple crystal structures. As the years have gone by and I have continued to think about these matters, my feeling of indebtedness to him has grown stronger. Of course, if Lawrence Bragg had not discovered the Bragg equation when he did, it probably would have been discovered within a few years, perhaps, however, too late to have led to my introduction to X–ray crystallography in 1922.

I was sent notice of my acceptance as a graduate student in chemistry in the California Institute of Technology in the spring of 1922. A month or two later, Professor Arthur Amos Noyes, Chairman of the Division of Chemistry and Chemical Engineering of the California Institute of Technology, wrote to me, saying that he had decided that I should carry on my research with Dr Roscoe Gilkey Dickinson, who was the first person to have received a PhD degree from that Institute (1922), and was then a National Research Council Fellow. I do not know why Noyes decided that I should work in that field, but it was a fortunate decision for me.

I then had the book *X–Rays and Crystal Structure* sent to me by the Oregon State Library in Salem, and I read it carefully during the summer. I found it interesting, especially because as a boy I had collected some minerals and had read books about mineralogy, and also because I had become interested in the general theory of the nature of the chemical bond, and it was evident that the interatomic distances in crystals provided information about chemical bonding.

When I arrived in Pasadena in late September 1922, Dickinson began at once to instruct me in the techniques of X–ray crystallography. He pointed out that the techniques available then were especially powerful for locating atoms in crystals with cubic symmetry, and I searched the literature for cubic crystals of substances that seemed to me to be possibly interesting. During the next three months I grew crystals of about twenty substances, and carried out preliminary X–ray analysis of several of them, under the supervision of Dickinson. They turned out to be so complex that the methods available then did not suffice to permit the determination of the atomic parameters. Within three months, however, Dickinson and I had determined the structure of molybdenite, and during the following months and years I was kept busy working in this field, using the powerful technique that Bragg's discovery had provided. Much of my later work, of course, such as that on the alpha helix and the pleated sheets in proteins, involved X–ray diffraction, or could be considered an outgrowth of the early X–ray diffraction work.

Also in 1922 and in 1923 I read the earlier literature, including Bragg's papers and Bragg's effort to assign radii to atoms. This paper stimulated me to begin collecting experimental values of interatomic distances and to attempt to analyse them, in searching for basic principles about chemical bonding.

In the spring of 1930, my wife and I and our eldest son Linus Jr, then five years old, spent one month in Manchester. Lawrence Bragg was helpful and kind to us, especially in that he arranged for a house in which we could live and for a maid. He also asked one of his assistants to work with me in making some measurements of the intensities of X–ray diffraction maxima from the principal planes of a crystal of epidote that I had brought with me, using the Bragg ionisation X–ray spectrometer in the laboratory.

Despite Bragg's helpfulness in these ways, the stay in Manchester was a disappointment to me. I had determined the structures of some silicate minerals, as had also Bragg and his co–workers, and I had published a paper about structural principles for silicates and other minerals in which the bonds have a considerable amount of ionic character, amplifying and extending the principle of close packing of oxygen atoms that had been formulated by Bragg. I had anticipated that there would be discussions between Bragg and me about these matters, and that Bragg would ask me to give a seminar talk about this work and other work that I had been doing during the preceding years, such as the discovery that in some crystals molecules are rotating rather freely. In fact, however, Bragg did not ever ask me to discuss scientific matters with him, and I, his junior by eleven years, did not have courage enough to ask for such a discussion with him or to suggest that I might give a seminar. It astonished me to discover that the scientific atmosphere in Manchester was much different from that in Pasadena. In Pasadena I was accustomed to attending about three seminars per week, in chemistry, physics, and astronomy, whereas there were no seminars in Manchester during the month that I spent there. Cambridge was different. Science was livelier there, and when we stopped in Cambridge for a few days, Bernal asked me to give a seminar on the rotational motion of molecules in crystals, which provoked a lively discussion.

In the spring of 1948, when I was Eastman Professor in Oxford, we visited Cambridge and were graciously received by Bragg and Lady Bragg. Our youngest son Crellin, then nine years old, lived with the Braggs for a week, while my wife and I were on a lecture tour. At that time, too, Bragg and I did not have any serious discussions about science, whereas every time that I came in contact with Bernal we were at once engaged in a lively interchange of ideas. Some years later I was told that Bragg resented my having intruded into the fields of crystallography and mineralogy in which he was working, and that he considered me to be a competitor. This information came as a shock to me. I had thought of Lawrence Bragg as a member of an older generation of great scientists , who had made very important discoveries, and in a sense I had thought of him as one of my scientific heroes. In retrospect, I am sure that in 1930 I would have rejected the idea that I was a competitor of Bragg. I did not think of my own scientific work as being competitive; I found it engrossingly interesting for its own sake. In 1930 I was still thinking of myself as a student, with Bragg the professor, the member of the older generation who had made the great discovery of determining the structure of crystals by X–ray diffraction. Bragg was always courteous and gentlemanly. I now regret that I did not have enough insight to have enabled me to take such action as would have permitted a more intimate friendship to have been developed between us.

Without having much supporting evidence, I surmise that circumstances during the second half of the 1920s may have influenced Bragg's life. At that time, although still quite young, he held an important position in science, involving administrative and teaching duties, as well as the direction of research. As a result, when quantum mechanics was discovered he was not in a position to devote enough time to this rather complicated and somewhat abstruse subject to master it. I suggest that he may have felt handicapped by this lack, and that it may have kept him from entering into lively scientific arguments and discussions.

I am glad to remember my association with a fine man, Lawrence Bragg. I wish that it had been closer.

# Bragg's Broomstick and the Structure of Proteins

## SIR JOHN KENDREW, CBE FRS

I first encountered Bragg in Cambridge in 1946 after I had emerged from the Second World War; I went to see him on the advice of Desmond Bernal, with whom I had collaborated on war work. Bragg, hearing that I was a chemist interested in biology, proposed that I should work with Max Perutz on protein structure. This suggestion surprised Bernal, who said "You've never learnt X–ray crystallography as a student and it's a very tedious subject". However, it was very much in line with Bragg's policy as Cavendish Professor, and I was glad to accept it.

Bragg was under criticism from the nuclear physicists for not supporting their own subject more strongly in a laboratory world–famous for its reputation in nuclear physics under J.J. Thomson and Rutherford – and indeed for not being a nuclear physicist himself. Of course, the criticisms should have been directed at the electors to the chair, rather than at the incumbent, but in any case, it would have been financially impossible for the Cavendish to continue after the war as a major centre of nuclear physics research, and Bragg's great contribution was to foster two quite new subjects – radio astronomy and molecular biology – both of which became very important during the years he was in Cambridge. As a matter of fact I never found him very interested in biology – nor even in the chemical structure of the compounds the structures of which he analysed (see, for example, the note by Lord Todd in the present volume). Basically he was a puzzle–solver; to him the great fascination was to interpret the complicated diffraction pattern, say of a protein crystal, in terms of its three–dimensional structure. As far as I could determine, Bragg was the *only* crystallographer in Cambridge – apart from Max Perutz – who did not believe we were wasting our time on a project much more complicated than had previously been attempted by the methods of X–ray crystallography. But we were carried along by his continuous enthusiasm – a most valuable characteristic that he displayed in all his research activities – and together with David Keilin (Professor of Parasitology and a very distinguished biochemist) he persuaded the Medical Research Council to support a research programme which produced no results, except wrong ones, for the following ten years. Can one imagine such a thing happening today?

He combined enthusiasm with a certain formality; I remember one day, hearing me talking to Max, his saying to me that he felt simply unable to refer to us except as Perutz and Kendrew; for him Christian names just could not be used outside the family. Very occasionally the formality verged on pomposity; at a Friday evening dinner that I attended at the Royal Institution in later years, Alice Bragg shouted down the table to her husband at the other end "Don't get on your high horse, Willie" (of course, no one else would have dreamed of calling him Willie). But as one came to know him better one realised that the occasional pomposity was simply a cover for shyness. And he greatly enjoyed social occasions with students; I remember one Christmas party at the Cavendish where he appeared dressed up in the bright blue robes of an honorary degree he had collected in Spain, surmounted by a kind of blue fez topped with a long golden tassel – this seemed to him a suitable dress in which to participate, as he vigorously proceeded to do, in all sorts of rather juvenile games.

Bragg was one of the last of the classical physicists, who never involved himself much with the ideas of quantum theory or of particle physics. Scientifically he possessed in high degree the classical physicist's power of making intuitive order–of–magnitude calculations in his head; the ability to see the likely result without even the traditional back–of–the–envelope to help him. And he liked simple methods; he distrusted electronic computers, as I discovered when I was first using the EDSAC Mk I in Cambridge to calculate Fourier synthesis. As David Phillips has described in detail in his article in the present volume, one of our problems in using the now famous heavy atom method was to determine the actual co-ordinates of the heavy atom in the cell. Of course, I devised a Fourier method to do this, and used the EDSAC to carry out the calculations; Bragg came into the laboratory with a drawing on a single sheet of paper and although he was ready to admit that my results *might* be more accurate, his were certainly not much in error.

He liked models too, and made them himself with a boyish enthusiasm. I remember when we had calculated for the first time three–dimensional Fourier synthesis of a protein molecule showing features that might be Pauling's α–helices, he found an old broomstick which he chopped up into lengths with his own hands, and on which he then marked the positions of the atoms in an α–helix; meanwhile he got me to make, on the same scale, a cylindrical section through one of the dense features of the Fourier synthesis. Sliding my section, drawn on a rolled up sheet of tracing paper, onto his broomstick immediately showed in the most direct possible way that the density did indeed exactly fit the α–helix, and this was the first direct evidence of its presence in a protein molecule.

Like all good scientists, he was passionate – or as some would say, obsessional – about subjects which interested him; but in addition he approached problems with all the enthusiasm and fresh pleasure a child would display on getting a new toy, and this childlike quality was allied to a physical intuition so strong that the combination was extremely powerful. These characteristics also made him one of the best lecturers one had ever encountered, as several other contributors to this volume have emphasised. He used to say that the secret of giving a good lecture was never to make more than one point, or at the most two, during the course of a single lecture – a piece of advice that was certainly very useful, but was by no means a sufficient recipe for his own success.

I do not believe Bragg would have approved of computer searches through databases, had such things existed during his lifetime. He always recommended browsing in the journals for original articles rather than going through abstracts or reviews; the value comes, he used to say, from the articles you see by accident as you turn the pages, rather than from the one you are looking for. Indeed, he did not encourage one to read the literature very systematically or thoroughly at all; he thought you should not look too hard or too often, or you might come to the conclusion that the research you were thinking of doing had all been done before and that there was no point in going over the ground again.

Bragg was extremely helpful to individuals, even if he could not bring himself to use their first names. When Desmond Bernal still worked in Cambridge he was in some trouble because of his left–wing political views, combined with his somewhat unconventional personal life, but he still got the strongest support from Bragg, even though both characteristics were anathema to the latter. When Bernal's new laboratory at Birkbeck was inaugurated by Bragg, his speech began "When I see Bernal, I see red", but the rest of the speech was enormously supportive. He did not like unconventional personal behaviour; when a student of mine was sent down from Cambridge for having committed offences that would attract no notice at all today, Bragg took him in at the R.I., to which by now he had migrated as Director, without asking any questions. Next time I was there, Alice Bragg took me into a corner and asked me "What did X really do?"; I told her in detail and her comment was "For Heaven's sake don't tell Willie, he would be so upset". I also remember his discussing with me the fact that Jim Watson had asked him to contribute a foreword to *The Double Helix*; "Should I do it?" he said, "It's very strong stuff". He eventually did, though he included the phrase "those who figure in the book must read it in a very forgiving spirit"; indeed Bragg himself must have done just that.

Bragg's hobbies were gardening, bird watching, watercolour painting and boats. When he went to the Royal Institution he no longer had a garden, since he lived "above the shop", so he went *incognito* to a London club and offered his services free to look after its garden. Later someone who knew Bragg personally and spotted him working there caused considerable surprise in the management when he asked them "why was Sir Lawrence Bragg working in their garden?".

When he eventually retired he moved to Waldringfield in Suffolk where he could indulge his love of boats as well as of gardens. I myself had recently bought a house with a large garden and he gave me not only a great deal of advice (which I badly needed) but also a number of plants which I still have growing today. And retired though he might be, his interest in complex crystal structures was still intense, so that any of us with new results had to drive over to Waldringfield to demonstrate them. Doing this was a pleasure, as indeed had been all my contacts with Bragg over twenty–five years.

If anyone ever deserved the old–fashioned (and now discredited) appellation of gentleman it was Bragg, even though his outward appearance and behaviour were rather those of a prosperous farmer, dressed not quite in the latest fashion. But this appearance was as deceptive as his apparently over–simple approach to scientific problems – an approach which in fact concealed an extraordinarily acute and intuitive mind. He was guide and mentor to successive generations of students, among whom I count myself privileged and fortunate to have been included.

# Taking Penicillin to the R.I.

## DOROTHY HODGKIN, OM FRS

I first saw W.L. Bragg through the memories of J.D. Bernal, the stories of the past he used to tell us when I began work with him at Cambridge in 1932. He himself had finished Physics Part II at Cambridge in 1921 and had been encouraged to go to Sir William H. Bragg in the Royal Institution in London where he was collecting a group of young persons from different parts of the world who were interested in using the discovery of X–ray diffraction to work out the structures of actual crystals. Bernal himself, as an undergraduate at Cambridge, had worked on the theory of space groups, using quaternions, which he had offered to W.H. Bragg as an inducement before he came to London. Bragg looked at it with some admiration but was not really interested. Two of the young persons working with him, Bill Astbury and Kathleen Yardley, had already come across the theory of space groups, and were working out together how they could be used to assist in X–ray analysis. It was with difficulty that W.H. Bragg was persuaded to recommend the publication of their paper to the Royal Society. He believed that structure analysis should be carried out as W.L. Bragg had shown, completely from first principles. Not surprisingly, this did not always work and W.L. Bragg was called to help them out. So all the structures that seemed particularly difficult to W.H. Bragg were sent to W.L. Bragg for his assistance. He was the structure solver 'par excellence' of the world who was guiding a group of young research students in Manchester along paths that were gradually transforming chemistry. He had begun with simple ionic compounds, sodium and potassium chloride, and gradually studied more complicated ones like iron pyrites. I remember him saying, "a very complicated arrangement with interpenetrating twofold screw axes'. Then gradually silicate structures with still more complex large ions – diopside, a structure with many parameters, other kinds of chemicals, diamond and graphite, the 'metallic state'. He left larger organic compounds to his father who gradually grew new crystallographers to take them over – J.M. Robertson, in particular.

I visited the Royal Institution with Bernal myself in the early 1930s, and I suspect I first saw W.L. Bragg some time then. I remember him best from a visit I first paid to Manchester soon after I returned to Somerville in 1935. I had gone to attend a scientific meeting and stayed overnight when it ended. I had been reading 'Beevers and Lipson' on calculating Fourier series, and I thought I should like to meet them in the Physics Department. So I went over early in the morning, before returning to Oxford. They welcomed me to see the work they had done, particularly on copper sulphate, and described the strips they had used to help them in summing the Fourier series, and sold me straight away two boxes of the necessary strips – £5 each, I think. We then went down to lunch in the department and there Bragg joined us. I was tremendously impressed that he should come to talk with us. It was clear that he was delighted with Henry Lipson and Arnold Beevers and their work on copper sulphate, the first crystals of which diffraction data had been obtained at all, and now the first 'heavy atom' compound, as Bragg called it, recognising the outline of the heavy atom method of proceeding with structure analysis through the use of Fourier analysis and the power of Fourier analysis to show the electron density in the crystal.

It is one of the curious facts of history that W.H. Bragg, in the Bakerian Lecture in 1915, pointed out that a crystal structure could be viewed as a Fourier series, and the X–ray diffraction effects derived as the components of the series, if correctly summed, would show the electron density, but the first actual calculations of the electron density were not made till the papers of Havighurst and Duane in 1924 and 1925. Duane pointed out that though they used the phases given by Bragg's determination of the structure of sodium chloride, this was not necessary; the phases were given either by chloride, the heaviest atom in the crystal or by the differences between sodium and potassium chlorides. Henry Lipson told me that when he prepared the signs to be used in calculating the projection from Bragg's diopside he noticed that nearly all were given by the heaviest atom, calcium, in the crystal. Bragg commented to me that his first Fourier calculations were all of projections, whereas the first calculations published were lines in the three dimensional electron density.

The next time I met W.L. Bragg he was presiding over rather primitive papers of ours on the first measurements we had made on peptides and proteins. Nothing has stayed in my memory of that time – just before the war – except that at the end of it, in closing the meeting, he said he looked forward to "the structures of proteins which we shall all live to see". I thought, "does he realise how difficult their structure analysis will be?" He was already deeply interested.

In the middle of the war he was involved in the new arrangements made for Oxford when our old Professor T.L. Bowman was to retire. He came into the department and found me hard at work on penicillin, my main project at that time. He was very encouraging about the progress we were making and said, "I suppose you are working on this full time". "Oh yes", said I and thought, quite untruthfully, as I was just finishing off a paper on cholesteryl iodide for the Royal Society and looking over some Patterson calculations that Kate Dornberger was helping me with on insulin, to say nothing of the college teaching and looking after the children. Still, the day came and it was a very proud day, when I took the model of the three–dimensional electron density of penicillin to show at an X–ray analysis group meeting in the Royal Institution. My sister, Elizabeth, had drawn the electron density on plastic sheets, drawn to scale and stacked to be regularly placed one above the other in a wooden frame that Frank had made. It was a great joy building the model slowly, sheet by sheet, from the ground up, before Bragg, and seeing the atoms growing to full spheres of the right electron density before his eyes.

After the war, research on all fronts could begin again. Bragg had been appointed Cavendish Professor and returned to Cambridge where he could arrange for Max's grant for work on haemoglobin. I meant to work on insulin but was distracted by beautiful crystals of Vitamin $B_{12}$ brought in in 1948. I would go over to Cambridge from time to time to see how haemoglobin was doing. Max did a number of measurements of the intensities of the shrinking of haemoglobin following an idea discussed with Bernal, of tracing the Fourier transforms. The main shrinkage of haemoglobin was in one dimension and the changes of the intensities that could be followed of the 001 reflections permitted sign determination in one direction only. Bragg had taken a main series of sheets of the intensities of the different layers home with him, and invited me to lunch to see them – spread out on the two beds in the spare room, a good place for maps, I thought, when I copied him later. Bragg was very pleased with the accuracy of the phase definition but worried a little about where to move next. Max has described his excitement and pleasure with the finding of the mercury derivative of haemoglobin with which the structure was finally solved.

Bragg was anxious to continue protein work when he moved to the Royal Institution on retirement from Cambridge. His first suggestion, to take John Kendrew with him, failed. John wanted to continue his work in Cambridge. Bragg did then, somewhat tentatively, suggest that I might like to come – saying that by my age most scientists tended to cease day to day measuring operations and move to more administrative levels. But I had B12 on my hands. I suggested two crystallographers who I knew needed jobs – Jack Dunitz and David Philips. Bragg tried and got both. David Philips took over proteins but Jack only agreed to come following his own wanderings, and left when offered a professorship appointment at Zurich. Bragg was sad to see him go, and said, "I think I never realised how good he was, until he left me".

In 1980 Bragg celebrated his 80th birthday with a scientific symposium at the Royal Institution covering in four sessions the highlights of his life's work, and a dinner in the evening. His colleagues and past students came from all over the world. It was a tremendous meeting where I sat by accident next to an elderly Hungarian scientist, Professor Naray Szabo. He told me that he had come as a student to work with Bragg in Manchester in 1928 and had joined in the structure analysis of silicates and other minerals, such as apatite. But there was one mineral they could not solve, epidote. Linus Pauling, who had come for the experience of working with Bragg, asked Naray Szabo if he might take the data and try his hand. After a month he returned it unsolved. He admitted !I've wasted a month of my life on these crystals". They remained unsolved until quite recently. They were examined by several crytallographers, including Professor Belov, but were solved completely by T. Ito in Japan. Naray Szabo returned to Hungary, and for a time all went well. He became a professor and then a fellow of the Hungarian Academy of Sciences. But the country was engulfed by the war, occupied first by Germany, then by Russia, and after the war became a communist state, riven by suspicion, stories of spies involving everyone who had had friendly relations with Western Europe. Naray Szabo was caught up in these suspicions, thought to be plotting against Hungary, sentenced to imprisonment for twelve years and disgraced.

Better days were to come after 1956. Professor Kalman, with the help of Bernal, was able to clear Naray Szabo of the charges against him and rehabilitate him as an academician. Kalman then decided to organise a Hungarian crystallographic meeting which should be a pilot European meeting. From outside Hungary he invited Belov, Guinier and me to come and planned that the evening lecture should be given by Naray Szabo to celebrate his freedom.

Unfortunately, Naray Szabo suffered from old wounds caused by shrapnel in his legs and these had become inflamed. He was taken to hospital and operated on successfully but he was not well enough to come to the meeting. We visitors asked if we might see him in hospital. The doctors replied that they would allow only one person to visit him and he had chosen me. So I was able to see him again, thin and pale in hospital, but oddly cheerful and sensible, just waiting for a chance to talk again about Bragg and solving structures in Manchester with him, even the structure they did not solve. It was clearly the high point of his life.

# A Recollection of Sir Lawrence Bragg

## LORD TODD, OM FRS

I came to Cambridge in the autumn of 1944 as Professor of Organic Chemistry and Head of the Department of Organic and Inorganic Chemistry. As such I was located in the old University Chemical Laboratory in Pembroke Street on the south side of the university's so–called New Museums Site. The Cavendish Laboratory where Bragg operated was also on the New Museums Site, about a hundred yards across the courtyard from my laboratory. Despite the proximity, Bragg never, to my knowledge, set foot in the Chemical Laboratory from the date of my arrival until one day – I think it must have been in 1950 – when he came to my room in a somewhat agitated state of mind, bearing a bunch of papers in his hand. I said it was nice to see him in chemistry and asked what had led to this unexpected visit.

Now, only a couple of days before this visit I had received, from my old friend Linus Pauling, the manuscript of a paper he had sent off for publication in which he put forward the α–helical structure for the fibrous proteins. Accordingly, when Bragg produced a copy of the same manuscript I told him I had already had a copy from Linus. This apparently upset Bragg for a few minutes, for he wanted to know why a copy should have been sent to me. He quietened down when I explained that Linus Pauling and I had been friends for a dozen or so years and then he said that Pauling couldn't simply put down the particular structure in the paper as the X–ray evidence did not distinguish it from at least two others – "Have you seen our paper published last year in the *Proc. Roy. Soc.*?" "I'm afraid I haven't", said I: "I am not directly interested in protein structure and I don't normally read the *Proc. Roy. Soc.* which never publishes the kind of chemistry with which I'm concerned." "Well," he said (pushing a reprint of his paper across my desk) "you will see there that on the X–ray data (the same as Pauling's) there are three structures which fit and one cannot differentiate between them." I looked at them and said "Well, if I were considering these structures I would certainly choose the one which Pauling did." "But," said Bragg, "that structure could only be correct if the peptide linkage can be planar." I replied, "Why shouldn't it be?" "Come, come," said Bragg "–CO–NH– can't be planar." "But the peptide –CO–NH– linkage is a resonance hybrid" said I " and accordingly it has a hybrid form (–C(OH)=N) which is planar." I think that, given the evidence, any organic chemist would accept Pauling's view. Indeed, if at any time since I have been in Cambridge you had come over to the Chemical Laboratory, I – or for that matter any of my organic colleagues – would have told you that. Don't you take any chemical advice when you do this kind of work?" "Oh yes" he said "we get advice when we need it from X." Which might have been all right except that X was not an organic chemist!

This terminated our discussion of the α–helix, but it had one consequence worth recording. Bragg decided then and there that in future he would not allow any of his people to publish a structure for an organic compound from his lab based only on X–ray measurements without having me first have a look at it, and pronounce it acceptable. That is why, a year or two later, when Watson and Crick produced the double helical structure for DNA I was asked to go across to the Cavendish and vet their model before they were allowed to submit their now famous paper to *Nature*.

# Manchester and Cambridge

## SIR NEVILL MOTT, FRS

My first job was with Bragg at Manchester. This was for the year 1929–30. I had had three years of research, in Cambridge, Copenhagen and Göttingen, and had published some papers on collision theory and nuclear reactions. Bragg offered me the job and I had no doubts about accepting. At this time there were only two important physics schools in England, Cambridge and Manchester. An established position with tenure was welcome, and £400 a year was a very tolerable salary. The prestige of the job was considerable; it was a lectureship once held by Bohr, theorist to the department.

Rutherford told me (according to a letter that I wrote to my mother): "I always believe in young men leaving Cambridge; I find that after about five years in Cambridge they get a sort of paralysis of the will, don't you know. I've had to send away a lot of young men from my lab. Now *I* went to Canada when I was 27, and *I've* stood on my own feet ever since."

In 1929, quantum or wave mechanics was three years old, and few people in the UK understood it yet. Bragg wanted me to give lectures to his staff, including himself, and this I did – learning (I hope) the technique of lecturing as I went along. I remember Bragg vividly – how interested and approachable he was. He also set me to work demonstrating in the practical class – an experience I have not had anywhere since. And, of course, fresh from Bohr and Rutherford, this was my first experience of crystallography and solid state physics. A paper of mine on the scattering of electrons by atoms (*Proc. Roy. Soc. A*, **127**, 658, 1930) comparing X–ray and electron scattering in the context of diffraction, was a direct result of Bragg's influence.

Towards the end of the year I was offered a university lectureship and a fellowship at Caius College at Cambridge – too good to refuse, but I was sorry to leave Manchester.

In 1933 I moved from Cambridge to Bristol as Professor of Theoretical Physics, and in response to some of the experimental work in progress at Bristol, I turned to solid state physics. This bought me from time to time in contact with Bragg, and I remember particularly his bubble model for the movement of dislocation. Then came the war, and after it I had the choice of staying at Bristol and within two or three years succeeding Arthur Tyndall as head of the laboratory, or responding to Bragg's invitation to take up the Chair of Theoretical Physics at Cambridge, vacant through Ralph Fowler's untimely death. Many factors lead me to choose Bristol. I had a delightful university house on the campus, rented for £70 per annum. Moving house with two young children at a time of post war shortages, was not attractive. Bristol under its new Vice Chancellor, Philip Morris, was ambitious – and I knew I could work with him, and above all I wanted my own show. It was a little discouraging that Bragg suggested I might share his secretary.

When Bragg went to the Royal Institution, and I succeeded him at Cambridge in 1954, naturally I discussed the situation with him more than once. I remember asking him what consumed most of his time there, and he said "visitors". I know what he meant. But on a more serious level, I don't think Bragg's time at Cambridge could have been entirely easy. The Cavendish in the 1930s under Rutherford was the world centre for nuclear physics; in the later part of the years before the war, many of his outstanding men took over the dormant physics departments elsewhere, such Liverpool, Manchester, Birmingham, Edinburgh and Glasgow, started work there and resumed it after the war, with all the prestige of the nuclear bomb to help them. Bragg was offered the Cambridge job by the electors, I have to assume because they the Cavendish needed a new line. Or did they just feel that Manchester should succeed to Cambridge, as York should (in the view of some) to Canterbury? I do not know – but I know of the tendency at that time of the nuclear fraternity to feel and express the view that what isn't nuclear isn't (fundamental) physics. And I believe that Bragg felt this, and the attitude was still present when I took over in 1854. I guess Bragg may have suffered from it.

In the event, however, how right the electors were. Under Bragg and with his most effective help, the Cavendish housed the most important scientific advances of the post–war period, molecular biology and the discovery of the genetic code.

# Bragg – the Cavendish Professor

### SIR BRIAN PIPPARD, FRS

W.L. Bragg's election to the Cavendish chair of experimental physics in Cambridge was taken by many as a threat to the great tradition of fundamental physics research established by J.J. Thomson and, especially, Rutherford. The first third of the century had seen a revolution in which they had played leading parts, and surely there were younger members of the Rutherford school who could have maintained the pre-eminence of the Cavendish in this most important branch of natural science. The choice of a crystallographer, however distinguished, was a blow to many hopes. This was not simply a reaction of disappointed personal ambition, for the shock was felt afar – as late as 1955 I was told by a leading American physicist that since Rutherford's death, the Cavendish had produced nothing of significance. Yet when one looks back on Bragg's tenure of the chair one sees that the seeds sown then had already, by the time he left, shown great potential, and shortly afterwards came to fruition in advances and discoveries that rivalled, perhaps even eclipsed, any from Rutherford's Cavendish. The radioastronomy of Ryle's group, and the partnerships in molecular biology of Perutz and Kendrew, Crick and Watson, have changed our view of the world more radically than the discovery of the neutron and of artificial disintegration; and these are only the most conspicuous successes from the post–war era of intellectual ferment. Bragg deserves great credit for creating an environment in which a multitude of ideas could prosper, and for his enthusiastic support (or at least, in the case of Crick and Watson, long-suffering tolerance) of every promising venture, whether or not it was directed at obviously fundamental problems.

He had hardly installed himself in the laboratory when war broke out and most of the senior members disappeared into radar and other military projects. At the end of the war there were chairs elsewhere to be filled, while atomic energy also beckoned; as a result, no member of staff from Rutherford's time, except the ionospheric physicist Jack Ratcliffe, returned to Cambridge. There were, of course, those who had been research students in the thirties and who, experienced by now in novel techniques, filled vacant posts and began the process of reconstruction. But it fell largely to Bragg and Ratcliffe, together with Norman Feather until he went to Edinburgh in 1945, to decide which of many applicants should receive postgraduate research awards. The laboratory photograph, taken in the Summer of 1946, is studded with young faces destined for senior chairs and other posts of distinction, testimony to the soundness of their choices. The details of their deliberations are in the university archives, material perhaps for a minor historical study.

Bragg was no autocrat in the Rutherford mould - there were indeed those who felt he was too readily swayed by his closest counsellors - and he knew he could not hold together a spontaneously diversifying empire unless he devolved power to the research groups. But he still had overall responsibility, and to carry out this duty he drew on the experience of government research institutions in which he and so many of his colleagues had worked during the war, and where they had learnt the value of competent day-to-day administration. In spite of a considerable shortage of money for new appointments Bragg managed (by what means I do not know) to persuade the university authorities to establish posts for a graduate departmental secretary and an accounts officer. The idea soon spread to other large departments and thus a system came into being that has lasted and evolved, and is now taken for granted as the only sensible way of running an extended research enterprise. This was perhaps the beginning for us of the gradual process of specialisation endemic to the whole world of science, which has led to the present almost complete divorce between different branches of physics. At first the regular meetings of the Cavendish Physical

Society and of other societies like the Kapitza Club and the $\nabla^2 V$ club served to keep different specialities united in an appreciation of interesting developments in other fields. The clubs have long since faded away, and the Cavendish Physical Society is no more the institution which, in the days of Rutherford and Bragg, everyone was expected to attend; but there still remains the most potent unifying influence of all, the shared responsibility for undergraduate teaching, and this continues to give the Cavendish a corporate identity.

Fragmentation, however, was still some time in the future during Bragg's reign, and in any case of no concern to us youngsters who had our way to make in the world and cared little whether the Professor took the personal interest in other work that was, according to legend, characteristic of Rutherford's centralised command. We rarely spoke with him except to ask him to communicate a paper to the Royal Society, which he always seemed to undertake so readily as to imply that the request had made his day for him, or if he enquired whether one had considered applying for some vacant post. I recall with shame that when he suggested I might try for the Manchester Chair, I remarked unthinkingly that it wasn't at all a bad prospect since Blackett had held it; he said with only a hint of reproach, "It wasn't bad in my time".

Too many of us, young and arrogant that we were, thought of Bragg as a kindly old buffer, well past his prime; and he didn't help his image by getting excited about using rafts of bubbles as models of dislocated crystals. It was only when the eminent Cyril S. Smith of Chicago, passed through and also got excited that we began to concede that there must be something in what the old man was doing; and as the protein work thrived under his aegis we came to acknowledge that the Professor, after all, was a master of his craft.

The avuncular manner was strongly in evidence in his optics lectures to undergraduates, to such a degree on the first occasion he gave them (during my third year), that he soon lost from his audience many who, had they persevered, would have found in their notes a treatment that excelled any textbook for clarity and insight. I have heard that his failure to capture our hearts distressed him, but he continued to give the course throughout the time he was in Cambridge, and in the later years took great trouble to set up in a dark room demonstrations of diffraction and interference, with the best available optical equipment, which were certainly appreciated by the students.

The material he presented in these lectures showed the characteristic English school of physics at its best, in the way inessentials were stripped off to lay bare the physics at the heart of a complex problem. This was typical of Bragg, to reduce a problem to such simplicity that intuition (and his was very strong) could serve as a guide; once on the scent he was indefatigable. Mathematics for its own sake held no attraction, and a practical demonstration was much to be preferred over an unsupported calculation if only because, as he once remarked to me "I always have to get the wrong answer three times before getting it right". The occasion was the only time we collaborated in a research project, small as it was, and of course at his bidding. I have no idea why he thought I could help with a problem that arose when Perutz measured the optical birefringence of a protein crystal; what, Bragg asked, could it tell us about the shape of the molecule? By chance, during my student days, one of the lecturers had drawn attention to a paper by C.G. Darwin on the refractive index of the ionosphere. In those days students had time to read original papers, and this one developed an approach which was just the thing for Bragg's problem. Later the method came to be called the excluded volume approach, but to me it was Darwin's method until Perutz, drawing on his remarkable memory, showed me a genuinely obscure paper of 1912 by Wiener, which presented the same idea. The reason for recalling this now quite unimportant collaboration, which lasted no more than two or three days, is that it brings to mind the glow of pleasure that lit up Bragg's face when he saw how neat was the final result. For him beauty and economy were the touchstones of a physical argument or an experiment, and unless one sympathised with his quest for these ideals one missed his intellectual power and subtlety. It was not that he was too delicate for hard and dirty labour – he was after all a keen gardener – but the job was not complete until the tools had been cleaned and put away. This little lesson in the aesthetics of research epitomises for me a great physicist whom the Cavendish should always remember with gratitude.

# An Appreciation

## H.S. LIPSON, CBE FRS

I claim that W.L. Bragg is the most successful scientist in history. I accept that Newton and Einstein have greater reputations, but although all three did their greatest work in their early twenties, Newton and Einstein essentially spent the rest of their lives polishing up their ideas; Bragg went on for the whole of his life transforming different branches of science. He first of all revolutionised chemistry, then mineralogy, then metallurgy and finally biology.

### Chemistry

At the beginning of this century, the great physical problem was the nature of X–rays, which had been discovered in 1895. Bragg's father, W.H. Bragg, had incontrovertible proof that they were particles (we now know that he was observing quantum effects), but Barkla had equally incontrovertible proof that they were waves. In 1912, Laue, Friedrich and Knipping, by diffracting X–rays from a crystal, showed that X–rays were indeed waves. W.L. Bragg, who was then a research student working under J.J. Thomson at Cambridge, was upset that his father had apparently been proved wrong. But he could not help thinking about the problem and produced his bright idea that diffracted waves could be regarded as 'reflexions' from planes of atoms. This gave the now–famous Bragg's Law:

$$n\lambda = 2d \sin\theta$$

Laue, a much more accomplished theoretical physicist, had produced a complete theory of three–dimensional diffraction but it was too complicated to use: Bragg's Law was not.

He was encouraged to try his idea on rock salt, which chemists believed to be composed of molecules of NaCl. He showed that it was in fact composed of regular sequences of Na and Cl atoms. Chemistry was transformed!

In 1919, after the First World War, he was appointed Professor of Physics at Manchester, and built up a powerful research group. But he did not want to continue in the inorganic field, and looked round for other worlds to conquer.

## Mineralogy

The Vice–Chancellor at Manchester was Sir Henry Miers, a noted mineralogist. The chemical compositions of many minerals were known, but little sense could be made of them, and so Bragg decided to see if their crystal structures could help. As he said later, their X–ray diffraction photographs seemed impossibly complicated compared with NaCl, but he and his collaborators now had considerable experience, and were very successful; beryl, for example, was worked out in an afternoon!

It turned out that the basis of minerals was the $SiO_4$ tetrahedron, which could be separate, could be joined at corners or at edges, but not share faces. Other atoms could fit into interstices. Everything fell into place.

## Metallurgy

Up to now (about 1925), all work had been carried out on single crystals, but it had been shown in the USA that for simple structures diffraction patterns from powders could be interpreted, and many elements were studied in this way. Bragg wanted to see what Manchester could contribute, and sent one of his research students, A.J. Bradley, to see what he could learn in Sweden from Westgren and Phragmen. Bradley was soon educating them! He worked out the structure of $\alpha$–manganese, and then went on to a useless form of brass, $Cn_5Zn_8$ – a very brittle alloy.

Bradley, who was perhaps the most single–minded person that I have ever met, was fascinated by the problem, not realising its importance. He solved the structure by quite unconventional methods. Bragg realised the importance of his result, and arranged a series of discussions with people like Mott, Bethe and Hume–Rothery, and out of this was formed the modern theory of the metallic state. Mott and Jones published the ideas in their book, *The Theory of the Properties of Metals and Alloys*.

Bragg's contribution to this work is not usually cited but I am sure that it was his part in bringing people together that was of supreme importance.

**Crystal–Structure Methods**

In the 1930s, crystal–structure work was becoming mainly trial–and–error, and Bragg's department in Manchester was undoubtedly the leading centre of this work. But Bragg was not satisfied; he did not want to be classed as a crystallographer but as a physicist – he wanted his subject to be a branch of optics.

He was inspired by his father's ideas of the introduction of Fourier series, as expressed in the 1915 Bakerian Lecture to the Royal Society. He tried to see whether the projection of a structure on a plane could be represented by a two–dimensional Fourier series and applied his ideas successfully to the structure of a mineral, diopside – $CaMg(SiO_2)_2$.

This led to a revolution in crystal–structure work. Beevers and I were led to try out his ideas in a new crystal structure, copper sulphate, and invented a method of summing two–dimensional Fourier series which became very popular. After that *all* papers on this subject had to have a Fourier diagram in them.

This was a fine example of his perspicacity; he would not tell us how he summed the series for diopside; he merely said that it was useful to have a billiard table – as he had in his house – for laying out his papers!

**Biology**

On Bragg's appointment as Cavendish Professor in Cambridge in 1937 he made his last great contribution. We had all thought that biological problems, with tens of thousands of atoms in the molecules, would be too difficult to tackle by X–ray methods. But he became involved in Perutz's work on haemoglobin, started by Bernal around 1930. Bernal was just the man to start such a problem, but not the one to solve it! (He was a generalist rather than a specialist).

Around 1960, with new devices and methods that came into use, the problem *was* solved. Bragg said that the problem to him seemed no more difficult than the minerals had seemed in 1930.

**Optical Analogies**

At Cambridge, Bragg put forward some new ideas on the relationship between X–ray and optical image formation. I like to think that I was his best supporter; some of my colleagues in Cambridge thought that he was in his dotage! But he was not. His ideas influenced me considerably when I was in Manchester, and I was flattered when he said that I had taken his ideas further then he thought possible.

**General Character**

Bragg was a great man to work with but not necessarily helpful in one's career. He used to say, "If a researcher is any good, he will not need pushing". This may be so in an ideal world, but the world is not ideal. When Bradley was elected to the Royal

Society Bragg was very pleased, but he said to me, "It was not *my* doing". I thought that it ought to have been. He was quite different from Rutherford, a large proportion of whose colleagues were elected to the Royal Society.

He was also rather demanding in one's work; most research students knew that whatever results they would produce, he would expect more. I was extremely proud that, when I produced some diagrams for a joint paper with him, he said "Oh, Lipson, you *have* been working hard".

But these were small failings, and he was, without doubt, a genius for getting new things done, things that most people would not have thought possible.

# Cavendish Days

### W COCHRAN, FRS

Sir Lawrence Bragg was Cavendish Professor during the first eight of my eighteen years at Cambridge. He visited the crystallography group every two or three weeks to see what was going on. Usually his interest was a stimulus, but sometimes he stimulated me to greater effort by refusing to see the value of what I was doing, as when my diffractometer took longer to work than it should – the apparent instability in its operation I eventually traced to the cyclotron four floors down. Bragg's contacts with other laboratories were often useful and he pushed several interesting problems my way. In fact, in writing this account I have come to realise more fully the sum total of his influence on me. I had no great regard for him as a theorist and I was surprised to learn years later that his first degree had been a first class honours in mathematics from Adelaide. W.H. Taylor managed the group in a very diplomatic style but those of my age scarcely appreciated the part he played in holding together a group which contained a number of prima donnas. Helen Megaw was working on ferroelectric structures and I learnt something of the subject from some lectures which she gave. She had also, in common with Taylor, an interest in mineralogical structures. I did not know John Kendrew and Max Perutz very well at that time and the former was always a rather reserved person. Hugh Huxley and Francis Crick joined them about 1949. I was prepared to concede that protein structures were of great interest and importance, but impossibly difficult to determine, I thought, after my experience of attempting to determine the crystal structure of sucrose when I was a research student in Edinburgh. Fortunately, they had never tried to determine simpler crystal structures, and so were not deterred.

Social life centred on coffee parties in the late evenings, occasional dinners and sometimes a sherry party in a college, but we were an abstemious lot. The Braggs once or twice gave a Christmas party, and I remember Sir Lawrence acting a charade of hay–mow–glow–bin. I was a fairly regular attender at meetings of the Kapitza

Club, run by David Shoenberg, and gave at least one talk about crytallographic computing using the Hollerith punched–card system. I remember being questioned by H. Bondi, who was unimpressed. During this period I undertook supervisions only at Part I level; although they took up about six hours per week in the evenings I did not have to spend much time on preparation. Most of my 'spare' time was given over to thinking about my research. I remember reading, after I became a demonstrator, that I could claim an additional payment from the university if I did not undertake more than six hours of college teaching. The concept of payment for not working was so foreign to me that I did not claim it, until after a year or so I found that other members of staff in science departments did so as a matter of course. It was in fact a sensible enough scheme, designed to encourage research, but unnecessary in my case as I never thought for a moment that I had been appointed to teach, rather than to do research. There were times when I felt dissatisfied with crystallography as a topic and wondered whether the nuclear physicists were perhaps justified in looking down on us – as I believe they did. Bragg had not been entirely forgiven for not being a nuclear physicist, and crystallography's golden age and second crop of Nobel Prizes was still out of sight, a decade away in the future.

Towards the end of 1950, Bragg suggested that I should apply for leave to work with Ray Pepinsky on XRAC, an electronic analogue computer, in Pennsylvania State University for six months, and to report on XRAC on my return. So with support from the Rockefeller Foundation I travelled on the *Queen Elizabeth* in December, 1950.

I look back on 1951 as the most eventful year of my life – I worked and travelled in America, attended my first conference, met my future wife, got my first tenured appointment and became a bachelor Fellow living in College.

I acted as consultant sometimes to the protein–crystallography group, and this occasionally led to a joint paper. Bragg was always keen to involve me in this work, but I was pessimistic about its prospects, and later, when the use of the isomorphous replacement method held out hopes of ultimate success, it would have looked as if I were clambering on to the band–wagon. Bragg borrowed a semi–crystalline specimen of poly–methyl–glutamate, a synthetic polypeptide, from members of a Courtaulds research group, and my diary for 2nd October 1951 notes: "The Prof shows a touching faith in my ability to extract a complicated crystal (sic) structure from almost no data." Later, Bragg was sent, I think as a referee, a paper by V. Vand on the theory of X–ray diffraction by atoms arranged on a helix. He passed it on to me, and with my knowledge of the theory of Fourier transforms I was able to conclude in a short time that Vand's answer was correct for a continuous helix but not for atoms on a helix. Francis Crick also saw the paper, and when we compared notes the following day we found we had arrived at the same (correct) answer by very different routes. A day or two later I suddenly realised, without having been conscious of thinking about the problem, that the photographs of poly–methyl–glutamate, which I had put aside a month or so before, could be explained as the diffraction pattern of atoms on helices of different radii. My diary for 7th November remarks: "... and I've retreated from my position of extreme scepticism to admit in this instance that Pauling may be right." Francis and I published a joint paper in *Nature*, which was the first conclusive evidence for the existence of a helical structure at the molecular level. My involvement in both experiment and theory I owe to Bragg. Watson, in his fascinating book *The Double Helix* has part of the story right, but in thinking that the experimental evidence was "Max's X–ray diagrams" (of haemoglobin) he is quite wrong.

In the early 1950s, Bragg became impatient for the completion of Volume III of the series which he had begun with Volume I. It was on crystal structure determination, and Henry Lipson had been working at it for some years. I was persuaded to lend a hand, and I contributed three chapters to the first edition which appeared in in 1953. As a lecturer I had to devote rather more time to teaching than before, but I believe that I also missed the spur of Bragg's interest after he moved to the Royal Institution in 1954, and my interests changed to other topics such as lattice dynamics and ferroelectricity.

# The Bird Life of Albermarle Street

## U.W. ARNDT, FRS

It was my good fortune to have been under Sir Lawrence Bragg's influence during three periods: as an undergraduate reading physics in Cambridge in 1942–44, as a research student in the Crystallography Laboratory at the Cavendish Laboratory during 1944–49, and in the Davy–Faraday Laboratory of the Royal Institution from Bragg's arrival there in 1954 until 1963.

During the war years, we undergraduates did not see a great deal of the august Cavendish Professor, but among his many duties he found time to give some lectures to the Part II class. In our preoccupation with the more fashionable aspects of the syllabus, that is, with quantum mechanics and nuclear physics, we probably did not respond to the appeal of what was not yet called solid–state physics, nor did we all appreciate the professor's physical insight and his ability to see the physical meaning in a mathematical statement. I well remember the stamping of the young sophisticates which greeted Bragg when, in a Part II lecture, he said, "we shall take a little bit of $x$, we shall call it d$x$ and we shall think of it as delta $x$". His beautiful demonstration of dislocations, before these were seen in electron micrographs, by means of the bubble raft was gently lampooned in a 'poem', of which I can only remember the lines in which Bragg is made to say to Orowan:

> I could have saved you all your troubles
> Because I
> and John Nye
> Have done it all with our soap bubbles.

It was only when I had been a research student for some time that I came to recognise how very genuine was his enthusiasm for a 'really pretty' X–ray photograph or electron micrograph which showed some new effect more clearly than before. Good electron micrographs were then a rarity, even though the instrument, a lend–lease RCA Type B electron microscope, was in the meticulous hands of George Crow, formerly Rutherford's personal assistant, to whom Bragg was 'little Willie' and 'the Prof' still meant Rutherford. Bragg was not greatly amused when Henry Lipson, in his presence, described one of my micrographs as "nothing to brag about, I mean, nothing to crow about". I was told, but cannot vouch for the accuracy of the story, that Bragg would not accept a much better Siemens electron microscope, 'liberated' from a German laboratory, or other German instruments, because he did not want German scientists to find their own equipment at the Cavendish when visits started again after the war.

In spite of his dignity, the Cavendish Professor could be approached at any time and he showed great kindness to all of us. I have always considered that the speediness of my own naturalisation as a British subject immediately after the war owed much to the more–than–generous reference which Bragg wrote for me to the Home Office.

Having moved to the Royal Institution in 1950, I was followed there by Bragg a few years later, and his farewell dinner at Trinity was a welcome dinner as far as I was concerned. His good–bye present from the Cavendish was a pair of binoculars. "So useful", as Lady Bragg said at the time, "for observing the bird–life of Albemarle Street".

In the more intimate surroundings of the small group at the Royal Institution we got to know Sir Lawrence – he was never "the professor" at the R.I. – and his family well. We were all treated as family and were included in activities, such as the Braggs' skating parties on St James Park pond. All members of the laboratory were guests at his daughter Patience's wedding, and one of the high–spots of the year was the annual staff outing to the Braggs' country home at Waldringfield. Lady Bragg's Christmas tree was fitted into its stand at the R.I. workshop – the only time I have seem a micrometer used on a tree trunk.

Modes of address at the time were different from those of today. Among scientific colleagues in the laboratory we were just beginning to use first names instead of surnames without titles, but the workshop staff were Mister Faulkner and Mister Thirkell. Bragg continued to address everyone by surname in the old style for many years, long after Lady Bragg had discovered and used our first names.

Scientifically, the Davy–Faraday Laboratory flourished under Bragg. He organised the work and recruited staff, so that at first we could function as a support group for the MRC Unit in Cambridge, with Max Perutz and John Kendrew becoming readers in protein crystallography at the R.I. Always the home of rotating–anode X–ray tubes, the laboratory was equipped with three modern generators built in the workshop, and with two automatic single–crystal X–ray diffractometers which were world firsts. The second of these instruments was the direct descendant of the original ionisation spectrometer used by W.L. and W.H.

Bragg in their pioneering experiments. Later on, with Bragg's constant encouragement, and under David Phillips, the laboratory became a major centre in its own right for solving protein structures.

The lecture programme at the R.I. achieved new heights under Bragg, in a large measure because of the quality of his own lectures and his unequalled ability to convey his enthusiasm. To this day, his *Advice to Lecturers* is handed to all visiting lecturers at Brookhaven National Laboratory. I well remember his tip that the best method of achieving spontaneity when reading from a prepared script consists of changing the occasional 'thus' to a 'therefore'; such alterations produce just sufficient of a hesitation to make the presentation sound natural. It would be good if more lecturers heeded his advice to restrict the number of slides to one every five minutes, and the number of concepts to one every twenty minutes.

Bragg was a talented artist; he could draw a perfect circle free hand on the blackboard, putting in the centre first. His landscapes in oils and some of his portraits of colleagues were of a very high quality. He painted some of the figures used in lecture demonstrations himself, such as that of a somersaulting clown who was rolled down an inclined plane in a Christmas lecture. His R.I. lectures to school children were enormously popular; one of the highlights was when he demonstrated the field–free region inside a Faraday cage by climbing into the cage himself, which was then charged by the original Whimshurst machine. He would explain that his hair would stand on end if he cautiously raised his head out of the trap on top, but as he had no hair he would content himself with raising a stick to which paper streamers had been attached.

A very special occasion was the celebration of the fiftieth anniversary of the award of Bragg's Nobel Prize in 1965, which was attended by a glittering array of Nobel Laureates. Bragg's gold medal was on display in the library; in the preparation of the exhibits the medal had been laid down in the preparation room on a drop of mercury and collected an unsightly stain. Messrs Johnson–Matthey, on consultation, prescribed the exact temperature of the heat–treatment needed to drive off the mercury. Bill Coates, the lecture assistant, claimed that he had lost several years of his life before the medal emerged in its pristine glory from the oven. I do not believe Sir Lawrence was ever told the story.

Sir Lawrence Bragg's scientific career was obviously a happy one and he derived great satisfaction from seeing the subject of X–ray crystallography, of which he was the prime initiator, growing into an all–embracing discipline. Yet one sometimes wondered whether he did not brood too much on what he regarded as his failures, such as the fact that he was pipped at the post by Pauling's discovery of the $\alpha$–helix. (The model of Bragg, Kendrew and Perutz's chemically impossible $4_{13}$ helix is almost indistinguishable to the untutored eye from that of the structurally correct $\alpha$–helix). His delight in solving crystal structures was obvious: his was the unique achievement of going on from determining the simplest crystal structure of all, that of rock salt, to solving the structure of the most complicated inorganic molecules, the silicates, and to having a major share in the elucidation of the most complicated organic molecules, the proteins. It was this delight, rather than the prospect 'of solving the riddle of life itself' to which he often paid lip service, which seemed to drive him and which served as an inspiration to several generations of crystallographers.

# Golden Rules

## ANDRÉ GUINIER

It was in the early fifties at the Crystallographic Laboratory in Cambridge. I remember that, one day, during tea time, W.L. Bragg told us that he used to give to newcomers a few 'golden rules'. After 35 years, I still have in mind two of them, because they are typical of the spirit of the Bragg laboratory and because they are also linked to problems which are permanent in science.

### "Never follow the fashion."

It happens that new subjects appear to be very promising and attractive. A change of the line of research is legitimate if the researcher feels that he can contribute new ideas; it is not if he is only able to duplicate the work of other laboratories, and if he is motivated by the easier funding of fashionable topics. Two years ago we were the witnesses of the extraordinary phenomenon of the superconductor rush. Thousands of physicists or chemists decided overnight to work on oxides of the family used by Bednorz and Muller in their original experiment. Some laboratories have been successful, but how many now regret not having followed Bragg's wise advice?

Unfortunately, it seems that the pressure of fashion is heavier nowadays than it was in Bragg's time. When, in 1958, the first transistor was built, that did not upset the laboratories. However, the opening towards the solid–state electronics was far more important than the discovery of the high $T_c$ superconductors will probably ever be.

### "Never be afraid to carry on an experiment which is declared stupid by the theoreticists of the laboratory."

The form of the sentence is deliberately provocative, but its meaning is profound. History shows that at the very beginning of many major advances of modern physics, there is an unsuspected observation. For instance, a diffraction pattern of a crystal with an 'impossible' five–fold symmetry revealed the existence of the quasi–crystalline state. A theoreticist could not have imagined this type of atomic order because it is too complicated, and the reason for the complexity is unknown. Afterwards, the observations were fully explained; the development of the new idea came from a very close collaboration between theoreticists and experimentalists. But it was essential that the first strange observations were not immediately rejected as trifling artefacts because they did not conform to the generally accepted ideas.

The young and enthusiastic scientist should not hesitate to try some hazardous experiments. Of course, there will be many failures; it is the price to pay to have, perhaps only once, the extraordinary joy of seeing something which has never been seen before.

Beginners are often more attracted by a 'clean' theory than by an endless struggle with matter as it is. The mathematical solution of a problem seems more rewarding than the realisation of an apparatus which works. (At least this is the case in France where mathematics have a prominent place in elementary teaching.)

The 'rule' of W.L. Bragg indeed touches a very sensitive point of methodology. In spite of the ingenuity of our models and the success of our logic, in many cases the progress of physics requires, and will always require, an empirical approach. W.L. Bragg has shown the value of a quite uncertain experimental trial. When the first diffraction pattern of a haemoglobin crystal was made in his laboratory, the chances of determining the structure of so large a molecule were really very remote.

# W.L. Bragg: A Few Personal Recollections

## FRANCIS CRICK, FRS

I did not meet Bragg till I was about 33. I was much in awe of him. As the founder of X–ray crystallography, he was already a legendary figure. He obtained his Nobel Prize for this pioneer work in the year before I was born. As head of the Cavendish, he held the senior physics chair in Britain. He was in addition the boss of my supervisor, Max Perutz (I had yet to obtain a PhD), and took a keen and fairly constant interest in Perutz and Kendrew's attempts to solve the three–dimensional structure of a protein.

Due to Jim Watson's chatty account of our experiences at the Cavendish between 1951 and 1953, it is public knowledge that Bragg did not always find my company entirely agreeable. He felt I was too critical, partly because of my detailed comments on the current work in the group, but mainly because I had argued, at a fairly public meeting, that most of their efforts stood little chance of succeeding. "Crick," he said to me "you're rocking the boat."

He also thought I talked too much and, I suspect, in too fast and complicated a manner, often about scientific subjects that he probably felt had little to do with X–ray crystallography. I'm told that he confided to others that "Crick makes my head buzz". (He always addressed us by our surnames, as was then the custom. In turn, we addressed him as 'Professor'. Even if I had known that his close friends called him 'Willie', it would have been unthinkable for me to do so. How times have changed!)

Nevertheless, I learned a lot from Bragg. He was a major influence on my scientific career. Perhaps the most useful and lasting lesson was how to approach a scientific problem. One example will explain what I mean. I had been trying to deduce, mainly from Perutz's data, the approximate overall shape of the haemoglobin molecule. I started off in the right way, but I got bogged down in details. Also, I did not look around for other evidence. Bragg quite independently took up the problem, made some bold simplifying assumptions, was not too pernickety about the exact fit with the experimental data as I had been and, with Perutz, came up with a good first approximation to the shape that fitted several distinct unit cells. It was a lesson I have never forgotten.

I also learnt from one of Bragg's few mistakes. He wanted to find, by model building, whether there was a regular fold to the polypeptide chain. He started off in the right way by making the correct, bold assumptions. (Again, I was impressed.) But then he (together with Perutz and Kendrew) went astray. In brief, they neglected to make the peptide bond planar, and they even assumed (due to some bad advice from a theoretical chemist) that the nitrogen might sometimes be pyramidal. Their main blunder was a more subtle one. They were trying to fit Astburg's X–ray data on $\alpha$–keratin. This showed a 5.15 Å reflection on the meridian. Bragg made the obvious deduction that the structure must have an integral screw axis, and so their models were built using this restriction. To Bragg's dismay they all looked terrible. In fact, one of them was topologically an $\alpha$–helix, but they had forced the poor thing to have a 4–fold axis, so that it looked extremely uncomfortable. When Linus Pauling came out with the correct structure for the $\alpha$–helix, with a 3.6–fold helix, Bragg was greatly cast down.

It turned out that a straight $\alpha$–helix has no reflection at 5.15 Å on the meridian, but a strong one of about that spacing off the meridian. We now know that in $\alpha$–keratin small groups of $\alpha$–helices coil slowly round one another, and it is this structure that gives the meridianal 5.15 Å, but who could ever have imagined that before the $\alpha$–helix was discovered.

Jim Watson and I were strongly influenced by this very forgivable mistake. We became acutely aware that no single piece of experimental data was to be trusted, not merely because it might be wrong, but because it might be correct but misleading. While worrying about the structure of DNA we kept this possibility constantly in mind.

The other thing I learnt from Bragg was how to give a lecture, or rather, how not to give a lecture. Bragg had been asked to speak at a small meeting at the Cavendish on a topic in which I also was closely interested. Without realising it I had outlined in my head how I would have given the lecture. When Bragg delivered his short talk it was not like my version at all. He made a few simple points that set out the main aspects of the work. Each was explained very clearly in a straightforward way, without too many technical details. I realised that had I given the talk all the emphasis would have been on the details and the broad conclusions would have been submerged beneath a mass of technicalities.

Bragg subsequently wrote a paper on how to give a lecture. His acid test was what one of his listeners would tell his wife about the lecture at breakfast the next morning. The lecture was to be judged a success if the listener could remember one item from it. Bragg believed this was about as much as you could expect to get over in a single talk!

Bragg's attitude to me changed drastically after the DNA double helix. He went out of his way, as he told me much later, to make up for his earlier poor opinion of me. I myself had always liked him, both for his gentlemanly personality and for his boyish enthusiasm for science, another thing I like to think I acquired from him. We were too different both in age and experience, to become friends, but in later years he was always cordial to me. I remember his giving me good advice on various types of shrub when I told him I was thinking of growing roses in our cottage garden in the country.

But my image of Bragg as a person and as a gardener is best illustrated by an anecdote he told me many years later. I cannot end better than by quoting what I wrote about it recently:

"Sir Lawrence Bragg was... also a keen gardener. When he moved in 1954 from his large house and garden in West Road, Cambridge, to London, to head the Royal Institution in Albemarle Street, he lived in the official apartment at the top of the building. Missing his garden, he arranged that for one afternoon each week he would hire himself out as a gardener to an unknown lady living in The Boltons, a select inner–London suburb. He respectfully tipped his hat to her and told her his name was Willie. For several months all went well until one day a visitor, glancing out of the window, said to her hostess, "My dear, what *is* Sir Lawrence Bragg doing in your garden?" I can think of few other scientists of his distinction who would do something like this."

# Bragg's Foreword to *The Double Helix*

## JAMES D. WATSON, For. Mem. RS

I had come to England for the fall of 1965 to finish *The Double Helix*. Harvard had granted me a sabbatical leave and the Guggenheim Foundation one of their prized fellowships. Sydney Brenner had arranged for me to live in Kings, in rooms looking out to Clare and I had virtually completed the manuscript by mid December. At that time a one day meeting was held at the British Biophysical Society at Queen Elizabeth College located off Campden Hill Road in Kensington. Listening to the talks I was diverted by a very good looking young woman to whom, during the coffee break, I introduced myself. She was Louise Johnson, a crystallographer at the Royal Institution working for her PhD with David Phillips on the structure of lysozyme. We went to lunch together at a nearby pub and without asking I got the unmistakable impression that she was fond of a man that she did not wish to identify. Her beauty, however, was not easily dismissible, and when I was next in London, I arranged to stop by the R.I.

Then in mid January I was on my way to Kenya for six weeks in East Africa lecturing to students under the auspices of the Ford Foundation. The last chapter of *The Double Helix* had been finished while I was back in the States in early January. Tom Wilson, the director of Harvard University Press, was among the first to read it and immediately said he wanted to publish it, provided that his lawyers could reassure him that no one was libeled, and even better if he could also obtain permission from key figures like Francis Crick, Maurice Wilkins and Sir Lawrence Bragg. I knew that some awkward moments lay ahead of me.

Immediately upon arriving at the Mayfair Hilton, I phoned Peter Pauling, then a Lecturer in Chemistry at University college, asking him who was the beauty at the R.I., the site where he had done his PhD. I had no doubt that he would know, and we arranged to meet the next day. Just before noon we called in at the R.I. to see if we could get Louise, and others of her group that Peter knew, well to join us for lunch. Happily she did, as did Tony North whom I first knew at the Cavendish. Soon we were walking down Dover Street and into Wheelers where I explained the awkward moments that I must face soon when I gave my manuscript to Sir Lawrence.

Possibly helping me was the fact that Sir Lawrence had written to me at Harvard almost a year before suggesting that, before my recollections fade, I write up my detailed memories of the finding of the double helix. On the other hand, he was bound to find himself portrayed in an unfavourable manner in the early chapters. After we were on our second bottle of Chablis, Tony North came up with the initially seemingly perverse idea of my asking Sir Lawrence to do the Foreword. Quickly, however, everyone saw this scheme would be the perfect way to give Bragg the respect he deserved without destroying my attempt to tell the story as if it were a novel, as opposed to a more conventional autobiography.

Upon my return from Kenya, I was to be at Alfred Tissiere's lab in Geneva for several months. Soon, I flew from there to London to give Sir Lawrence a copy of the manuscript. After arranging an appointment with his secretary, I went up to his flat within the R.I. Graciously he told me that he wanted me to tell my side of the story since, given Francis Crick's brilliance, my contributions might well be thought those of a minor contributor. I told him that what he was to read would not be at all what he had asked for. My aim was to write an account where the characters as first portrayed were not always what they later turned out to be. So I was concerned he might not like the way I first introduced him. If, however, I were to describe his interactions with Francis in any other way than Francis described them to me, my book as a work of literature would be badly compromised. Our meeting lasted less than half an hour, it being arranged that I would return the following week upon my return from a visit back to Cambridge.

I was naturally nervous when I approached his office the second time. But I began to relax when he greeted me with the statement that he couldn't sue me for libel if he wrote the Foreword. Telling me that he was at first very upset by what he read, and had so told his wife Alice, he had calmed down and saw what I was trying to do. Clearly he appreciated the virtue of his writing the Foreword. He would be acting in a magnanimous as opposed to a petty way, and show that he was above flattery. With his consent in hand, I flew to Geneva, knowing that a great hurdle had been crossed, though I had to fear that Sir Lawrence might change his mind if he found that others featured in the book thought that its publication should be blocked.

Tom Wilson was equally relieved when later told of Bragg's reaction. Immediately he wrote to Sir Lawrence that Harvard University Press did indeed want to publish my book which still at that time I called "Honest Jim", knowing of the past literary successes of Lord Jim and Lucky Jim. Bragg's Introduction arrived at Harvard in the mid fall of 1966. By then we were clearly apprehensive that a serious attempt would be made to block its appearance. Francis Crick did not think it was academic enough for a university press, and President Pusey of Harvard, fearing the scandal of being caught up in a fight between noted scientists, told the Press not to publish the book. Happily, Tom wilson still ended up with the book, since, knowing of his imminent retirement because of his age, he had arranged to move on as a senior editor to Athenaeum, a publisher of serious literature in New York. I worried that Sir Lawrence might back off during the ensuing controversy, but he held his ground and the book was published as *The Double Helix* in New York in February 1968. The English publisher was Weidenfeld and Nicolson, whose edition appeared in May 1968. Six weeks earlier I was married to Elizabeth Lewis and we arranged later to visit Sir Lawrence and Lady Bragg at their home near the Suffolk coast. This was to be the last occasion we ever met and I was most touched by his pleasure in showing us his garden that so pleased him, as did those of his previous homes on West and Madingly Roads in Cambridge.

In retrospect I do not know whether I would have had the courage to see the publication of *The Double Helix* through to its end without Sir Lawrence's backing. In writing it, I thought science would be helped by its appearance. But certain of my friends and most definitely my father worried that I might be in for more trouble than I could handle. It meant much to me in the pre–publication years to have behind me a man of such integrity and intelligence.

## Foreword to *The Double Helix* by Sir Lawrence Bragg

This account of the events which lead to the solution of the structure of DNA, the fundamental genetical material, is unique in several ways. I was much pleased when Watson asked me to write the foreword.

There is in the first place its scientific interest. The discovery of the structure by Crick and Watson, with all its biological implications, has been one of the major scientific events of this century. The number of researches which it has inspired is amazing; it has caused an explosion in biochemistry which has transformed the science. I have been amongst those who have pressed the author to write his recollections while they are still fresh in his mind, knowing how important they would be as a contribution to the history of science. The result has exceeded expectation. The latter chapters, in which the birth of the new idea is described so vividly, are drama of the highest order; the tension mounts and mounts towards the final climax. I do not know of any other instance where one is able to share so intimately in the researcher's struggles and doubts and final triumph.

Then again, the story is a poignant example of a dilemma which may confront an investigator. He knows that a colleague has been working for years on a problem and has accumulated a mass of hard–won evidence, which has not yet been published because it is anticipated that success is just around the corner. He has seen this evidence and has good reason to believe that a method of attack which he can envisage, perhaps merely a new point of view, will lead straight to the solution. An offer of collaboration at such a stage might well be regarded as a trespass. Should he go ahead on his own? It is not easy to be sure whether the crucial new idea is really one's own or has been unconsciously assimilated in talks with others. The realization of this difficulty has led to the establishment of a somewhat vague code amongst scientists which recognizes a claim in a line of research staked out by a colleague – up to a certain point. When competition comes from more than one quarter, there is no need to hold back. This dilemma comes out clearly in the DNA story. It is a source of deep satisfaction to all intimately concerned that, in the award of the Nobel Prize in 1962, due recognition was given to the long, patient investigation by Wilkins at King's College (London) as well as to the brilliant and rapid final solution by Crick and Watson at Cambridge.

Finally, there is the human interest of the story – the impression made by Europe and by England in particular upon a young man from the States. He writes with a Pepys–like frankness. Those who figure in the book must read it in a very forgiving spirit. One must remember that his book is not a history, but an autobiographical contribution to the history which will some day be written. As the author himself says, the book is a record of impressions rather than historical facts. The issues were often more complex, and the motives of those who had to deal with them were less tortuous, than he realized at the time. On the other hand, one must admit that his intuitive understanding of human frailty often strikes home.

The author has shown the manuscript to some of us who were involved in the story, and we have suggested corrections of historical fact here and there, but personally I have felt reluctant to alter too much because the freshness and directness with which impressions have been recorded is an essential part of the interest of this book.

W.L.B.

# Blowing Bubbles with Bragg

## W.M. LOMER

My close contact with Sir Lawrence extended over only a year. I had come to Cambridge to read Part II Physics of the Natural Science Tripos, holding a London degree (awarded from Exeter), and following that examination was fortunate enough to get a DSIR grant to do research in the Cavendish on the mechanical properties of crystals with Egon Orowan as my supervisor. Then, a week or two after starting, Bragg asked for someone to persue the properties of the self crystallising rafts of bubbles and I was transferred – or more accurately, lent – to him for a year.

A few months earlier Bragg had noticed, in the washing–up bowl at home, a steady stream of bubbles from some submerged dish, which floated together to form a surprisingly regular hexagonal array. As they pushed each other, the rows slid and reorganised themselves without destroying the crystalline nature of the mass. No sooner seen than copied. He went to the laboratory and his technician, Crow, assembled soap solutions, aspirators and glass jets to reproduce the effects. It was not so easy, and John Nye was temporarily diverted from his PhD studies on glaciology to get it all working – recorded triumphantly in Bragg and Nye (1947). And then it seemed worth while to calculate the forces between the bubbles; small ones seemed to be 'hard' and large ones 'soft' in some sense, and to behave slightly differently. Nicholson made one attempt to do this but it did not lead far.

The main observations were that shape changes of bubble rafts occurred when bubbles in one half of the mass were displaced by one spacing relative to the other half, not by a rigid motion of the whole, but by the motion of a localised disturbance in the crystal pattern, the dislocation. This was precisely what Orowan, Polyani and others had postulated for the plasticity of metals, but which was failing to convince many classical metallurgists in the mid 1940s. Bragg, as ever, had early seen that the dislocation theory must be right, and his excitement at having it all there, before his very eyes, was intense and infectious. For those who did not share his insight, or live with crystals, his favourite explanation of what dislocation was ran like this. If you have a large, heavy carpet on the floor and want to move it an inch or two, you do not try to drag it all over at once. You will take a little ruck in one corner and work it along by shuffling your feet – most of the carpet at any moment is stationary in the old position or in the new, and no big effort is needed to move the ruck. A dislocation in a crystal, like the ruck in the carpet, marks the boundary between two areas, one of which has moved relative to its original position and the other which has not.

In the same way as for the ruck in the carpet, it takes little force to move a dislocation, which is why metals, where dislocations abound, are easily deformed. It would clearly be informative to determine the forces between bubbles, and the stress needed to move dislocations, to asses the relationship between them. So we embarked on a campaign to get bubbles of a lasting quality, and techniques for handling them, that would let us measure forces of deformation and compare them with calculations. But this contribution is not about the details of that work (for that see Bragg and Lomer, 1949; Lomer, 1949). The point is that with this new visual aid, dislocation models of plasticity very rapidly swept all before them in a heady rush, and the concept could never again be questioned.

Now, throughout my work, Bragg's main excitement was the work with Max Perutz on the crystallography of proteins. I well remember his roughly fortnightly forays to my bench to look at the latest bubble photographs or graphs. Five minutes would be enough for me to summarise what I had done, and one minute for him to catch on, catch up, overtake and suggest my next actions. And then, what was obviously a great pleasure to him, a quarter of an hour explaining carefully, in non–specialist terms, what the last set of protein X–ray pictures meant to him. The shape of molecules deduced by subtracting results from crystals containing water from those containing salt solution. Patterns from layers of ellipsoids perpendicular to a plane compared with patterns from tilted ellipsoids. Not only could he see them, I could too (whilst he was there!) Throughout my year with him, despite this mounting excitement and the duties of Cavendish Professor, he never once left me unattended for more than my usual two weeks.

After, I suppose, some eight or nine months we had skimmed the cream from the bubbles, and we both got carried away with the idea of introducing mass into the two–dimensional models, to exhibit melting, thermal vibrations and rate processes such as ordering. Bragg saw one day, in the biology school, a demonstration of the effect of electric field induced dipoles causing a mutual repulsion between spheres – deemed to be of some relevance to the behaviour of lipid layers on cell membranes. A few mustard seeds were floated on the surface of a pool of mercury, and a vertical electric field set up by putting a horizontal conducting (*i.e.* damp) piece of glass above it with a few thousand volts on it. The mustard seed then disperses from the cluster into an open hexagonal lattice. The induced polar repulsion is of shorter range than the capillary attraction of the mercury, and a stable lattice results. But the mustard seeds were neither spherical nor uniform, and the mercury surface far from flat because of the vessel walls. The surface of the mercury quickly skinned over as impurities in it oxidised, and the floating particles on it locked.

So Crow manufactured a vessel with side walls champfered to the angle of contact of mercury. High purity mercury which did not oxidise was obtained. Ball bearings were floated on it, but no electric field would separate them. Analysis of the forces showed that the dipole was never strong enough if the density of the ball was above 2. So we needed light, uniform, spherical, cheap balls. Bragg's first idea was pills. I was despatched to the chemist to buy 100 pills (black) and 100 pills (white), hand made to normal pharmacy standards of uniformity. It took a little while, in front of the dispensing queue, to convince them that I really did mean pills with no drug content at all. Back in the laboratory they were not nearly uniform or spherical enough. Then we tried tiny glass balls as used for making reflecting greeting cards.

A Heath Robinson sorting device which sorted them for size was made, allowing them to fall through, or to be carried up, a rising column of liquid. We got good uniformity, but it quickly appeared that the dynamics of the system were really the dynamics of waves on mercury rather than of the balls. (Maybe this could have been the first model for electron phonon interactions had we seen it!) After a couple of months we gave up. Perhaps the Health and Safety Commission might nowadays consider that it was indeed time enough to have spent hours a day with my nose a foot away from a large open pool of mercury.

Then, of course, we had the fun of writing up, publishing and lecturing. In less than a year, thanks to his inspiration and leadership, there were three papers in the bag and a series of lecture invitations. Impressive as our slides were, cine film would convey more of the excitement of watching plastic deformation actually happening, with dislocations dashing about. Amateur efforts failed, but finally Norman McQueen, who ran a small film unit of his own, was located, and over a hectic weekend, when the bubbles themselves took stage fright time after time, some good footage was shot and the film made available as a teaching aid. Sadly, McQueen died, the firm taken over, and the film rights lost. Later, a full scale 16 mm film designed for sale was produced at the Royal Institution and has had a long history of success.

So much for bubbles, and my first year. My research continued with Orowan for two productive and stimulating years. Then Orowan, who did not hold a satisfactory permanent post at Cambridge, left to go to the USA, leaving four or five of us with incomplete PhD studies. We were well into our studies, and Bragg willingly assumed the role of supervisor. My own research grant from the DSIR terminated after three years, but when I wrote up my thesis I hit difficulty. To my dismay, and Bragg's fury, I fell foul of Regulations. During my first grant year, with Bragg, I was still registered as an undergraduate because I needed two years residence to qualify, under affiliated student rules, for my BA. The work I had done with Bragg could not also count towards my PhD. We had published the work with dates on that proved the overlap, and the work had to be disregarded. Bragg was most distressed, and even tried introducing a special resolution of Senate. It did not work and his distress on my behalf was touching. He found me a post as 'Assistant in Research' to give me time to repair the lacuna left by the elimination of the bubble work, and helped me devise extensions of my work to fit the need. As part of my duties, I looked after the (tiny) group budget for the residue of Orowan's group. A part of the drama that I never confessed to Bragg was the considerable effort needed in changing over from a grant paid quarterly in advance to a salary paid quarterly in arrears! At the end, it all came to a satisfactory conclusion and I left in 1952 with my Doctorate and fond memories of the Cavendish.

Bragg was a gentle man, and a gentleman. He never embarrassed anyone and my every contact with him was a pleasure. When he met me showing my fiancee around the little museum on the second floor of the Austin Wing one Saturday afternoon, he came and talked to us about the exhibits, full of enthusiasm as ever, and was so very pleasant that to this day my wife will hear nothing against him. And nor will I.

## A Parenthetic Anecdote

Bragg always had his eyes open and his wits about him. The flow of ice in glaciers and the formation of crevasses intrigued him, and John Nye was following up some of the measurements made by Perutz at the Jungfraujoch. I shared a laboratory with Nye, who gave me a flying start with my bubble work. Bragg had noticed at home at mealtimes that substances like porridge or blancmange could flow like viscous solids, but when partially set, could also fracture or tear like glass. So, for a lecture, I believe at the Royal Institution, Nye must make a four–foot long tank with a plaster of Paris model of a mountain valley in it, half fill it with a boiled flour paste; then, at the proper time, tilt it so that the flow down the valley would start. After some quarter of an hour, crevasses developed in exactly the right configuration to match observations of real glaciers.

After the success, the tank lay for some weeks in the corner of our laboratory. Finally we recognised it as the source of a peculiar smell, and we put ourselves to the revolting task of persuading the paste to go down the conventional sink in the laboratory. It was not, I suspect, the best way of disposing of it, but Nye and I did not have the benefit of Bragg's advice on that part of the problem!

## References

Bragg, W.L. and Nye, J.F. 1947. *Proc. Roy. Soc. A*, **190**, 474.
Bragg, W.L. and Lomer, W.M. 1949. *Proc. Roy. Soc. A*, **196**, 171.
Lomer, W.M. 1949. *Proc. Roy. Soc. A*, **196**, 182.

# Encounters with Bragg

## JACK D. DUNITZ, FRS

My first encounter with Sir Lawrence Bragg was a one–sided affair. I was one of the countless anonymous readers of a book he had written. In the summer of 1943 I was nearing the close of a crash course in chemistry at Glasgow University. J. Monteath Robertson had recently been appointed as Gardiner Professor of Chemistry, and I was taking his course on crystal structure analysis. We were told that the final examination would be based on Chapters III, V, VI and IX of Bragg's book. As this volume was in steady demand in the departmental library and the photocopying machine had not yet been dreamt of, I must have decided to buy the book for I still have it on my bookshelf, inscribed with my name and the date, Aug. 1943. Although I cannot remember exactly what it cost, the figure of 25 shillings (nowadays, £1.25) comes to mind. Whatever it was, it must have been a considerable expense for a poor student. Perhaps I persuaded my parents to buy it for me. In any case, I became (and still am) the possessor of *The Crystalline State*, edited by Sir W.H. Bragg, OM, KBE, DSc, PRS and W.L. Bragg, DSc, FRS, Volume I, *A General Survey*, by W.L. Bragg, Bell, London, 1933, reprinted 1939.

The four chapters we were supposed to read dealt with Experimental Methods of Crystal Analysis, Crystal Symmetry, Principles of Structure Analysis, and X–ray Optics. I found them fascinating. I read and re–read them, and most of the other chapters as well. Bragg was an excellent teacher, and his book was an ideal introduction to the subject. At last I felt I understood how it was possible to determine the atomic arrangements in crystalline solids with a high degree of certainty. Although the analysis of molecular structures was then still limited to fairly simple problems, it was quite clear to me that by these methods molecules could be associated with definite spatial arrangements of atoms and thereby achieve a kind of objectivity that had eluded them in the more old–fashioned teachings to which I had been exposed until then.

About the same time, again as a reader, I encountered another great figure of twentieth century science, Linus Pauling. His book, *The Nature of the Chemical Bond*, also assigned as reading for our final examinations, was a revelation. It set out to explain how the structures and energies of molecules could be explained in terms of a few simple principles. Pauling showed that the essential first step in understanding chemical phenomena was to establish the atomic arrangement in the substances of interest. Bragg's book showed how this could be done. Through Bragg and Pauling, I decided that my future was to be in structural chemistry. When Robertson offered me the opportunity to stay on at Glasgow as a research student to determine crystal structures of organic molecules by X–ray analysis, I accepted immediately.

About four years elapsed before I actually met Bragg and talked to him, or rather, he talked to me. By that time I had finished my research training with Robertson, had acquired my PhD, and had left Glasgow to work with Dorothy Hodgkin in Oxford. From time to time, interesting visitors turned up at Dorothy's laboratory in the old University Museum; among them was Bragg. He was courtesy itself. He would excuse himself for intruding on my valuable time: "Mrs Hodgkin tells me you're engaged in some very interesting work and have some extremely exciting results. Tell me about them". I would then attempt to sketch the background of the work I was doing on the structures of calciferol and of cyclobutane derivatives. Bragg listened, but more, I imagine, out of politeness than of genuine interest. He had little background in chemistry, so I often needed to explain rather elementary concepts to him. The problems I was working on were probably too chemical to attract his curiosity, the methods too standard to secure his attention. Sometimes even, I had the impression that although he appeared to be listening, nodding from time to time with his polite smile, his thoughts were elsewhere. Perhaps he was wondering whether the techniques we were then using could ever be developed far enough to allow the structure analysis of protein crystals. "Thank you very much, Dunitz, that was most interesting." he would say at the end of our conversation.

When he returned a few months later, he had usually forgotten most of what I had told him on his last visit, so I had to explain everything again from scratch. After I had become accustomed to meeting the great man, I began to enjoy those visits. They had a relaxing quality about them. And when I went to Cambridge, on Max Perutz's invitation, to give a seminar at the Cavendish Laboratory on my Glasgow work, Bragg welcomed me in his office as if I were an important visitor, attended my lecture and shook my hand afterwards. I felt I had arrived!

With Linus Pauling, my other hero from my student days, it was quite different. He arrived in Oxford towards the end of 1947 as Visiting Professor. He was a superb lecturer. I had never heard anyone quite like him, with his jokes, his relaxed manner, his seraphic smile, and his spontaneous flow of ideas (only much later did I realise that much of that apparent spontaneity was carefully studied). During the following months he was also an occasional visitor at Dorothy's laboratory. In contrast to Bragg's visits, conversation with Pauling was anything but relaxing. In spite of his easy–going manner, he soon made me aware of his superior knowledge and intelligence. He put up questions which, I realised, I should have been asking myself, but to which I had no answer. Whereas Bragg had made me feel confident about my work and myself, Pauling made me feel stupid. During discussions with him, my ignorance about my own field, about structural chemistry in general, was exposed to be exceeded only by my slowness of mind. It was a tremendous surprise when, in June, 1948, Pauling offered me a post–doctoral research Fellowship at Caltech. Although I was still slightly terrified of him, I knew that this was an opportunity I could not afford to miss.

During the next few years, there may have been occasional meetings with Bragg, but I have no clear memory of them. For me, three years in Pasadena were followed by a second two–year spell in Oxford, during which I made frequent visits to the Cavendish, but not to talk to Bragg – rather to Bill Cochran and the ebullient Francis Crick. Then another year in Pasadena. Bragg was certainly present there during the famous September 1953 conference on protein structure, where Pauling talked about α–helices and pleated sheets, Watson on the DNA double helix, and Perutz announced that he had been able to diffuse heavy atoms into protein crystals without destroying the crystalline order, and so produce changes in the X–ray diffraction patterns from which phases of the Fourier components could, in principle, be derived.

In September, 1954, I took up an appointment as Visiting Scientist at the US National Institute of Health in Bethesda, Maryland, in order to help Alexander Rich set up a laboratory for the study of biological materials by diffraction methods, but by that time I had already decided to return to Britain, at least temporarily. Otherwise, it seemed likely that I would soon drift into an academic career in the United States. I had no objection to a career in America, I liked it there and so did Barbara, my wife. There were far more opportunities than in Britain. But I did not want to drift into my future. I wanted to make a conscious choice, and the best way of doing this, it seemed to me, was to spend another few years in Britain, sounding out the possibilities. The only question was: where? I had asked Dorothy Hodgkin to make some enquiries on my behalf. She talked to Bragg, who had recently left Cambridge to take up the position as Director of the Royal Institution, the position that his father had held for so many years, and Bragg wrote to me.

In a letter dated August 12, 1954, he described the preliminary results obtained by Perutz on hemoglobin, and by Kendrew on myoglobin; the final paragraph read: "There is every chance that with a concerted drive on the problem, light will suddenly break and some key to the general structure of protein emerge. The more good people we get to work together here the better, and if you would like to be one of them, I will do all I can to make it possible."

In my reply, I told Bragg that although I was very interested in the possibility of working at the Royal Institution, I was not too enthusiastic about the idea of concentrating exclusively on protein research. "Had I complete freedom to choose a line of research for myself, I do not think I would concentrate on protein analysis. I might choose to apply modern X–ray techniques to some of the problems of inorganic structural chemistry which survived the attacks of yourself and others in the early days of crystallography. Especially in the complex coordination compounds of the transition metals there are many problems left. Another study interesting to me would be that of the specificity of molecular compounds and complex formation, where apparently very weak forces can achieve a high degree of specificity. Both of these fields would, of course, tie in with the study of proteins although in an indirect fashion. The first would be a good starting point for finding out something about the important prosthetic groups containing transition metals... The second might tie in with the study of the specificity of enzyme systems. But perhaps this is building castles in the air, and I only mention it to emphasise the fact that my present interests are in regions far from direct protein structure analysis." After 36 years, I am not displeased with this statement of my intentions, but I had serious misgivings about it then, once my letter had been posted. While I did not wish to tell him outright lies, surely a little prevarication would have been preferable to this blunt statement. As the months went past without any word from London. the prospect of joining Bragg's group at the Royal Institution became more and more remote. I began to look into other possibilities.

In April, 1955, Bragg wrote to apologise for his delay in replying to my letter and offered me a five–year appointment as Senior Research Fellow at the Davy–Faraday Research Laboratory. He explained that much of his energy was going into the venture of trying to change the character of the Royal Institution and make it fit better to modern conditions. "I cannot see my way clearly in all directions yet. I am not clear of the financial tangle and many plans are still uncertain, but if you would like to join the venture and help with the research side, I will do all I can to give you a good time. Once again, I am sorry I did not write to you at once. I could not have been more definite about plans at that stage but I should have acknowledged your letter." With all my misgivings about the tone of my letter, here was Bragg apologising to me! By the end of May, I had agreed to join in, and Bragg had obtained the approval of the Managers for my appointment. I suggested that I might initiate X–ray work on heme itself or some other simple porphyrin derivative (sans protein!), a proposal that found immediate favour with Bragg (although nothing ever came of it because of lack of suitable crystals). It was agreed that I should begin work in London in January, 1956.

As things turned out, it was just as well that I had not committed myself, neither to Bragg nor to myself, to work on protein structure, for there were probably not enough suitable problems to go around. In Cambridge, Perutz was busy with hemoglobin, Kendrew with myoglobin. In London, next door to my office, Uli Arndt and David Phillips were beginning to develop the linear diffractometer. There was an orthorhombic form of ox hemoglobin under investigation by David Green, and Helen Scouloudi was comparing diffraction patterns from various myoglobin crystals. Tony North was making X–ray photographs of lactoglobulin crystals. There was some surprise, I recall, when crystals of a new modification of ox haemoglobin were recognised to belong to a cubic space group. While it was interesting for me to talk to these colleagues, there was really nothing useful that I could contribute. The plan to study simple porphyrin derivatives was stagnating because of the difficulty of obtaining suitable single crystals.

I returned to my plan to look at the structures of coordination complexes of transition metals and soon became involved in a collaboration with Leslie Orgel on the role of the Jahn–Teller effect in inducing distortions from higher symmetry in the solid state. I had known Leslie since my Oxford days, and we had already worked together, both there and later at Caltech, on a variety of structural problems and their theoretical interpretation. He had now taken up a position at Cambridge. Once I had settled in London we used to meet regularly. Our new collaboration began with a comparison of closely related pairs of structures containing divalent cobalt or copper, but we soon realised that it was of much wider generality. We found, in particular, that it could explain some puzzling features of the structures of spinels, an important group of oxides with the composition $AB_2O_4$. The typical spinel structure is cubic, based on a close–packed arrangement of oxide anions, with the trivalent B cations in octahedral interstices and the divalent A cations in tetrahedral ones. But in some spinels the symmetry is lowered by distortion of the regular octahedral or tetrahedral coordination sites, and in others the cationic arrangement is inverted, with divalent A cations in the octahedral sites and the trivalent B cations distributed over tetrahedral and octahedral ones. The reasons for these anomalies had been unknown, but Leslie and I could show that they followed by simple application of a few rules, based on crystal field theory and the Jahn–Teller theorem.

When Bragg learned about these results he was immediately interested. After all, he had himself laid down the foundations of structural mineralogy, he was aware of the existence of distorted and inverse spinels, and he was genuinely curious and eager to understand the explanation that we were proposing. There was a difficulty. As Pauling and others have pointed out, Bragg was a classical physicist and had never found the need to learn the elements of quantum theory; our explanation was based on a rudimentary application of quantum theoretical ideas, involving splitting of the atomic energy levels in fields of lower than spherical symmetry, ideas that have since found their way into elementary courses on structural inorganic chemistry. But they were relatively novel then. Bragg was then engaged in preparing a revised edition of his book, *Atomic Structure of Minerals*, and he wanted to include in it an account of our new results. Day after day, week after week, he struggled with these, for him, new–fangled ideas. It was a brave attempt on the part of a man in his late sixties. The revision took much longer than expected. Eventually, it was published in 1965 as Volume IV of *The Crystalline State, Crystal Structures of Minerals*, with G.F. Claringbull as co–author. The question of the cation distribution in spinels was discussed, with due credit to our work, in the chapter on metal oxides; the theoretical background was neatly evaded as being beyond the scope of the book – which, of course, it was.

In December, 1956, I received an invitation to come to Zurich to discuss the possibility of my setting up an X–ray analysis group in the Organic Chemistry Laboratory of the ETH. Leopold Ruzicka, due to retire the following year, offered me a Professorship in this world–famous Institute that he had directed for so many years. But he demanded a speedy decision on my part: I had to accept his offer before the end of the Christmas–New Year break or he would look elsewhere. He was in a hurry to fill this post, there was no time to waste. Although I was attracted by the offer, I also felt a certain obligation towards Bragg and the Davy–Faraday; less than a year of my five–year fellowship had elapsed. Bragg made my mind up for me. Congratulations, Dunitz! This was the opportunity of a lifetime, one that I could not afford to pass by. It had been very interesting and useful to have me at the Royal Institution, but it was now time for me to move on to set up a research group of my own. The following September I said goodbye to Bragg, to my friends and colleagues at the Royal Institution, to London. to England, and set out for Zurich, where I have been ever since.

In my life I have met many of the great scientific figures of the twentieth century. In the multi–dimensional space describing their various qualities, gifts and talents, any comparison becomes impossible. Sir Lawrence Bragg stands out among them through the simplicity and directness of his physical intuition, and for something else: he was one of the last of a disappearing variety of human being – he was a gentleman.

# It's a Black Ibis

## S. CHANDRASEKHAR, FRS

The time that I spent at the Royal Institution was a memorable period for me. The protein crystallographers at the Davy–Faraday Research Laboratory, working in collaboration with the Cambridge group, were on the threshold of solving the structures of myoglobin, haemoglobin and other large molecules. Preparations were going on constantly for the famous Royal Institution lectures, the scope of which was being enlarged so as to reach a wider audience through films and television. The place was humming with activity, and there was a general feeling of excitement and expectancy in the air. Sir Lawrence Bragg was, of course, the inspiration behind it all, as well as being an enthusiastic participant. We attended as many of the Friday evening Discourses as we possibly could; in particular, Bragg's lectures, whether they were Discourses, research seminars or lecture demonstrations for school-children, were a special treat that we looked forward to with much eagerness. He was unquestionably the finest expositor of science that I have had the privilege to know.

My own work was not part of the mainstream of activity at the Davy–Faraday Laboratory, but Bragg himself was very much interested in it as it was about a problem that he had grappled with in the early years of crystallography. It concerned the phenomenon of extinction in imperfect crystals. I had proposed a method of estimating the extinction factor by the use of polarised X–rays, and had carried out some measurements in Dame Kathleen Lonsdale's laboratory at University College to confirm the validity of the method. The aim here was to set up a more convenient experimental arrangement in order to study the phenomenon with greater accuracy. David Phillips and I designed a rotating X–ray tube device for rotating the plane of polarisation of the X–ray beam. Bragg used to come to the laboratory frequently whilst the apparatus was being set up and offer suggestions. His first love being the optical principles of X–ray diffraction, this was indeed an investigation after his own heart. To test the apparatus, David and I repeated C.G. Barkla's classical experiment demonstrating the polarisation of X–rays, of course, with very much greater precision than was possible in 1906, and Bragg was delighted. When the studies were complete, we prepared a note for *Nature*, which he read through critically and suggested modifications. We tried to persuade him to be a joint author, but with characteristic generosity he declined.

Early in 1961 I accepted an offer of a Professorship in the University of Mysore to start a new postgraduate department of Physics, and we left England in March of that year. A few months before we left, I remember Bragg telling us at a Friday evening dinner how much he enjoyed reading Malcolm Macdonald's lovely book *Birds in my Indian Garden*, and we knew then that his heart was set on coming to India.

We met the Braggs when they arrived in Bangalore nearly three years later. (An earlier visit had to be cancelled because of his illness.) They were both looking splendid – relaxed and extremely fit. The weather was just perfect and we set off by car to Mysore. It was a journey to remember. Every so often Sir Lawrence would ask me to stop the car so that he could take a closer look at some interesting bird he had sighted. "Do you see it – it's a black ibis". He would stroll into the fields by the roadside and examine the bird through his field–glasses. Then he and my wife, who is herself a keen bird–watcher, would go off into a discussion on birds, whilst Lady Bragg and I looked on. (We managed to find him a copy of Salim Ali's *Book of Indian Birds*, which was then out of print, and he wrote to us afterwards that he had identified nearly a hundred birds described in that book.) We made slow progress but enjoyed ourselves enormously. It was getting to be tea–time, and on impulse I decided to make an unscheduled stop at Scott's Bungalow, a sequestered and beautiful place by the river near the small town of Seringapatam. The place had recently been acquired by some friends of ours, who were only too glad to receive us. After the introductions were over and we were settling down to tea, the host, a medical man, asked me in a low voice, "Not the Bragg of Bragg's Law?" As it happened, Sir Lawrence overheard this and was greatly amused.

When I was setting up the new department in Mysore, I made up my mind to change my field from solid crystals to liquid crystals. My knowledge of these 'intermediate phases' at that time was limited to the brief accounts that I had come across as a student more than ten years earlier in books published in the 1930s, but I was determined to make the change. With some trepidation, I mentioned this to Bragg, hoping that he would not be too disappointed that I was wandering off into an unfashionable and long–forgotten field. His response was, in fact, just the opposite, for which I was truly grateful. He started a serious discussion on the subject and I felt jubilant. He knew more about these substances than I had expected, perhaps because he was familiar with Sir William Bragg's renowned Friday evening Discourse on *Liquid Crystals* given in 1934. In retrospect, the work that I did in London stood me in good stead in my early studies on liquid crystals. For example, I was able to show that the reflection of circularly polarised light from a cholesteric liquid crystal bears a close analogy with the reflection of X–rays from a crystal. Thus the consequences of primary extinction and other effects predicted by the dynamical theory of X–ray diffraction could be studied directly by optical observations. An extension of this to include absorption led to the first experimental demonstration of the optical analogue of the Borrmann effect. Bragg would have been fascinated by these results, but unfortunately this work was completed some years later and I did not have the opportunity to discuss it with him.

In Mysore, he gave two lectures which kept the audience spellbound, and after each lecture he was practically mobbed by young undergraduates and schoolchildren for autographs. The return drive to Bangalore a few days later was equally interesting – more birds were sighted and identified. I was getting a little worried about reaching the airport in time, but Sir Lawrence was quite unperturbed and refused to be hurried. In the end everything turned out well and they boarded their flight to Delhi. Sadly, that was the last time we saw Sir Lawrence Bragg. We did, however, have the pleasure of renewing our friendship with Lady Bragg in 1987 when we were in Cambridge.

# W.L.B. at the R.I.

## LORD PORTER, OM PRS

I first heard Sir Lawrence lecture immediately after the war, in Cambridge, when he was giving a Part 1 course in general physics at the Cavendish Laboratory. At the time I also attended lectures by other great physicists; Dirac's lectures were blackboard presentations of theoretical physics, and Bertrand Russell's were popular talks on general science, admixed with a little philosophy. But Bragg's course on general physics is the one I remember to this day, especially because of the experimental demonstrations.

The art of the lecture demonstration was dying out in the universities after the war, and, in a department like the Cavendish, there was a tendency to regard demonstrations as somewhat frivolous – playing to the gallery. Yet even today I remember many of the demonstrations in those lectures and little of the words chalked on the blackboard.

But, although Bragg was liked by all, he probably derived little credit or respect for these masterly lectures from his colleagues. Furthermore, the majority were particle physicists in the great tradition of the Cavendish Laboratory, and the very presence of a Cavendish Professor who, however distinguished, was not in the direct J.J. Thomson–Rutherford line was though by many of the staff to be unfortunate. Yet today Bragg must be given eternal credit for recognising where the new world of science was to be, and for having the courage to take those of his colleagues who did not kick and scream too much, into the second half of the twentieth century.

In 1955, when the success of the molecular biology at the Cavendish Laboratory was assured, Sir Lawrence Bragg again dissented from the establishment. He left Cambridge to become Research Director (and eventually the first "Director") of the Royal Institution in London. To understand why this shocked the establishment it is necessary to know a little about the goings–on of the R.I. at that time.

The Royal Institution, in the hands of Count Rumford, Thomas Young, Humphry Davy, and Michael Faraday, was the most famous laboratory and theatre of science in Britain for much of the last century. Although increasing competition appeared from the Universities in the second half of the century, the Davy–Faraday Laboratory, as it later became, had an enviable reputation right up to the beginning of the Second World War, when its Director, Lawrence Bragg's father, Sir William Bragg. directed the most successful laboratory of X–ray crystallography in the world.

When W.H. Bragg died in 1942, Sir Henry Dale, who was President of the Royal Society at the time and also a Nobel Laureate, agreed to become a "caretaker" Director of the R.I. until the war was over. Sir Eric Rideal left his Chair in

Cambridge to become Director of research in 1946, but soon found that he was far from being Director of the Institution itself. He had difficulties with the management, and the financial situation of the Institution was at least as bad as that of the rest of the country. After a brave try, Sir Eric resigned in 1950 and Professor E.N. da C. Andrade enthusiastically took his place.

The next few years are almost too painful to relate. Like Rideal, Andrade found the management situation intolerable. Both had come from positions of almost total authority as professors and heads of departments in large universities and had had complete freedom in research and most other things as well. But Andrade's personality was quite different from that of Rideal. He was autocratic and was determined to do as he wanted. He removed several long–serving staff and brought in his own. There would soon have been trouble even in a much more stable organisation; in the R.I. of that time conflict was inevitable.

The President, Lord Brabazon, acted as diplomatically as possible. But one quaint endowment of the R.I. statutes had left it *two* managing bodies, a Board of Managers and a Committee of Visitors. The latter was not what its name implies but was a second, elected body of members which duplicated most of the work of the managers and challenged almost every decision on principal. Naturally these two bodies took sides in the "Andrade affair". After a large meeting of members, Andrade was dismissed, and he immediately sued the R.I. for compensation. The most unfortunate aspect of the whole case was that the Royal Society, with Sir Robert Robinson as President, was asked to be arbitrator in the case. The Royal Society were seen to have found in favour of Professor Andrade FRS and against the Royal Institution, its management and its President, Lord Brabazon. It was expensive for the R.I. and its finances, as well as its position in the world of science, were now at a very low ebb.

There had been some jealousy at various times between the Royal Society and the Royal Institution, though mostly there was close collaboration and mutual respect. But now the situation was icy estrangement, with speculation, and perhaps even hope in a few cases, that the Royal Institution would die. At this point Sir Lawrence Bragg stepped into the breech. Although he was doubtless warned against any such madness by most of his acquaintances, one or two of his closest friends encouraged it. Lord Adrian, the master of his college, Trinity, Cambridge, told Bragg quite simply that it was the only way of saving the R.I. and it was expected of him.

Of course, Lawrence Bragg knew the R.I. extremely well and the thought of its demise must have caused him much remorse. His father and mother had been host and hostess there, and on Lady Bragg's death in 1929, Lawrence's sister, Gwendolen, took over and lived, with her husband, in the R.I. until Sir William's death. The place was almost a Bragg family institution. But if, for Sir Lawrence, it was like going home geographically, (and the Director's flat was magnificent as ever, especially after Andrade's attentions), it was no longer a happy place. Lady (Alice) Bragg recognised this but threw herself into the task of helping her husband to restore it.

It was fairly clear what had to be done, but how to do it? First, confidence and good will had to be restored between the "Resident Professor" and the management. Then cash must be found to carry out the many essential repairs to the buildings and laboratories. Then the post of Director of the Royal Institution must be created, as the chief executive officer of the Institution as well as Director of Research. The last step was to think the unthinkable – to get rid of *both Managers and Visitors* in their present form and have a properly elected council, officers and President with fixed terms of office.

Against the odds, this was all achieved. In his last year Bragg was appointed the first Director of the Royal Institution. His name alone would have helped to restore the once great reputation of the Institution and, under his direction, the research flourished more than even he could have hoped. He was able to raise adequate funds for research from the Medical Research Council, and made Herculean efforts to raise money, through schools lectures (his most successful innovation) and courses for civil servants, for the general expenses of the Institution.

The final step came some years later. Even whilst he was Director, moves were afoot to rewrite the statutes so that the Director was the true executive and the duties and terms of appointment of the honorary officers were clearly defined. I had been a lecturer at the R.I., and then the Professor of Chemistry, giving schools lectures and occasional Discourses for several years and in 1964 was appointed successor to Sir Lawrence, two years before he was to retire. We therefore had an interregnum during which we could work together on all the changes that were necessary. Had I been given my head at that time I would probably have gone the way of Andrade; Sir Lawrence was a wise and moderating influence on my impatience. His attitude in handing over the Directorship of the R.I. was as if, in his outstretched hands, he was offering me a delicate egg and asking me to see that I didn't drop it.

We sat on the Managers together for a year or two and so began the long and delicate process of reorganisation. Although some of this happened after he ceased to be Director, it was only made possible by his pioneering work and, fortunately, he lived to see most of it come to fruition. In the event, even those who had seemed to be the strongest advocates of the old regime, like the Secretary, Brigadier Hopthrow, became enthusiastic supporters of the new. The President, Lord Fleck was most supportive of the changes as was his successor, Lord King's Norton and gradually the R.I. became the happy place that it had been in earlier times and is, again, today.

I saw a great deal of Sir Lawrence at this time, and he told me that his time at the Royal Institution, in spite of all the difficulties, had been the happiest of his life.

One night, in the time when he was still Director, he invited me after dinner, to accompany him to a room, called the Model Room, that was part of the Library store, in number 19 Albemarle Street. As we entered and closed the door behind us, it was clear that he had something very special to show me and was excited about it. On a table in the middle of the room, illuminated by one electric bulb, was a pile of perspex sheets, on each of which had been drawn the electron density cross sections of a very large molecule. It was lysozyme, the first enzyme structure to be worked out at high resolution, which had just been solved in the Davy–Faraday laboratory by David Phillips and colleagues, under the encouraging and ever helpful eye of Sir Lawrence. I listened to his happy story of how this had happened, the importance of introducing a heavy atom for phase determination, how the structure showed a cleft which had to fit the carbohydrate molecules of the cell wall that were to be broken, how the molecule had been discovered in the first place by Alexander Fleming and many other wonderful things which infected the listener with the narrator's own excitement.

When it became late and time to leave we found that we had locked ourselves into this uninhabited part of the building. We eventually escaped when Bragg remembered an internal telephone in some cupboard by which he was able to communicate with Jackson, the caretaker in his penthouse flat. Only those who have walked at night through the creaky corridors of the R.I. and imagined they saw some of its immortals, will fully appreciate the magic for me of that close encounter with one of them.

My other clearest recollections are of his lectures. Few who have experienced them will ever forget Bragg seated on a stool in front of that kidney shaped bench, surrounded by his "Paget models" which mimicked the vowel sounds of the human voice..."ba–by", or then the French, "bé–bé." Or those elegant models in his lecture on waves.... with the dumb–bells attached to a steel strip from the floor to the ceiling of the theatre thirty feet above it. Or the "Vinecombe" model with the waves damped spectacularly by a little resonant pendulum. Or the bubble rafts and magnetic arrays showing atomic arrangements, the models of soap molecules poured out of a soap packet into water, forming a monomolecular layer, or the fluid–bed of sand on which a "ship of the desert" miraculously surfaced. Fortunately Bragg recorded the best of his demonstrations on twelve films just before he retired.

Bragg's lectures were a "tour de force", a term he used himself to describe what demonstration lectures should be. If, sometimes, they seem to belong to another era, one can only wish that the era could return.

# Reminiscences of Sir Lawrence Bragg

### SIR AARON KLUG, FRS

I came to the Cavendish Laboratory as a research student in 1949 from the University of Cape Town where I had studied under R.W. James, who had worked with Bragg in Manchester for many years before taking up the chair of Physics in Cape Town in 1937. Indeed his association with Bragg went back to their undergraduate years in Cambridge and sound–ranging in France during the Great War.

In the twenties, James shared in many of the crucial experiments that established X–ray crystallography as a quantitative science, for example, by showing that the intensity of the X–ray reflections of several crystals was effectively proportional to the square of the structure factor rather than to the amplitude, as might have been expected for a perfect crystal. The reason lies in the *mosaic* character of most crystals, the theory for which had been worked out in two remarkable papers by C.G. Darwin in 1914. On the other hand, the German school, following Ewald's dynamical theory, believed that the observed intensity should be directly proportional to the structure factor. As a result they were doubtful of the validity of Bragg's determination of crystal structures involving several parameters, *e.g.* iron pyrites, where the atomic positions do not depend merely on the lattice and the space–group symmetry.

James told me how, after the war, the British and German schools met at a conference at Holzhausen on the Ammersee in Bavaria in 1925 to discuss these differences. Bragg had summoned Darwin as the British champion, someone who could hold his own with the powerful German theoreticians. In the event Darwin, who was by now working in other fields, had not done his homework, and had forgotten his theory, resulting in a fiasco. Bragg was not amused, but the result was to stimulate him to write a paper with James and Darwin (*Phil. Mag.*, 1926) which summarised the earlier papers and discussed how far crystals conform to the idealised models adopted in the theories. This was historically important in the use of quantative data in crystal analysis.

The difference in approach between British and Continental science is illustrated by another story of James's. In 1931 he went as a Rockefeller Fellow to Leipzig, which counted among its reigning luminaries both Heisenberg and Debye, What struck James was the impressive learning in theoretical physics and mathematics not only of the leaders, as might have been expected, but also of all the junior workers. As Cambridge undergraduates in physics they had hardly been exposed to any formal teaching in mathematics, and James had learned it only as it was needed in various parts of physics.

James had gone to work with Debye to investigate the influence of temperature on the scattering of X–rays by molecules in the gas phase. He recounted how Debye could write down without notes the quantum–mechanical Hamiltonian for the electromagnetic field, or work out the asymptotic form of Bessel functions, relevant to the problem of the distribution of the intensity of light near the focal point of an optical system. The lack of rigorous training among their English contemporaries had not gone unnoticed by their German counterparts. "Tell me", said one of James's colleagues, emboldened after several months acquaintance, "How does Bragg discover things? He doesn't know anything." I do not, of course, remember the exact words in which James told me this story, but they were close to these.

I would imagine that the man in Leipzig must have been further astonished some three years later when Bragg and Williams produced their theory of order–disorder in metals, the beginning of the subject of cooperative phenomena in physics. It seems unlikely to me that Bragg would have known the hybrid formalism of thermodynamics and statistical mechanics employed (that is surely due to Williams) but his hand is unmistakable. In the first presentation of the theory, the energy of interaction between an atom and its neighbours is assumed to depend upon the degree of order in the whole assembly. Elsewhere Bragg made the analogy that the energy keeping any given member of a society in its right place is dependent on the degree to which its neighbours are in their right places, that is, on "public opinion". The theory surely reflects Bragg's imaginative insight into the physics of the phenomenon.

When I came to the Cavendish I had hoped to work on a topic in X–ray crystallography different from the straight analysis of crystal structures of small molecules, for example, on proteins, in the embryonic MRC Unit, or on order–disorder phenomena in alloys. Bragg told me the Unit was full and that the work on copper–iron–nickel alloys was not to be continued. He suggested the complexities of the plagioclase series of feldspar silicates, then being studied by W.H. Taylor, but I did not relish the idea, partly because in my ignorance I did not know how fascinating minerals could be. In the end, through letters back and forth to Cape Town, James put me in touch with former colleagues of his at Manchester, Professors D.R. Hartree and J.E. Lennard–Jones, and in the end I gravitated to the former to work on a problem involving a phase transition in a solid, which he thought required a crystallographer. During this unsettled period, Bragg was kind and considerate and let me go my own way, which I very much appreciated. So I did not learn any physics or crystallography directly from him but I did learn one useful thing for living in England. One evening at a reception in Bragg's house in West Road, he called me to come and help him stoke the boiler, a magnificent contraption in the basement, and quite foreign to me as a newcomer from warmer climes. He told me about the necessity for good air flow and how to remove the ash and clinker. The demonstration stood me in good stead later on.

At the time Bragg was busy with his bubble rafts, models for illustrating the flow and deformation of metals through the movement of dislocations. This provoked some amusement amongst my fellow research students, who could not see the point of "Bragg blowing bubbles", because the study of imperfections in solids was not regarded as main line physics, and the average physicist could not see its importance, nor that a new science was being created. Bragg indeed had already published a number of papers in this field, for example, one as early as 1940 on dislocations in grain boundaries, and another on the yield point of metals in the famous 1948 Bristol Conference Report on the Strength of Solids. I followed this work out of its intrinsic interest and because I thought, wrongly, that it might be of help to me in my problem. The papers were not directly useful, but one learned from them in seeing how Bragg tried to reduce a problem to its simplest features.

In 1954, Bragg left Cambridge for the Directorship of the Royal Institution in London, where he set up a research group in the X–ray crystallography of proteins (see Arndt and Phillips, this volume). As part of the effort, Uli Arndt constructed two high power rotating–anode X–ray tubes; later John Finch and I, then working in J.D. Bernal's department at Birkbeck College, London, were given permission to use them for our work on spherical virus crystals. We had been using Ehrenberg–Spear microfocus tubes built at Birkbeck, which gave high resolution but lacked the power of the Royal Institution apparatus. In 1956, we had obtained three–dimensional X–ray data from the crystals of turnip yellow mosaic virus with a unit cell of 706 Å, and had shown the particle to possess icosahedral symmetry. To collect X–ray data systematically, even to the relatively low resolution of 20 Å, required more powerful X–ray sources; after we had grown better crystals, we set out to do this at the Royal Institution.

Bragg followed the work with interest, and when we obtained good precession photographs, I took one to show him. He held up the X–ray film I had proudly handed him, looked at the small dark circle in the midst of the sheet of blank film, a circle less than a centimetre across, created by the 2° precession, crowded with hundreds of spots arising by diffraction from the large unit cell. The "spikes" of high intensity characteristic of the icosahedral symmetry of the virus could just be discerned marching diagonally across the film, I explained. He contemplated it for a while. "Is this the 'mosaic' crystal?", he asked (all plant viruses seemed to him, as to others, to be called 'something–or–other mosaic'). "Yes", I said expectantly. He went on: "Why did you use such a large piece of film?". Somewhat deflated, I realised that in his day X–ray film was precious and did not come ready packaged in sizes to fit various cameras. One cut up film to suit the experiment. The immediate feeling of being a wastrel did not last long, since Bragg went on to ask more about these intriguing structures with their non–crystallographic symmetry. But, in turn, to this day I try to restrain myself when I encounter what my generation sees as waste, and the younger generation as convenience.

About ten years later, Ken Holmes and I were trying to solve (to low resolution) the structure of tobacco mosaic virus (TMV), using the method of isomorphous replacement. TMV is a rod shaped particle, which does not crystallise, but forms nematic liquid crystals, that is, ordered gels. The X–ray diffraction pattern is cylindrically averaged, scrambling three–dimensional data in two dimensions, and hence requires non–conventional methods of analysis. I found that a method Bragg had developed for single crystals could be adapted for determining the relative positions of heavy atoms in the various isomorphous derivatives. This method, which we called "Bragg ellipses" was the subject of his last scientific paper (*Acta Cryst.*, **11**, 70–75, 1958).[*] Its essence is as follows: if the scattering factor contributions of the heavy atoms in two different isomorphous derivatives are of the form $\Delta F_1 = f_1 \cos 2\pi h x_1$ and $\Delta F_2 = f_2 \cos 2\pi h x_2$, then a plot of $\Delta F_1/f_1$ against $\Delta F_2/f_2$ as a function of $h$ should fall into an ellipse – a Lissajous figure – whose eccentricity would depend on the difference of position, $x_1 - x_2$.

---

[*] Bragg had tried his method on Kendrew's different heavy atom derivatives of myoglobin and found that it gave him the difference in the $y$–parameters of the heavy atoms that was needed to solve the phase problem in three dimensions. He has related how he "wept with joy" as he realised that the structure was now open to solution.

We used this successfully for one of the helical projections of TMV, and showed it to Bragg. He was delighted. Later, this geometrical construction, so pleasing in its simplicity, was inevitably superseded by computer methods. Some of the romance was lost and with it, I believe, the need for the physical understanding so necessary in the early days of the subject.

The pictorial representation that Bragg devised to solve this particular problem was a very minor affair among Bragg's large output and great achievements, but to me it is a small illustration that exemplifies his style: that of a man who had the gift of the imagination to see into patterns at the heart of matter. At the same time, Bragg could be an acute experimentalist. Bragg's law is known to all students, but how many learn that what helped him to arrive at the notion of X–rays being reflected by a crystal was his observation of the change of shape of the diffracted spots, as the distance between the crystal and photographic plate was varied in his experiments. This is described in Bragg's first and great paper submitted in November 1912. I used to give a copy of it to my new research students or associates to bring to life a great scientist at work. I remembered Bragg's observations when, in 1972, our crystals of tRNA gave X–ray spots which had different shapes in different regions of the film. The thin plate–like crystals were being bent by contact with the glass wall of the capillary tube, and reflecting as from a curved mirror. So, sixty years later, Bragg's great paper still had a resonance.

# An Early Adventure in Crystallographic Computing

## HUGH HUXLEY, FRS

Sir Lawrence Bragg took considerable interest in everything that was happening in Perutz and Kendrew's protein crystallography group, and one of his interventions had a considerable, though somewhat indirect, influence both on the direction of my own work and on the development of crystallographic computing. Quite early in my research studentship, in 1949, when I was still working on lattice changes in haemoglobin crystals, Bragg suggested that it would be good for my soul to calculate a two–dimensional Patterson projection of one of the haemoglobin forms at moderately high resolution. This was a terrible chore with Beevers–Lipson strips and an adding machine cranked by hand. It took me about two weeks of solid work, with much loud complaining.

One of the people I complained to was my best friend, John Bennett, who was an engineer–mathematician from Australia, and a fellow research student at Christ's College. (I think this little story illustrates how valuable it can be to have acquaintances outside one's own immediate field, and to have things organised so that one meets other people and not just those in one's own laboratory.) Bennett sympathised with my complaints, and as it happened, was working on the original EDSAC computer in the Maths Laboratory with Wilkes. He immediately realised that the calculation that was giving me so much trouble was programmable. At that time, as I remember, the computer had only about 512 memory positions, so all the sines and cosines which we used had to be calculated by the program at each single step because there was nowhere to store them. Bennett produced a program which could do my two weeks work in about half an hour, although it did take about another half an hour to print out the results! However, by the time this system was operating properly, I had left the field of protein crystallography, having become convinced that it was very boring and would probably never work, and had switched my attentions to muscle. In a reversal of perhaps a more normal procedure, I turned over the developments of the crystallographic computations to my PhD supervisor, John Kendrew, who had a strong personal interest in computing Fouriers at that time. After much more work on that problem, he and Bennett got the system working really well with the Math Laboratory's computer so that it was all in place when the real work with isomorphous replacement began in the mid–fifties. An article on the system appeared in *Acta Crystallographica* in 1952 (Bennett and Kendrew, 1952). The paper is a classic; it is the first one written about this type of computation done with a digital computer. John Bennet subsequently became Professor of Computing at Sydney University.

Later on, during the later part of the fifties and in the sixties, in Cambridge and at the Royal Institution in London to which Bragg had gone, methods were worked out for recording the reflections on automatic diffractometers, and also for scanning film automatically, so that progressively more and more of the chores were taken out of the initial stages of crystallographic analysis.

# Of Shoes – and Ships – and Sealing Wax and String

## RONALD KING, FRS

The task facing Sir Lawrence Bragg when, in 1953, he was appointed Resident Professor and Director of the Davy Faraday Research Laboratory at the Royal Institution was, to say the least, a formidable one. In the previous three years the Institution had experienced probably the worst turmoil it had known in the century and a half since it was established.

The Institution, "an association of men and women for the advancement of natural knowledge" was, at that time, governed by "a President, fifteen Managers, fifteen Visitors, one Treasurer and one Secretary", chosen annually from among the

Members. The smooth ordering of the affairs of the Institution clearly depended upon harmonious relations between these officers and committees, and the Resident Professor upon whom the responsibility for the daily running of the Institution rested. This system had worked with little change over the years, though it had occasionally creaked. However, in 1950, Professor E.N. da C. Andrade had been appointed with the title, Director *in* the Royal Institution, as well as Fullerian Professor of Chemistry and Director of the Davy Faraday Research Laboratory. Full of reforming zeal, he at once set about making changes which soon put him at odds with the Officers and many Managers and Visitors. There followed a sorry saga of acrimony and recrimination, the resignation of the Secretary and some Managers and Visitors and litigation, ultimately leading to Andrade's resignation in 1952. The Institution was left financially straightened and with its reputation in many quarters sadly tarnished (Caroe, 1985).

Sir Lawrence was thus faced with restoring harmony to the relations of Members, their Committees and the Officers, reviving the confidence of an unhappy and somewhat bewildered staff and re–establishing the good reputation upon which the support, moral and financial, of outside bodies so much depended.

My own position at this time was Assistant Director of the Davy Faraday Laboratory, to which I had been appointed in September 1950, having previously been a Reader on Andrade's staff at University College. I had kept firmly clear of controversial issues and had stayed on after Andrade's departure as a Recognised Teacher of the University of London to supervise the PhD students in the laboratory. I was prepared to leave had Sir Lawrence so wished, but he was kindness itself, we got on well together and I soon found myself his deputy in the Superintendence of the House as well as the Laboratory.

The story of the great success of the Research Laboratory under his direction will, I am sure, be told by many; I shall restrict myself to the general activities of the Institution.

The tight control exercised by the Officers and Managers could make great demands on the tact and forbearance of the Resident Professor, particularly in the case of Sir Lawrence, who disliked committees anyway. Two examples will suffice to illustrate the detailed nature of the supervision. The Committee of Managers met on the first Monday of each month except January, August, September and October, during which months their duties were undertaken by a Vacation Sub–Committee. At each meeting, all invoices of accounts due for payment, except for petty items, were circulated for inspection and, if approved, cheques were signed by the appropriate number of Managers. This seemed unnecessarily time consuming and questions were sometimes provocative. Requests were sometimes received from other societies for the use of the Lecture Theatre or other rooms. All such requests had to be submitted to the Managers. One can well imagine how these and other restrictions would have incensed a man of Andrade's impetuous nature. In contrast, though intensely irritated on many occasions, Sir Lawrence was calm and courteous and only gave vent to his feelings when we retired to his study after such a meeting.

However, the level of supervision was gradually relaxed as the success of new ventures initiated by Sir Lawrence became apparent.

The first of these new ventures started in 1955. At that time, in addition to the Friday Evening Discourses and the Christmas Lectures, the programme included a number of short courses – three or four lectures on Tuesday and Thursday afternoons. Given by the Visiting Professors and other distinguished lecturers, these were open to the general public (at a charge of six shillings for a three lecture course, eight shillings for four lectures). Attendance at these lectures had fallen so embarrassingly low that on occasions members of staff were press–ganged into attending. Experiments were made with the timing of the lectures but produced no improvement. Sir Lawrence and I mulled over this problem several times. Then, one early evening as we talked around it, it occurred to me that the reason was that the lectures were not directed at any specific, identifiable audience. Remembering my own sense of isolation when a teacher in rural Wales, and how much I would have appreciated such lectures, I suggested that we might target schoolteachers specifically – a large identifiable potential audience in the London area. His response was not immediately enthusiastic, then as we talked I saw his interest quicken as he said, "Why not the children as well?". By the time I left he was bubbling with ideas and, as he walked with me to the door of the flat, I heard for the first time his "What fun!", said with that special intonation which meant he was really enthused.

With characteristic energy he got together a small committee of teachers to advise us and plans were pushed ahead.

The proposal for lectures for young people was not unanimously welcomed by the Managers. I remember being told very acidly by one member. "You know King, we are not going to let this place become a kindergarten!". But the lectures went ahead. At first they were short courses of three or four lectures but it was soon suggested by the teachers that single lectures would be better as they would enable more children to have the opportunity to experience a lecture at the R.I.

The first lectures were aimed at sixth formers and many teachers attended. I am sure that the degree of the popular success of the venture rested entirely upon Sir Lawrence's own lectures in the initial stages. As a scientific expositor he was superb at all levels, but when he spoke to young people his imagery and demonstration technique and above all his obvious enjoyment, established a special rapport.

Lectures to fourth formers and Preparatory Schools followed and the 'traditional' lectures were discontinued altogether. Other activities were arranged for schools. Refresher courses for teachers and research days on which groups of teachers spent an afternoon at the R.I., meeting the leader of a research laboratory and his team to hear about recent advances were organised, and opportunities were offered for teachers to acquaint themselves with a wide range of demonstration apparatus.

All these activities attracted interest and financial support, but it was the Schools Lectures which did most to restore the good name of the R.I. and its income through sponsorship and special grants.

Over the years, and with the indispensable assistance of Mr Bill Coates, we cooperated with other societies – in particular with the British Association, the Institute of Physics and the Institution of Metallurgists – in giving lectures at centres outside London. Sir Lawrence used to talk of a Repertory Theatre of Science.

1959 saw a cooperative venture with the BBC. Sir Lawrence gave a series of lectures on "The Nature of Things" before an invited audience in the R.I. Lecture Theatre. These were recorded and later broadcast with very satisfactory audience figures.

In 1964 we were invited to organise a course of lectures and seminars on fundamental science for administrative civil servants. The Visiting Professors participated in these lectures which were well received and continued until the Civil Service started its own establishment at Sunningdale.

All these activities point to the growing recognition of the importance of the R.I.'S contribution to science education under Sir Lawrence. The whole atmosphere of the place had changed. There were critics, but they were few. It was a happy ship.

Sir Lawrence was made the first Director *of* the Institution.

While we worked together on all aspects of the R.I.'s activities, Sir Lawrence and I got closest together in our enthusiasm for good lecture demonstrations. We did not think much of 'black box' demonstrations, particularly when the point could be better made with 'sealing wax and string'. I still remember the intense pleasure it gave me when he was genuinely excited by some of the demonstrations in my first Discourse.

We sat together in the Lecture Theatre on Friday evenings and I learned to recognise his reactions. I do not know how, but I always knew when he felt the lecturer was not doing justice to his demonstrations (a real sin) and working out how he would have presented them. He was never unkind in his criticism but I knew his comment would be something like "He had good material!".

I never heard him speak harshly of anyone critically. Yes, angrily occasionally. The most damning appellation I remember him apply to anyone was "Juggins". He hated any situation where a rebuke was necessary. He was sympathetic and understanding and, as is frequently the case with truly sympathetic people, vulnerable and depended so much on the marvellous support of Lady Bragg.

We still kept in close touch after his retirement in 1966. I was responsible for the Schools Lectures programmes and he continued to lecture until his death in 1971.

As I write, my eyes are frequently drawn to a treasured picture. It is a painting by Sir Lawrence – he was an accomplished water colourist – of the River Deben at Woodbridge and I am reminded with particular pleasure of a weekend spent at the Bragg 'cottage' at Waldringfield in Suffolk. Lady Bragg was away, so we fended for ourselves, preparing the meals, doing the washing up, gardening, which we both enjoyed, and bird–watching along the banks of the Deben. We talked of many things but not, I think, about R.I. matters. I remember discussing who–dun–its (he was a fan of Agatha Christie's), the function of soap in shaving, the virtue of storing coffee in the fridge and gardening matters – he did not like chrysanthemums whereas I grew them in profusion. Simple uncomplicated things.

But the highlight was our sailing trip. Sir Lawrence was an experienced sailor of light craft. I was the tyro. We set out on the Deben under sail in the family dinghy – a venerable boat. It was at that time a perfect day for sailing. All went well until in some shallows we got stuck in the mud. (I must have been at the helm.) It was then that we discovered that we had left the oars on the shore. So I got out to push us off. No problem; I was wearing plimsolls and shorts. It was just as well that I had the plimsolls because we soon realised that we were taking in water and had left the bailer with the oars. So my shoes became bailers. Two professors in a boat!

By this time the wind had turned gusty and Sir Lawrence was faced with bringing us in through the crowded moorings in front of the Clubhouse under sail when he would normally have rowed in. He was quite anxious but we got through with hardly a touch. Is it too fanciful of me to be put in mind of the way in which he steered the good ship R.I. through difficult waters under often very critical eyes?

**Reference**

Caroe, G. 1985. *The Royal Institution. An Informal History*, pp.113 *et seq.*. John Murray, London.

# Christmas Lectures to a Juvenile Auditory, 1959/60

## T.E. ALLIBONE, CBE FRS

It is possible that I was asked by W.L.B. to give these lectures as I had been connected with the R.I. for very many years. In March 1926, I came to hear Rutherford lecture on disintegration of the atom; I had an appointment with him the following week in Cambridge to ask him if he would accept me as a research student to try to disintegrate atoms with a very high voltage source of particles, and my Director said I must go to see the great man before going to Cambridge – "better for the dog to see the rabbit beforehand", he said.

My Cambridge work brought me in close touch with Rideal (later Sir Eric, Director of the R.I.) in 1928/30, and in 1947 he asked me to give a Friday Discourse on high–voltage spark discharges; this I did with a 400 kV generator. Sir Alfred Egerton led my wife to Faraday's Chair and told her, March 12, that that day I had been elected a FRS. I was not told till after the lecture!

Percy Andrade (who succeeded Rideal as Director of the R.I.) asked me to lecture on November 16, 1951, and I packed the stage with experiments on new materials in engineering.

In 1958, fusion was becoming almost successful in the USA, Russia and Great Britain, both in Harwell and in my lab in AEI, Aldermaston, and it was the subject of my Presidential Address, Section A, British Association, Glasgow. Whether Bragg was there I cannot remember but I was a Manager of the R.I. at the time. It might have been earlier in the year for my diary records preparing experiments in the early summer, and these were *not* for BA. So Bragg probably asked me to give a Discourse on December 12, 1958, on "Fusion", and it was full of experiments; my diary records, "Lecture went well; finished four seconds after 10 o'clock", and Bragg kindly wrote a superb letter of appreciation, "in the very best of tradition of the R.I.". It must have been within a few days of that that he asked me to give the Christmas Lectures, 1959, for I had tickets for the Christmas Lectures, 1958/59 and he *must* have given me these so that I could gauge the atmosphere. I attended December 30 and January 1, 1959.

We were making apparatus in the summer of 1959 and all the scripts were written by September/October. Coates came to Aldermaston to give advice on the apparatus we made, size, appearance, *etc.*, and the great day arrived; all was ready by early afternoon.

The first lecture was on the atom pre–nucleus. Experiments went without a hitch, but I felt it was a little dull, applause was good but not rapturous. Bragg noticed with his great experience that I was a bit disappointed (he may have been too, but was too kind to say so). He suggested that I should arrange to make one or two mistakes in the experiments; get a wrong result; let something not do what I said it would do, *etc.* So two days later on "The Nucleus" I made just two mistakes and corrected them with apologies; I got yells of applause, and from that moment onwards, with mistakes in the following four lectures, the atmosphere was marvellous and after each lecture the children crowded round for an hour asking questions, In the book I wrote "Peaceful uses of Atomic Energy", I made a special point of the pleasure I derived from their wild enthusiasm and their endless questions. Bragg's letter of appreciation was marvellous, for indeed, I have never been a lecturer; my whole life in industry giving almost 200 public lectures, I see. But he was too kind.

I had the marvellous assistance from my technical helper, Chivers, who later became a curate and later still vicar at Southampton, a dedicated friend, now dead, alas.

My final Discourse was under Porter, so I have given one under each post–war Director; that was for the Rutherford Centenary in 1971, and I performed every one of Rutherford's great experiments with apparatus exactly the size he used, but of course, the TV camera could present the small experiment to the large audience.

Happy days.

# As the Barnacles Stick to the Rock

## R.L. WAIN, CBE FRS

I have given three evening Discourses at the Royal Institution and the first is the most memorable.

It started with an invitation to have tea with Sir Lawrence and Lady Bragg, during which I was told at length about the great Discourse traditions and asked if I would give one the following year. I heard about the formal procedure – how, after dinner, the speaker retires to Michael Faraday's office to collect his thoughts and prepare to deliver his Discourse lasting exactly one hour. I heard, too, about the occasion when Professor Wheatstone took fright down the stairs just before he was due to enter the Theatre – and how Michael Faraday himself entered on the stroke of nine and gave a Discourse lasting exactly one hour.

Next came another tea invitation where, after much discussion, my title was agreed, "Plant Growth and Man–Made Molecules" – which Sir Lawrence had thought up and strongly favoured.

At this time, our discovery of a new weedkiller which destroyed weeds in legume crops was being widely publicised and was on exhibition as an elaborate mechanical display at the World Fair in Brussels. When Sir Lawrence heard about this, he tried to get it to show at my Discourse. To my surprise he succeeded, and the heavy contraption was delivered and assembled in the Lecture Theatre two days before my Discourse.

My recollection of the Evening itself are dominated by my nervousness as I sat alone on the horsehair couch in Faraday's office. I remember Sir Lawrence, a great traditionalist, coming into the room at 8.55, putting his hand on my shoulder and pointing to Faraday's specimen of rock crystal cased in one corner of the room. "May your Discourse be as clear as the crystal", he said. I nodded and was turned round to face a glass tank containing barnacles, "May you stick to your timing as the barnacles stick to the rock", he said. I promised to try to do so and we left the room to meet the President and other R.I. officials before proceeding to the doors leading to the Lecture Theatre. On the stroke of nine I went in – and it all began! "How does your garden grow, says the old nursery rhyme..."

# Optical Influences

## CHARLES TAYLOR

In 1940 I went up to Queen Mary College, London, to read physics, but because of the war, the college had been evacuated to King's College, Cambridge. As a result, I had the great good fortune to be able to attend Sir Lawrence's inspirational course on physical optics. I can honestly say that it determined my future career.

During the course he invited those of us who were interested to see an experiment that one of his demonstrators was doing. It was the "Two–wavelength microscope" – an instrument now known as an optical diffractometer – made out of two telescopes borrowed from the observatory, which reconstructed an image of a crystal structure by using the diffraction pattern of a mask representing the data obtained from its X–ray diffraction pattern.

The image was of diopside, and I was absolutely fascinated. I wrote to the physics master of my old school and told him that this was the outstanding feature of my physics course and was what I hoped to work on. War service intervened and I had forgotten about the incident, though remaining inspired by the course.

Towards the end of the war I began to apply to various universities to do research but was told that there was no future in physical optics (!) Then, in 1948, I applied for an assistant lectureship at what is now UMIST, and found to my amazement that the Head of Department was Henry Lipson, that he was the demonstrator who had shown us the two–wavelength microscope, and that he wanted me to take up work on optical and X–ray diffraction which would be a continuation of the work he had started with Sir Lawrence.

# A Personal View by his Elder Son

## STEPHEN LAWRENCE BRAGG

It has been my experience that good lecturers also find it easy to relate to children. The ability to respect the more limited background of those being addressed, and the patience to explain in simple terms, with analogies drawn from normal life, the key ideas on which a theory depends, are essential in establishing a rapport with both types of audience. My father (whom I shall refer to as WLB, since that is the way he signed his letters to me) was a superb lecturer and also got on very well with children. Indeed, I think his love of physics stemmed from the fact that it provided such simple explanations to account for observed phenomena, and he enjoyed sharing these with others. Mathematics, he once said, represented the peak of perfection in the sciences, with physics a little lower than the summit, and the technologies, which had not yet yielded to explanation on the basis of simple postulates, very much in the foothills. Only once do I remember getting a rather short answer to a childish enquiry. One day at lunch I asked "Can waves cross?". "Of course they can", was the reply, "Otherwise you could not see your brother across the table while I was looking at your mother".

Perhaps because of this love of order and explanation, my father found the variability and irrationality of personal relationships much more difficult. Certainly he had many friends among those who shared his interests in science or painting or gardening or birds. And his love for his family is evidenced by the emphasis on holidays and domestic activites in his autobiographical notes. But he disliked committees, and often returned from meetings agonising over what he might have said if he had thought of it in time. He had little interest in politics or in the theories of management and hated any form of deviousness or deceit. He worried over decisions which depended on factors which could not be determined in advance – unlike my mother's family, who never worried because, as she said, the thought that they could be wrong never entered their heads.

The decision to leave Cambridge and come to the Royal Institution was perhaps one of the most difficult WLB had to make. He consulted Lord Adrian, a close friend and at that time the President of the Royal Society. He eventually decided, with Adrian's support, that it was his duty to come to the rescue of the R.I., with which the family had close ties but which was then going through a most difficult period after the abrupt departure of Professor Andrade. WLB was acutely disappointed that his relationship with the Royal Society, many of whose members felt that Professor Andrade had not been well treated, suffered for a time as a result.

In spite of WLB's ease of communication with audiences and children, he could appear rather vague at times. This apparent lack of interest in his surroundings – for which, be it said, my mother amply made up – may have been associated with his intense powers of concentration. He could work at home in his study, quite impervious to domestic clatter or conversation going on around him, making an occasional grunt to show that he was conscious of others but not paying any attention to them. When he was disengaged, however, he was an excellent raconteur, who enjoyed a good joke and laughed uproariously both at his own stories and at those told by others.

WLB's love of order and explanation led to a delight in craftmanship and making things work. Not having the money to spend on expensive track, WLB himself constructed a fine model railway layout in the conservatory of our house in Manchester: the rails were wooden beading, steam–bent in the nursery bathroom, pinned to a baseboard, and the points were operated by string. To illustrate the Christopher Robin stories of A.A. Milne, WLB constructed a shadow theatre, consisting of a model stage covered with a thin sheet of translucent paper which was lit from behind. The audience then saw the silhouettes of cardboard cut–out figures of the principal actors performing a shadow play: sixty years later I can still remember the realism of the flood water rising around the marooned Pooh Bear while he sat astride a bough with his few remaining jars of honey.

These toys and many others, such as the crossbow and the model boat, were all constructed from the simplest materials. Plasticene, walnut shells, gelatine sheet (for windows) were all employed. On the other hand, WLB could not resist the lure of good tools, and rarely left an ironmonger's shop without having yielded to the temptation to make an unpremeditated purchase. Another example of his do–it–yourself ability was the garden "grow–through". WLB took a square of wire netting and bent it to roughly hemispherical shape over a pudding basin. He then placed this support over a plant which tended to flop over, such as a delphinium: as the plant grew, the support rose with the lower leaves, but remained concealed by the upper leaves and flowers, It was neat, effective and cheap.

Another factor on which I now look back with surprise is the amount of time that a physics professor before the war was able to spend with his family. Long vacations really were long in those days. Indeed in the sixties, when the attractions of university life were claiming all new graduates, WLB suggested to me that all industry had to do to transform its recruitment was to offer six weeks of holiday a year. Holidays were indeed a very important part of his life and his four children all benefited greatly from the amount of attention he so enthusiastically gave to them at those times.

Little of WLB's spare time was given over to sport. He enjoyed tennis, and played golf until an old elbow injury – the result of a tricycle accident as a child – prevented him. He was a swift runner over short distances, and won a 100 yards handicap race at a village sports in Norfolk at the age of 60! He was also keen on sailing. But his real interests, after science, were in nature – particularly birds and plants. As a boy he had collected shells and had found a previously unknown species on a South Australian beach. He imparted to me an enthusiasm for collecting butterflies, at a time when collection was not a sin against the environment. Wherever he went round the world he immediately bought a guide to the local birds and arranged that one day at least of any lecture tour should be spent birdwatching. He did not pursue his hobby competitively: he kept no records and made no lists of the birds he had seen. He just enjoyed watching and listening. He thought several times of ways of producing a shorthand description of bird song, though never had time to take this further.

WLB's gardening was originally confined to the occasional weeding of beds that were officially the preserve of his gardener. But during and after the war he steadily assumed more control of his own gardens, planning a new herbaceous border or maybe doing a little scything of the long grass before breakfast. Finally gardening became his major relaxation, not only in the doing of it but in the admiring and enjoying of his handiwork afterwards. He liked to tell the story of the two Americans who returned to the cottage in Waldringfield where they had been billeted during the War. They met WLB, who now lived there, in the garden. He was dressed in his working clothes, which usually included a hat well past its first youth, and naturally they were shown round. When they later called at the local pub they caused great amusement by recounting that "... the owner of Quietways was not at home, but they were shown round the grounds by the most delightful old gardener".

WLB's mother was an accomplished artist, and he must have been encouraged early to develop this talent. We still have a book full of attractive sketches of people and views from Adelaide days. This hobby was taken up again atfer the war, mostly using water colour or pen and ink, but occasionally pastel. I remember how fascinated WLB was by the effects that the Impressionists could produce with designs that were meaningless when viewed too close. He enjoyed trying to produce cloud effects in the same way. Of the other arts, he had little interest in music – though he enjoyed dancing, particularly the waltz and the polka – but liked the theatre and was extremely well read. A broad education at St Peter's College in Adelaide had given him a wide knowledge of the classics, which was useful when he turned to crossword puzzles for relaxation. It also helped him to write very good prose. He enjoyed telling of his pleasure at finding a typescript in which ideas similar to his own were expressed most beautifully, and reading it for some time before he remembered that he had written it himself years before!

Although a scientist of world repute, WLB was in many ways a simple man. His chief pleasures after science became his family, which latterly included ten grandchildren, to all of whom he was devoted, and his garden. His lectures conveyed his enthusiasm for understanding basic phenomena, but he also enjoyed observing the natural scene, and trying to record his enjoyment in line and colour. His family appreciated his greatness and returned his affection.

# Thoughts about my Father by his Daughter

## PATIENCE MARY THOMSON

I remember a winter's evening spent with my father in the study at the Royal Institution. He was measuring and cutting out for me a circular skirt, the fashion of the fifties. The difficulty was, of course, that my waist was elliptical and that I was not symmetrical back and front. It would have been much easier, he pointed out, if I had asked for a handkerchief. But we persevered and I wore the finished creation on my honeymoon. He would never have given up, nor would he have intimated in any way that he felt he was wasting his time on trivia. Far from it, it was a memorably enjoyable and companionable evening.

"Be careful what you set your heart on, for you shall surely get it." My father quoted this to me on several occasions. He was keen on establishing goals, large and small,long–term and short–term. He also loved problem–solving exercises. In my memory he was always actively doing something, whether it was pondering in his study over some absorbing new results, or leaning out of the window to shoot the starlings, who were spoiling his Williams pears, with his powerful home–made catapult. There was never any free–wheeling of the mind; it was always in gear, involved, interested, questioning, exploring.

My father involved himself quite happily in our more feminine interests. He adored my mother, and was delighted to have daughters and later grand–daughters to spoil and entertain. He was a magnificent present giver, always choosing the best available. In 1948 he found a pair of Wellington boots in Norfolk for me of genuine pre–war quality. He prudently bought them one size too large. I have them to this day and they are still too large, for alas, my feet had stopped growing. When the dolls' house lacked beds, he created perfect miniatures, which I painted in red and blue with two coats of paint, sand–papering between them punctiliously at his insistence. The results were professional. On my marriage he presented me with a set of tools on which he had carved my initials. They were in a box with a lock and key. "Share your toothbrush if you must with your husband, but never your tools," was his advice. In my parents' Suffolk retreat he regularly did the washing up. Long before the equality of the sexes was generally recognised he drew no demarcation lines, liked babies whose heads were still at the wobbly stage and regularly sat on the edge of the bath reciting stories to us at bedtime.

Perhaps because of his Australian origins, my father had something of the pioneer and the backwoodsman in him. On two occasions we went sailing alone together on the Broads. I was in my teens. The *Wild Rose* had no engine, my father would have considered it 'squalid' not to rely on one's wits, the wind and the tide. We quanted through bridges and were carried unceremoniously backwards in Great Yarmouth harbour, having failed to make it against the tide. In the evening, while the bitterns boomed in the background, my father would sketch from the deck while I wrote up the log and my dog, Scrap, splashed muddily through the reeds, returning quite filthy to curl up on my bunk. It was all part of the blissful freedom of this type of holiday.

This mongrel terrier had been bought by my father and myself while my mother was away; her disapproval was absolute, and any mess the puppy made had to be cleared up by the two of us. Conspiratorially my father and I concealed his thieving habits, half condoned his amorous and unpopular forays in the neighbourhood and encouraged him to climb trees in pursuit of the local cats. He loved animals. He bought a pony for my sister from the man who sold cockles and winkles on Cambridge market, but while leading it home in triumph from the other side of Cambridge it escaped on Midsummer Common and we had, as my father said, "one hell of a job" to recapture him.

"It is not what you do for your children, it is what you do with them," was another favourite maxim of my father's. I was the youngest child, alone at home and going on holidays with my parents after the others had grown up and departed. My father always seemed to find something unexpected, a praying mantis among Greek ruins or an otter in the moat of a French chateau on the Loire. It was strongly advisable not to stray out of earshot or one might well miss the punch line!

My father and I used to keep house together when my mother was away. Standards happily lapsed, time became immaterial, we reverted to nursery cooking and lived on scrambled eggs and chocolate semolina pudding. We ate when it suited us and I went to bed when I was tired. In retrospect, those times were golden. My father could talk fascinatingly on an incredibly wide range of subjects. He had had the broadest of educations. I remember experiencing a faint sense of bewilderment and anxiety when I discovered that he knew as much, if not more, than I did about the French author Loti, whom I was studying at the time as part of my degree course at Cambridge. It seemed unfair.

There were about a dozen books which he re–read every decade. These included the *Odyssey*, *Anna Karenina*, *Emma* and *The Voyage of the Beagle*. He would read aloud to us in the evenings, poems perhaps, or extracts from novels, or snippets from the newspaper. He particularly loved Browning. He read the Old Testament as literature, revelling in the poetry of the language of the Authorised Version and imparting his pleasure to the listener. He told wonderful stories, and loved playing with words. We had an elaborate game where we capped each other's puns, the sillier the better. "Why did the plaice leave the place?" "Because the smelt smelt." He wrote enchanting letters to us from Canada in the war, peppered with illustrations and actually enclosing such treasures as chunks of wood marked by the teeth of a beaver.

My father fancied a round of family bridge occasionally and taught us children before we were ten. It was not unknown for him absent–mindedly to redeploy an ace of trumps which had inadvertently fallen into his trouser turn–up. He played with tremendous verve and panache, and loathed post–mortems. I always wanted to be his partner.

He was a religious man in the broadest sense, comparing the awe and wonder of scientific discovery to an almost spiritual experience. At the time of my confirmation I asked him about the afterlife. He was quite unfazed, assuring me that arrangements were undoubtedly satisfactory. He would sit with my father–in–law, G.P. Thomson, of an evening and reform the Church of England, retaining favourite hymns and the language of the Bible and Prayer Book, but questioning much of the doctrine.

Not long after my marriage, I travelled to Berlin with my father, where he was giving a series of lectures. I had the latest protein model held safely on my lap, lest it should be damaged. To my excitement there was a well–known pop group on the plane, and at the airport there was a crowd of reporters and a huge bouquet of pink roses. It was with surprise and faint embarrassment that I discovered that they were for my father and not for the group.

When I was engaged, I asked my father the secret of a happy marriage, not really expecting a serious reply, if any at all. His response was immediate. "Never feel sorry for yourself," he said, "And never keep your husband in the dog–house for too long." It was, as always, excellent advice.

# Sir William Bragg and his Lecturer's Assistant

## W.A. COATES, MBE

One afternoon in the early 1950s I was repairing an X–ray target in the workshop at the Royal Institution when I suddenly became aware of our new Director standing beside me. After a friendly greeting and an inquiry as to what I was doing, he asked me if I knew that rubber contracted when heated. Rather taken aback by the question, I replied that I did, but had no idea why. He immediately gave me an explanation as to why this happened, and then enquired of the possibility of producing a model to demonstrate this action. After pondering on the idea, I produced a model in which the long molecules were meccano chains, and the heat was a large sheet of aluminium vibrated by blows from drumsticks. Sir Lawrence Bragg was very pleased with my answer to his rubber model, and he used it in his lectures on materials. Thus began an association with WLB which was to last over ten years.

I think the success of this demonstration was Bragg's love of the self–explanatory experimental demonstration, one in which the audience could follow and see all the stages in its performance and, he hoped, enjoy its success. I think he disliked the complex electronic 'black box' (as he called it) experiment. Only one of this type did we ever use, and this was a microwave setup, given by the Marconi Company, which we could use to show practically all the demonstrations in optics. Even then Bragg would rather use the sound detection system of the apparatus rather than the complex waveform displayed on the oscilloscope.

Sir Lawrence had a great love and skill in the art of lecture demonstration. He really enjoyed lecturing to young people. The success of the R.I. School Lectures, which he started, must have been the inspiration for many a budding young scientist. In later years, I have had many of these budding young scientists, now quite eminent, saying to me,"Do you remember when Bragg did this or that experiment?" After many years they had remembered the man and his experiments. I think WLB would have been quite amused.

Sir Lawrence always believed that a lecture, as he put it, should be given "standing on your feet", not with copious notes and scripts. His own lecture notes were very simple: a running order of the lecture, more for my benefit than his, and perhaps the odd date or number which might have been difficult to remember. He disliked intensely the lecturer who arrived with a full word for word script and, as WLB would say, talked to the script rather than to the audience.

Sir Lawrence's ability to break down complex science into a form easily understood came to me most vividly when he decided to include an explanation of a PN diode into his lectures on electricity and magnetism. I was called to his office and asked to explain the action of a PN diode. A few days later I was again called to his office and he gave me a drawing of a model to explain the PN junction which he had devised. It was simple, yet it contained all the necessary facts for explanation. I left the office wondering why I had not thought of that.

WLB loved to take his lectures on the road, as he called it, and I was very fortunate in going with him to many parts of England, Scotland and Ireland. The lectures were always extremely well received; and after a lecture, I think as a bonus to me, he always made a tour of places of interest in the town or city we were visiting. On one such visit to the University of St Andrews in Scotland, after the lecture, we were given a tour of the places of interest such as the stones on which the martyrs were executed by burning, and also the famous battle dungeon where they were kept prior to this event. Our party consisted of various dignitaries from the university, and our guide was a gentleman in full Highland dress. This man also carries a lighted lantern on the end of a long rope. On reaching the dungeon, he lowered the lantern down into it and gave his commentary. To me it sounded like "Ah reek a reek 1674. Ah re a reek 168" – I did not understand a word. On the way back to the university I asked Sir Lawrence if he had understood what the guide had said. "Not a word, Coates", was his reply, "but I'll find out." He turned to one of the university party, who I believe was the Dean, and enquired. The Dean's reply rather stunned Sir Lawrence and I. "I've been taking parties like this round for years", he said, "but still cannot understand a word he is saying."

The popularity of Sir Lawrence's lectures was very well demonstrated when he was asked to give a series of popular science programmes on the BBC. So successful were his explanations of popular science to the layman that a second series of "The Nature of Things" was produced.

I always remember WLB as a very even–tempered man – even the hustle on TV never seemed to worry him, except, I may say, on one occasion. At the start of each programme, Sir Lawrence would enter, a nice friendly smile, and a cheerful "Good evening". On one programme, just after the "good evening", the floor manager stopped him. "Must do it again, Sir", he said, "technical fault". Sir Lawrence duly left and re–entered on cue, only to be stopped again. By the fourth entrance the smile was beginning to wane and the 'good evening' a little tense. On the sixth entrance they got it right and WLB sailed through the programme as though nothing had happened.

The success of the TV lectures led to a filmed version being made by EFVA for loan to schools. This led to one amusing incident, although I don't think the producer of the film thought so. After the final shot of the final film, we all left for holidays. While on holiday, the producer rang me up to say that they needed to retake certain parts of one of the films. He asked me to warn WLB and get the necessary apparatus ready, but most important of all to ensure that Sir Lawrence wore the grey suit he had worn throughout the filming. I got in touch with Sir Lawrence who informed me that unfortunately Lady Bragg had disposed of the important grey suit to a jumble sale. Great panic ensued and a great search for the person who had bought the suit which was vital for the continuity of the film. With great relief the buyer of the jacket was found, but alas, never the trousers. So with great care, the inserts were filmed of Sir Lawrence only from the waist up.

WLB's lectures were always well rehearsed and filled with experiments. He was always looking for new ways of getting his point across. To this end, he would often try out an experiment on a member of the staff. On one occasion he asked me how far I could throw a wooden dart. I replied that I was not quite sure. He produced a two foot length of dowel stick with a paper flight attached and invited me to throw it down the long red corridor at the R.I. I tried and made a throw of about fifteen feet – the corridor must be at least fifty feet long. WLB's reply was to take the dart and cut a small notch in the dowel stick near the flight. To this he added a piece of string rolled at one end. Hitching the string to the dart and round his hand, he hurled the dart the whole length of the corridor such that it slammed into the far wall, narrowly missing a large oil painting. "Simple leverage!, said WLB. "This was used by the Australian spearthrower when hunting". I agreed, but have often wondered how, if the dart had gone through the oil painting, I would have explained to the Managers of the R.I. that the damage had occurred while playing darts with the Director.

Sir Lawrence had, I think, a wonderful expression when planning his lectures – "Always, if possible Coates, never talk about science, *show* it to them", and this he practised throughout all his lectures. His enthusiasm and method of lecturing must have inspired countless young people to enter science. Even after his retirement and in his eighties, his love of the demonstration lecture never waned. WLB came to see me just a fortnight before he died, still planning his next school lecture with the same care to content, care to detail and enthusiasm as he had done all those years ago when we first started.

After his death, the Institute of Physics awarded a medal for excellence in demonstration lectures. It is called the Bragg Medal, and I am very proud to possess a medal bearing that name.

# Memories of the Workshop

### S. BRUCE MORRIS

The period I was employed at the Royal Institution, under Sir Lawrence Bragg as Director, was comparatively short. However, in that time, I realised he was indeed "a man for all seasons". As a member of staff, he always always found time to give one an acknowledgement, no matter what he was engaged in or whom he was with.

He also had a unique method of letting us know he was to 'visit' our Departments – in my case the Workshop. He would stand outside the door, and stamp his feet! If we were, at that moment, doing something not strictly correct, we stopped!

I have one particularly happy – and hilarious – memory of him. He brought a saucepan to the Workshop for repair. My then engineer, Mr Fred Simmons, and I decided that it was well–nigh impossible to do any further repair on said saucepan. It already had five or six repair washers in the bottom! We decided the only answer to the problem was to buy a new saucepan, and beat the "heck" out of it, which is what we proceeded to do. We then put two repair washers in the bottom, and with judicious use of a very rough emery cloth, made it look suitably "well used". Not a word was said when the "finished article" was returned to Sir Lawrence. But by the twinkle in his eye, he was in no doubt as to what we had done!

Finally, Bill Coates and I one day took the chance to ask him a personal question, that of all the honours that had been bestowed upon him, which was the one that meant the most to him? The answer? "The Companion of Honour, of course."

Sir Lawrence Bragg was, to me, a great Edwardian gentleman.

# From Near and Far

## JOHN M. THOMAS, FRS

The thrill of understanding is second only to that of original discovery: it stimulates and sustains the student, just as it inspires and propels the teacher. Our pleasure is intensified when one recognises that certain concepts, and the equations that they engender, have hidden depths and far–reaching repercussions, which may be conveyed to those who least suspect that they can understand them. Thoughts of this kind spring to mind whenever I contemplate an incident that occurred in the practical laboratory of the Department of Chemistry at the University College of Swansea one Thursday in November 1951. Though he was not present, it was my introduction to W.L. Bragg.

Earlier in the week, during a lecture by R.H. Davies outlining important developments in physics and chemistry in the early decades of the twentieth century, it was stated that, using simple concepts in crystal physics, it was possible to determine afresh the magnitude of Avogadro's number. This, on first hearing it, I could not fathom; so I resolved , with a certain amount of trepidation characteristic of the undergraduate of the age, to seek further clarification from the lecturer, whom I knew would be supervising our efforts in gravimetric analysis in the inorganic chemistry laboratory later that week. "Think of the Bragg equation", he said, "and what you can deduce from knowing the density of a solid".

Armed with this advice, I delved into my Glasstone, and consulted a few other books, including Moelwyn Hughes'. The gradual realisation that, from X–ray analysis, thanks to Bragg's work, one could ascertain the separation distances of atomic planes, the nature, content and volume of the unit cell, and hence set up a simple equation relating X–ray density to atomic or molecular mass, which includes Avogadro's number, thrilled me. Shortly thereafter, I realised that this equation could also be the basis, and was already being used, for the determination of the molecular weight of the constituents of an insoluble crystal, and that the Bragg equation, apart from being the foundation stone of *all diffraction* by periodic structures, also played a central role in the practice of X–ray *spectroscopy* with crystals of different spacings being used as monochromators.

When, in the late 1950s, I became a university lecturer, I found that, in service teaching especially, the attention of audiences, particularly those ill–equipped in or who had an aversion for mathematics, could be rivetted by re–enacting the joy that had engulfed me as a student on contemplating the cascade of consequences, and outlining the derivation, of the Bragg equation ($n\lambda = 2d\sin\theta$). As others have doubtless discovered, the emergence, significance and application of the Bragg equation constitute a singularly well–suited topic for the popularisation of science among lay audiences. It formed the basis of one of my regular evening Welsh lectures delineating the essence of scientific discovery and knowledge, to WEA classes and to extra–mural and adult audiences in Anglesey and other regions of North Wales.

Bragg had become one of my heros; and by the mid 1960s, my knowledge of his work, and the genius of simplicity associated with his insight, was adequate for me to add a human dimension to discussions of his equation. When, in 1965, the BBC broadcast "Fifty Years a Winner", my admiration of him as a scientist, as a teacher and as a human being, knew no bounds. I particularly cherished the story told by Max Perutz in that programme, recalling Bragg's Cambridge days. At the appropriate time in the course of a scientific investigation, following numerous exploratory discussions with those involved, Bragg, so we were told, would request the laboratory notes and experimental results of the investigator(s) in question and take them home of an evening. He would return the following day with a complete, handwritten manuscript, essentially devoid of any corrections, already in a state suitable for transmission to the *Phil. Mag.* or *Proc. Roy. Soc.*. In describing this quality possessed by Bragg, Perutz recalled Mozart, "who composed the Overture to *The Marriage of Figaro* in one sitting".

To my eternal regret, I never actually met Bragg, though I came very near to it once. In 1971, he attended a Royal Society Soireé in Carlton House Terrace to which, at the instigation of Kathleen Lonsdale, my group at Aberystwyth had been invited to exhibit our work on the chemical consequences of imperfections in solids. My enthusiastic young post–doctoral colleague, J.O. Williams (now Professor of Chemistry at UMIST), not recognising the distinguished–looking gentleman exuding gracious curiosity, who had arrived at our display, enquired of Bragg: "How much can I assume that you know about diffraction?" "A little", came the urbane and twinkling reply. Unaccountably, and perhaps uncharacteristically, I resisted the temptation to join in the ensuing discussion. The opportunity never arose again, for a few months later Sir Lawrence had passed away.

Bragg's influence, exerted in multifarious ways by a kind of intellectual osmosis, has been with me ever since I first heard of him on that autumnal Thursday in 1951. Fresh opportunities arose of learning more about his inner thoughts when I took up my duties at the R.I., to the heritage and reputation of which, as others have described in this volume, Bragg made incalculable contributions.

Among the Bragg papers in our Archives are his notes on some of his most important scientific publications. Apart from recording his own assessment of his contributions, they reveal his essential humility and characteristic generosity of spirit. Here are some excerpts.

"The Diffraction of Short Electromagnetic Waves by a Crystal. *Proc. Camb. Phil. Soc.*, XVII(1), 43, 1912.

> This was my first paper, written in Cambridge before I started working with my father. I explained Laue's pictures of the diffraction of X–rays by zincblende, as characteristic of a crystal with a face–centred cubic lattice: it was in fact the first determination of the structure of a crystal by X–rays."

"The Structure of Some Crystals as Indicated by their Diffraction of X–rays. *Proc. Roy. Soc. A.*, **89**, 248, 1913.

> This paper was written after my father had developed the X–ray spectrometer. My determination in Cambridge of the structure of rocksalt was confirmed by the earliest spectrometer results."

"The Analysis of Crystals by the X–ray Spectrometer. *Proc Roy. Soc. A.*, **89**, 468, 1914.

> This, apart from the joint paper on diamond with my father, was the first series of crystal structures to be worked out after the original rocksalt structure."

"The Intensity of Reflexion of X–rays by Rock–salt. (With R.W. James and C.H. Bosanquet.) *Phil. Mag.*, XLI, 309, 1921.

The Intensity of Reflexion of X–rays by Rock–salt, Part II. (With R.W. James and C.H. Bosanquet.) *Phil. Mag.*, XLII, 1, 1921.

The Distribution of Electrons around the Nucleus in the Sodium and Chlorine Atoms. (With R.W. James and C.H. Bosanquet.) *Phil. Mag.*, XLIV, 433, 1922.

> After the War, James, Bosanquet and I set out to get accurate quantitative measurements of X–ray diffraction. These papers represent an exhaustive enquiry into the phenomena from a quantitative point of view."

"The Structure of Argonite. *Proc Roy. Soc. A.*, **105**, 16, 1924.

> I have underlined this paper because it was the first structure of any complexity to be worked out, for which several variable parameters had to be determined."

"The Refractive Indices of Calcite and Argonite. *Proc. Roy. Soc. A.*, **105**, 370, 1924.

The Influence of Atomic Arrangement on Refractive Index. *Proc. Roy. Soc. A.*, **105**, 370, 1924.

These papers broke new ground. Born had produced a very elaborate theoretical treatment of double refraction. In these papers, on the basis of known structures, I calculated the refractive indices of calcite and argonite and some other crystals and obtained results which were in quite good agreement with observation."

"The Structure of Beryl, $Be_3Al_2Si_6O_4$. *Proc Roy. Soc. A.*, **111**, 691, 1926.

This was one of the first silicates to be worked out, a quite complex structure."

"The Structure of Phenacite, $Be_2SiO_4$. *Proc. Roy. Soc. A.*, **113**, 642, 1927.

Phenacite was the first example of the application of our quantitative methods to a quite complex crystal of low symmetry. I remember well that when I published the structure our German colleagues, particularly, thought it was much too daring and speculative, and that one could not possibly work out such a complex structure by X–ray diffraction. The results were however quite sound."

"A Technique for the X–ray Examination of Crystal Structures with Many Parameters. (With J. West.) *Zeit. Für Krist.*, **69**(1/2), 118, 1928.

In this paper West and I summarised the strategy of investigating complex structures by quantitative methods."

"The Structure of Diopside, $CaMg(SiO_3)_2$. (With B. Warren.) *Zeit. Für Krist.*, **69**(1/2), 168, 1928.

The analysis of diopside was a turning point in our ideas about silicate structures. It showed that the "$SiO_3$" which appears in the chemical formula does not represent $SiO_3$ acid groups but a string of $SiO_3$ groups joined by shared oxygen atoms. It was a crucial step in showing that silicon always occurs in a tetrahedral group of oxygen atoms."

"The Determination of Parameters in Crystal Structures by means of Fourier Series. *Proc. Roy. Soc. A.*, **123**, 537, 1929.

This paper should really have been written with my father. He produced a crucial idea about two–dimensional Fourier series; I happened to have all the experimental data which showed how such a series could be used. It was the first paper in which Fourier series were used for parameter determination."

"The Structure of Silicates. *Zeit. Für Krist.*, **69**(3/4), 118, 1928.

In this paper I summed up all we had found out about silicates, the main constutuents in the mineral world."

"The Effect of Thermal Agitation on Atomic Arrangement on Alloys. (With E.J. Willimas.) *Proc Roy. Soc. A.*, **145**, 699, 1934.

The Effect of Thermal Agitation on Atomic Arrangement on Alloys, Part II. (With E.J. Willimas.) *Proc Roy. Soc. A.*, **151**, 874, 540, 1935.

These papers by Williams and myself had a great influence in drawing everyone's attention to the 'order–disorder' phenomenon. They were not as original as we thought when we published them. We discovered afterwards that Johan and Linde and others had put forward similar ideas.

But the papers were put in a very simple way and we had some striking experimental work to support them, and so they caught everyone's attention and stimulated much work on similar phenomena."

"X–ray analysis with the Aid of the 'Fly's Eye'. *Nature*, **156**, 332, 1945.

This, though not a very serious paper, was the start of quite a lot of work on optical methods of solving crystal structure."

"A Dynamical Model of a Crystal Structure. (With J.F. Nye.) *Proc. Roy. Soc. A.*, **190**, 474, 1947.

A Dynamical Model of a Crystal Structure, Part II. (With J.F. Nye.) *Proc. Roy. Soc. A.*, **196**, 171, 1949.

These papers described the 'bubble model'. I found that one could repeat phenomena observed in metals, such as dislocations, slips and faults, by a model of small regular bubbles. Though not deeply scientific, the model caught everyone's fancy and is widely used by metallurgists to illustrate the properties of metals."

"The External Form of the Haemoglobin Molecule. I. (With M.F. Perutz.) *Acta Cryst.*, **5**, 227, 1952.

The External From of the Haemoglobin Molecule. II. (With M.F. Perutz.) *Acta. Cryst.*, **5** 323. 1952.

The Structure of Haemoglobin. (With M.F. Perutz.) *Proc. Roy. Soc. A.*, **213** ,423, 1952.

The Structure of Haemoglobin. VI. Fourier Projections on the 101 Plane. (With M.F. Perutz.) *Proc. Roy. Soc. A.*, **222** ,33, 1954

These papers represent collaboration with Perutz when we were attacking the structure of haemoglobin. The final triumph of working out the positions of the atoms in the vast protein molecules belongs to Perutz and Kendrew, and marked a major breakthrough in science. My part in all this, I think, was to keep them encouraged and help to glean small bits of the solution which kept us all keen until eventually the final answer came out."

As a communicator, Bragg had few equals. Fortunately, his advice to lecturers has been recorded for posterity.[*] A few excerpts merit repetition here. This is what he says on holding the interest of an audience:

"There is a most important principle which I think of as the 'detective story' principle. It as a matter of order. How dull a detective story would be if the writer told you who did it in the first chapter and then gave you all the clues. Yet how many lecturers do exactly this. One wishes to give the audience the aesthetic pleasure of seeing how puzzling phenomena become crystal clear when one has the clues and thinks about them in the right way. So make sure the audience is first puzzled. A friend

[*] Copies of the article "The Legacy of Lawrence Bragg" are available from the Royal Institution. Please write to the Appeals Office, The Royal Institution of Great Britain, 21 Albermarle Street, London, W1X 4BS, for further information.

of mine, a barrister, told me that, when presenting a case to a judge, if he could appear to be fumbling toward a solution and could entice the judge to say 'But, Mr X, isn't the point you are trying to make this or that?' he had as good as won the case. One wants to get the audience into this frame of mind, when they are coaxed to guess for themselves what the answer is. Again I fear I am saying the trite and obvious, but I can assure you I have often sat and groaned at hearing a lecturer murder the most exciting story just by putting things in the wrong order."

And on the first ten minutes we are told:

"A lecture is made or marred in the first ten minutes. This is the time to establish the foundations , to remind the audience of things they half know already, and to define terms which will be used. Again this seems obvious, but I have listened to so much splendid material lost to the audience because the lecturer failed to realize that it did not know what he was talking about, whereas, if the precious first ten minutes had been spent on preparation, he would have carried his listeners with him for the rest of his talk."

"A guiding principle of the popular lecture is that of starting with something with which the audience is thoroughly familiar in everyday life, and leading them further with that as a basis. The survey of the new country must be tied on to fixed points which are already in their minds. This is one of the most difficult tasks facing the popular lecturer. He may be honestly trying to avoid technical language; but it goes further than that. He has to put himself in the place of the intelligent layman and realize that ideas and experiences so familiar to him are unexplored country to his listener. This may seem to be stressing the obvious; but I venture to stress it because I have rather special opportunities to assess the effect of popular scientific talks, and they often pass completely over the heads of the audience because an otherwise excellent talk does not establish an initial *rapport* with the listener's knowledge and experience."

Bragg left a lasting impression on members of staff of the R.I., as others have described elsewhere in this volume (see for example contributions by David Phillips and Ronald King). Three of the present staff, Bill Coates, Bruce Morris and Jean Conisbee, continue to recall with affection their debt to, and their recollections of him. There is one reminiscence of Bragg that I find especially poignant. I am grateful to Max Perutz for drawing it to my attention.

"Although I was 15 when I entered Adelaide University, I think my emotional age was about twelve or less, and my fellow students were mature young men and women. Such a disparity has a cumulative effect. Anyone handicapped in this way is debarred from taking part in the normal activities of his age group, and the very fact that he cannot enter into their plans, schemes, differences of opinion, exercise of authority and so forth, means that he loses the earlier experience which would teach him how to take his part later in life in the world of affairs. He loses touch with what is going on around him and he thinks of the people who guide the course of events as 'they', not as 'we'. He develops a defence mechanism to hide his inexperience from those he meets, and this again makes him shy of asking the questions the answers to which would keep him in touch. He is like a hermit crab with a formidable array of whiskers and claws in front, but with a soft white tail which it has to conceal in a protecting shell."

"How is such a one to face in later life the demands made upon him when his position is one of authority? He is greatly helped and fortunate if he can find a colleague who will act as a 'blind-man's dog' who provides a pair of eyes to guide him through the jostling contacts with other people and across the roaring traffic of current events. He cannot fully see the obstacles and dangers himself. His disability has a compensation in that his very lack of appreciation of what is going on around him gives him a power of internal concentration and enables him to excel in the subjects of his interest. His colleagues, however, seeing his competence in these special lines, expect him to have at least an ordinary competence in the affairs of life, and their disappointment when they realize his failures can be very mortifying to him. I can never be sufficiently grateful to those colleagues who have so often helped and guided me."

*Handicaps of an Infant Prodigy*, W.L. Bragg Autobiography.

# Extracts from W.L.B.'s Publications

In this section, some of W.L.B.'s articles are reproduced in full,
others only partly, yet others in abstract form.

**Editors**

Reprinted from the
*Proceedings of the Cambridge Philosophical Society*, 1912, volume 17, Part I

*The Diffraction of Short Electromagnetic Waves by a Crystal.*
By W. L. BRAGG, B.A., Trinity College. (Communicated by
Professor Sir J. J. Thomson.)

[*Read* 11 November 1912.]

[PLATE II.]

Herren Friedrich, Knipping, and Laue have lately published
a paper entitled 'Interference Phenomena with Röntgen Rays*,'
the experiments which form the subject of the paper being carried
out in the following way. A very narrow pencil of rays from an
X-ray bulb is isolated by a series of lead screens pierced with fine
holes. In the path of this beam is set a small slip of crystal,
and a photographic plate is placed a few centimetres behind the
crystal at right angles to the beam. When the plate is developed,
there appears on it, as well as the intense spot caused by the
undeviated X-rays, a series of fainter spots forming an intricate
geometrical pattern. By moving the photographic plate backwards or forwards it can be seen that these spots are formed by
rectilinear pencils spreading in all directions from the crystal,
some of them making an angle of over 45° with the direction
of the incident radiation.

When the crystal is a specimen of cubical zinc blende, and one
of its three principal cubic axes is set parallel to the incident
beam, the pattern of spots is symmetrical about the two remaining axes. This pattern is shown in Plate II. Laue's
theory of the formation of this pattern is as follows. He considers the molecules of the crystal to form a three-dimensional
grating, each molecule being capable of emitting secondary
vibrations when struck by incident electromagnetic waves from
the X-ray bulb. He places the molecules in the simplest possible
of the three cubical point systems, that is, molecules arranged in
space in a pattern whose element is a little cube of side '$a$,' with
a molecule at each corner. He takes coordinate axes whose
origin is at a point in the crystal and which are parallel to the
sides of the cubes. The incident waves are propagated in a
direction parallel to the $z$ axis, and on account of the narrowness of
the beam the wave surfaces may be taken to be parallel to the $xy$
plane. The spots are considered to be interference maxima of the
waves scattered by the orderly arrangement of molecules in the
crystal. In order to get an interference maximum in the direction

* *Sitzungsberichte der Königlich Bayerischen Akademie der Wissenschaften.*
June 1912.

whose cosines are $\alpha$, $\beta$, $\gamma$, for incident radiation of wave-length $\lambda$, the following equations must be satisfied

$$a\alpha = h_1\lambda, \quad ap = h_2\lambda, \quad a(1-\gamma) = h_3\lambda \ldots\ldots\ldots\ldots(1)$$

where $h_1\ h_2\ h_3$ are integers.

These equations express the condition that the secondary waves of wave-length $\lambda$ from a molecule, considered for simplicity as being at the origin of coordinates, should be in phase with those from its neighbours along the three axes, and that therefore the secondary waves from all the molecules in the crystal must be in phase in the direction whose cosines are $\alpha\ \beta\ \gamma$.

The distance of the crystal from the photographic plate in the experiment was 3·56 cm. The pencil of X-rays on striking the crystal had for cross-section a circle of diameter about a millimetre, and the dimensions of the spots are of the same order. The plate of crystal was only ·5 millimetre thick. It is thus easy to calculate with considerable accuracy from the position of a spot on the photographic plate the direction cosines of the pencil to which it corresponds, since the pencils of rays may be all taken as coming from the centre of the crystal. Laue found, on doing this for each spot, that as a matter of fact the values for $\alpha\ \beta\ 1 - \gamma$ so obtained were in the numerical ratio of three small integers $h_1\ h_2\ h_3$ as they should be by equations (1).

For instance, a spot appears on the photographic plate whose coordinates referred to the $x$ and $y$ axes are

$$x = \cdot28 \text{ cm.}, \quad y = 1\cdot42 \text{ cm.}$$

The distance of the crystal from the photographic plate, 3·56 cm., gives $z$.

Thus since $\qquad \alpha : \beta : \gamma :: x : y : z$

$$\frac{\alpha}{\cdot28} = \frac{\beta}{1\cdot42} = \frac{\gamma}{3\cdot56} = \frac{1}{\sqrt{(\cdot28)^2 + (1\cdot42)^2 + (3\cdot56)^2}} = \frac{1}{3\cdot83}.$$

Thus $\qquad\qquad\qquad \dfrac{\alpha}{\cdot28} = \dfrac{\beta}{1\cdot42} = \dfrac{1-\gamma}{\cdot27},$

or $\qquad\qquad \alpha : \beta : 1 - \gamma :: 1 : 5 : 1.$

Laue considers some thirteen of the most intense spots in the pattern. Owing to the high symmetry of the figure, the whole pattern is a repetition of that part of it contained in an octant. Thus these thirteen represent a very large proportion of all the spots in the figure. For these spots he obtains corresponding integers $h_1\ h_2\ h_3$ which are always small, the greatest being the number 10. But even if one confines oneself to integers less than 10, there are a great many combinations of $h_1\ h_2\ h_3$ which might give spots on the photographic plate which are in fact not there, and there is no obvious difference between the numbers $h_1$ $h_2$ $h_3$ which correspond to actual spots, and those which are not represented.

To explain this Laue assumes that only a few definite wavelengths are present in the incident radiation, and that equations (1) are merely approximately satisfied.

Considering equations (1) it is clear that when $h_1$ $h_2$ $h_3$ are fixed $\dfrac{\lambda}{a}$ can only have one value. However if $h_1$ $h_2$ $h_3$ are multiplied by an integral factor $p$, equations (1) can still be satisfied, but now by a wave-length $\dfrac{\lambda}{p}$. By adjusting the numbers $h_1$ $h_2$ $h_3$ in this way, Laue accounts for all the spots considered by means of five different wave-lengths in the incident radiation. They are

$$\lambda = \cdot 0377a$$
$$\lambda = \cdot 0563a$$
$$\lambda = \cdot 0663a$$
$$\lambda = \cdot 1051a$$
$$\lambda = \cdot 143a.$$

For instance, in the example given above, where it was found that

$$\alpha : \beta : 1 - \gamma :: 1 : 5 : 1$$

these numbers are multiplied by 2, becoming 2.10.2. Then they can be assigned to a wave-length

$$\frac{\lambda}{a} = \cdot 037,$$

approximately equal to the first of those given above.

However, this explanation seems unsatisfactory. Several sets of numbers $h_1$ $h_2$ $h_3$ can be found giving values of $\dfrac{\lambda}{a}$ approximating very closely to the five values above and yet no spot in the figure corresponds to these numbers. I think it is possible to explain the formation of the interference pattern without assuming that the incident radiation consists of merely a small number of wavelengths. The explanation which I propose, on the contrary, assumes the existence of a continuous spectrum over a wide range in the incident radiation, and the action of the crystal as a diffraction grating will be considered from a different point of view which leads to some simplification.

Regard the incident light as being composed of a number of independent pulses, much as Schuster does in his treatment of the action of an ordinary line grating. When a pulse falls on a plane it is reflected. If it falls on a number of particles scattered over a plane which are capable of acting as centres of disturbance when struck by the incident pulse, the secondary waves from them will build up a wave front, exactly as if part of the pulse had been reflected from the plane, as in Huygen's construction for a reflected wave.

The atoms composing the crystal may be arranged in a great many ways in systems of parallel planes, the simplest being the cleavage planes of the crystal. I propose to regard each interference maximum as due to the reflection of the pulses in the incident beam in one of these systems. Consider the crystal as divided up in this way into a set of parallel planes. A minute fraction of the energy of a pulse traversing the crystal will be reflected from each plane in succession, and the corresponding interference maximum will be produced by a train of reflected pulses. The pulses in the train follow each other at intervals of $2d \cos \theta$, where $\theta$ is the angle of incidence of the primary rays on the plane, $d$ is the shortest distance between successive identical planes in the crystal. Considered thus, the crystal actually 'manufactures' light of definite wave-lengths, much as, according to Schuster, a diffraction grating does. The difference in this case lies in the extremely short length of the waves. Each incident pulse produces a train of pulses and this train is resolvable into a series of wave-lengths $\lambda, \frac{\lambda}{2}, \frac{\lambda}{3}, \frac{\lambda}{4}$ etc. where $\lambda = 2d \cos \theta$.

Though to regard the incident radiation as a series of pulses is equivalent to assuming that all wave-lengths are present in its spectrum, it is probable that the energy of the spectrum will be greater for certain wave-lengths than for others. If the curve representing the distribution of energy in the spectrum rises to a maximum for a definite $\lambda$ and falls off on either side, the pulses may be supposed to have a certain average 'breadth' of the order of this wave-length. Thus it is to be expected that the intensity of the spot produced by a train of waves from a set of planes in the crystal will depend on the value of the wave-length, viz. $2d \cos \theta$. When $2d \cos \theta$ is too small the successive pulses in the train are so close that they begin to neutralize each other and when again $2d \cos \theta$ is too large the pulses follow each other at large intervals and the train contains little energy. Thus the intensity of a spot depends on the energy in the spectrum of the incident radiation characteristic of the corresponding wave-length.

Another factor may influence the intensity of the spots. Consider a beam of unit cross-section falling on the crystal. The strength of a pulse reflected from a single plane will depend on the number of atoms in that plane which conspire in reflecting the beam. When two sets of planes are compared which produce trains of equal wave-length it is to be expected that if in one set of planes twice as many atoms reflect the beam as in the other set, the corresponding spot will be more intense. In what follows I have assumed that it is reasonable to compare sets of planes in which the same number of atoms on a plane are traversed by unit cross-section of the incident beam, and it is for this reason that I have chosen the somewhat arbitrary parameters by which the planes will be defined. They lead to an easy comparison of the effective density of atoms in the planes. The effective density is the number of atoms per unit area when the plane with the atoms on it is projected on the $xy$ axis, perpendicular to the incident light.

Laue considers that the molecules of zinc-blende are arranged at the corners of cubes, this being the simplest of the cubical point systems. According to the theory of Pope and Barlow this is not the most probable arrangement. For an assemblage of spheres of equal volume to be in closest packing, in an arrangement exhibiting cubic symmetry, the atoms must be arranged in such a way that the element of the pattern is a cube with an atom at each corner and one at the centre of each cube face. With regard to the crystal of zinc-blende under consideration zinc and sulphur being both divalent have equal valency volumes and their arrangement is probably of this kind. It will be assumed for the present that the zinc and sulphur atoms are identical as regards their power of emitting secondary waves.

Take the origin of coordinates at the centre of any atom, the axes being parallel to the cubical axes of the crystal. The distance between successive atoms of the crystal along the axes is taken for convenience to be $2a$.

All atoms in the $xz$ plane will have coordinates

$$pa \quad o \quad qa$$

where $p$ and $q$ are integers and $p + q$ is even. See fig. 1 in text.

The same holds for atoms in the $yz$ plane. Therefore any reflecting plane may be defined by saying that it passes through the origin, and the centres of atoms

$$pa \quad o \quad qa$$
$$o \quad ra \quad sa$$

For instance, the plane on which the triangle $OAB$ lies passes through the origin and

$$a \quad o \quad 3a$$
$$a \quad o \quad a$$

The planes can now be classified by the corresponding values of $p$, $q$, $r$, $s$ as parameters.

The direction cosines of a plane $p\ q\ r\ s$ will be

$$\frac{rq}{\sqrt{p^2s^2+q^2r^2+p^2r^2}}, \quad \frac{ps}{\sqrt{p^2s^2+q^2r^2+p^2r^2}}, \quad \frac{-pr}{\sqrt{p^2s^2+q^2r^2+p^2r^2}}.$$

If these are called $l\ m\ n$ the direction cosines of the reflected beam are

$$2ln, \quad 2mn, \quad 2n^2-1,$$

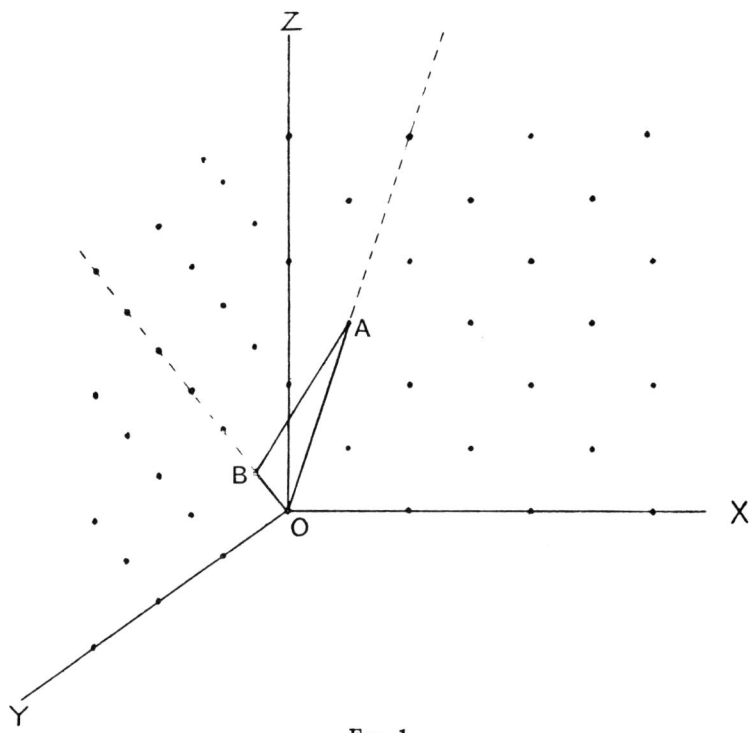

Fig. 1.

and the position of the interference maximum on the photographic plate can be found in terms of these quantities.

The corresponding wave-length is $2d \cos\theta$ where $d$ is the perpendicular distance between successive planes. Now $\theta$ is the angle of incidence, therefore $\cos\theta = n$ above. It is easier to find the intercepts which successive planes cut off on the $z$ axis, than their perpendicular distance apart. Calling these intercepts $l$, then

$$\lambda = 2d \cos\theta = 2 \cdot l \cos\theta \cdot \cos\theta = 2ln^2.$$

Consider the atoms as arranged in vertical rows parallel to the $z$ axis in the figure. A plane for which $p = 1$ and $r = 1$ passes through one atom in every one of these vertical rows (see fig. 3). Therefore the next plane to it passes through a set of atoms all $2a$ above the corresponding atoms in the first plane. Thus for this set of planes, $l = 2a$ and the wave-length $\lambda = 4an^2$. The effective density of atoms on such a set of planes is the greatest possible.

If $p = 1$, $r = 2$, each plane now passes through atoms in one half of the vertical rows. For instance, the plane through the origin contains no atoms in those vertical rows for which $r$ is odd. The successive planes must cut the $z$ axis at intervals $\dfrac{2a}{2}$, since the effective density of atoms in each is half as great as before and the whole number of atoms in unit volume of the crystal remains constant. Similarly if $p = 1$, $r = 3$ $l = \dfrac{2a}{3}$ and so forth.

In the general case $l = \dfrac{2a}{\text{L.C.M. of } p \text{ and } r}$.

In the tables given below planes with the same effective density of atoms on them, and therefore the same values of $l$, are grouped together.

The position of the spot reflected by each system of planes considered has been calculated, also the wave-length of the reflected train expressed for convenience in the form $\dfrac{a}{\lambda}$, and when in the photograph a spot is visible in the position calculated, its intensity is denoted by star according to an arbitrary scale.

✳     ✱     ✲     ✦     •

When no spot appears in the calculated position, I have put 'invisible' opposite that plane.

There is no need to go any further than the set for which $l = \dfrac{2a}{4}$, to obtain all the spots in the photograph. Indeed only one spot is given by this last set.

Only one spot on the plate is to be assigned to planes of this class. It is curious that the value of $\dfrac{a}{\lambda}$ corresponding to this spot should be as great as 11·2. It is noticeable in the photograph that all spots at any distance from the centre of the pattern tend to become very faint, and the values of $p$, $q$, $r$, $s$ which do give a spot in Table IV are the only ones to be found giving a spot at all near the centre. In the first three tables the parameters corresponding to a value of $\frac{a}{\lambda}$ between 6 and 9 are represented by the most intense spots.

Every spot in the photograph is accounted for in the following Tables. I think it is evident that the sets of planes which actually reflect spots can be arranged in a very complete series with few or no gaps. Though at first sight it may appear that in the

TABLE I.

*Planes for which* $p=1$, $r=1$, $l=2a$, $\lambda=4an^2$.

| $p$ | $q$ | $r$ | $s$ | $\dfrac{a}{\lambda}$ | Intensity | $h_1$ | $h_2$ | $h_3$ |
|---|---|---|---|---|---|---|---|---|
| 1 | 1 | 1 | 3 | 2·8 | * | 1 | 3 | 1 |
| 1 | 1 | 1 | 5 | 6·8 | ⁂ | 1 | 5 | 1 |
| 1 | 1 | 1 | 7 | 12·8 | * | 1 | 7 | 1 |
| 1 | 1 | 1 | 9 | 20·8 | Invisible | 1 | 9 | 1 |
| 1 | 3 | 1 | 1 | 2·8 | * | 3 | 1 | 1 |
| 1 | 3 | 1 | 3 | 4·8 | * | 3 | 3 | 1 |
| 1 | 3 | 1 | 5 | 8·8 | ⁂ | 3 | 5 | 1 |
| 1 | 3 | 1 | 7 | 14·8 | + | 3 | 7 | 1 |
| 1 | 3 | 1 | 9 | 22·8 | Invisible | 3 | 9 | 1 |
| 1 | 5 | 1 | 1 | 6·8 | ⁂ | 5 | 1 | 1 |
| 1 | 5 | 1 | 3 | 8·8 | ⁂ | 5 | 3 | 1 |
| 1 | 5 | 1 | 5 | 12·8 | * | 5 | 5 | 1 |
| 1 | 5 | 1 | 7 | 18·8 | Invisible | 5 | 7 | 1 |
| 1 | 7 | 1 | 1 | 12·8 | * | 7 | 1 | 1 |
| 1 | 7 | 1 | 3 | 14·8 | + | 7 | 3 | 1 |
| 1 | 7 | 1 | 5 | 18·8 | Invisible | 7 | 5 | 1 |
| 1 | 9 | 1 | 1 | 20·8 | Invisible | 9 | 1 | 1 |

Range of values of $\dfrac{a}{\lambda}$, all possible up to 15.

tables the parameters are selected in a somewhat arbitrary way, they are in reality the simplest possible. For instance, in Table III the first values for $p$, $q$, $r$, $s$ considered are 1, 1, 3, 5. This is so because '$r+s$' must be positive. If $r=1$, $s$ must be odd.

1, 1, 3, 1 and 1, 1, 3, 3 would reflect the beam so as to miss the photographic plate. 1, 1, 3, 5 and 1, 1, 3, 7 are considered. 1, 1, 3, 9 has already been considered as 1, 1, 1, 3, and 1, 1, 3, 11 gives a value for the wave-length outside the 'visible' range.

In fig. 3, Plate II, is given a photograph of the interference pattern which Laue obtained. In fig. 4, Plate II, the key to the pattern has been drawn, showing in what planes the spots are to be considered as reflected.

## TABLE II.

*Planes for which* L.C.M. *of p and r = 2, l = a,* $\lambda = 2an^2$.

| $p$ | $q$ | $r$ | $s$ | $\dfrac{a}{\lambda}$ | Intensity | $h_1$ | $h_2$ | $h_3$ |
|---|---|---|---|---|---|---|---|---|
| 1 | 1 | 2 | 4 | 3 | • | 2 | 4 | 2 |
| 1 | 1 | 2 | 8 | 9 | * | 2 | 8 | 2 |
| 1 | 1 | 2 | 12 | 19 | Invisible | 2 | 12 | 2 |
| 2 | 4 | 2 | 0 | 2·5 | Invisible | 4 | 0 | 2 |
| 2 | 4 | 2 | 4 | 4·5 | • | 4 | 4 | 2 |
| 2 | 4 | 2 | 8 | 10·5 | • ? | 4 | 8 | 2 |
| 1 | 3 | 2 | 0 | 5 | * | 6 | 0 | 2 |
| 1 | 3 | 2 | 4 | 7 | * | 6 | 4 | 2 |
| 1 | 3 | 2 | 8 | 13 | • ? | 6 | 8 | 2 |
| 2 | 8 | 2 | 0 | 8·5 | • | 8 | 0 | 2 |
| 2 | 8 | 2 | 4 | 10·5 | • ? | 8 | 4 | 2 |
| 1 | 5 | 2 | 0 | 13 | Invisible | 10 | 0 | 2 |

Consider a reflecting plane which passes through the atom at the origin and a neighbouring atom, let us suppose the atom whose coordinates are $a, o, a$. As the plane is turned about the line through these two points the reflected beam traces out a circular cone, which has for axis the line joining the two points and for one of its generators the incident beam. This cone cuts the photographic plate in an ellipse. If the atom through which the plane passes is in the $xz$ plane as above, the ellipse touches the $y$ axis on the photographic plate at the origin. Now take a plane passing through the origin and a point $0, a, 3a$. The

TABLE III.

*Planes for which* L.C.M. *of* $p$ *and* $r = 3$, $l = \dfrac{2a}{3}$, $\lambda = \dfrac{4an^2}{3}$.

| $p$ | $q$ | $r$ | $s$ | $\dfrac{a}{\lambda}$ | Intensity | $h_1$ | $h_2$ | $h_3$ |
|---|---|---|---|---|---|---|---|---|
| 1 | 1 | 3 | 5 | 3·6 | Invisible | 3 | 5 | 3 |
| 1 | 1 | 3 | 7 | 5·6 | • | 3 | 7 | 3 |
| 1 | 1 | 3 | 11 | 11·6 | Invisible | 3 | 11 | 3 |
| 3 | 5 | 3 | 5 | 4·9 | Invisible | 5 | 5 | 3 |
| 3 | 5 | 3 | 7 | 6·9 | * | 5 | 7 | 3 |
| 3 | 5 | 3 | 11 | 12·9 | Invisible | 5 | 11 | 3 |
| 3 | 7 | 3 | 1 | 4·9 | Invisible | 7 | 1 | 3 |
| 3 | 7 | 3 | 5 | 6·9 | * | 7 | 5 | 3 |
| 3 | 7 | 3 | 7 | 8·9 | * | 7 | 7 | 3 |
| 3 | 7 | 3 | 11 | 14·9 | Invisible | 7 | 11 | 3 |
| 1 | 3 | 3 | 1 | 7·6 | * | 9 | 1 | 3 |
| 1 | 3 | 3 | 5 | 9·6 | + | 9 | 5 | 3 |
| 1 | 3 | 3 | 7 | 11·6 | Invisible | 9 | 7 | 3 |

Range of values of $\dfrac{a}{\lambda}$, 5·6 = 9·6.

TABLE IV.

*Planes for which the* L.C.M. *of* $p$ *and* $r = 4$, $l = \dfrac{2a}{4}$,

$$\lambda = \frac{4an^2}{4} = an^2.$$

| $p$ | $q$ | $r$ | $s$ | $\dfrac{a}{\lambda}$ | Intensity | $h_1$ | $h_2$ | $h_3$ |
|---|---|---|---|---|---|---|---|---|
| 1 | 1 | 4 | 10 | 8·2 | Invisible | 4 | 10 | 4 |
| 1 | 1 | 4 | 14 | 16·2 | Invisible | 4 | 14 | 4 |
| 2 | 4 | 4 | 10 | 11·2 | + | 8 | 10 | 4 |
| 1 | 3 | 4 | 6 | 12·2 | Invisible | 12 | 6 | 4 |

locus of the reflected spot as it turns is again an ellipse, which now touches the $x$ axis. The intersections of the two ellipses will give the position of a spot reflected by a plane passing through all three points, the origin, the point $a$, 0, $a$, and the point 0, $a$, $3a$.

The ellipses are drawn in the figure, and the plane corresponding to any spot can be found by noting the ellipses at the intersection of which the spot lies. Only those ellipses have been drawn which give the points in Table I. It will be seen that a very large proportion of the spots in the photograph lie at the intersection of these.

The analysis involved in this way of regarding the interference phenomena must be fundamentally the same as that employed by Laue. In fig. 1, suppose the phase difference between vibrations from successive atoms along the three axes, when waves of wavelength $\lambda$ fall on the crystal, to be $2\pi h_1$, $2\pi h_2$, $2\pi h_3$. Then in order that the vibrations from those atoms, which are arranged in the figure at the centres of the cube faces, should also be in phase, one must have

$$\frac{h_1}{2} - \frac{h_3}{2} = \text{an integer,} \qquad \frac{h_2}{2} - \frac{h_3}{2} = \text{an integer.}$$

This condition is simply expressed by saying that $h_1$, $h_2$, $h_3$ must all be even or all odd integers. When $h_1$, $h_2$, $h_3$ are given, the value of $\lambda$ follows from

$$\frac{\lambda}{2a} = \frac{2h_3}{\sqrt{h_1{}^2 + h_2{}^2 + h_3{}^2}},$$

since here $2a$ has been taken as the distance between neighbouring molecules along the three axes.

If the three simplest values of $h_1$, $h_2$, $h_3$ for a spot on the plate are not all odd, or all even, then these numbers must be doubled to make them even and the wave-length accordingly halved.

When this is done, it can be seen that for each value of $h_3$ there is a series of values of $h_1$ and $h_2$. These numbers all give spots in the photograph if the corresponding value of $\frac{a}{\lambda}$ lies within a certain range. The smaller the number $h_1$, the larger is the range of $\frac{a}{\lambda}$ for which spots are visible. Spots whose $\frac{a}{\lambda}$ lies near the extremity of the range are very faint, those whose $\frac{a}{\lambda}$ is in the middle of the range are intense. In the tables the values of $h_1$, $h_2$, $h_3$ corresponding to each spot are set down.

It is quite probable that the qualitative explanation put forward here to account for the intensities of the spots is not the right one, other explanations being possible. For instance, one might substitute for the factor termed 'effective density' above, one which expressed the fact that, other things being equal, spots nearer the centre of the pattern were more intense than those farther out. This, together with the right curve for the distribution of energy in the spectrum of the incident radiation, could be made to account for the intensities quite reasonably. This does not vitiate the conclusion that the spots in the pattern represent a series which is complete, and characteristic of a cubical crystalline arrangement. The other arrangements of cubical point systems cannot, as far as I can see, give such a complete series. The other possible arrangements have for elements of their pattern (1) a cube with a molecule or atom at each corner, the arrangement which Laue pictured, or (2) a cube with a molecule at each corner and one at the centre. Neither arrangement will fit the system of planes given above. It is only the third point system, the element of whose pattern has a molecule at each corner and one at the centre of each cube face, which will lend itself to the system of planes found to represent spots in the photograph.

This last system, seeing that it forms an arrangement of the closest possible packing, is according to the results of Pope and Barlow the most probable one for the cubic form of zinc sulphide.

In one of the photographs taken by Messrs Friedrich and Knipping the crystal was so oriented that the direction of the incident radiation made equal angles with the three rectangular axes of the crystal. In this case a figure is obtained in which the pattern is a repetition of the spots contained in a sector of angle $\frac{\pi}{6}$. Regarding the spots as reflections of the incident beam in planes as before, these planes can be found almost as easily as those which reflect the spots in the square pattern, and indeed in many cases the planes are identical. I will not give the calculations here, but one point is of especial interest. A photograph was taken of the crystal oriented so that the pattern obtained was perfectly symmetrical. The crystal was then tilted through 3° about a line perpendicular to the incident beam and to one of the cubical axes. This distorted the pattern considerably, but corresponding spots in the two patterns are easily to be recognised. The points which I wish to consider especially are the following.

In the first place, the spots in the distorted pattern are all displaced exactly as would be expected if they were reflections in planes fixed in the crystal. For instance, when the reflecting plane contains the line, about which the crystal was tilted through 3°, it can be ascertained that the movement of the spot corresponds to a deviation of the reflected beam through 6°. This alone is, I think, strong evidence that the wave-length $\lambda$ is elastic, and not confined to a few definite values, and that equations (1) are satisfied rigorously and not merely approximately.

Besides the distortion of the figure due to the tilting of the crystal, a very marked alteration in the intensity of the spots is to be noticed. This is especially marked for those spots which are near the centre of the pattern, but not on or near the axis about which the crystal is tilted. This is probably due to the fact that for these spots a considerable change in wave-length has taken place.

When the angle of incidence $\theta$ of the primary beam on a set of reflecting planes varies, the value of $2d \cos \theta$ is altered and the alteration for the same $\delta\theta$ is greater the greater $\theta$ is.

One spot in particular changes from being hardly visible in the symmetrical pattern to being by far the most intense when the crystal is tilted. It is the spot reflected in a plane passing through the origin and

$$3a, \ 0, \ a; \quad 0, \ 3a, \ a.$$

Planes parallel to this have for $d$, the shortest distance between successive planes, the value $\dfrac{4a}{\sqrt{11}}$. It can easily be calculated from the position of the spot that the value of $\cos \theta$ changes from ·19 to ·12 when the crystal is tilted. This corresponds to a change in the value of $\dfrac{a}{\lambda}$ from 4·3 to 6·5, and it was found before for the square pattern that spots corresponding to the former wave-lengths were weak, those corresponding to the latter intense.

A curious feature of the photographs may be explained by regarding the spots as formed by reflection. As the distance of the photographic plate from the crystal is altered, the shape of each individual spot varies. At first round, they become more and more elliptical as the plate is moved further away. A reason for this is found in the following. If the incident beam is not perfectly parallel, but slightly conical, rays will strike the crystal at slightly different angles. Regard the crystal as a set of reflecting planes perpendicular to the plane of the paper (fig. 2). The rays striking the reflecting planes on the upper part of the crystal on the whole meet them at a less angle of incidence than those striking the planes at the bottom; the latter are deflected more, and the rays tend on reflection to come to a focus in a horizontal line. On the other hand, rays deviating from the axial direction in a horizontal plane diverge still more after reflection. Thus as the plate is removed from the crystal, the spots up to a certain distance become more and more elliptical.

The atoms of a crystal may be arranged in 'doubly infinite' series of parallel rows, as well as in 'singly infinite' series of planes. The incident pulse falls on atom after atom in one of these rows, if the row is not parallel to the wave front, and secondary waves are emitted, one from each atom, at definite time intervals. Along any direction lying on a certain circular cone with the row of atoms as axis, these secondary waves will be all in phase, one generator of the cone being, of course, parallel to the direction of the incident radiation. If the row of atoms makes a small angle with the direction, this cone with vertex at the crystal slip may now be considered to cut the photographic plate in an almost circular ellipse passing through the big central

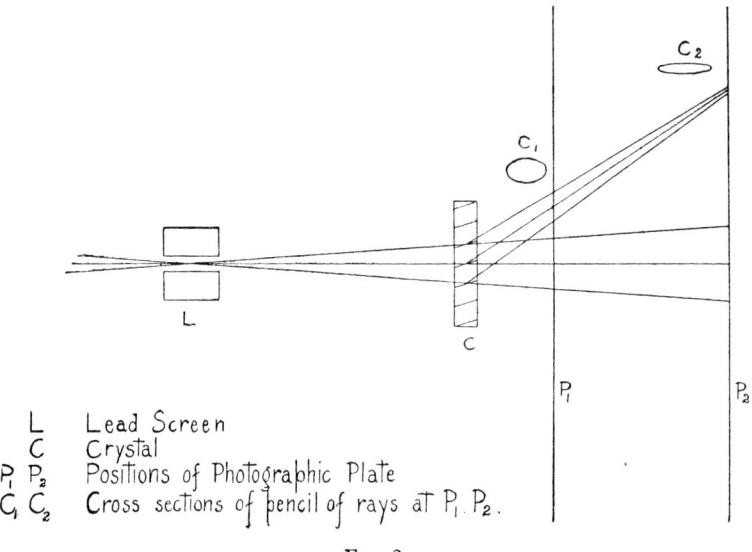

L      Lead Screen
C      Crystal
$P_1$  $P_2$    Positions of Photographic Plate
$C_1$  $C_2$    Cross sections of pencil of rays at $P_1$ $P_2$.

Fɪɢ. 2.

spot. Drawing the ellipses which correspond to the most densely packed rows of the crystal, a spot is to be expected at the intersection of two ellipses, for this means that pulses from a doubly infinite set of atoms are in that direction in agreement of phase. Thus it ought to be possible to arrange the spots in the photograph on these ellipses, in whatever way the crystal is oriented, and indeed they appear in all cases. They come out very strongly in the photographs taken with copper sulphate crystals.

So far it has been assumed that the atoms of zinc and sulphur act in an identical manner with regard to the production of secondary waves, but this assumption is not necessary. What is brought

Phil. Soc. Proc. Vol. XVII. Pt. I. Plate II.

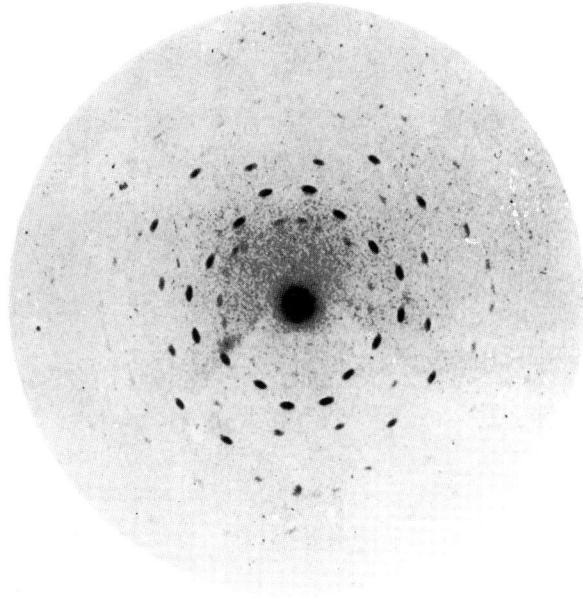

Fig. 3.

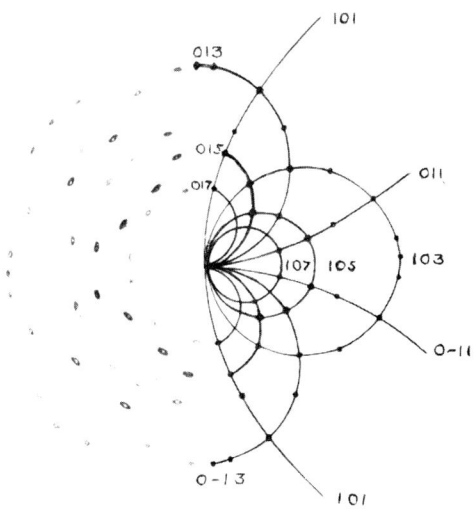

Fig. 4.

out so strongly by the analysis is this; that the point system to be considered has for element of its pattern a point at each corner of the cube and one at the centre of each cube face.    In the arrangement assigned to cubical zinc sulphide and similar crystals by Pope and Barlow, this point system is characteristic of both the arrangement of the individual atoms regarded as equal spheres, and of the arrangement of atoms which are in every way identical as regards nature, orientation, and neighbours in the pattern.  The atoms of zinc, for instance, in the zinc blende are grouped four together tetrahedron-wise, and as these little tetrahedra are all similarly oriented and are arranged themselves in the above point system, atoms of zinc identical in all respects will again be arranged in this point system.   Which of these factors it is that decides the form of the interference pattern might be found by experiments with crystals in which the point system formed by the centres of all the atoms differs from that formed by the centres of identical atoms.

In conclusion, I wish to thank Professor Pope for his kind help and advice on the subject of crystal structure.

Reprinted from *Nature*, 1912, volume 90, page 410

### The Specular Reflection of X-rays.

It has been shown by Herr Laue and his colleagues that the diffraction patterns which they obtain with X-rays and crystals are naturally explained by assuming the existence of very short electromagnetic waves in the radiations from an X-ray bulb, the wave length of which is of the order $10^{-9}$ cm. The spots of the pattern represent interference maxima of waves diffracted by the regularly arranged atoms of the crystal. Now, if this is so, these waves ought to be regularly reflected by a surface which has a sufficiently good polish, the irregularities being small compared with the length $10^{-9}$ cm. Such surfaces are provided by the cleavage planes of a crystal, which represent an arrangement of the atoms of the crystal in parallel planes, and the amount by which the centres of atoms are displaced from their proper planes is presumably small compared with atomic dimensions.

In accordance with this, the spots in Laue's crystallographs can be shown to be due to partial reflection of the incident beam in sets of parallel planes in the crystal on which the atom centres may be arranged, the simplest of which are the actual cleavage planes of the crystal. This is merely another way of looking at the diffraction. This being so, it was suggested to me by Mr. C. T. R. Wilson that crystals with very distinct cleavage planes, such as mica, might possibly show strong specular reflection of the rays. On trying the experiment it was found that this was so. A narrow pencil of X-rays, obtained by means of a series of stops, was allowed to fall at an angle of incidence of $80°$ on a slip of mica about one millimetre thick mounted on thin aluminium. A photographic plate set behind the mica slip showed, when developed, a well-marked reflected spot, as well as one formed by the incident rays traversing the mica and aluminium.

Variation of the angle of incidence and of the distance of plate from mica left no doubt that the laws of reflection were obeyed. Only a few minutes' exposure to a small X-ray bulb sufficed to show the effect, whereas Friedrich and Knipping found it necessary to give an exposure of many hours to the plate, using a large water-cooled bulb, in order to obtain the transmitted interference pattern. By bending the mica into an arc, the reflected rays can be brought to a line focus.

In all cases the photographic plate was shielded by a double envelope of black paper, and in one case with aluminium one millimetre thick. This last cut off the reflected rays considerably. Slips of mica one-tenth of a millimetre thick give as strong a reflection as an infinite thickness, yet the effect is almost certainly not a surface one. Experiments are being made to find the critical thickness of mica at which the reflecting power begins to diminish as thinner plates are used. The reflection is much stronger as glancing incidence is approached.                    W. L. Bragg.

The Cavendish Laboratory, Cambridge,
                      December 8.

Reprinted from
*Proceedings of Royal Society, A*, 1913, volume 89, pages 248-260

# The Structure of Some Crystals as Indicated by their Diffraction of X-rays.

### By W. L. BRAGG, B.A.

(Communicated by Prof. W. H. Bragg, F.R.S.   Received June 21,—Read
June 26, 1913.)

[PLATE 10.]

A new method of investigating the structure of a crystal has been afforded by the work of Laue* and his collaborators on the diffraction of X-rays by crystals.   The phenomena which they were the first to investigate, and which have since been observed by many others, lend themselves readily to the explanation proposed by Laue, who supposed that electromagnetic waves of very short wave-lengths were diffracted by a set of small obstacles arranged on a regular point system in space.   In analysing the interference pattern obtained with a zincblende crystal, Laue, in his original memoir, came to the conclusion that the primary radiation possessed a spectrum consisting of narrow bands', in fact, that it was composed of a series of six or seven approximately homogeneous wave trains.

In a recent paper† I tried to show that the need for assuming this complexity was avoided by the adoption of a point system for the cubic crystal of zincblende which differed from the system considered by Laue.   I supposed the diffracting centres to be arranged in a simple cubic space lattice, the element of the pattern being a cube with a point at each corner, and one at the centre of each cube face.   A simpler conception of the radiation then became possible.   It might be looked on as continuous over a wide range of wave-lengths, or as a series of independent pulses, and there was no longer any need to assume the existence of lines or narrow bands in its spectrum.

---

* W. Friedrich, P. Knipping, and M. Laue, 'Münch. Ber.,' June, 1912.
† 'Camb. Phil. Soc. Proc.,' November, 1912.

It is the object of this paper to extend the analysis used in the case of the zincblende to some other crystals, particularly those of the simple alkaline halides.

In treating the diffraction of waves by a space point system such as a crystal, that case is the most simple in which the diffraction is caused by a series of points arranged in a space lattice, of one of the 14 Bravais types. Here every point is identical with every other point of the arrangement, and it is always possible to find an element of the pattern consisting of a parallelepiped with a point at each corner : there will then be as many parallelepipeds as atoms in any space. The points can be referred to three axes parallel to the edges of the parallelepiped, and if one of the points is taken as the origin the co-ordinates of the others may be written

$$x = \pm pa, \qquad y = \pm qb, \qquad z = \pm rc,$$

where $p$, $q$, $r$ are any integers, and $a$, $b$, $c$ are equal to the sides of the parallelepiped, and therefore proportional to the axial ratios of the space lattice. When the axes are chosen in this way the co-ordinates of the points and the equations of the planes passing through given selections of points are expressed in the simplest manner possible.

Let a series of pulses fall on this space lattice, the direction of propagation having a given relation to the axes of the system. As any one pulse passes over each point, a diffracted wavelet spreads from it, and it will be shown that the wavelets from all the points due to one incident pulse will combine in certain directions to form trains of waves, which give rise to the patterns of spots appearing in Laue's diffraction patterns. This may be done in the following way :—

If the axial ratios of the space lattice be denoted by $a$, $b$, $c$, any plane which makes intercepts $pa$, $qb$, $rc$, on the axis ($p$, $q$, $r$ being any integers) is parallel to a whole set of planes on which the points of the system may be considered as arranged. It is such planes as these which form the faces of a crystal. When a pulse falls on a set of points on a plane the wavelets from the points combine to build up a wave front which will appear to be regularly reflected from the plane. As there are a series of planes regularly spaced one behind the other, a single pulse falling on them gives rise to a reflected wave train.

When therefore a narrow pencil of X-rays falls on a section of a crystal, part of its energy is transmitted undeviated, but there is also a part which is reflected on the crystal planes existing potentially in the body of the crystal. It is the series of narrow beams arising by reflection in this way which gives rise to the pattern of spots appearing in the photograph.

x 2

There can be assigned to each set of parallel planes integral indices $(h, k, l)$, as when naming the faces of a crystal, and a spot can be classified as being reflected in the $(h, k, l)$ set of planes. Here the integers $h, k, l$, are reciprocal to the intercepts which a parallel plane makes on the axis of reference. They are Millerian indices, the equation of the plane being

$$h\frac{x}{a} + k\frac{y}{b} + l\frac{z}{c} = \text{an integer.}$$

They may be considered as the parameters of each spot of the pattern, and are exactly equivalent to the parameters $(h_1, h_2, h_3)$ employed by Laue in his original treatment of the subject. Laue defines his parameters by saying that the diffracted wavelet from a point at the origin of co-ordinates lags $h_1, h_2, h_3$, wave-lengths in the directions under consideration behind the wavelets proceeding from its neighbours along the $x, y, z$ axes respectively. Thus the wavelets from all atoms in the plane

$$h_1\frac{x}{a} + h_2\frac{y}{b} + h_3\frac{z}{c} = 0$$

are in phase with that from the origin, and, in general, the wavelets from all points in the plane

$$h_1\frac{x}{a} + h_2\frac{y}{b} + h_3\frac{z}{c} = \text{an integer}$$

are in the same phase. We are led back to the same conclusion as before, that the direction of the diffracted wave front is one in which the primary beam is reflected by planes whose Millerian indices are $(h_1, h_2, h_3)$. But, as will appear presently, it is important to bear in mind the fact that crystal structure alone fixes the exact position of the interference maxima, quite independently of the existence of homogeneous components of definite wavelength in the incident rays, and therefore a method of treatment has been adopted in which all reference to the wave-length has been avoided.

It is possible for a spot to appear in a position corresponding to reflection in any set of planes having integral indices $(h, k, l)$. In an actual pattern obtained by allowing the diffracted X-rays to fall on a photographic plate, since there is not an infinite number of spots, only a selection of the planes can be operative. The spots forming the pattern are of very different intensities, and one can never say that spots are entirely absent but merely that in certain cases the rays are too weak to make an impression. It would seem, however, that by classification of the planes which reflect the principal spots of the pattern a clue can be got to the true point system arrangement of the diffracting centres. The point system which affords the most simple interpretation of the pattern is that which ought to be taken as representing the crystal structure.

When a photograph has been taken with a crystal an analysis is necessary in order to assign to each spot of the pattern obtained the correct parameters $h$, $k$, $l$, the Millerian indices of the face from which the spot is reflected. Having decided on the axes of reference of the crystal, the following method will be found to apply whatever their inclinations to each other and axial ratios may be.

The more important planes of the system are those densely packed with points, and from this fact it follows that these planes contain rows along which the points are closely packed. These are the important "point-rows" of the crystal, and each of these point-rows will have a set of important planes parallel to it. The three axes themselves are the most obvious examples of these point-rows. The "zone axis" of planes belonging to a common zone is also such a direction. There is a convenient relation between the points which are reflected in the planes belonging to any one zone. The reflected beam always lies on a circular cone with apex at the crystal section, the zone axis as axis, and the direction of the primary beam as one generator. This cone cuts the photographic plate in an ellipse passing through the central point of the pattern, and all spots reflected in planes of the zone lie on it. The arrangement of the spots on ellipses is very obvious in an interference pattern (see fig. 11), and the ellipses can immediately be drawn. A little calculation shows to which zone axis each ellipse must be assigned, and, by marking a given spot as lying on the intersection of two ellipses, the calculation of the indices $h$, $k$, $l$, of that spot is made possible. For each zone of planes we have the relation $h\mathrm{U} + k\mathrm{V} + l\mathrm{W} = 0$ where $(\mathrm{U}, \mathrm{V}, \mathrm{W})$ is the zone symbol; that is to say, the set of direction ratios of the zone axis.

When representing diagrammatically an interference pattern it is very inconvenient to draw the ellipses at the intersections of which the spots of the pattern lie. It is simpler to employ an extension of the usual stereographic projection of crystallography. Reference to fig. 1 will make this clear. Let the section of crystal be situated at C, the centre of the sphere represented in the figure by the circle ABP, and let the direction of the incident rays be from P to C. The rays which traverse the crystal undeviated fall on the photographic plate AD at A. Let CZ represent the direction of a zone axis. The beams reflected in planes of this zone lie on a circular cone with vertex at C, of which CZ is the axis, and CA, CB are two generators.

This cone cuts the sphere in a circle of which AB is a diameter, and by the well known property of the stereographic projection, the projection of this circle on the plane AD from the pole P is also a circle. The centre of this circle is at Z, since $AZ = ZS'$, Z being the point where the zone axis cuts the photographic plate.

Let the pattern of spots be supposed to be made by the diffracted beams on the sphere ABP, and this pattern projected on the plane AD from the pole P. Spots corresponding to reflection in planes of a zone now lie on a circle, having its centre at the point where the zone axis cuts the plate AD. The spot at S made by the reflected beam CB becomes a spot at S′ of the

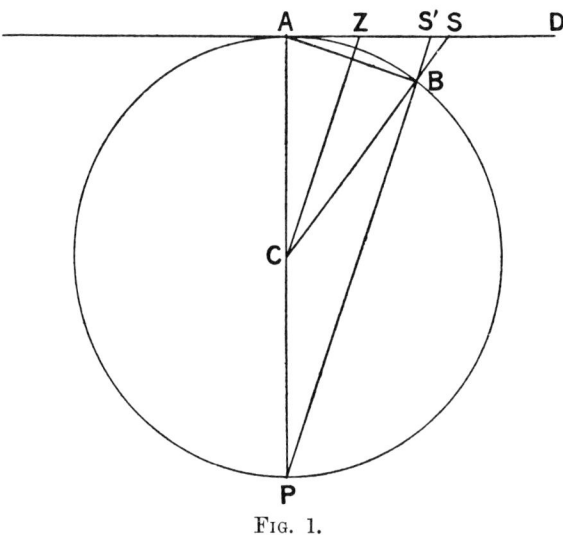

Fig. 1.

transformed pattern. The distortion of the pattern of spots by the transformation is very small except in the regions distant from the centre, and circles are much easier to draw than ellipses. This has been done in all the diagrams given in this paper. In constructing a diagram, a point is chosen as that in which the incident rays meet the photographic plate. This is A in the figure. Then the points such as Z, where the principal zone axes meet the plate, are found by a calculation, which is easy when the crystal is placed symmetrically to the pencil of X-rays. A circle is drawn with centre Z and radius ZA. This being done for each zone axis, the intersections of the circles give the stereographic projections of the reflected spots.

Let us take as an example of the application of this analysis the very simple case of potassium chloride. The diffraction pattern obtained when the X-rays fall normally on a plate cut parallel to the cube face (001) is reproduced in fig. 2, Plate 10, and its stereographic projection in fig. 3, which shows also the indices of the reflecting planes corresponding to the several points of the photograph.

Potassium chloride is cubic, and the indices given to the planes are those obtained when the edges of the cube are selected as axes of reference.

The circles correspond to zone axes for which

$$U = 0, \quad V = \pm 1 \atop U = \pm 1 \quad V = 0 \Big\} W = 0, 1, 2, 3, 4, 5,$$

and their intersections give the spots reflected in all planes of the form $(h\,k\,1)$ where $h$ and $k$ have any of the values

$$0, \ \pm 1, \ \pm 2, \ \pm 3, \ \pm 4, \ \pm 5.$$

In the diagram of the KCl pattern the spots are represented by dots, the magnitude of each dot indicating the strength of the corresponding spot in the

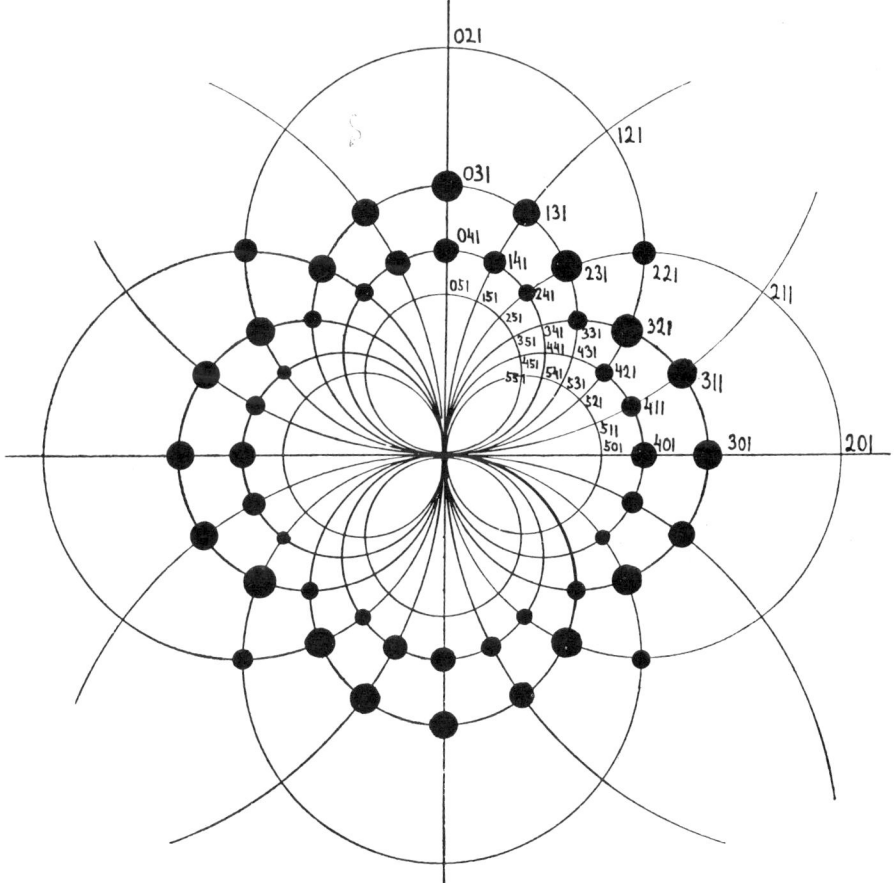

Fig. 3.—Potassium chloride.

photograph. It will be seen how complete the pattern is, and how within a certain range each intersection is represented by a spot in the photograph.

This may be put in another way. Below is a table of values of $h$ and $k$, $l$ being equal to 1. In the square corresponding to given values of $h$ and $k$

is placed a dot denoting the magnitude of the corresponding spot, the square being left empty if no spot is to be seen.

Table I.

KCl.

$h \longrightarrow$

| $k$ | 0 | 1 | 2 | 3 | 4 | 5 |
|---|---|---|---|---|---|---|
| 0 | | | | ✳ | ✳ | |
| 1 | | | | ✳ | ✳ | |
| 2 | | | ✳ | ✳ | + | |
| 3 | ✳ | ✳ | ✳ | + | | |
| 4 | ✳ | ✳ | + | | | |
| 5 | | | | | | |

This table contains a list of all the spots appearing in the photograph. It suggests that the diffraction is due to a simple cubic space lattice, for when the elementary parallelepiped is a cube and its edges are taken as axes the indices of the planes naturally take these simple forms.

For, let a series of planes be taken, for which two indices are constant and one varies, such as the series $031, 131, 231, 331, 431$, etc. These planes will be arranged in this order for all their properties, such as reticular density, distance apart, and so forth, if, and only if, the indices are referred to axes parallel to the sides of the elementary parallelepiped. If this condition is satisfied, then all the properties of the planes vary in an orderly manner as one passes along the series. The power of reflecting the X-rays is a particular property of the planes, which is seen from the photograph to vary continuously for any such series as the one given above, therefore the diffracting system is a space lattice with axes at right angles, and a cube for its elementary parallelepiped.

It may be objected here, that it is conceivable that a complex structure, and a radiation consisting of homogeneous components, just happen in the case of potassium chloride to give a deceptively simple pattern. That this is not the case can be seen by displacing the crystal from its symmetrical position, and obtaining the distorted interference pattern. It is still as straightforward as before, though of course no longer symmetrical. Corresponding spots in the two patterns are now made by different wave-lengths, and it is obvious that there can be nothing of the nature of homogeneous components of the incident radiation. The contrast of this pattern with those characteristic of potassium bromide and iodide, of rock salt, and of zincblende, which will shortly be given, will tend to make this more clear.

All the most intense spots of the photograph are at about the same distance from the centre of the pattern. A circle can be drawn such that the spots which lie near to it are very intense, while those further away are weaker and those at great distances are too faint to appear. All ellipse intersections lying near this circle are represented by a spot. Those planes reflect most strongly for which the glancing angle lies between 12° and 20° and it is in seeking to explain this fact that it is necessary to consider the question of the " wave-length " of the diffracted rays. This we must now do.

When a pulse falls on a series of planes regularly spaced one behind the other, it is reflected as a wave train, and the waves making any one spot must be considered to be of the lengths given by

$$n\lambda = 2d\sin\theta,$$

where $\theta$ = glancing angle, $d$ = distance between successive planes, and $n$ is an integer 1, 2, 3, etc. An alternative way of regarding the phenomenon is to consider the incident radiations as compounded of homogeneous wave trains of all wave-lengths, with a characteristic distribution of energy in the spectrum, when the parallel planes must be considered as reflecting only that part of the spectrum for which the relation $n\lambda = 2d\sin\theta$ holds good. In the case of the cubic space lattice considered here, this relation reduces to

$$n\lambda = \frac{2a}{l}\sin^2\theta,$$

where $a$ is the distance between neighbouring points along the cubic axes, for a simple calculation shows that $d = a\sin\theta/l$. Since $l$ is equal to unity for all the spots of the potassium chloride photograph, spots which have the same $\theta$, and lie at the same distance from the centre of the pattern, correspond to the same wave-length. The ring of intense spots in the pattern indicates strong reflection of a certain part of the spectrum of the incident radiation. Either conditions are especially good[*] for reflecting this wave-length, or the incident rays have a large amount of their energy in this part of the spectrum.

It is interesting to compare the simple pattern of potassium chloride with those of potassium iodide, potassium bromide, fluorspar, and zincblende.

The stereographic projection of KBr (100) is given in fig. 4, that of KI being very similar. Both of these are like the patterns of zincblende and fluorspar, and are in marked contrast to that of KCl.

---

[*] The most important condition in this connection is probably the thickness of the crystal section used. As will be shown later, the use of a thin crystal section favours the reflection of the longer wave-lengths, the corresponding spots coming out strongly, while the use of a thick section favours the reflection of the shorter.

It is evident that some factor has now entered which destroys the simplicity of the arrangement of spots characteristic of potassium chloride. Spots no longer appear at every intersection of the ellipses within a certain region, as

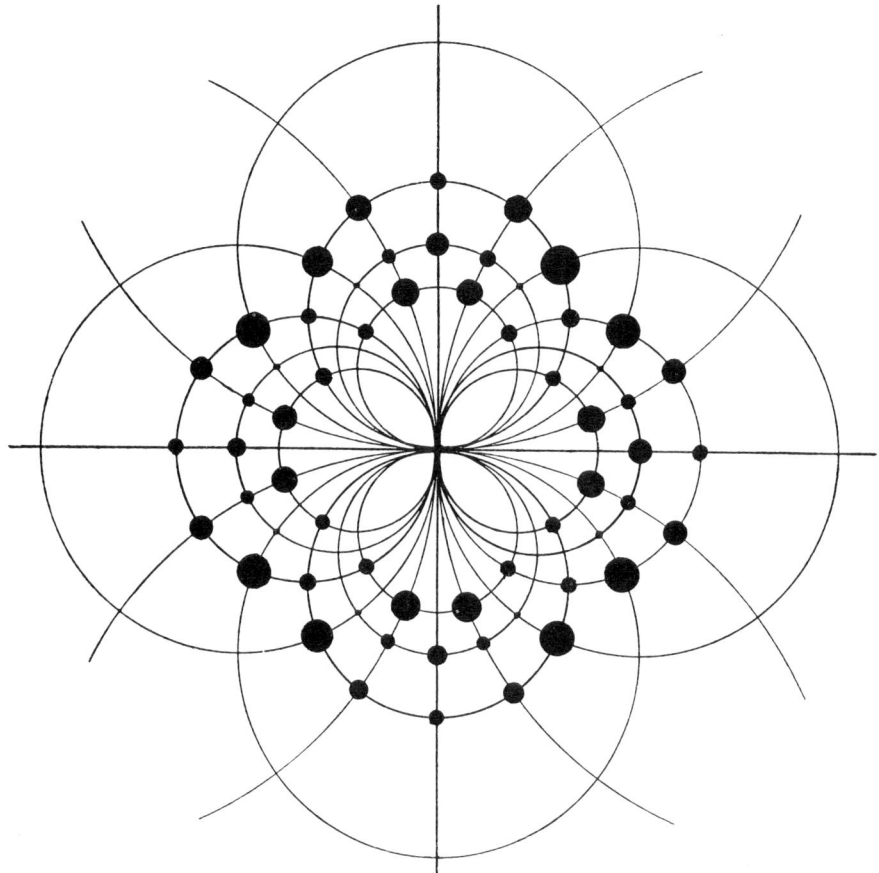

Fig. 4.—Potassium bromide.

in fig. 3. A tabulation of the intensities of the spots in the zincblende and potassium bromide patterns will make this clear. (See Tables II and III.)

There are also in the case of zincblende several spots for which a value 3 must be assigned to $l$, if $h$ and $k$ are to be integers, but not many. It was a consideration of Table II which led in a former paper* to the conclusion that the diffracting centres of the zincblende crystal are arranged on the face-centred cubic space lattice.

An examination of the planes in which reflection takes place shows that there is a differentiation between those whose indices are wholly odd and

* 'Camb. Phil. Soc. Proc.,' November, 1912.

Table II.

Zn.S.

h →

| k | 0 | 1 | 2 | 3 | 4 | 5 | 6 | 7 |
|---|---|---|---|---|---|---|---|---|
| 0 |   |   |   | + |   |   |   |   |
| 1 |   |   | • | + | ✳ | ✳ |   | + |
| 2 |   | • | • | ✳ | + |   |   |   |
| 3 | + | + | ✳ | + | + | ✳ |   | + |
| 4 |   | ✳ | + | + |   |   |   |   |
| 5 |   | ✳ |   | ✳ |   | + |   |   |
| 6 |   |   |   |   |   |   |   |   |
| 7 |   | + |   | + |   |   |   |   |

Table III.

K.Br.

h →

| k | 0 | 1 | 2 | 3 | 4 | 5 |
|---|---|---|---|---|---|---|
| 0 |   |   |   | + | ✳ |   |
| 1 |   |   | ✳ | + | ✳ |   |
| 2 |   |   | ✳ |   |   |   |
| 3 | + | ✳ | ✳ | + |   | ✳ |
| 4 | ✳ | + |   |   |   |   |
| 5 |   | ✳ |   | ✳ |   |   |
| 6 |   |   |   |   |   |   |
| 7 |   |   |   |   |   |   |

those which have one or more even indices. If those planes alone are considered which have odd indices, as in the following table, the scheme is as complete as it was for the spots of the KCl crystal.

Table IV.

Zn.S.(odd indices only)

h →

| k | 1 | 3 | 5 | 7 | 9 |
|---|---|---|---|---|---|
| 1 |   | + | ✳ | + |   |
| 3 | + | ✳ | ✳ | • |   |
| 5 | ✳ | ✳ | + |   |   |
| 7 | + | • |   |   |   |
| 9 |   |   |   |   |   |

Odd planes, ZnS.

Table V.

Zn.S. (even indices) only

h →

| k | 0 | 1 | 2 | 3 | 4 | 5 |
|---|---|---|---|---|---|---|
| 0 |   |   | + |   |   |   |
| 1 |   | • |   | ✳ |   |   |
| 2 |   | • | + | ✳ | • |   |
| 3 | + |   | ✳ |   | • |   |
| 4 |   | ✳ | • | • |   |   |
| 5 |   |   |   |   |   |   |

Even planes, ZnS.

The same is true for those with an even index* except that the intense spots are all further removed from the centre of the picture.

This difference can be explained without our being forced to assume that the diffracting system is anything more than a simple system of identical points. It is sufficient to suppose that the point system has points at the centres of the cube faces as well as at the cube corners. Let a cubic point system of the first kind be taken which has points at cube corners alone, and let points be introduced at the cube face centres in order to turn it into a

* The spot 041 forms an exception, indeed evidence is not lacking that the assumption of diffraction by the face-centred space lattice does not completely account for the pattern. The reason for this will appear when the parts played by the atoms of two kinds in the diffraction are discussed.

point system of the so-called " third kind." (The " second kind " is the centred cube.) The spacing of the planes which have odd indices ($h$, $k$, $l$) is not altered by the introduction of the new points, for they all lie on the original planes and only increase their point density. On the other hand, in the case of planes having an even index, some of the new points lie half-way between the original planes, the distance between the successive planes of this type must now be halved, and so must therefore the wave-lengths of the reflected beams.

The interpretation of the zincblende pattern is now simple. We have seen that the planes with odd indices only are a complete set. There are fewer spots corresponding to reflection in planes with an even index, for these planes are, relatively to the former, less closely packed, and of a more complex nature. Moreover, they are, at the same time, less widely separated, and therefore the intense spots with even indices are further from the centre; the angle of incidence must be increased in order to make these planes reflect that region of the spectrum which gives intense spots. By assuming the third cubic space lattice instead of the first, all the intense spots of the pattern again correspond to the same wave-length region.

The difference between the diffraction by the two cubic space lattices may be put in a much clearer way on analysis of the patterns of threefold symmetry, obtained when the incident rays fall normally on a plate cut perpendicular to a trigonal axis. If the points of the space lattices are con-sidered from this aspect, they are special cases of the trigonal rhombohedral space lattice, one of the Bravais types.

The axes to which the spots ought to be referred are not the same for the two cubic lattices. When the points are at cube corners alone, the axes along which they are nearest neighbours are the cube edges, and the cube itself is the elementary parallelepiped. When there are also points at the centres of the cube faces, three semi-diagonals of cube faces meeting in a corner form three edges of the elementary parallelepiped. The angles between the axes are right angles in the first case, in the second they are 60°.

It will now be clear that when the stereographic diagram is constructed, giving the positions of the spots reflected from the simple planes of a trigonal rhombohedral space lattice, one such diagram will represent the patterns of all rhombohedral lattices, the alteration of the angle between the axes, *i.e.*, the rhombohedral angle, only causing an alteration of the scale of the diagram. The radius of the sphere used in the projection is, of course, supposed to be always the same.

Given the points where the three axes of the lattice meet the diagram, the corresponding points for the other zone axes can immediately be found and the whole diagram drawn. Such a diagram is shown in fig. 5, X, Y, Z, being these axial points. Now, our study of the patterns of fourfold symmetry given by potassium chloride and zincblende has shown that the axes of the

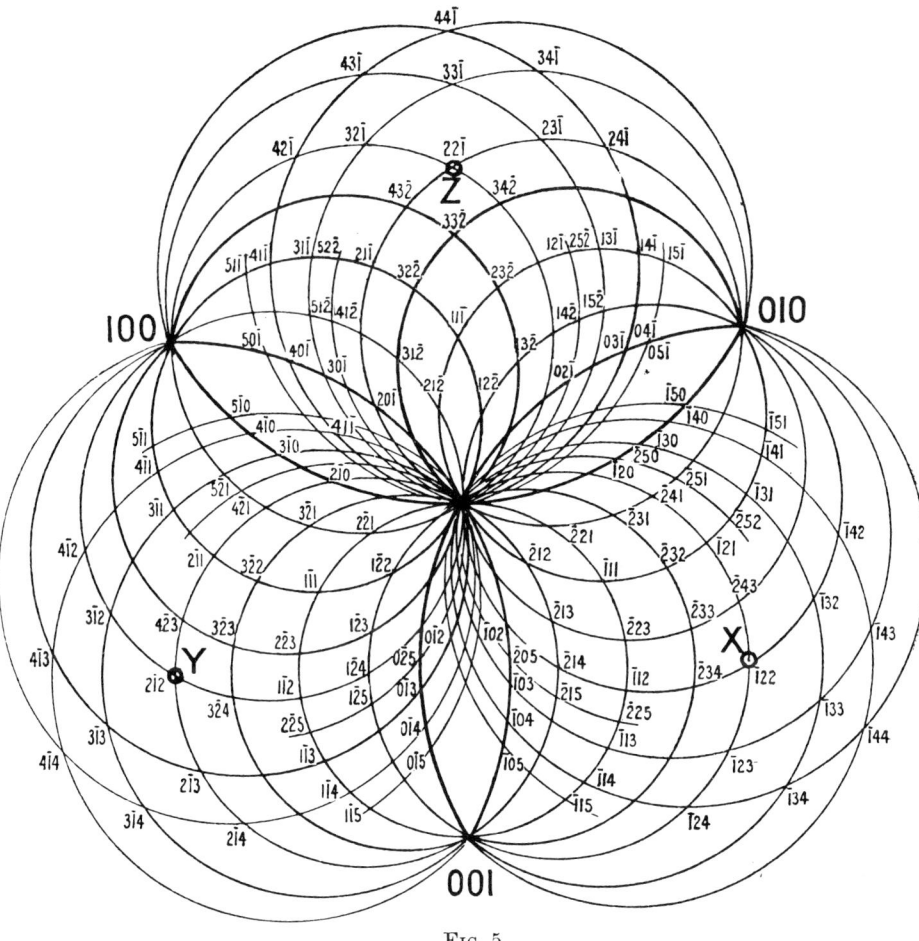

FIG. 5.

lattice, which is from this aspect a special case of the rhombohedral lattice, make angles of 90° with each other in the first case, and of 60° in the second. Therefore it ought to be possible to refer the threefold patterns of potassium chloride and zincblende to the same trigonal lattice diagram, the scale being different, however, in the two cases. This conclusion is exactly confirmed by experiment. The pattern given by zincblende was published by Laue in his original memoir. The stereographic projections of the zincblende and potassium chloride patterns are given in figs. 6 and 7. The object of this comparison is to show that the spots of the KCl pattern fall naturally on a diagram twice the size of that on which the spots of the ZnS pattern are arranged, the points where the axes making 90° with each other cut the plate, being just twice as far apart as for axes making 60° with each other.

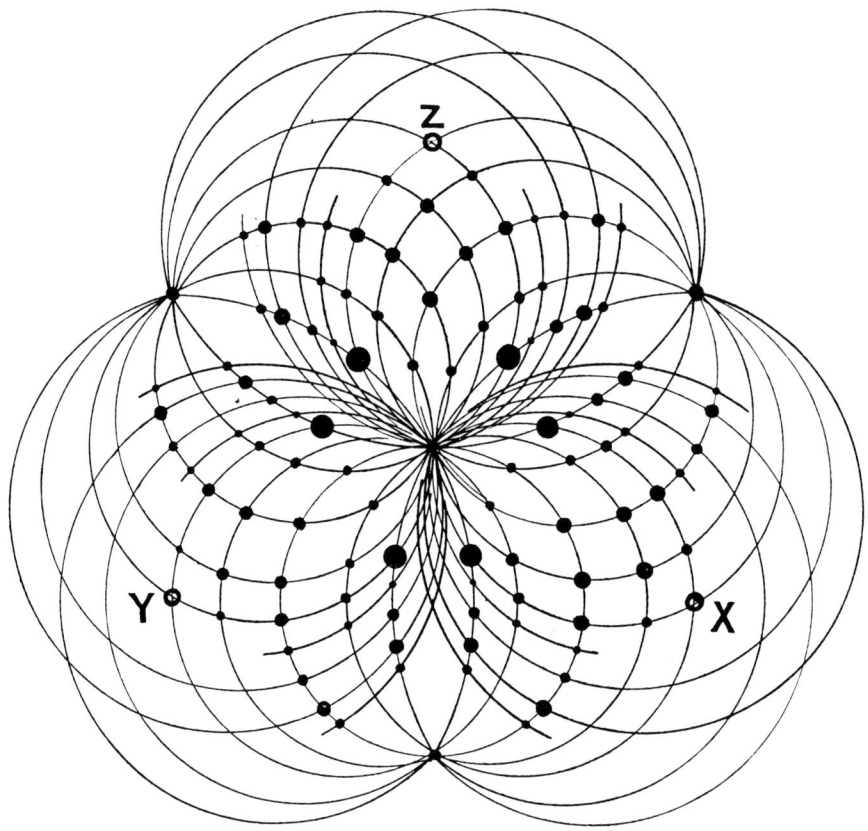

FIG. 6.—Zincblende.

The following table will illustrate the awkwardness of referring either pattern to the wrong diagram.

If the spots of the zincblende pattern are referred to the cubic axes, their indices become very much more complicated, and the pattern is no longer complete. The converse is true for the potassium chloride pattern, the indices in this case being simpler when referred to cubic axes. In Table VI a list of indices of the spots of each pattern is set down referred to (A) the cube edges, (B) the cube face diagonals, *i.e.*, three edges of the regular tetrahedron, as axes.

It will be seen that in the case of zincblende it is the B series, in the case of the potassium chloride the A series, which is simple, and which gives a complete series of indices over a certain range. I do not think there can be any doubt which space lattice is the right one in either case.

Reprinted from *Nature*, 1919, volume 104, page 187

## SOCIETIES AND ACADEMIES.

### MANCHESTER.

**Literary and Philosophical Society**, October 21.—Mr. William Thomson, vice-president, in the chair.—Prof. **W. L. Bragg** : Sound-ranging. A sound spreads from the point where it originates as a spherical cone moving with constant velocity. If it is intercepted by three or more stations the positions of which are accurately known, and if the time-intervals elapsing between its arrival at the stations are measured, a simple construction gives the position of the sources of the sound. Soon after the commencement of hostilities it became clear that the struggle was going to take the form of trench warfare. This gave rise to the idea of locating the enemy guns by sound in the way described. The French made experiments with sound-ranging in October, 1914, and showed that it was feasible, and the British Army was encouraged by their success to send an experimental sound-ranging section to the Front. This section started operations in October, 1915, taking up its position opposite Wytschaete. The first results obtained were poor, but they improved with experience and better apparatus. The original section became a training school for officers and men, and sufficient sections were formed to cover the whole of our Front. Each section had six microphones spaced along a base opposite the German front line. The microphones were connected to a chronographic instrument at a central headquarters, and when the sound reached each microphone it sent an electric signal recorded by the instrument. In front of the base there were two observation posts so placed that the sound reached them a few seconds before it reached the microphones, which gave time for an observer at the post to press a key which started the recording apparatus at headquarters. By studying the record the time-intervals could be measured and the position of the gun plotted on the map and telephoned to the artillery. There were between thirty and forty sections along the Front. They could locate batteries between 10,000 and 15,000 yards away with a mean error of about fifty yards. Each section sent in about one thousand results in the year.

Reprinted from
*Proceedings of the Royal Institution of Great Britain*, 1920, volume 23, pages
190-205

# Royal Institution of Great Britain.

## WEEKLY EVENING MEETING,

Friday, May 28, 1920.

Sir James Crichton-Browne, J.P. M.D. LL.D. F.R.S.,
Treasurer and Vice-President, in the Chair.

W. Lawrence Bragg, M.A., Langworthy Professor of Physics,
Manchester University.

### Crystal Structure.

1. The examination of the structure of crystals by means of X-rays
has made it possible to discover the arrangement of the atoms in a
number of the simpler crystal forms. We owe to Laue the original
experiments, first published in June, 1912, which placed this
power in our hands. In seeking for some means of diffracting
X-rays and thus investigating their nature, he was led to use a crystal
as a diffraction grating for the rays, the regular arrangement of the
atoms in the crystal structure performing the same function as the
lines ruled on a grating. The success of his experiment has resulted
in investigations which have vastly increased our knowledge of
X-rays, of crystal structure, and of the structure of the atom itself.

The problem of crystal structure, which forms the subject of this
Discourse, has been attacked in various ways. In his original work
Laue obtained diffraction patterns by passing a fine beam of X-rays
through a thin plate of crystal, and allowing the diffracted beams to
fall on a photographic plate which recorded their geometrical distribution. Though this clearly showed that the X-rays consisted of
electromagnetic waves of very short wave-length, diffracted by the
atoms of the crystal, the complexity of the resulting pattern on the
photographic plate made it difficult to draw conclusions as to the
arrangement of the diffracting atoms. A simpler method of attack
was realized in the X-ray Spectrometer devised in 1913 by Sir W. H.
Bragg. In the course of experiments with which the author was
associated, the structure of crystals such as diamond, sodium chloride,
zincblende, fluor spar, and the carbonates of the divalent metals were
fully worked out, the arrangement of the atoms being determined.

Large crystals are necessary for these methods of analysis, and in
order to examine crystalline substances which could not be obtained
except as a mass of minute crystals, Debye employed another experimental arrangement which he published in December, 1915. Instead
of using a single crystal, Debye passed the X-rays through a mass of
finely-powdered material, consisting of crystalline fragments oriented in

A

all directions, the diffraction of the X-rays resulting in the appearance
of a set of " halo " rings on a suitably placed photographic plate.    He
analysed graphite, and showed that so-called " amorphous " carbon
consists in reality of minute graphite crystals.    The arrangement of
the atoms in silicon, tungsten, tin, gold, aluminium and other elements has been discovered by Debye's method.    Sherrer has found
that colloidal gold and silver consist of minute crystals, the dimensions
of which are so small that they are only four or five atoms deep in
any direction, and which yet retain exactly the same crystal structure
as massive gold and silver.    The same method was arrived at inde-

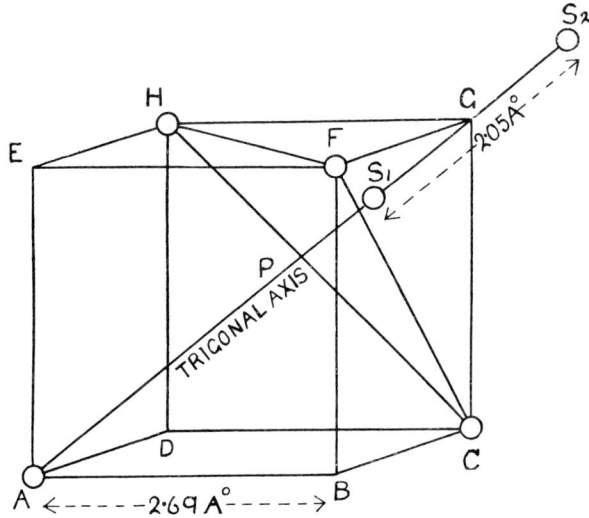

UNIT OF IRON PYRITES STRUCTURE

FIG. 1.

pendently by Hull, and he has extended it to a number of interesting crystals.    We now know the atomic arrangement for a very
large proportion of the crystalline elements and simple compounds.
  2.  The essential principle of these methods of crystal analysis
may be compared to that involved when a diffraction grating is cali-
brated by means of monochromatic light, the wave-length of which is
known accurately.    By finding the angle at which the light is
diffracted by the grating, the distance apart of the lines ruled on the
grating can be calculated.    The planes on which the atoms of a crystal
are arranged correspond to the lines of a diffraction grating.    A beam

of X-rays of known wave-length falls on the crystal, and it is found
that when the beam makes a certain glancing angle with the planes
of the structure it is strongly diffracted. By measuring this angle it
is possible to calculate the distance between the planes of the crystal
structure, just as the distance between the lines of the grating is
obtained by employing monochromatic light. The distance between
the planes in all directions is thus measured up, and leads to the
fixing of the atoms in the crystal structure at their intersections. In
this way the crystalline arrangements of some twenty or thirty
elements, of compounds such as NaCl, MgO, ZnS, the carbonates, the

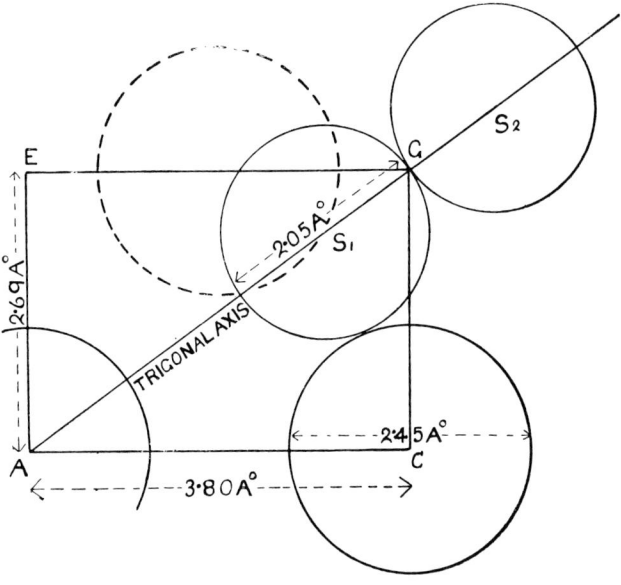

Fig. 2.

spinel group of minerals, the alums, the oxides insomorphous with
ruby, pyrites, fluor, galena and many others have been analysed.

3. In many simple crystalline substances the atoms are so arranged
that their exact positions are determined by the symmetry of the
crystal. In the diamond, for example, each carbon atom is at the
centre of four other carbon atoms. In the cubic crystal of potassium
chloride, the atoms are arranged so that potassium and chlorine atoms
alternate at the corners of the cubes in the structure. Every potassium
atom is surrounded symmetrically by six chlorine atoms, every
chlorine atom by six potassium atoms. The atoms cannot be displaced

A 2

from these positions without destroying the symmetry of the structure, and their exact positions are therefore defined. Such structures are illustrated by the models of potassium chloride and zincblende in Plates I. and II.

In contrast to this, the positions of the sulphur atoms in the crystal of iron pyrites, $FeS_2$, are defined by symmetry alone. Plate I., Fig. ($a$), and Figs. 1 and 2 illustrate this structure. The sulphur atoms lie on certain axes of three-fold symmetry, illustrated by the model, and every atom occupies the same relative position along the appropriate axis, but this position must be determined by quantitative investigations of the diffraction of the rays. The ratio of the parts into which the cube axis is divided by the centre of the sulphur atom may be taken as the parameter fixing its position, and this parameter may have any value. In the case of the ruby, $Al_2O_3$, two parameters are necessary to define the crystal structure; in quartz, $SiO_2$, four parameters must be determined. The complexity of the crystal structure, and the difficulty of analysing it, increase greatly with the number of these parameters, and it is this which has limited to the simpler forms the types of crystal so far worked out.

4. In trying to find some method of simplifying the analysis of these complex structures, the author has been led to a manner of regarding the crystalline structure which is similar to the well-known theory proposed in 1906 by Barlow and Pope. Barlow and Pope pictured the atoms of a crystal as an assemblage of spheres, packed together tightly, the volume of the space in the crystal structure occupied by the sphere representing any atom being proportional to the valency of the atom. We now know the atomic arrangement of a number of crystals, and we know that the disposition of the atoms predicted by the "Valency Volume" theory, though in some cases it has been found to hold, is in general different to that which the X-rays have enabled us to discover. Nevertheless, Barlow and Pope's models of crystal structures may be modified so as to apply to crystals by substituting, for the valency volume law, one which assigns to the sphere representing any atom a constant size characteristic of that atom.

5. This may be illustrated by the iron pyrites structure already referred to. In this structure the iron atoms are situated on a face-centred cubic lattice. If the unit cube of this lattice be subdivided into eight cubes of half the linear dimensions, each of these latter will have an iron atom situated at four of its eight corners. Fig. 1 represents such a unit of the structure, the iron atoms being at the corners of A, C, H and F. One diagonal of each cube, the diagonal AG in the figure, is an axis of threefold symmetry, and the sulphur atom lies at some position along this axis. Since each corner of the cube is a centre of symmetry, there will correspond to the sulphur atom centred at $S_1$ a similar atom at $S_2$, where $S_1G = S_2G$. A pair of sulphur atoms are thus associated with each cube corner, since one

PLATE I.

FIG. (*a*).—Structure of Iron pyrites, FeS₂.

FIG. (*b*).—Potassium chloride, KCl; Calcium carbonate, CaCO₃.

PLATE II.

Fig. (*a*).—Zincblende, ZnS.

Fig. (*b*).—Alumina, $Al_2O_3$

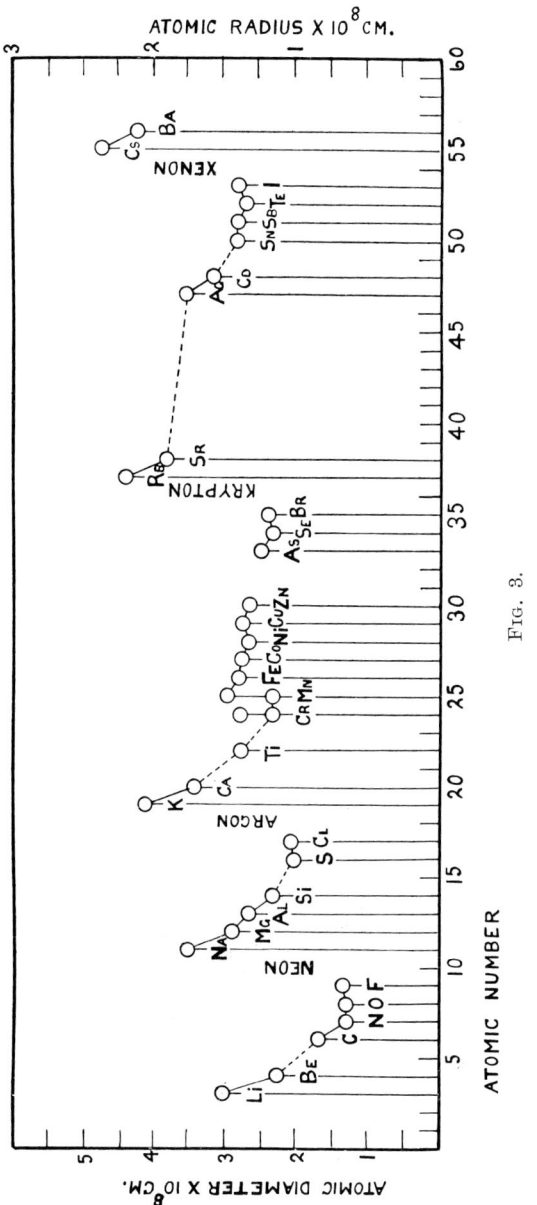

FIG. 3.

threefold axis passes through every corner, and the necessary proportion of two sulphur atoms to one iron atom is realized.

On the conception of the crystal as a set of spheres packed together, it will be seen that there are two possible positions for the sulphur atom. It may lie at the centre of the cube, where it is surrounded by the four iron atoms at A, C, H, and F, an arrangement which exists in the structure of fluor spar, $CaF_2$. Alternatively, it may move along the axis to a position $G_1$ on the other side of the plane HFC, where it will be packed between the three iron atoms at H, C and F, and the corresponding sulphur atom at $S_2$.

If the size of the sphere representing the iron atom is known, geometrical considerations fix the centre of the sulphur atom touching the iron atoms and the other sulphur atom. As a first approximation to the size of the iron sphere, the distance between atomic centres in metallic iron, first analysed by Hull, may be taken. This distance is $2 \cdot 47 \times 10^{-8}$ cm., or $2 \cdot 47$ Ångstrom Units. Using this value, the ratio $S_1G/AG$ is found to be equal to $0 \cdot 22$. The author originally deduced the value $0 \cdot 20$ for this parameter, and a more exact determination by Ewald gave it as $0 \cdot 226$, so it will be seen that the conception of the atoms as a set of spheres packed together leads to a determination of the parameter very near the true one. Further, the diameter of the sphere representing the sulphur atom follows to be $2 \cdot 05$ Å. Fig. 2 will illustrate the manner in which this result is arrived at.

6. The structure of zinc sulphide, and therefore the distance between the zinc and sulphur atomic centres, is known ; it is illustrated by Plate II., Fig. (*a*). Taking the diameter of the sulphur sphere to be $2 \cdot 05$ Å, that of the zinc sphere touching it is found to be $2 \cdot 65$ Å. From the zinc oxide structure the dimensions of the oxygen sphere can be calculated ; its diameter is found to be $1 \cdot 30$ Å. This difference of $0 \cdot 75$ Å between the diameters of the oxygen and sulphur spheres is also found to exist in a number of other crystals.

The rhombohedral carbonates typified by calcite, $CaCO_3$, provide a check on these figures. We have seen that the oxygen sphere has a diameter of $1 \cdot 30$ Å. In the diamond the distance between the carbon centres is $1 \cdot 54$ Å, and this may be taken to be the diameter of the carbon sphere. Every carbon atom in the carbonates is closely surrounded by three oxygen atoms, and we should therefore expect the distance between carbon and oxygen centres to be $\frac{1}{2}(1 \cdot 54 + 1 \cdot 30)$Å, or $1 \cdot 42$Å. As a matter of fact the X-ray measurements show it to be $1 \cdot 47$ Å, which is in fair agreement with the calculated value. Further, in zinc carbonate the zinc atom is surrounded by six oxygen atoms, the distance between the centres being $1 \cdot 99$ Å. Comparing this with the distance $1 \cdot 97$ Å between zinc and oxygen

centres in zinc oxide, we see that each of the atoms appears to occupy
a space of the same dimensions in all these crystals, sulphur in pyrites
and zinc sulphide, zinc in zinc sulphide, oxide, and carbonate, oxygen
in zinc oxide and carbonate, carbon in the carbonate and in diamond.

7. This will illustrate the manner in which the atomic diameters
shown in the diagram (Fig. 3) have been calculated. The results
may be summarized by saying that the distance between two
neighbouring atoms in a crystal structure is equal to the sum of two
constants characteristic of the atoms. We can therefore picture the
atoms as a set of spheres packed together so that they are in contact,
by taking these constants to be the radii of the spheres, and the
models which illustrate this lecture have been built up in this way.

In the figure the elements are arranged in the order of their
atomic numbers, and the ordinates represent the diameters of the
corresponding spheres, measured in Ångstrom Units. A comparison
of the distances found between the atoms in these structures which
have so far been determined, with the distance calculated by adding
the "atomic radii," shows that the average discrepancy between the
two is $0 \cdot 06$ Å, or between two and three per cent.

It will be seen that the atomic diameters lie on a series of regular
curves which show very strongly the periodic arrangement of the
elements. The monovalent electropositive elements have the greatest
diameters, the divalent metals the next greatest, and passing along
each period the diameter diminishes steadily until it approaches a
lower limit for the electronegative elements at the end of the period.
In the case of two of the elements, chromium and manganese, it
is necessary to suppose that the atom has a smaller diameter when
functioning as an electronegative element than as an electropositive
one.

The curve may be compared to Lothar Meyer's curve of atomic
volumes, but in the case considered above the volume is that occupied
by the atom in all the compounds into which it enters, so that the
curve has a wider application. The molecular volume of a compound often differs very greatly from the volume obtained by adding
the atomic volumes of its constituents, but if the crystalline structure is taken into account, this generalization shows that the space
occupied by each atom is approximately constant.

In some cases the distances between atoms do not agree with
those calculated from the diameters ; for example, this is the case for
many of the elements. In spite of this, the analysis of a complicated
crystal is greatly helped by this way of regarding the atomic arrangement. When marshalling the atoms together in trying to find some
arrangements which account for the diffraction effects, the necessity
of allowing each atom a certain space in the structure limits the
variable parameters to a small range and so simplifies the analysis.

8. The physical interpretation of these empirical relations must
be sought for in the structure of the atom, and in fact that theory of

atomic structure, which has been developed by the work of Kossel, Lewis, Born, Landé and many others, and which has been so strikingly summarize l and extended recently by Langmuir, affords a ready explanation of the relationships. An essential feature of this theory is the supposition that the electrons, which surround the positive atomic nucleus, are fixed at, or oscillate about, certain definite positions in the atomic structure. This may be contrasted with the type of atomic structure represented by the Bohr atom, when the electronic orbits are supposed to enclose the atomic nucleus. In the "fixed electron" atom the electrons are placed in certain definite positions in a series of concentric spherical shells surrounding the nucleus. The commencement of each period of the periodic table marks the commencement of a new shell, and the inert gases which separate the periods are the atomic systems in which the outer shell has in each case its full complement of electrons.

The arrangement of electrons in an inert gas is a very stable one, corresponding to the chemical inactivity of the elements. The chemical properties of the other elements are due to the tendency of the system to revert to a more stable arrangement, such as that of one of the inert gases. Argon, for example, with atomic number 18 has a stable system of 18 electrons surrounding the nucleus. Potassium has an atomic number 19, and the nucleus is surrounded by 19 electrons in a neutral atom. There is, therefore, a tendency for the potassium atom to lose an electron and revert to the stable argon arrangement of 18 electrons, so that potassium behaves as a monovalent electropositive element. Chlorine, on the other hand, with atomic number 17, tends to gain an electron, and is a monovalent electronegative element. The atoms which have thus lost or gained an electron are positively and negatively charged; they are the kations and anions of potassium and chlorine.

The atomic numbers of the inert gases tell us the number of electrons in the outer shell which each atom must have for complete stability. The atomic numbers of helium, neon, argon, krypton, xenon and niton are 2, 10, 18, 36, 54 and 86, so that the number of electrons which must be added to complete each successive shell must be 2, 8, 8, 18, 18 and 32.

9. On this theory, two different types of chemical combination may be distinguished. The first is that represented by such a compound as potassium chloride. Here the potassium atom has lost an electron in reverting to the argon arrangement of eighteen electrons, and the chlorine atom has gained one. The oppositely charged ions are held together by the electrostatic attraction of their resultant charges. In the crystal of potassium chloride the positive potassium ion tends to surround itself with as many negative ions as possible. This is realized in the crystal structure (Plate I, Fig. (*b*) ), where each ion is surrounded by six of the opposite sign. The fact that the " molecule " of KCl has no apparent existence in the

crystal structure receives a natural explanation on this theory. The valency of the ion of either sign is due to an electrostatic attraction and can be subdivided to any extent.

The other type of chemical compound is that of two electronegative elements. Each element in this case has a smaller number of electrons than is necessary for complete stability. In order that the empty spaces in the outer shell may be completely filled, the atoms share electrons, the valency bonds corresponding to a pair of electrons held in common by both atoms. It is in this way of regarding the combination of electronegative elements that the Langmuir theory finds one of its strongest supports ; the complicated valencies of elements such as nitrogen and phosphorus are readily explained by a consideration of the ways in which these atoms can fill up their outer shells by holding electrons in common with other atoms.

10. It has been seen that the potassium chloride crystal consists of alternate ions. The structure of calcite (Plate I, Fig. (*b*)) presents the same alternation of ions, only in this case one of the ions, the $CO_3$ group, is complex. The calcium atom has lost two electrons in reverting to the argon arrangement of electrons, and it is therefore a doubly charged positive ion. The $CO_3$ group has absorbed into its system two additional electrons, and the four atoms in the group are surrounded by the total complement of electrons for stability, some of the electrons being held in common. In this crystal both types of chemical combination are illustrated : the calcium and $CO_3$ ions are held together by their charges ; the carbon and oxygen atoms are bound together into the $CO_3$ group by holding electrons in common. The crystal is therefore divisible into units, each unit having a continuous outer electron shell. One unit is the calcium nucleus surrounded by its proper electron cloud, the other is the $CO_3$ group again surrounded by its electron cloud. Some repulsive force must be supposed to exist between the outer electrons which keeps the ions apart, opposing their electrostatic attractions for each other. The arrangement of the ions in potassium chloride and calcite is the same, except that in the latter case the substitution of the complex $CO_3$ ion for the Cl ion distorts the cube into a rhombohedron (cp. figure).

11. The empirical relations summarized by Fig. 3 can readily be interpreted on this theory. In calcium carbonate, for example, the proximity of the carbon and oxygen centres leads to a small diameter being assigned to the spheres representing these atoms, while the comparative isolation of the calcium atoms leads to a large diameter being taken for the corresponding sphere. We now see that the carbon and oxygen atoms are close together because they share electrons ; the calcium atom is isolated because it has no electrons in common with the other atoms. The large diameter assigned to the electropositive elements does not therefore indicate that the outer electrons are any further from the nucleus than they are in the

electronegative elements of the same period ; it expresses the fact that the electropositive atom never shares electrons with the neighbouring atoms, and is therefore always found to be at a distance from the other atomic centres as if it occupied a large domain in the crystal structure.

12. In each period the divalent ion is assigned a smaller diameter than the preceding monovalent ion. Sodium fluoride and magnesium oxide, for example, have exactly the same atomic arrangement, that of potassium chloride. The dimensions of the magnesium oxide structure are, however, smaller than those of sodium fluoride : the side of the unit cube is $4 \cdot 22$ Å, as compared with $4 \cdot 78$ Å. Since other data assign practically identical dimensions to oxygen and fluorine, the difference in the dimensions is accounted for by taking a smaller diameter for magnesium than for sodium. A comparison of the identical stuctures, magnesium carbonate and sodium nitrate, leads to the same result. We may ascribe this closer grouping of the atoms in the magnesium oxide or carbonate to the fact that the charges on the ions are double those in sodium fluoride or nitrate, so that the forces of attraction are more than four times as great. For the same reason the trivalent elements appear to occupy a still smaller domain in the crystal structure.

13. At the end of each period the diameters approach a lower limit. Since the electronegative elements are holding electrons in common, an estimate of the size of the outer electron shell can be formed from the distances which separate the atoms. The limiting values for the periods are, approximately :—

| | |
|---|---|
| Neon . . . . . . | $1 \cdot 30$ Å |
| Argon . . . . . | $2 \cdot 05$ Å |
| Krypton . . . . . | $2 \cdot 35$ Å |
| Xenon . . . . . | $2 \cdot 70$ Å |

The diameters of the outer electron shells would appear to be equal to, or slightly less than, these values.

14. We can now review the types of crystalline structure. In what follows the various points have either been made by Langmuir or are direct consequences of the atomic theory which has been described above.

The crystals of a salt have been discussed above. Crystals of sodium chloride, or calcium carbonate, consist of ions of opposite signs. The ions are surrounded each by its own electron cloud ; they are held together by their electric charges, and kept apart by repulsive forces which must be supposed to exist between the outer electron shells. Diamond represents yet another type of crystal. The carbon atoms have each four electrons in the outer shell, and the complement of eight is attained by each carbon atom holding in common a pair of electrons with the four other atoms surrounding it symmetrically. The whole crystal is one molecule, all the atoms being linked up by electron sharing, a view which is supported by the density and hardness of the diamond. A crystal such as quartz probably has the same type of structure. The structure of carborundum resembles very much that of diamond, and here again every atom shares electrons with all its neighbours.

The crystal of an electropositive element, such as lithium or potassium, has a different structure. Each atomic nucleus has a stable arrangement of electrons surrounding it, corresponding to one of the inert gases, and in addition one or more electrons must be associated with each atom according to its valency, as the whole mass of the metal is electrically neutral. The crystal may be regarded as composed of ions and electrons, the electrons having no definite place in the crystalline structure. If an electromotive force is applied to the metal they are driven through it ; in other words, the metal is a conductor of electricity.

Still another type of association is that represented by water of crystallization, where some residual forces of attraction must be supposed to hold the electrically neutral water molecules in the crystalline structure.

15. Crystals where all the atoms hold electrons in common are characterized by great hardness ; large forces are necessary to break the atoms apart. The typical salt, on the other hand, is soft, as in parting the atoms the only forces which have to be overcome are the electrostatic attractions between the atoms. An exception occurs when the ions have a double or treble charge and are close together, as in magnetite, $Fe_3O_4$, and ruby, $Al_2O_3$, for then the forces must be supposed to be so great as to give the crystalline structure considerable hardness.

In the crystal of a metal the ions, held together by electrons which probably have no fixed positions in the structure, are still freer to move past each other and give the metal its characteristic malleable and ductile properties.

Since the first two classes of crystals have no free electrons, they are non-conductors of electricity. This is the case for crystals of the electronegative elements where the atoms hold electrons in common. It is the last class of crystals, those of the electro-positive elements, which are conductors.

16. In studying crystal structure we are studying the arrangement of the atoms in the solid state, for all true solids are crystalline in nature. It is the extremely short wave-length of the X-rays which makes this feasible. The limit to the minuteness of detail which it is possible to see under the microscope is fixed by the wave-length of the light used to illuminate the object, for it is impossible to distinguish two objects which are closer together than that wave-length. In the case of X-rays the wave-length is ten or twenty times smaller than the distances between the atoms, so that by illuminating the crystal with X-rays the atomic arrangement may be

analysed. It may be possible to push the analysis still further, and find in a direct manner the arrangement of the electrons around the nucleus. Experiments on these lines have already been carried out; for example, Debye's experiments on lithium fluoride.

17. I have tried to indicate the contribution which the study of crystals has made towards the solution of the problem of atomic structure, and the lines on which it may be expected to afford a still greater insight into that problem in the future. In considering the broadest aspects of the question it has been impossible to avoid generalizations to which many exceptions occur. I hope, however, to have shown that crystal structure has a wider significance than may perhaps be obvious at first sight. In a crystal the atoms and atomic groupings are ranged in perfect geometrical regularity, and it is by observing their concerted effects on the X-rays that we can investigate the intimate structure of solid bodies.

[W. L. B.]

Reprinted from *Nature*, 1921, volume 107, page 107

### The Dimensions of Atoms and Molecules.

CERTAIN relations which are to be traced between the distances separating atoms in a crystal make it possible to estimate the distance between their centres when linked together in chemical combination. On the Lewis-Langmuir theory of atomic constitution, two electro-negative elements when combined hold one or more pairs of electrons in common, so that the outer electron shell of one atom may be regarded as coincident with that of the other at the point where the atoms are linked together. From this point of view, estimates may be made (W. L. Bragg, *Phil. Mag.*, vol. xi., August, 1920) from crystal data of the diameters of these outer shells. The outer shell of neon, for example, was estimated from the apparent diameters of the carbon, nitrogen, oxygen, and fluorine atoms, which show a gradual approximation to a minimum value of $1.30 \times 10^{-8}$ cm. The diameters of the inert gases as found in this way are given in the second column of the following table :

| Gas | Diameter $2\sigma$ (Crystals) | Diameter $2\sigma'$ (Viscosity) | Difference $2\sigma' - 2\sigma$ |
|---|---|---|---|
| Helium | — | 1.89 | — |
| Neon ... ... | 1.30 | 2.35 | 1.05 |
| Argon ... | 2.05 | 2.87 | 0.82 |
| Krypton ... | 2.35 | 3.19 | 0.84 |
| Xenon ... | 2.70 | 3.51 | 0.81 |

In the third column are given Rankine's values (A. O. Rankine, Proc. Roy. Soc., A, vol. xcviii., 693, pp. 360–74, February, 1921) for the diameters of the inert gases calculated from their viscosities by Chapman's formula (S. Chapman, Phil. Trans. Roy. Soc., A, vol. ccxvi., pp. 279–348, December, 1915). These are considerably greater than the diameters calculated from crystals, but this is not surprising in view of our ignorance both of the field of force surrounding the outer electron shells and of the nature of the electron-sharing which links the atoms together, for it is quite possible that their structures might coalesce to a considerable extent. The constancy of the differences between the two estimates given in the fourth column shows that the *increase* in the size of the atom as each successive electron shell is added is nearly the same (except in the case of neon), whether measured by viscosity or by the crystal data. Further, Rankine has shown that the molecule $Cl_2$ behaves as regards its viscosity like two argon atoms with a distance between their centres very closely equal to that calculated from crystals, and that the same is true for the pairs $Br_2$ and krypton, $I_2$ and xenon.

We see, therefore, that the evidence both of crystals and viscosity measurements indicates that (*a*) the elements at the end of any one period in the periodic table are very nearly identical as regards the diameters of their outer electron shells, and (*b*) in passing from one period to the next there is a definite increase in the dimensions of the outer electron shell, the absolute amount of this increase estimated by viscosity agreeing closely with that determined from crystal measurements.

A further check on these measurements is afforded by the infra-red absorption spectra of HF, HCl, and HBr. The wave-number difference $\delta v$ between successive absorption lines determines the moment of inertia I of the molecule in each case, the formula being

$$\delta v = \frac{h}{4\pi^2 c I},$$

where $h$ is Planck's constant and $c$ the velocity of light.

It is therefore possible to calculate the distances between the centres of the nuclei in each molecule, for

$$s^2 = \frac{m+m'}{mm'} \cdot \frac{h}{4\pi^2 c m_H \delta v},$$

where $m$ and $m'$ are the atomic weights relative to hydrogen and $m_H$ the mass of the hydrogen atom. The following table gives these distances (E. S. Imes, *Astroph. Journal,* vol. 1., p. 251, 1919). It will be seen that there are again increases in passing from F to Cl and Cl to Br, which agree closely with the increases in the radii $\sigma$ of the electron shells given by the crystal and viscosity data.

| $s \times 10^8$ | | | | $\sigma \times 10^8$ (Crystals) | | $\sigma' \times 10^8$ (Viscosity) | |
|---|---|---|---|---|---|---|---|
| H F | 0·93 | | Neon | (= F) ... | 0·65 | | 1·17 | |
| | | *0·35* | | | | *0·37* | | *0·26* |
| H Cl | 1·28 | | Argon | (= Cl) ... | 1·02 | | 1·43 | |
| | | *0·15* | | | | *0·15* | | *0·15* |
| H Br | 1·43 | | Krypton | (= Br) ... | 1·17 | | 1·58 | |
| | | | | | | *0·18* | | *0·17* |
| H I | — | | Xenon | (= I) ... | 1·35 | | 1·75 | |

The increase from fluorine to chlorine of $0.35 \times 10^{-8}$ cm. confirms the estimate given by crystals of $0.37 \times 10^{-8}$ cm., as against the estimate $0.26 \times 10^{-8}$ cm. given by viscosity data. It follows from the above that the distance between the hydrogen nucleus and the centre of an electro-negative atom to which it is attached is obtained by adding $0.26 \times 10^{-8}$ cm. to the radius of the electro-negative atom as given by crystal structures. The radius of the inner electron orbit, according to Bohr's theory, is $0.53 \times 10^{-8}$ cm., double this value. The crystal data, therefore, predict the value $\delta v = 13.0$ cm.$^{-1}$ for the HI molecule, corresponding to a distance $1.61 \times 10^{-8}$ cm. between their atomic centres.

This evidence is interesting as indicating that the forces binding the atoms together are localised at that part of the electron shell where linking takes place.

W. L. BRAGG.<br>H. BELL.

Manchester University, March 16.

Reprinted from
*Manchester Memoirs*, 1925, volume 69, No. 4

## IV. Model Gratings to Illustrate the Diffraction of X-Rays by Crystals.

### By W. L. BRAGG, O.B.E., M.A., F.R.S.

THE gratings described in this note were prepared in order to
illustrate a lecture given to the British Optical Society in
March 1924.  When light is scattered by a diffraction grating
of the usual type, the intensities of the different orders of
spectra depend on the way in which the lines have been ruled
on the grating.  If the individual lines scatter light strongly
in a certain direction, the spectra which are in or near to this
region will be strong.  An extreme instance is found in the
case of the echelette grating, where the groove is so ruled that
the greater part of the incident light energy is thrown in the
direction of the spectral region which it is desired to examine.
Experiments made by Wood and Trowbridge (*Phil. Mag.*
Oct. 1910) on the energy distribution in the different spectra
are described in Wood's " Optics " (p. 230, 2nd edition).  The
reflexion of X-rays by the planes of a crystal is governed by
similar intensity laws, for the planes of the crystal form a
pattern repeated at regular intervals as are the lines of a
grating.  In all but the most simple crystals, each " plane "
is complex in character, actually consisting of a group of
planes on which the centre of atoms of different kinds are
situated.  As a consequence, the intensities of the different
orders of reflexion depend on the structure of the group, the
reflexion being strong when the planes in the group conspire
to produce a strong diffraction of X-rays, and weak when the
diffracted waves destroy each other by interference.  In
X-ray analysis of crystal structure, the examination of intensities is our most important guide to finding the structure of
the planes which cause the observed effects, and so to
determining the positions of the atoms in the crystal.

A grating may be made to reproduce the effects observed

*February 27th, 1925.*

with X-rays and crystals. For instance, when X-rays are reflected from the face (111) of rock-salt, the odd orders of spectra are weak compared with the even orders. This is due to the existence in the crystal of a set of planes in which chlorine atoms are centred, with planes half-way between them on which are placed sodium atoms which have a smaller scattering power than the chlorine atoms. The waves reflected by the chlorine planes are partially destroyed by interference with the waves reflected by the sodium planes in the odd orders, whereas their effects are added in the even orders. A grating in which lines which scatter the light to different extents are arranged alternately at regular intervals produces in the same way weak first, third, and fifth spectra, and strong second, fourth, and sixth spectra. If in the grating lines are ruled in pairs, so that the distance between two lines of a pair is one-quarter the distance between successive pairs, the second order spectra is cut out, just as the second order disappears with X-ray reflexion from diamond (111) where there is a corresponding arrangement of planes. Gratings to illustrate these effects were ruled by the National Physical Laboratory for W. H. Bragg and shown at the Royal Instiution in 1914.

The present note describes a very simple method of making gratings of any desired kind in order to copy the effect of the crystal on X-rays. Various devices were experimented with before a satisfactory one was developed. For instance, the lines were ruled on a large scale and a small scale copy produced by photography. The ruling of the lines with sufficient distinctness for each type of grating required is very laborious. A slit was illuminated, and an image thrown on a photographic plate. The slit was moved by a micrometer screw through successive intervals, an exposure being taken at the end of each movement. This was again a long process and the lines were somewhat irregularly spaced.

The device finally adopted gave very good results and was quick in operation. I am indebted to professor Wilberforce for the suggestion that a plate such as is used in the half-tone printing process might be used. These plates may be obtained ruled with several hundred lines to .the inch, and are beautifully regular. The lines are so made that the transparent and opaque portions are equal in area and form a grating which shows 15 to 20 spectra on either side of the central image. One lent by Professor Wilberforce with 400 lines to the inch was used in the present case. A print may be taken on a fine grained photographic plate by laying the grating with its ruled side in contact with the plate and exposing to a pointolite lamp at a distance of six feet for some seconds. It is found that the width of the lines in the print depends on the time of exposure, the lines being very narrow if it is short and as wide as the original transparent portion if it is long. In making a complex grating, the original grating was laid on the photographic plate and kept in position by being pressed with springs against a micrometer screw. Several exposures were taken on the same plate, the original grating being moved a fraction of 1/400 inch between each exposure, so that when the plate was developed it showed complex groups of lines, spaced so that there were 400 groups to the inch. By varying the time of the exposure and the length of the movement, any desired type of group could be obtained. Gratings made in this way show about a dozen spectra on either side of the central image, if a monochromatic source of light be viewed through them, and the intensities of the orders depend in the most striking way on the arrangement of the lines.

The photographs in the plate which illustrates this paper were taken by the method of crossed spectra. The grating and a prism of small angle were placed in contact with the lens of the camera, and a distant point source of light was focussed on the negative. The grating spread the light horizontally and the prism vertically. It is difficult to do justice in the reproduction to the brilliancy of the spectra seen through the original gratings, since the central orders are so strong that over-exposure results if an attempt is made to reproduce the high orders. Beside each set of spectra is a microphotograph of the grating which produced it. The connection between diamond and rocksalt arrangements, and their corresponding spectra, will be clear. In the case of the diamond arrangement of lines, the second order spectrum is not quite cut out on one side owing to some assymetry of the lines in the grating.

The photograph at the bottom of the plate shows a device in which two reproductions of the original grating are mounted on each other so that the lines are exactly parallel, and the faces of the gratings are in contact. The upper grating can be moved over the lower grating by means of a screw. The intensities of the different orders vary as the screw is moved, the higher orders altering extremely rapidly while the lower orders do so slowly. The spectra can be projected by throwing an image on to a screen. At a distance of six metres the spectra are about 5 cm. apart.

I am indebted to Professor Wilberforce for the loan of the original ruled plate. The construction of the gratings was carried out by Mr. W. Kay of the Physics Laboratory, Manchester University, to whom I wish to express my thanks for his assistance.

### EXPLANATION OF PLATE.

The photographs are of gratings of 400 lines to the inch which are enlarged about 40 times. The spectra were taken by placing the grating, which diffracted light horizontally, in contact with a prism of small angle which gave a vertical spectrum, and photographing a distant point source of light through the combination.

Figure 1. Photograph of original plate from which gratings were printed.

Figure 2. Photograph of print taken from the original plate, showing how narrow lines may be obtained by a short exposure.

Figure 3. Photograph of spectra produced by simple grating, showing a regular falling away in the orders.

Figure 4. Photograph of grating with " rock-salt (111) " arrangement of lines.

Figure 4a. Spectrum produced by grating shown in Fig. 4

Figure 5. Photograph of grating with a " diamond (111)" arrangement of lines.

Figure 5a. Spectra produced by grating shown in Fig. 5.

Figure 6. Device for superimposing two parallel gratings and moving one relatively to the other.

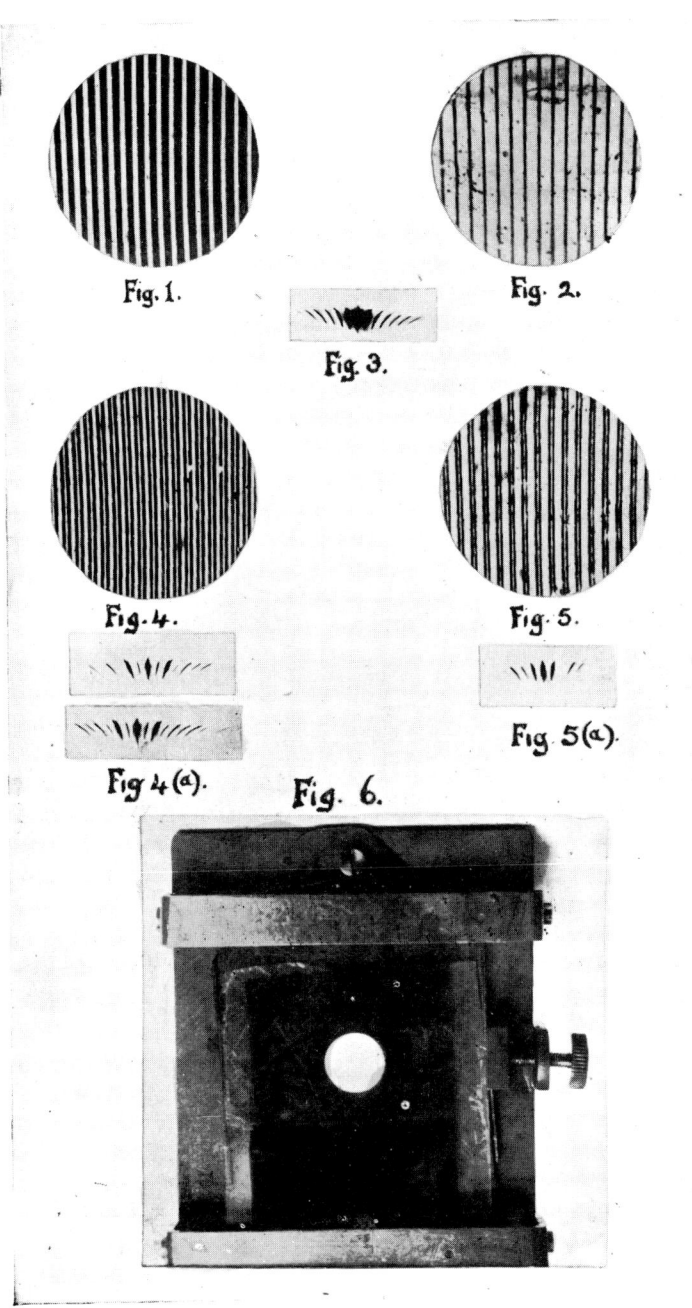

Fig. 1.

Fig. 2.

Fig. 3.

Fig. 4.

Fig. 5.

Fig 4 (a).

Fig. 5 (a).

Fig. 6.

Reprinted from the
*Proceedings of the Royal Society*, *A*, 1926, volume III, page 691

## *The Structure of Beryl,* $Be_3Al_2Si_6O_{18}$.

By W. Lawrence Bragg, F.R.S., Langworthy Professor of Physics,
Manchester University, and J. West, John Harling Fellow, Manchester
University.

(Received May 21, 1926.)

1. The structure of beryl, described in this paper, has some interesting features.
In the first place, the ratio of silicon to oxygen atoms in the molecule is that
of a metasilicate.  As far as we know, no other example of a metasilicate has
as yet been completely analysed (Wyckoff* has made some measurements on
diopside $MgCa(SiO_3)_2$, but has only succeeded in determining its space group).
Although the ratio of silicon to oxygen is as one to three, we find no $SiO_3$
groups in beryl.  We find instead an arrangement of oxygen atoms around a
silicon atom of exactly the same conformation as the groups $(SiO_4)^{==}$ in
typical orthosilicates such as olivine† and garnet.‡  In this metasilicate the
ratio of one silicon to three oxygen atoms is effected by a sharing of two oxygen
atoms of each tetrahedral $SiO_4$ group with neighbouring groups.  Thus the
structure forms an intermediate stage between the orthosilicates and the
structures of quartz§ and christobalite‖ where every oxygen atom is shared
by silicon atoms.  This interesting feature may throw some light on the
structure of other metasilicates.  In the second place, we have analysed the
structure by making careful quantitative measurements of the absolute
intensity of X-ray reflexion, and interpreting these measurements by the
formulæ which have proved to hold for simpler cases.  The structure is one of
moderate complexity, depending on seven parameters.  We hope to show
that all these parameters can be directly and accurately fixed.  The analysis
is greatly simplified when quantitative data are available, and there appears to
be no reason why structures with many more parameters should not be
attacked in the same direct manner.

Reprinted from *Z. Kristallogr Kristallgeom*, 1928, volume 69, page 168

# The structure of diopside. $CaMg(SiO_3)_2$.

By

## B. Warren,

Research Student, Massachusetts Institute of Technology,

and

## W. Lawrence Bragg,

Professor of Physics, Manchester University.

Diopside is a typical crystal of the large Pyroxene group of minerals. The present investigation has, we believe, determined the positions of all the atoms in the structure, and has brought to light an interesting arrangement of the silicon and oxygen atoms in this metasilicate. The silicon atoms are surrounded by four oxygen atoms as in other silicates, but two oxygen atoms of each tetrahedral group are held in common with neighbouring groups in accord with the three to one ratio of oxygen to silicon atoms. The tetrahedra thus linked together by shared oxygen atoms form endless chains parallel to the $c$ axis of the crystal; they lie side by side and are held together by calcium and magnesium atoms. All three cleavages of the crystal (110), (100), (010), are parallel to these chains, evidence of their relatively great strength. The pyroxene minerals are closely related to another group, the amphiboles, in which many types of fibrous crystals, such as asbestos, occur. It is therefore highly interesting to discover in a typical pyroxene these chains of silicon and oxygen atoms forming a "grain" in the structure, for this feature may prove to be common to a number of minerals.

The structure is shown in fig. 8. It is determined by fourteen parameters, and the analysis affords practical examples of methods described in a paper "A technique for the X-ray analysis of crystals with a large number of parameters" by Mr. J. West and one of the authors (W.L.B.). In order to illustrate these methods, the steps by which the structure was unravelled are described in detail in sections 4, 5, 6 and 7; the reader who is not interested in the details of analysis will find a general summary in section 3. The evidence for the correctness of the structure is examined in section 8, and its features are discussed in section 9.

Reprinted from the
*Proceedings of the Royal Society*, A, 1929, volume 123, pages 537-559

## The Determination of Parameters in Crystal Structures by means of Fourier Series.

By W. Lawrence Bragg, M.A., F.R.S., Langworthy Professor of Physics, Manchester University.

(Received February 9, 1929.)

### 1. *Introduction.*

The Fourier representation of the results of X-ray analysis was first suggested by W. H. Bragg.* It was developed independently by Duane, and used by Havighurst and Compton† to give striking representations of the distribution of scattering matter in crystals. Duane and Havighurst were first in applying the method to the much more accurate X-ray measurements available in 1925, and in showing how useful it could be.

Duane used a formula derived by Epstein and Ehrenfest.‡ They showed that the intensity of an X-ray reflexion from a plane $(h\ k\ l)$ of a crystal is proportional to the square of the coefficient of a term in the Fourier series, representing the density $\rho\ (x,\ y,\ z)$ of the diffracting material in the crystal as a function of $x$, $y$, $z$. The general term may be written

$$\mathbf{A}\ (h\ k\ l)\ \sin\ (2\pi hx/a\ -\ \delta_h)\ \sin\ (2\pi k/b\ -\ \delta_k)\ \sin\ (2\pi lz/c\ -\ \delta_l)$$

Duane reversed the line of thought, and showed that it is possible to deduce the density in the crystal from the measured intensities of X-ray reflexion. The X-ray measurements give the values of $(\mathbf{A}\ (h\ k\ l)\ )^2$ but not the phase angles $\delta_h$, $\delta_k$, $\delta_l$. This difficulty, Duane showed, could be surmounted in certain simple cases.

Havighurst§ used this triple Fourier series to determine the density of scattering matter in such crystals as rock-salt, NaCl. The calculations are lengthy. and Havighurst confined himself to evaluating the series along certain lines (cube edges or face-diagonals). Later, he used the same series for the determination of crystal parameters and analysed by its aid the mercurous halides which have structures with two parameters.

Compton made the further step of correlating the coefficients $\mathbf{A}\ (h\ k\ l)$ with

* 'Phil. Trans.,' A, vol. 215, p. 253 (1915).

† Duane, 'Proc. Nat. Acad. Washington,' vol. 11, p. 489 (1925); Havighurst, *ibid.*, vol. 11, p. 502 (1925); Compton, "X-rays and Electrons," p. 151.

‡ 'Proc. Nat. Acad. Sci.,' vol. 10, p. 133 (1924).

§ 'J. Amer. Chem. Soc.,' vol. 48, p. 2113 (1926).

the absolute value F $(h\,k\,l)$ of the structure factor.  F $(h\,k\,l)$ is the ratio of the wave amplitude scattered in a given direction by all atoms in the unit cell, to that which would be scattered according to the classical formula by a single electron under the same conditions.  Using the values of F, and adding to the series a suitable constant term, Compton showed that the series represents the " electron density " at any point in the crystal.  He used a simple Fourier series to express the distribution of scattering matter in sheets parallel to a given plane ; for this the values of F for the different orders of reflexion by parallel planes are alone required.  He also developed a formula for the radial distribution of scattering matter in an atom ; for this a knowledge of the atomic scattering curve (F curve) is necessary.

The first Fourier representations of distribution of scattering matter by Havighurst and Compton were based on measurements of the quantity F $(h\,k\,l)$ by Bragg, James and Bosanquet.*  Compton's formula for the sheet distribution of scattering matter has been used to check the results of crystal analysis (beryl, topaz and alum)† and to measure the thermal agitation of atoms.‡

It is interesting to note that the formula of Duane is implicitly developed in a paper by Ewald in 1921 on the reciprocal lattice, referred to more fully below. It was formulated by A. B. Porter for a corresponding optical problem in 1905, and W. H. Bragg's treatment in 1915 is based on Porter's equations.  Porter based his work on Abbe's diffraction theory of microscopic vision.  The correlation of the intensities of spectra with coefficients in the terms of a Fourier series is indeed a well-known optical principle due originally to Abbe fifty years ago, and used by him to discuss the resolving power of microscopes ; it is now becoming clear that it has its most far-reaching and perfect expression in the interpretation of X-ray diffraction.

## 2. *The Double Fourier Series.*

In Havighurst's calculations, although a triple Fourier series in $x$, $y$, $z$ is used, the density is only calculated for a series of points along a chosen line in the crystal.  In Compton's calculations the density in sheets parallel to a plane, or the radial density distribution, is measured.  In both cases the density is in effect expressed as a function of one variable (distance along a line, perpendicular to a plane, or along an atomic radius), though theoretically the

* ' Phil. Mag.,' vol. 41, p. 304 (1921), and vol. 42, p. 1 (1921).

† Beryl—Bragg and West, ' Roy. Soc. Proc.,' vol. 111, p. 691 (1926) ; Topaz—Alston and West, ' Z. Kryst.,' vol. 69, p. 149 (1928) ; Alum—Cork, ' Phil. Mag.,' vol. 4, p. 688 (1927).

‡ James and Firth, ' Roy. Soc. Proc.,' A, vol. 117, p. 62 (1927).

formula may be used for a complete expression of the density throughout the crystal. The difficulty of dealing with all three variables is one of calculation, as, in order to get a passably accurate expression for the density, hundreds of terms must be evaluated and summed for every point $x$, $y$, $z$.

The present paper describes evaluations of the series which are more extensive than those previously carried out, in that the density is *calculated for values of two variables*. The values of F $(h\,k\,l)$ are measured for all crystal reflexions around a given zone ; for instance, if the zone is the $a$ axis of the crystal, the values of F $(0\,k\,l)$ are used. A Fourier series is formed in which these values appear as coefficients, the variables being the co-ordinates $y$ and $z$. Values of $y$ and $z$ are taken at convenient intervals, and the Fourier series is summed for every pair of co-ordinates. The result is a series of figures in rows and columns which indicate the distribution of scattering matter in the unit cell, as projected on the face (100). The direction of projection is parallel to the $a$ axis.

The calculations can be made quite rapidly. In the cases described below, the required range of each co-ordinate is divided into 24 intervals in one direction and 12 in the other, and the Fourier series of about 40 terms is summed for 288 points.* This is done for the $a$, $b$ and $c$ axes as zone axes in turn, leading to projections of the unit cell upon its faces (100), (010) and (001). The projections (shown as contoured diagrams in figs. 1$a$, 2$a$ and 3$a$) indicate clearly the spatial distribution of scattering matter throughout the unit cell when they are considered in combination. They enable the atomic parameters to be measured, and the number of electrons in each atom to be counted. It is the object of the present paper to describe this analysis, and to compare its results with those obtained by other ways of analysing a crystal.

In order to form the Fourier series which represents the density distribution, it is necessary to know both the amplitudes and the phase constants of all the terms. X-ray measurement determines the former, but not the latter, for it is concerned with intensities which depend on the square of the amplitude coefficients alone. If, however, the crystal has centres of symmetry, and the

---

* A comparison shows that the amount of calculation required for projection on a plane is much less than that required for a complete survey of density throughout the unit cell. Suppose that F $(h\,k\,l)$ values for the general planes were used, which represented reflexion up to as high an angle as those taken into account in the present calculations for planes around each zone. The number of terms in the Fourier series representing the density at a point then proves to be between 200 and 300 instead of 40, and the series would have to be summed for 48 times as many points.

origin of co-ordinates is taken to be at one of these centres, the equations
assume a much more simple form.

It will be assumed that the crystal has a centre of symmetry at the origin,
and that the formula for the projection on the face (100) is required. The axes
of the unit cell are of lengths $a$, $b$, $c$, and make angles $\beta$, $\beta$, $\gamma$ with each other,
so that $bc \sin \alpha$ is the total area of the face on which projection is made. Let
$\rho(y, z)$ be the density of scattering matter per unit area of the projection at the
point $y$, $z$. It may then be shown that

$$\rho(y, z) = (1/bc \sin \alpha) \cdot \sum_{-\infty}^{+\infty} \sum_{-\infty}^{+\infty} F(0\,k\,l) \cos 2\pi (k\,y/b + lz/c). \qquad (1)$$

In this formula, there are no phase-constants, but $F(0\,k\,l)$ must be given the
correct sign. It is positive or negative, according to whether the scattering
matter in the unit cell diffracts a wave in the same or the opposite phase to
that scattered by an electron at the origin. All positive and negative values
of $k$ and $l$ are taken into account (*i.e.*, although $F(0\,k\,l)$ is identical with
$F(0\,\bar{k}\,\bar{l})$ the corresponding terms are counted as separate contributions to the
series).

In the special case where $k = 0$, $l = 0$, the value of $F(0\,0\,0)$ must be taken to
be Z, the total number of electrons in the unit cell. The corresponding
member of the Fourier series is a constant. When integrating $\rho(y, z)$ over the
face (100), all terms vanish, except the term involving $F(0\,0\,0)$. Thus

$$\int_{-b/2}^{+b/2} \int_{-c/2}^{+c/2} \rho(y, z)\, dy\, dz \sin \alpha = F(0\,0\,0) = Z. \qquad (2)$$

Formula (1) is an extension, to two dimensions, of the formula derived by
Compton for the distribution of scattering matter in sheets, and holds for a
cell of any shape provided that it has a symmetry centre. It may be proved
by forming the expression for $F(0\,k\,l)$

$$F(0\,k\,l) = \int_{-b/2}^{+b/2} \int_{-c/2}^{+c/2} \rho(y, z)\, dy\, dz \sin \alpha \cos 2\pi (ky/b + lz/c). \qquad (3)$$

When a series $\sum\sum A(q, r) \cos 2\pi (qy/b + rz/c)$ is substituted for $\rho(y, z)$ all terms
vanish on integration except those for which $q = k$, $r = l$ and $q = -k$,
$r = -l$. Remembering that $F(0\,k\,l) = F(0\,\bar{k}\,\bar{l})$, this shows that the coefficient
$A(k, l)$ of the series is equal to $F(0\,k\,l)/bc \sin \alpha$.

It will readily be seen that formula (1) gives the projection of scattering
matter in the unit cell, in a direction parallel to any zone axis, on any crystal
plane. The zone axis is taken as one axis of reference, and two other axes

of reference are chosen in the plane. A set of indices $(h\,k\,l)$ becomes a set such as $(0\,\mathrm{K\,L})$ referred to the new axes, and $\mathrm{F}\,(h\,k\,l)$ must now be labelled $\mathrm{F}\,(0\,\mathrm{K\,L})$. Formula (1) then applies.

The formula quoted above is a special case of the general formula for the density at the point $x$, $y$, $z$ in a crystal cell of any shape and symmetry. The reflexion from the plane $(h\,k\,l)$ must now be characterised by both an amplitude and a phase constant. Following Ewald (*loc. cit.*) $\mathrm{F}\,(h\,k\,l)$ may be expressed as a complex quantity

$$\mathrm{F}\,(h\,k\,l) = \mathrm{F}\,(h\,k\,l)\ e^{i\theta\,(h\,k\,l)},$$

$$= \frac{\mathrm{V}}{abc} \int_{-a/2}^{+a/2} \int_{-b/2}^{+b/2} \int_{-c/2}^{+c/2} \rho\,(x,\,y,\,z)\ e^{2\pi i\,(hx/a + ky/b + lz/c)}\ dx\ dy\ dz. \tag{4}$$

V is the volume of the unit cell, and $a$, $b$, $c$ are the lengths of its edges.

If we assume a series for $(x,\,y,\,z)$ of the form

$$\rho\,(x,\,y,\,z) = \overset{+\infty}{\underset{-\infty}{\Sigma}}\ \overset{+\infty}{\underset{-\infty}{\Sigma}}\ \overset{+\infty}{\underset{-\infty}{\Sigma}}\ \mathrm{A}\,(pqr)\ \cos\,(2\pi\,(px/a + qy/b + rz/c) + \alpha\,(pqr)\,),$$

a formal solution is given by

$$\mathrm{A}\,(h\,k\,l) = \mathrm{F}\,(h\,k\,l)\ \cdot \frac{1}{\mathrm{V}}\cdot$$

$$\alpha\,(h\,k\,l) = -\ \theta\,(h\,k\,l).$$

The series for $(x,\,y,\,z)$ is thus

$$\rho\,(x,y,z) = \frac{1}{\mathrm{V}} \overset{+\infty}{\underset{-\infty}{\Sigma}}\ \overset{+\infty}{\underset{-\infty}{\Sigma}}\ \overset{+\infty}{\underset{-\infty}{\Sigma}}\ \mathrm{F}\,(h\,k\,l)\ \cos\,(2\pi\,(hx/a + ky/b + lz/c) - \theta\,(h\,k\,l)\,). \tag{5}$$

As before, $\mathrm{F}\,(0\,0\,0)$ is equal to Z, the total number of electrons in the unit cell. In this general case $\mathrm{F}\,(h\,k\,l) = \mathrm{F}\,(\bar{h}\,\bar{k}\,\bar{l})$ and $\theta\,(h\,k\,l) = -\ \theta\,(\bar{h}\,\bar{k}\,\bar{l})$. All terms except the constant term in the series occur in identical pairs, but it is convenient to keep the series in this form for the sake of symmetry of expression.

### 3. *Application of the Double Fourier Series.*

The Fourier series is applied in this paper to a crystal which has already been analysed by other methods.* The crystal is diopside, $\mathrm{CaMg}\,(\mathrm{SiO}_3)_2$, the structure of which depends on 14 parameters. Extensive measurements of $\mathrm{F}\,(0\,k\,l)$, $\mathrm{F}\,(h\,0\,l)$, $\mathrm{F}\,(h\,k\,0)$ are available and are quoted in the paper referred to above. All 14 parameters had been determined by Warren and Bragg, and it is therefore of interest to see how closely the former values agree with the

* Warren and Bragg, ' Z. Krist.,' vol. 69, p. 167 (1928).

parameters deduced from the projections of density on the cell faces. The average difference, in this quite complex crystal, proves to be only $0 \cdot 5$ per cent. Other interesting points arise from a consideration of the projections, which are dealt with below.

The main point which it is desired to emphasise, is one discussed by West and the author* in a recent paper on the analysis of complex crystals. If absolute measurements of X-ray diffraction are available, the analysis of complex crystals is far more simple and certain than it is when merely comparative or qualitative estimates of diffraction are made. The paper on the structure of diopside was intended to be an illustration of the use of these measurements. The 14 parameters of the crystal can be deduced by using the absolute measurements without making any assumptions as to the probable arrangement of the atoms. In the present paper, the values of the parameters are derived in a quite different way, and the agreement in the results shows that the crystal has been analysed correctly.

The two methods of analysis are not independent, for the former analysis was used to give the correct sign to each coefficient $F(h\,k\,l)$. If the sign could be determined otherwise, the complete analysis could be made by the Fourier series. This point is briefly discussed in section 9 of the paper by Bragg and West. In the previous analysis of diopside, atomic scattering curves (F curves) for the atoms were used, and values of the parameters were found which made the observed and calculated values of $F(h\,k\,l)$ agree, signs being of course disregarded. For convenience, we may denote by $|F(h\,k\,l)|$ the quantity we can deduce from X-ray measurements of intensity, and by $F(h\,k\,l)$ the coefficient of the Fourier series. When the analysis of the structure was completed it was possible to give the right sign to each coefficient, *i.e.*, to determine $F(h\,k\,l)$. In the present analysis, therefore, the magnitudes of the Fourier coefficients depend only on X-ray measurement, but their signs are found by a previous analysis. It will be realised, however, that there is in general very little doubt about the sign of each coefficient, once an approximate analysis of the crystal has been made. It is determined in most cases by the positions of the heavier atoms of calcium, magnesium, and silicon, and quite approximate estimates of their parameters will suffice. The sign is only doubtful when F is very small, and in that case it does not matter.

As was emphasised by Duane, any given set of X-ray results may be explained even in the case of a centrosymmetrical crystal by as many different arrangements of scattering matter as there are permutations of signs in the Fourier

* Bragg and West, ' Z. Krist.,' vol. 69, p. 118 (1928).

coefficients. The test for the correct solution is that it is reasonable, or that it indicates a distribution of scattering matter which outlines atoms such as we know to exist in the crystal. In the former analysis, the existence of four molecules of $CaMg(SiO_3)_2$ in the unit cell was assumed from the start, and these atoms were moved about until the experimental results were explained. In the present analysis we show in effect that a certain set of signs given to the measured values of $|F(h\,k\,l)|$ leads to a distribution of density which (a) gives consistent projections on all three cell faces ; (b) gives the correct number of atoms in the unit cell ; (c) gives the correct number of electrons to each atom. The evidence for the correctness of the solution is set forth, using the Fourier series, in a new form which is perhaps more attractive and easy to grasp.

It must be realised, however, that the analysis by assigning parameters to atoms which make observed and calculated results agree, and the analysis by finding a suitable set of signs for Fourier terms, fundamentally depend upon precisely the same criteria for their success. We assume as one criterion, for instance, that the calcium atom contains about 18 electrons with a spatial distribution which we have been able to estimate. In the first type of analysis this yields an F curve for the scattering by calcium, and such F curves are used in comparing calculated and observed results. In an analysis entirely con-ducted by the Fourier method, signs would be adjusted till the series outlined a recognisable calcium atom, again with the number of electrons and spatial distribution which we expect. Every step in the one type of analysis may be paralleled by a similar step in the other.

### 4. *Tabulation of Experimental Results for Diopside.*

The crystal diopside is monoclinic, with $a = 9 \cdot 71$ Å, $b = 8 \cdot 89$ Å, $c = 5 \cdot 24$ Å, $\beta = 74° 10'$. The unit cell contains four molecules of $CaMg(SiO_3)_2$, hence the total number Z of electrons in the unit cell is 432. The space group is $C_{2h}^6$ $(2Ci - 6)$.

The projections dealt with in this paper are upon the three faces (100), (010) and (001) of the unit cell. Sets of values of $F(0\,k\,l)$, $F(h\,0\,l)$, $F(h\,k\,0)$ are required which are as extensive as possible. These values, taken from the paper on diopside, may be put in the form of tables such as those below.

In Table I, for example, $l$ varies along the rows and $k$ along the columns. Owing to the conditions imposed by the space group, only even values of $k$ appear, and also $F(0\,0\,l)$ is zero when $l$ is odd. The complete table would show negative values of $k$ as well as of $l$. This is unnecessary because $F(0\,k\,l) = F(0\,\bar{k}\,\bar{l})$ ; we may say that every table has a centre of symmetry at the value

432 corresponding to F (0 0 0). Negative values of F are denoted by a bar above the figure. As mentioned above, the magnitudes of F are in every case determined by experimental measurement. The sign of each coefficient is determined by a previous analysis of the crystal, which need only be assumed to be approximately correct.

### Table I.—Values of F (0 $k$ $l$).

When $k = 0$, $l$ is even.    $k$ is always even.    When $l$ is odd, F (0 $k$ $l$) $= -$ F (0 $k$ $\bar{l}$).

| Index $k$ | $\bar{8}$ | $\bar{7}$ | $\bar{6}$ | $\bar{5}$ | $\bar{4}$ | $\bar{3}$ | $\bar{2}$ | $\bar{1}$ | 0 | 1 | 2 | 3 | 4 | 5 | 6 | 7 | 8 |
|---|---|---|---|---|---|---|---|---|---|---|---|---|---|---|---|---|---|
| 0 | 38 | — | 29 | — | 136 | — | $\overline{175}$ | — | 432 | — | $\overline{175}$ | — | 136 | — | $\overline{29}$ | — | 38 |
| 2 | 0 | 0 | 0 | 0 | 0 | 0 | 75 | $\overline{44}$ | 19 | 44 | 75 | 0 | 0 | 0 | 0 | 0 | 0 |
| 4 | | 26 | 33 | $\overline{26}$ | 0 | 50 | 72 | $\overline{82}$ | 0 | 82 | 72 | $\overline{50}$ | 0 | 26 | 33 | $\overline{26}$ | |
| 6 | | | 0 | 29 | 0 | $\overline{44}$ | 88 | 50 | 94 | $\overline{50}$ | 88 | 44 | 0 | $\overline{29}$ | 0 | | |
| 8 | | | | 0 | 0 | 0 | 28 | 25 | 0 | $\overline{25}$ | 28 | 0 | 0 | 0 | | | |
| 10 | | | | | | | | | 66 | | | | | | | | |
| 12 | | | | | | | | | 29 | | | | | | | | |

### Table II.—Values of F ($h$ 0 $l$).

For all reflexions, $h$ and $l$ are even.

| Index $h$ | $\bar{8}$ | $\bar{6}$ | $\bar{4}$ | $\bar{2}$ | 0 | 2 | 4 | 6 | 8 |
|---|---|---|---|---|---|---|---|---|---|
| 0 | 38 | $\overline{29}$ | 136 | $\overline{175}$ | 432 | $\overline{175}$ | 136 | $\overline{29}$ | 38 |
| 2 | 0 | 0 | 19 | $\overline{88}$ | 0 | 46 | 0 | $\overline{36}$ | 0 |
| 4 | 0 | $\overline{72}$ | 90 | $\overline{128}$ | 15 | $\overline{80}$ | 77 | $\overline{49}$ | 0 |
| 6 | | 0 | 0 | 0 | 100 | $\overline{82}$ | 59 | $\overline{30}$ | |
| 8 | | | 33 | $\overline{51}$ | 76 | $\overline{32}$ | 0 | | |
| 10 | | | | $\overline{63}$ | 56 | $\overline{44}$ | | | |
| 12 | | | | | 0 | | | | |

Table III.—Values of $F(h\,k\,0)$.

For all reflexions, $h+k$ is even. $F(h\,k\,0)=F(h\,\bar{k}\,0)$.

| Index $h\rightarrow$ | 0 | 1 | 2 | 3 | 4 | 5 | 6 | 7 | 8 |
|---|---|---|---|---|---|---|---|---|---|
| Index $k$   0 | 432 | | 0 | | 15 | | 100 | | 76 |
| 1 | | 0 | | 76 | | $\overline{63}$ | | 41 | |
| 2 | 19 | | $\overline{51}$ | | $\overline{23}$ | | $\overline{19}$ | | $\overline{32}$ |
| 3 | | 13 | | 50 | | 37 | | 0 | |
| 4 | 0 | | 16 | | $\overline{50}$ | | 0 | | |
| 5 | | $\overline{84}$ | | $\overline{55}$ | | 0 | | $\overline{96}$ | |
| 6 | $\overline{94}$ | | 31 | | 29 | | 0 | | |
| 7 | | 0 | | 0 | | 40 | | | |
| 8 | 0 | | $\overline{17}$ | | | | | | |

In order to get a perfect representation of the scattering power in the crystal. it would be necessary to measure all values of F up to indices so high that the values become vanishingly small. It will be clear from the tables that the experimental results fall far short of the ideal. All values of F have been measured up to a glancing angle represented by $\sin\theta=0\cdot45$ for planes $(0\,k\,l)$ and $(h\,0\,l)$, and $\sin\theta=0\cdot30$ for the planes $(h\,k\,0)$, using rhodium K$\alpha$ radiation for which $\lambda=0\cdot615$ Å. Hence the Fourier representation will be in all cases imperfect, and particularly so for the projection on the $c$ face where values of $F(h\,k\,0)$ are used.

### 5. *Ewald's Reciprocal Lattice.*

The figures in these tables may be given an interesting interpretation by the elegant method of the "Reciprocal Lattice*" which we owe to Ewald.† Every set of parallel planes of a crystal is represented by a point in the reciprocal lattice. The line joining this point to the origin of the reciprocal lattice is at right angles to the crystal planes, and its distance from the origin is inversely proportional to their spacing. Since there is a definite structure-factor for each set of planes, a corresponding figure or "weight" can be attached to the point of the reciprocal lattice. The structure factors for first, second and

* It will be realised that each point in the reciprocal lattice corresponds to a simple sinusoidal distribution of density in the crystal, and that the complete representation of a given set of parallel crystal planes is an extended row of points.

† 'Z. Krist.,' vol. 56, p. 129 (1921).

high orders of X-ray reflexion become a set of figures attached to points in a row at equal intervals, the first order being nearest the origin. The assemblage of points corresponding to reflexion by all planes of the crystal builds up a space lattice, the reciprocal lattice.

We may consider the " weights " attached to the points of reciprocal lattice as being, in our notation, the values F ($h\ k\ l$). In general F ($h\ k\ l$) is a complex quantity, according to Ewald, representing both the amplitude and phase of the scattered wave. In the particular case considered here, it is real but positive or negative. The indices $h$, $k$, $l$ give the co-ordinates of the point with reference to the axes of the reciprocal lattice. We attach a weight F (0 0 0) to the origin equal to Z, the number of electrons in the unit cell of the crystal.

If this convention be adopted, it will be seen that the figures in Tables I, II and III represent *plane sections, through the origin, of Ewald's reciprocal lattice.* The origin of the lattice is always at the figure 432. The Fourier representation may therefore be summed up as follows. Any plane of the reciprocal lattice passing through the origin has a two-dimensional array of figures. These are the coefficients of a Fourier series, which gives the projection of the scattering matter in the crystalline cell on a plane. The direction of projection is that of the zone axis corresponding to the plane section of the reciprocal lattice. The orientation of the crystal plane on which projection takes place is obviously immaterial. Any convenient plane inclined to the zone axis, and any axes of reference in that plane, can be chosen. The indices ($h\ k\ l$) must, of course, be transformed into indices ($h'\ k'\ l'$) to correspond to the new axes which have been chosen. This merely means that having chosen our axes of reference in the crystal plane, we must choose a corresponding frame of reference for the network of points in the central section of the reciprocal lattice.

It is interesting to note that the whole development of the Fourier representation is implicitly contained in the paper by Ewald referred to above. He develops it, however, only in respect to a set of scattering points in the crystal, and not to a continuous distribution of scattering matter.

### 6. *Summation of the Fourier Series.*

The Fourier series for projections on (100), (010) and (001) faces of the unit cell are summed in Tables IV, V and VI. The figures in these tables correspond to series

$$S\,(y,\,z) = \Sigma\,\Sigma\ F\,(0\ k\ l)\,\cos\,2\pi\,(ky/b + lz/c)$$
$$S\,(x,\,z) = \Sigma\,\Sigma\ F\,(h\ 0\ l)\,\cos\,2\pi\,(hx/a + lz/c)$$
$$S\,(x,\,y) = \Sigma\,\Sigma\ F\,(h\ k\ 0)\,\cos\,2\pi\,(hx/a + ky/b).$$

To make the tables more compact, the actual sums of the series are divided by 10. The density per unit area at any point in a projection is given by

$$S(y, z)/bc \sin \alpha, \qquad S(x, z)/ac \sin \beta, \qquad S(x, y)/ab \sin \gamma.$$

(Since the crystal in the present example is monoclinic, $\sin \alpha = \sin \gamma = 1$.) Thus in order to derive the density per unit area from the figures in the tables, they must be multiplied by 10 and divided by the area of the face on which projection is being made.

The origin is taken to be at the centre of the unit cell. This origin is marked in each table, and the range of the figures in the $a$, $b$ or $c$ direction is indicated. It is not necessary to calculate the density all over the cell face as it repeats by symmetry. Since an atom in the general position becomes eight atoms in the unit cell, owing to the symmetry elements, it follows that it is only necessary to plot the density distribution over one-eighth of the surface of each face. The continuation of these sets of figures over the whole of each face will be clear if they are considered in conjunction with the contoured diagrams of figs. 1A, 2A, 3A.

Table IV.—Projection on Face (100).

$$S(y, z) \times 10^{-1}.$$

| 163 | 122 | 58 | 29 | 2 | 6̄ | 3 | 6̄ | 2 | 29 | 58 | 122 | 163 |
|---|---|---|---|---|---|---|---|---|---|---|---|---|
| 129 | 83 | 40 | 24 | 6 | 4̄ | 33 | 4̄ | 6 | 24 | 40 | 83 | 129 |
| 65 | 30 | 17 | 25 | 30 | 42 | 76 | 42 | 30 | 25 | 17 | 30 | 65 |
| 28 | 9 | 24 | 52 | 75 | 134 | 191 | 134 | 75 | 52 | 24 | 9 | 28 |
| 22 | 22 | 48 | 83 | 112 | 214 | 285 | 214 | 112 | 83 | 48 | 22 | 22 |
| 17 | 29 | 51 | 69 | 91 | 212 | 289 | 212 | 91 | 69 | 51 | 29 | 17 |
| 2 | 13 | 21 | 24 | 33 | 143 | 210 | 143 | 33 | 24 | 21 | 13 | 2 |
| 0 | 4 | 0 | 5̄ | 6̄ | 67 | 111 | 67 | 6̄ | 5̄ | 0 | 4 | 0 |
| 12 | 11 | 0 | 1 | 6 | 29 | 49 | 29 | 6 | 1 | 0 | 11 | 12 |
| 24 | 16 | 4 | 22 | 35 | 25 | 25 | 25 | 35 | 22 | 4 | 16 | 24 |
| 29 | 16 | 3 | 37 | 68 | 44 | 36 | 44 | 68 | 37 | 3 | 16 | 29 |
| 31 | 13 | 0 | 42 | 78 | 76 | 79 | 76 | 78 | 42 | 0 | 13 | 31 |
| 33 | 8 | 6̄ | 31 | 70 | 112 | 137 | 112 | 70 | 31 | 6̄ | 8 | 33 |
| 31 | 5 | 8̄ | 20 | 54 | 142 | 193 | 142 | 54 | 20 | 8̄ | 5 | 31 |
| 29 | 4 | 5̄ | 15 | 40 | 156 | 224 | 156 | 40 | 15 | 5̄ | 4 | 29 |
| 24 | 4 | 2 | 12 | 27 | 139 | 213 | 139 | 27 | 12 | 2 | 4 | 24 |
| 12 | 1̄ | 2 | 7 | 12 | 93 | 159 | 93 | 12 | 7 | 2 | 1̄ | 12 |
| 1̄ | 1̄2 | 2̄ | 1̄ | 2̄ | 45 | 97 | 45 | 2̄ | 1̄ | 2̄ | 1̄2 | 1̄ |
| 2 | 5̄ | 7 | 12 | 15 | 37 | 74 | 37 | 15 | 12 | 7 | 5̄ | 2 |
| 17 | 13 | 21 | 33 | 45 | 66 | 95 | 66 | 45 | 33 | 21 | 13 | 17 |
| 22 | 18 | 16 | 31 | 50 | 86 | 111 | 86 | 50 | 31 | 16 | 18 | 22 |
| 28 | 21 | 2̄ | 6 | 23 | 68 | 91 | 68 | 23 | 6 | 2̄ | 21 | 28 |
| 65 | 50 | 3 | 5̄ | 4̄ | 34 | 52 | 34 | 4̄ | 5̄ | 3 | 50 | 65 |
| 129 | 99 | 38 | 12 | 6̄ | 10 | 19 | 10 | 6̄ | 12 | 38 | 99 | 129 |
| (163) | 122 | 58 | 29 | 2 | 6̄ | 3 | 6̄ | 2 | 29 | 58 | 122 | 163 |

$\dfrac{b}{2}$ (left margin)   $\dfrac{c}{2}$ (bottom centre)

Origin←

Table V.—Projection on Face (010).

$$S(x, z) \times 10^{-1}.$$

| 364 | 291 | 138 | 33 | 20 | 48 | 55 | 48 | 76 | 127 | 162 | 159 | 150 | 159 | 162 | 127 | 76 | 48 | 55 | 48 | 20 | 33 | 138 | 291 | 364 |
|---|---|---|---|---|---|---|---|---|---|---|---|---|---|---|---|---|---|---|---|---|---|---|---|---|
| 330 | 242 | 121 | 25 | 14 | 39 | 36 | 34 | 71 | 131 | 167 | 160 | 136 | 128 | 125 | 101 | 70 | 63 | 74 | 64 | 23 | 21 | 117 | 264 | 330 |
| 249 | 206 | 76 | 8 | 8 | 19 | 24 | 20 | 54 | 115 | 146 | 128 | 91 | 78 | 74 | 68 | 72 | 77 | 94 | 78 | 29 | 9 | 82 | 192 | 249 |
| 150 | 106 | 24 | $\overline{13}$ | 3 | 27 | 17 | 9 | 40 | 95 | 109 | 82 | 52 | 28 | 32 | 45 | 57 | 87 | 109 | 97 | 34 | $\overline{3}$ | 31 | 114 | 150 |
| 73 | 36 | $\overline{14}$ | $\overline{24}$ | 16 | 26 | 20 | 5 | 18 | 59 | 67 | 40 | 7 | 0 | 14 | 36 | 63 | 98 | 127 | 87 | 50 | $\overline{5}$ | 1 | 52 | 73 |
| 32 | 5 | $\overline{30}$ | $\overline{26}$ | 8 | 30 | 20 | 19 | 17 | 38 | 40 | 15 | $\overline{10}$ | 7 | 14 | 40 | 66 | 104 | 130 | 117 | 59 | 8 | $\overline{2}$ | 24 | 32 |
| 17 | $\overline{4}$ | $\overline{25}$ | $\overline{21}$ | 6 | 18 | 14 | 8 | 13 | 25 | 13 | 1 | $\overline{13}$ | $\overline{4}$ | 18 | 41 | 65 | 94 | 110 | 100 | 57 | 10 | 3 | 20 | 17 |
| 18 | 4 | $\overline{14}$ | $\overline{16}$ | $\overline{5}$ | 1 | 4 | 8 | 16 | 16 | 4 | $\overline{7}$ | $\overline{12}$ | 2 | 16 | 34 | 53 | 71 | 82 | 70 | 46 | 16 | 14 | 23 | 18 |
| 21 | 10 | $\overline{3}$ | $\overline{11}$ | $\overline{16}$ | $\overline{16}$ | $\overline{8}$ | 11 | 25 | 14 | 2 | $\overline{8}$ | $\overline{7}$ | 2 | 21 | 21 | 36 | 51 | 56 | 46 | 27 | 16 | 18 | 24 | 21 |
| 18 | 14 | 3 | $\overline{5}$ | $\overline{12}$ | $\overline{7}$ | 11 | 33 | 35 | 34 | 6 | 2 | 2 | 4 | 5 | 13 | 28 | 43 | 35 | 32 | 17 | 13 | 14 | 20 | 18 |
| 21 | 16 | 14 | 0 | 2 | 14 | 34 | 61 | 56 | 36 | 10 | 12 | 12 | 12 | 6 | 19 | 30 | 56 | 54 | 37 | 22 | 26 | 14 | 14 | 21 |
| 12 | 14 | 17 | 21 | 19 | 33 | 50 | 78 | 68 | 43 | 21 | 18 | 22 | 18 | 15 | 27 | 55 | 74 | 66 | 40 | 28 | 33 | 17 | 10 | 12 |
| (2) | 8 | 19 | 25 | 29 | 45 | 73 | 87 | 71 | 39 | 21 | 24 | 24 | 24 | 21 | 39 | 71 | 87 | 73 | 45 | 29 | 25 | 19 | 8 | 2 |

Origin←————————————————————————— $\frac{a}{2}$ —————————————————————————→

(left axis label) $\frac{c}{4}$

Table VI.—Projection on Face (001).

$$S(x, y) \times 10^{-1}.$$

| 122 | 87 | 22 | $\overline{15}$ | 5 | 50 | 80 | 80 | 67 | 47 | 30 | 11 | 6 | 11 | 6 | 47 | 67 | 80 | 80 | 50 | 5 | $\overline{15}$ | 22 | 67 | 122 |
|---|---|---|---|---|---|---|---|---|---|---|---|---|---|---|---|---|---|---|---|---|---|---|---|---|
| 54 | 31 | 0 | $\overline{3}$ | 31 | 68 | 79 | 65 | 49 | 43 | 37 | 22 | 10 | 8 | 27 | 51 | 81 | 95 | 85 | 40 | $\overline{5}$ | $\overline{7}$ | 68 | 157 | 216 |
| 17 | 5 | $\overline{4}$ | 12 | 48 | 76 | 70 | 44 | 34 | 35 | 39 | 26 | 11 | 4 | 19 | 45 | 78 | 94 | 82 | 38 | $\overline{5}$ | 8 | 100 | 217 | 273 |
| 14 | 1 | $\overline{12}$ | $\overline{11}$ | 32 | 57 | 47 | 20 | 10 | 14 | 24 | 14 | 2 | $\overline{6}$ | 2 | 20 | 46 | 58 | 55 | 25 | $\overline{4}$ | 15 | 102 | 207 | 258 |
| 40 | 21 | $\overline{8}$ | $\overline{16}$ | 6 | 25 | 21 | 1 | $\overline{6}$ | $\overline{5}$ | 6 | 5 | 3 | 5 | 6 | 9 | 10 | 15 | 19 | 12 | $\overline{12}$ | $\overline{2}$ | 58 | 137 | 174 |
| 85 | 56 | 3 | $\overline{25}$ | $\overline{11}$ | 18 | 29 | 15 | 0 | $\overline{11}$ | $\overline{6}$ | 5 | 28 | 47 | 55 | 31 | 4 | $\overline{11}$ | $\overline{5}$ | 2 | $\overline{1}$ | $\overline{3}$ | 21 | 60 | 83 |
| 151 | 116 | 46 | 4 | 15 | 52 | 74 | 62 | 31 | 6 | 1 | 25 | 75 | 121 | 135 | 96 | 37 | $\overline{2}$ | $\overline{4}$ | 12 | 17 | 6 | 6 | 14 | 23 |
| 189 | 154 | 78 | 36 | 51 | 91 | 115 | 101 | 56 | 19 | 7 | 36 | 103 | 170 | 197 | 155 | 80 | 23 | 13 | 29 | 37 | 22 | 5 | 4 | 5 |
| 171 | 140 | 78 | 44 | 60 | 102 | 119 | 97 | 54 | 9 | $\overline{5}$ | 17 | 87 | 163 | 203 | 173 | 102 | 39 | 21 | 30 | 32 | 16 | 0 | $\overline{4}$ | $\overline{1}$ |
| 118 | 96 | 50 | 30 | 46 | 75 | 82 | 61 | 28 | $\overline{4}$ | $\overline{18}$ | $\overline{7}$ | 44 | 111 | 156 | 150 | 104 | 57 | 36 | 31 | 18 | 0 | $\overline{8}$ | 0 | $\overline{10}$ |
| 66 | 51 | 23 | 13 | 28 | 46 | 42 | 27 | 18 | 7 | $\overline{6}$ | $\overline{11}$ | 5 | 47 | 94 | 113 | 104 | 85 | 66 | 44 | 14 | $\overline{9}$ | $\overline{11}$ | 5 | 20 |
| 37 | 26 | 12 | 11 | 21 | 26 | 16 | 10 | 21 | 30 | 26 | 2 | $\overline{8}$ | 14 | 58 | 98 | 117 | 122 | 108 | 78 | 33 | 1 | 0 | 26 | 43 |
| (25) | 20 | 12 | 13 | 20 | 22 | 11 | 9 | 28 | 47 | 45 | 16 | $\overline{8}$ | 7 | 44 | 93 | 126 | 139 | 129 | 94 | 42 | 7 | 10 | 40 | 59 |

Origin←————————————————————————— $\frac{a}{2}$ —————————————————————————→

(left axis label) $\frac{b}{4}$

The positions of the atoms are revealed by the figures. A heavy atom makes the figures rise to an obvious maximum. A light atom (oxygen) is sometimes so close to a heavier neighbour in a projection that its position is not shown by a separate maximum value.

Some of the figures are negative, indicated by a bar above them. In a case of X-ray diffraction such as this, where anomalous scattering does not occur, negative scattering matter has no significance. The density should be positive everywhere, approaching a zero value in the regions between the atoms. The appearance of negative values may be partly due to errors in measurements of F, but even if these were perfect, negative values are to be expected because the Fourier series is not complete. Additional values of F for higher indices would make the figures correspond more closely to the ideal values.

The diagrams in figs. 1A, 2A and 3A were made by plotting the figures giving the density distribution in their positions on each face of the unit cell, and then drawing contour lines through points of equal density. The contours are drawn at intervals of 40, corresponding to intervals of 400 in the actual values of

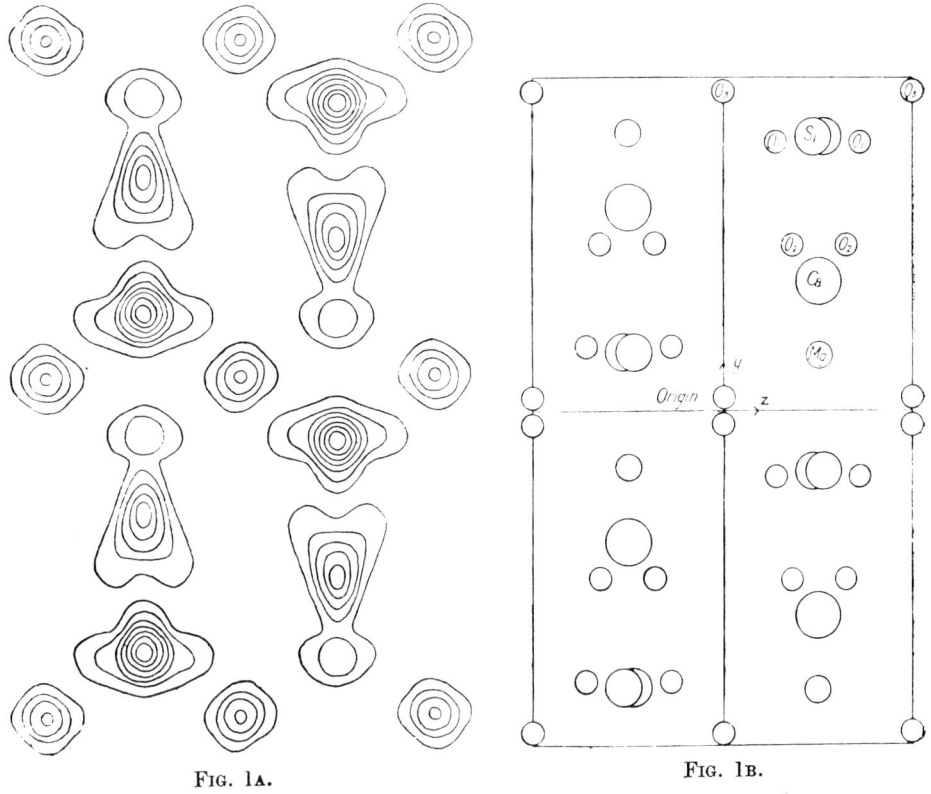

FIG. 1A.        FIG. 1B.

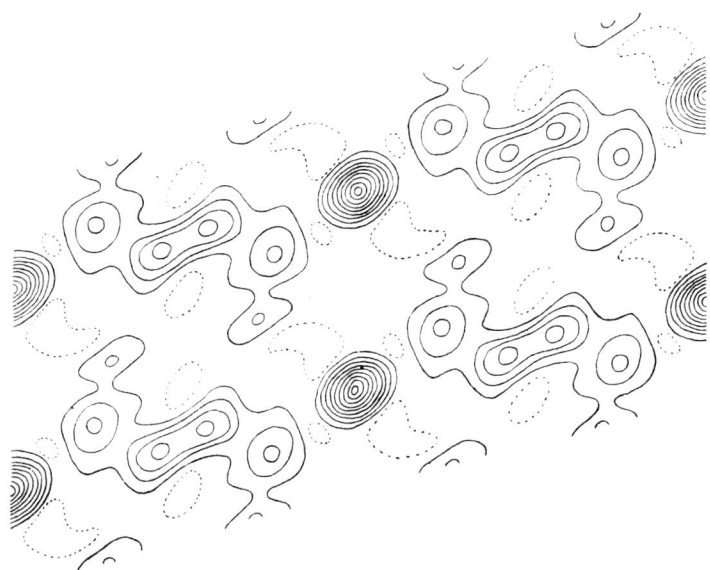

FIG. 2A.

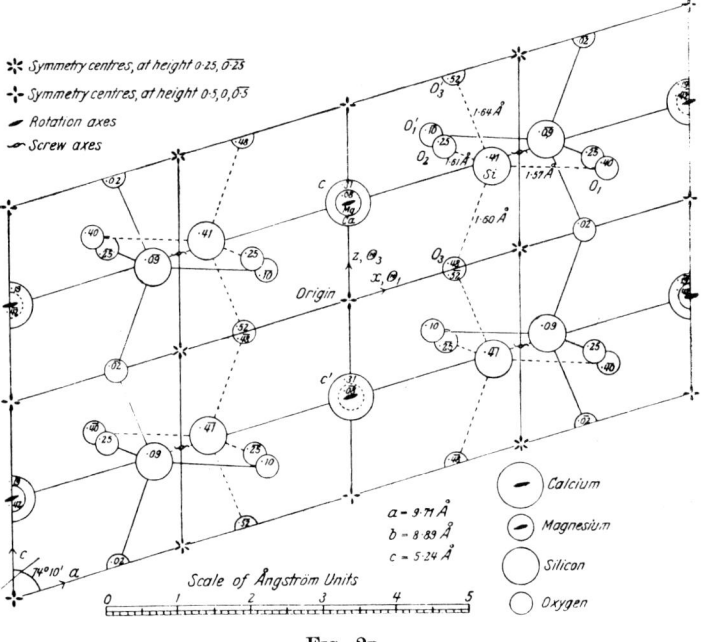

FIG. 2B.

$S(y, z)$, etc. The positions of the atoms as found in the previous paper on diopside are shown in figs. 1B, 2B, 3B, and the two sets of figures are seen to correspond very closely. In the projection on (010) the areas enclosing

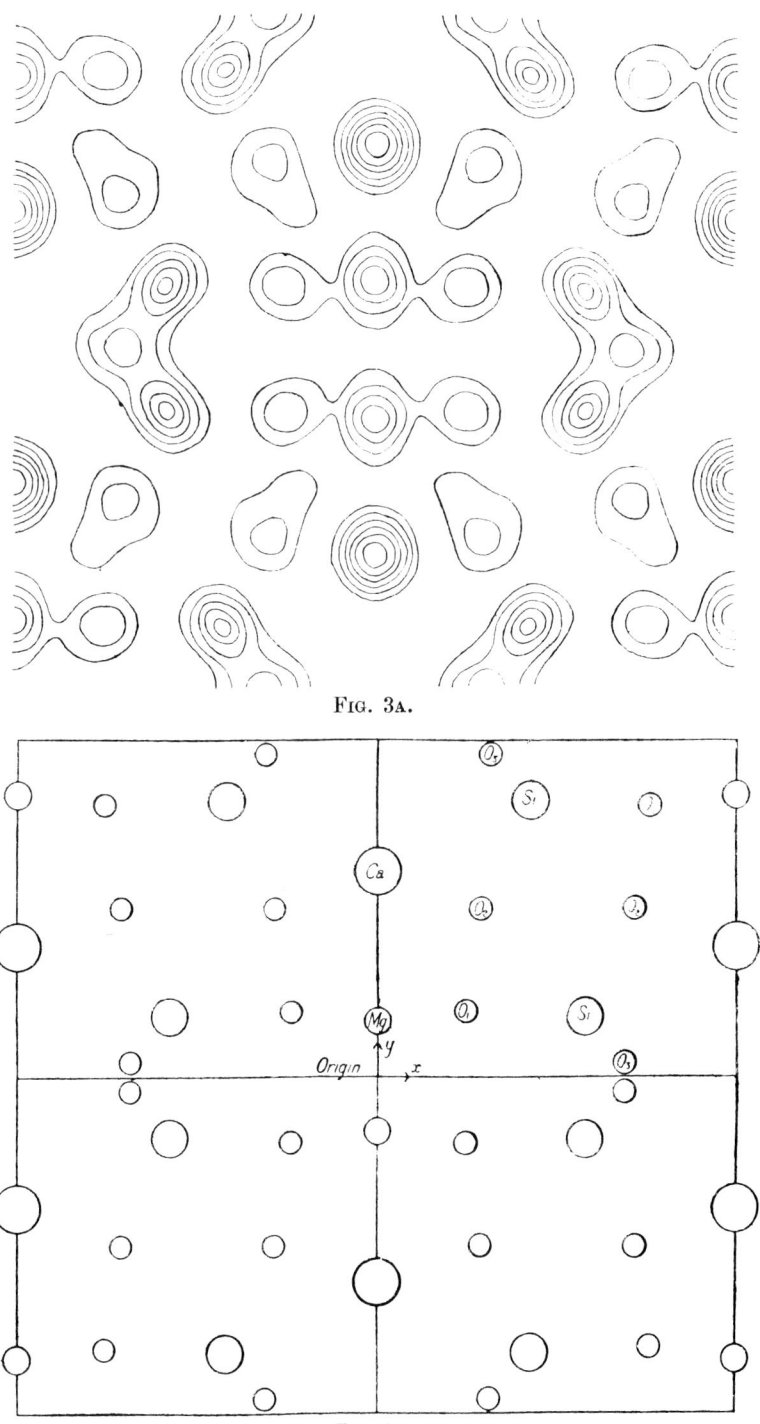

Fig. 3a.

Fig. 3b.

negative values are marked by dotted lines, these lines being the contours of zero level where $S(x, z) = 0$. The zero contours are not marked in the other projections. The first continuous contour line around each atom or group passes through all points where S is 400, the next through points where it is 800, and so forth.

### 7. *The Number of Electrons in the Atoms, and their Identification.*

The density in the space between the atoms is in general quite small. Since this is the case, it is possible to draw an approximate boundary around each atom or group of atoms in a projection and to calculate the total number of electrons in that area. We may take, as an instance, the projection on (010), and count the number of electrons in the most obvious rounded mass shown in that projection, where the contour lines rise to a peak of 364 (3640). The figures S are plotted at intervals $a/24$, $c/24$. The density per unit area is equal to

$$S(x, z)/ac \sin \beta$$

and this density may be taken to be the average density over a cell with sides $a/24$, $c/24$. This little cell of area $ac \sin \beta/24^2$ contributes an amount

$$(S(x, z)/ac \sin \beta) \cdot (ac \sin \beta/24^2) = S(x, z)/2304.$$

Thus the total number of electrons in the whole mass of scattering matter is given by

$$\Sigma S(x, z)/2304,$$

where $\Sigma S(x, z)$ is 10 times the sum of all the numbers in Table V which outline the atom or group in question. Although the boundary enclosing these numbers is somewhat indefinite, trial shows that it does not matter much where it is drawn because the density between the atoms is so small. In the case considered, the number of electrons proves to be $28 \cdot 3$, corresponding to a superimposed calcium atom and magnesium atom $(18 + 10)$. The remaining atoms in the projection (010) are so superimposed that it is difficult to disentangle them, but all atoms stand out clearly in one projection or another. The following table shows the electron-count in all cases where it is possible. There are three kinds of oxygen atom, $O_1$, $O_2$ and $O_3$.

Projection on (100).

| Atoms. | | No. of electrons. |
|---|---|---|
| $Ca + 2O_2$ | ...... | 35·3 |
| $Si + O_1$ | ...... | 20·1 |
| Mg | ...... | 13·3 |
| $O_3$ | ...... | 8·0 |

Projection on (010).

| Atoms. | | No. of electrons. |
|---|---|---|
| $Ca + Mg$ | ...... | 28·3 |
| $O_3$ | ...... | 7·7 approx. |

Projection on (001).

| Atoms. | | No. of electrons. |
|---|---|---|
| Ca | ...... | 16·6 |
| Mg | ...... | 12·6 |
| $Si + O_3$ | ...... | 19·8 |
| $O_2$ | ...... | 9·6 |
| $O_1$ | ...... | 8·0 |

Two points of interest may be noted. The average number of electrons in the oxygen atoms is distinctly less than 10, being in fact 8·3. It is thus much nearer to the value 8 for a non-ionised atom than to the value 10 for $O^{-2}$. The average number for $Si + O$ is equal to 20, so that according to these figures the number of electrons in the silicon atom is 11·7, and in the oxygen atom is 8·3. The estimate of 9·6 electrons for $O_2$ in the (001) projection is at variance with these estimates, and the discrepancy shows that too much reliance must not be placed upon them. Nevertheless it is interesting to see that the figures do not correspond to ions $Si^{+4}, O^{-2}$ each with 10 electrons. They suggest, on the other hand, that both the oxygen atoms and the silicon atoms are only partially ionised. As against this, if the estimates given above for the numbers of electrons in all the atoms of the projection on (001) are added, the sum for the molecule $CaMg(SiO_3)_2$ is 104 which does not check with the correct number 108. Some electrons have been missed in the count, and the missing electrons may belong to the diffuse oxygen atoms. It is indeed difficult to make estimates for the oxygen atoms, since their boundaries are not precise and the incomplete Fourier series leads to irregular variations of the density between the atoms. For instance, it is possible to see in the figures of Table VI at the point $a/2$, 0, a small mass of scattering matter which cannot be associated with any atom, and is a kind of optical " ghost."

The other point of interest is the division of electrons between calcium and magnesium. The total number is found to be 28, corresponding to the figures $18 + 10$ which we would expect. The magnesium atom, however, appears to have more than its due share of these electrons. The material is reported to contain $1 \cdot 12$ per cent. of FeO, and if this iron replaces magnesium it would raise the average number of electrons in the Mg position from 10 to $10 \cdot 5$. The number of magnesium in the projections is, however, between 12 and 13 whereas calcium appears to have about 16 electrons instead of 18. The possibility that calcium and magnesium interchange their positions to a certain extent is suggested. In view of the complexity of the crystal, and the difficulty of allowing for extinction in correcting some of the observed intensities, it would be misleading to stress any of these figures unduly.

It is quite clear that the atoms can be successfully identified by counting the electrons in them.

8. *The Parameters of the Structure.*

The position of an atom as shown in a projection may either be taken to be the point where the density shows a maximum, or to be the centre of gravity of the whole mass of scattering matter. For the oxygen atoms the latter has been determined, but this can only be done when the atom stands out clearly separated from its neighbours. In some cases overlapping is so extensive that no precise co-ordinates can be found. An interesting special case is shown in the projection on (100) fig. 1a. Two oxygen atoms overlap at the centre of the figure, forming a single rounded mass. These oxygen atoms are derived from each other by inversion at the centre. It is clear that their co-ordinates in both $b$ and $c$ directions are very nearly equal to zero, but it is impossible to find their precise values. The information derived from the various projections is tabulated below.

Table VII.

| Projection. | (100). | | | (010). | | | (001). | | |
|---|---|---|---|---|---|---|---|---|---|
| | $\theta_1$. | $\theta_2$. | $\theta_3$. | $\theta_1$. | $\theta_2$. | $\theta_3$. | $\theta_1$. | $\theta_2$. | $\theta_3$. |
| Ca | — | −107 | 90 | 0 | — | 90 | 0 | −108 | — |
| Mg | — | 30 | 90 | 0 | — | 90 | 0 | 34 | — |
| Si | — | 146 | (90) | 78 | — | 85 | 74 | 147 | — |
| $O_1$ | — | (148) | (50) | 137⎫ | — | ⎧ 55 | 135 | 151 | — |
| $O_2$ | — | (100) | (115) | 43⎭ | — | ⎩125 | 51 | 91 | — |
| $O_3$ | — | (180) | (0) | 52 | — | 0 | 52 | (180) | — |

The figures in brackets are approximate because of overlapping of atoms. The values for $O_1$ and $O_2$ in the (010) projection are bracketed because the position of the centre of gravity of the pair can be placed at the co-ordinates given in the table although these two atoms cannot be resolved.

The parameters deduced from all three projections are combined below, and are compared with the parameters deduced by the analysis in a previous paper.

Table VIII.

| | Parameters determined by Fourier analysis. | | | Values given in previous paper on diopside. | | |
|---|---|---|---|---|---|---|
| | $\theta_1$. | $\theta_2$. | $\theta_3$. | $\theta_1$. | $\theta_2$. | $\theta_3$. |
| | ° | ° | ° | ° | ° | s |
| Ca | 0 | $-107 \cdot 5$ | 90 | 0 | $-110$ | 90 |
| Mg | 0 | 32 | 90 | 0 | 30 | 90 |
| Si | 76 | $146 \cdot 5$ | 85 | 76 | 148 | 85 |
| $O_1$ | 135 | 151 | (50) | 136 | 145 | 50 |
| $O_2$ | 51 | 91 | (115) | 51 | 90 | 115 |
| $O_3$ | 52 | (180) | 0 | 56 | 173 | 0 |

Even when the results of the three projections are combined, certain co-ordinates of the oxygen atoms remain doubtful. They might be obtained by taking, for instance, the calcium atom as outlined in the (001) projection and subtracting it from the group Ca + 2O in the (100) projection, so as to leave the oxygen atoms clearly defined, but the figures are perhaps not sufficiently accurate to make such a process sure. It seems better to give in the table definite values only in those cases where they can be read directly from the projections.

The parameters are given in degrees, in accordance with the notation in the previous paper. The average difference between the two sets of values, for all figures except those in brackets, is $1 \cdot 6°$. If the parameters are expressed as fractions $u$, $v$, $w$ of the axial lengths $a$, $b$, $c$, this corresponds to an average difference of $0 \cdot 005$ in these fractions. For a crystal with 14 parameters this is a small difference, and the agreement is evidence of the effectiveness of quantitative measurements in analysing complex structures.

Table IX.

| | Parameters determined by Fourier analysis. | | | Values given in previous paper on diopside. | | |
|---|---|---|---|---|---|---|
| | *u.* | *v.* | *w.* | *u.* | *v.* | *w.* |
| Ca | 0 | −0·299 | 0·25 | 0 | −0·306 | 0·25 |
| Mg | 0 | 0·089 | 0·25 | 0 | 0·083 | 0·25 |
| Si | 0·211 | 0·407 | 0·236 | 0·211 | 0·411 | 0·236 |
| $O_1$ | 0·375 | 0·419 | (0·14) | 0·378 | 0·402 | 0·139 |
| $O_2$ | 0·142 | 0·253 | (0·32) | 0·142 | 0·250 | 0·320 |
| $O_3$ | 0·145 | (0·50) | 0·00 | 0·155 | 0·480 | 0·00 |

## 9. *Analysis by Fourier Series.*

The diopside crystal was first analysed by making calculated and observed values of $|F(h\,k\,l)|$ agree. This determined the sign of $F(h\,k\,l)$ and it was possible to form the Fourier representation of the distribution of scattering matter. It is interesting to see whether any of the labour of finding suitable parameters could have been shortened by employing the Fourier analysis at an earlier stage.

This appears to be the case. Consider the projection on (010) where calcium and magnesium atoms are superimposed, fig. 2A. In Table II it will be seen that $F(h\,0\,l)$ is positive when $\pm\,l$ is 0, 4, 8 and negative when $\pm\,l$ is 2, 6. This means that the sign of $F(h\,0\,l)$ is determined by the position of the calcium and magnesium atoms, so that all terms in the Fourier series

$$\Sigma\,\Sigma\,F(h\,0\,l)\cos 2\pi\,(hx/a + lz/c)$$

are positive at the point $x = 0$, $z = c/4$, where these atoms are situated. The sole exception is $F(202)$. It so happens that for this spectrum alone oxygen and silicon contributions to $F(202)$ more than neutralise those of calcium and magnesium.

If therefore some hint had been obtained at an early stage of the analysis that the calcium and magnesium atoms were superimposed in this projection, and that they determined the sign of $F(h\,0\,l)$, it would then have been possible to use the Fourier series to find the projection on (001) and so the $x$ and $z$ co-ordinates of all the atoms. This would have been done without the labour of trying different values for the parameters, and seeing which gave the best agreement between calculated and observed values of $F(h\,0\,l)$.

There is no such simple rule for the signs of $F(0\,k\,l)$ and $F(h\,k\,0)$, and it is necessary to analyse the crystal in order to determine these signs. However

a study of the contribution of the various atoms to these F values shows that,
in every case except F (022), the sign is determined by the calcium, magnesium,
and silicon atoms.   Therefore a knowledge of the positions of these heavy atoms
would make it possible to form the Fourier series, and so to fix the oxygen
atoms.   This would be of great advantage in analysis, because the determination of the oxygen parameters is a troublesome matter owing to their
small scattering power.

To sum up, a preliminary analysis of the crystal which gives approximate
positions of the heavy atoms, suffices to fix the signs of the coefficients F.   The
Fourier series may thus be formed, and the positions of all the atoms accurately
read off on the projections.

It is interesting to re-interpret the ordinary process of analysis by the
conceptions of the Fourier series.   In particular, a study of the effect of extinction is very illuminating.   Extinction affects the most powerful reflexions, and
allowance for it is an uncertain matter.   When comparing calculated and
observed values of F, the discrepancies for the powerful reflexions are very
obvious, and might seem to cast doubt on the success of the analysis.   In our
analyses of complex crystals by quantitative measurements we have always
held, however, that this doubt is not justified, and that the agreement for a
large number of reflexions of high order is ample evidence for the correctness
of the solution.   When now the Fourier series is formed, it is clear that the
effect of allowance for extinction on the calculated distribution of scattering
matter is very small.   For instance, in the (010) projection of diopside, the
position of the superimposed calcium and magnesium atoms is shown by a
peak rising to 3640.   The strongest reflexion is (002) and F (002) is taken to
have a value of 175.   It may be in error by 30 units owing to incorrect allowance
for extinction, but clearly this will hardly affect the peak of 3640.   The density
is determined by a large number of F values not affected by extinction, and
the few reflexions at low angles which are so affected are relatively unimportant.

If the form of the Fourier series

$$\Sigma \, \Sigma \, \text{F} \, (0 \, k \, l) \cos 2\pi \, (hx/a + lz/c)$$

be considered, it will be seen that each term represents a series of periodic
undulations of density, parallel to a line whose slope is determined by the
indices $k$, $l$.   The higher the indices $k$ and $l$, the shorter is the wave-length.
We may thus distinguish the effect on the projection of the different terms.
Those with low indices group the density into certain masses which begin to
outline the atoms.   The terms with high indices trim the outlines, and give

precision to the atoms.  The number of electrons in each atom is determined by the terms with low indices.  Since these are affected by allowance for extinction, the numbers of electrons counted in section 7 must be accepted with reserve.  On the other hand, the precise positions of the atoms are almost entirely determined by the terms with high indices.  Hence the values of the parameters may be relied on to be correct.

This is merely another way of regarding the familiar consideration that reflexions with low indices must be measured accurately if we are to tell whether the atoms are ionised or not, and that reflexions with high indices serve to fix the positions of the atoms with precision.

## Summary.

The representation of the scattering matter in a crystal by Fourier series, first used by W. H. Bragg and later developed by Duane, Havighurst and Compton, is applied here to the determination of the parameters in a complex crystal.

A series is used which gives the projection of the scattering matter in the unit cell on each of its faces in turn.  For instance, when projection is made on the face (100) of the cell, the formula for the density $\rho(y, z)$ of the scattering matter at a point $y, z$ is as follows :—

$$\rho(y, z) = (1/bc \sin \alpha) \sum_{-\infty}^{+\infty} \sum_{-\infty}^{+\infty} F(0\,k\,l) \cos 2\pi (ky/b + lz/c).$$

In this formula, $F(0\,k\,l)$ is the value of the structure factor for the reflexion $(0\,k\,l)$ measured in absolute units.  The formula applies to a cell of any shape, provided that it has a centre of symmetry.  $F(0\,0\,0)$ is taken to be the number of electrons in the unit cell.

This series is evaluated for the crystal diopside $CaMg(SiO_3)_2$.  The signs of the coefficients $F(0\,k\,l)$ had been fixed by a previous analysis of the crystal. The projections are shown as contoured diagrams in figs. 1A, 2A and 3A.  The positions of the atoms agree very closely with those given by the previous analysis, figs. 1B, 2B and 3B, made by finding values for the parameters which gave agreement between calculated and observed values of $F$.  A comparison of the two sets of 14 parameters is shown in Table IX.

It is possible to count the numbers of atomic electrons in the projections. They are approximately as follows :—Ca 16·5, Mg 12·5, Si 11·5, O 8·5–9. It is interesting to note that the oxygen does not appear to be an ion $O^{-2}$ with 10 electrons.

The groups of F values used for any projection may be conveniently described as the weights attached to a network of points on a central section of Ewald's reciprocal lattice.

The employment of Fourier series in analysing complex crystals is discussed, and it is concluded that it may be used in conjunction with an analysis of the usual type made by assigning parameters to the atoms, and may considerably shorten the labour of analysis. The series is particularly of value in discovering the positions of the lighter atoms and in leading directly to precise values of the parameters.

In a recent paper by Mr. West and the author in the ' Zeitschrift für Krystallographie,' entitled " A Technique for the X-ray Examination of Crystal Structures with many Parameters," examples were given to show that the use of absolute measurements of X-ray diffraction enabled these complex crystal structures to be solved with directness and accuracy. The use of the same measurements in the method of Fourier series affords further evidence in support of the effectiveness of such absolute measurements.

It is with great pleasure that I acknowledge my indebtedness to my father, Sir William Bragg, for suggestions which materially contributed to the work described in this paper. At the time when I was following up the connection between our usual methods of analysis and the analysis by Fourier series, a connection briefly treated in the paper by Mr. West and myself, my father showed me some results which he had obtained by using relative values of the first few terms of two- and three-dimensional Fourier series to indicate the general distribution of scattering matter in certain organic compounds. It was largely as a result of his suggestions that I was encouraged to make all the computations for these two-dimensional series, using the extensive absolute measurements which we had made on certain crystals.

Reprinted from
*Proceedings of the Royal Society, A,* 1934, volume 145, page 699

## The Effect of Thermal Agitation on Atomic Arrangement in Alloys.

By W. L. Bragg, F.R.S., and E. J. Williams, D.Sc., Manchester University.

(Received December 29, 1933.)

Forming the subject of the Bakerian Lecture by Professor W. L. Bragg, F.R.S.
(Read June 28, 1934.)

*Summary.*

An alloy phase has two characteristics. The first is the pattern of sites occupied by atoms irrespective of their nature. Each phase of an alloy system has a different pattern of sites, and therefore a change from one phase to another involves their complete re-arrangement. The second characteristic is the distribution of the atoms amongst these sites. This distribution may vary continuously without change of phase, from being random at high temperatures to being partially regular at low temperatures. The effect of thermal treatment upon the arrangement of the atoms forms the subject of the present paper.

The equilibrium states of the alloy are first considered, and the degree of order of the structure as a function of temperature is calculated. The ordered structure has a lower potential energy than the disordered structure, but thermal agitation promotes disorder. It is shown that above a certain critical temperature the structure is completely random. As the temperature is lowered, order sets in abruptly at the critical temperature, and at first rapidly increases. It only becomes complete as absolute zero is approached.

This characteristic sudden onset of order indicated by the theory causes a sharp inflexion in curves which show the variation of resistivity, lattice spacing and specific heat with temperature. These inflexions simulate a phase-change, though there is actually no such change. β brass, Au-Cu alloys, and Fe-Al alloys are cited as examples.

The second section of the paper deals with the rate at which an alloy, not in equilibrium, relaxes towards equilibrium. A general law for the dependence of rate of relaxation upon temperature is deduced, which enables the effects of annealing and quenching to be predicted. The rate of relaxation depends upon the magnitude of the " activation energy " required to surmount a potential barrier when two atoms interchange position.

The alloy is a system of dynamical equilibrium. Although interchange of atomic position at room temperature is infrequent, the alloy has received its character at some previous point in its history when the temperature was just sufficiently high for interchange to be important. Maxima and minima in physical properties at certain relative proportions (*e.g.*, $Fe_3Al$ and $AuCu_3$) are statistical effects, and do not imply the existence of corresponding compounds.

Reprinted from *Nature*, 1939, volume 143, page 678

### A New Type of 'X-Ray Microscope'

A STANDARD method of X-ray analysis consists in measuring the strength of the diffracted beams corresponding to a series of reflections around a crystal zone (for example, the reflections with indices $h0l$ around the $b$ axis), and then forming a double Fourier series with the amplitudes $F$ as coefficients.

$$\Sigma\Sigma \, F(h0l) \cos \left\{ \frac{2\pi hx}{a} + \frac{2\pi lz}{c} + \alpha(h0l) \right\}$$

The sum of this series gives the density of scattering matter at a point $x,z$ when the contents of the unit cell are projected on the face (010). In the case of a

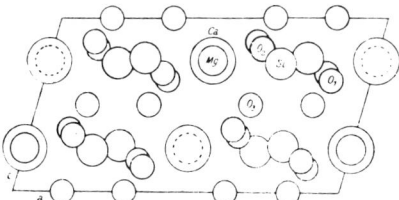

FIG. 1.

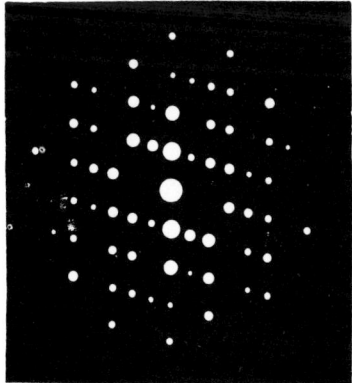

FIG. 2.

centro-symmetrical projection $\alpha(h0l)$ is either 0 or $\pi$, and if there are sufficiently heavy atoms at the centre of symmetry, it is zero for all reflections. The present note describes a simple and rather striking optical method of effecting the summation for a case where $\alpha(h0l)$ is always zero.

Holes are drilled in a thin plate of brass, one for
each reflection $h0l$. The area of the hole is proportional to $F(h0l)$ and the holes are arranged in the
positions of cross-grating spectra. The plate represents, in fact, a section through the reciprocal lattice
containing all $h0l$ reflections. The plate is placed
between a pair of good lenses, of about 6-ft. focal
length. A point source of monochromatic light (a
pin-hole in front of a mercury vapour lamp) is placed
at the focus of one lens, and the image of the pin-hole
at the focus of the other lens is viewed through a
microscope. The diffraction of the light by the holes

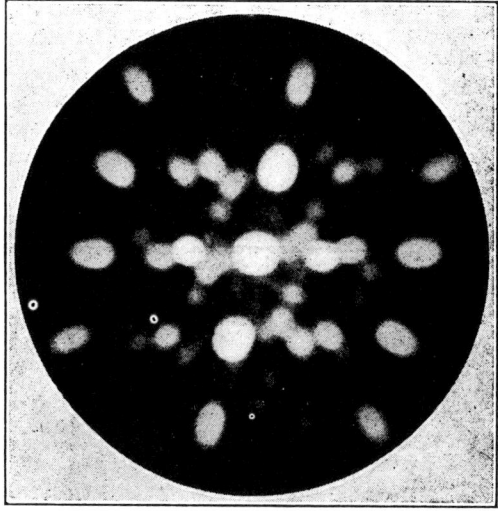

FIG. 3.

in the plate results in a very realistic image of the
crystal structure being seen through the microscope.
Each pair of holes $F(h0l)$ and $F(\bar{h}0\bar{l})$ forms a set of
parallel diffraction fringes, and these sets have the
right amplitude, spacing and phase to build up the
double Fourier series given above.

Fig. 1 shows the projection of diopside, $CaMg(SiO_3)_2$ [1],
on the plane (010). The largest circles represent
superimposed Ca and Mg atoms at symmetry centres
of the projection, these atoms being so heavy that
$\alpha(h0l)$ is zero for all reflections. The intermediate
circles are silicon, the smallest are oxygen. Fig. 2 is
twice natural size and is from a contact print of a
brass plate drilled with holes to correspond to the
$h0l$ spectra given by the crystal (see[2] Fig. 3*b*). Fig. 3
is a photograph of the diffraction image seen in the

microscope when this plate is placed between the lenses as described above, and it will be seen that it is a faithful reproduction of the crystal structure shown in Fig. 1.

We are now searching for a device for dealing with the more general case of values of 0 or $\pi$ for $\alpha(h0l)$, for example, a ready way of placing a film with a half-wave retardation over certain holes. If this can be found, the method may prove to be of practical use in crystal analysis.

Cavendish Laboratory,  W. L. BRAGG.
Cambridge.

[1] *Z. Krist.*, **69**, 168 (1928).
[2] *Z. Krist.*, **70**, 475 (1929).

Since writing this note my attention has been drawn to a paper by von H. Boersch in "Zeitschrift für Technische Physik", page 337, 1938, in which similar experiments with arbitrary patterns of holes are described, and the suggestion is made that the method might be used for building up an image of crystal structure by using the determinations for X-ray diffraction.

I was unaware of this paper when I wrote the note, and take this opportunity of making due acknowledgement.

Reprinted from *Nature*, 1945, volume 156, page 332

## X-Ray Analysis with the Aid of the 'Fly's Eye'

In a note in *Nature*[1], an example was given of the use of the 'fly's eye' for X-ray analysis. The reflexions of X-rays by planes around a crystal zone correspond in intensity to the optical spectra produced by a cross-grating, the pattern of which is that of the crystal structure projected on a plane perpendicular to the zone. The 'fly's eye' enables such cross-gratings to be made. The spectra they produce can be compared with the observed X-ray reflexions, thus avoiding the labour of calculation, at any rate in the first stages of the usual trial-and-error method of seeking the solution.

The original type of 'fly's eye' was a multiple pin-hole camera, the holes being in a square array, forty to the centimetre. Each hole produces an image of a single illuminated object representing the unit of structure. An example of a cross-grating made in this way by Bunn is shown in Fig. 1*a*. It represents phthalocyanine and gave a good correspondence with observation (see *Nature, loc. cit.*). It has the disadvantages, however, that the images are diffuse be-

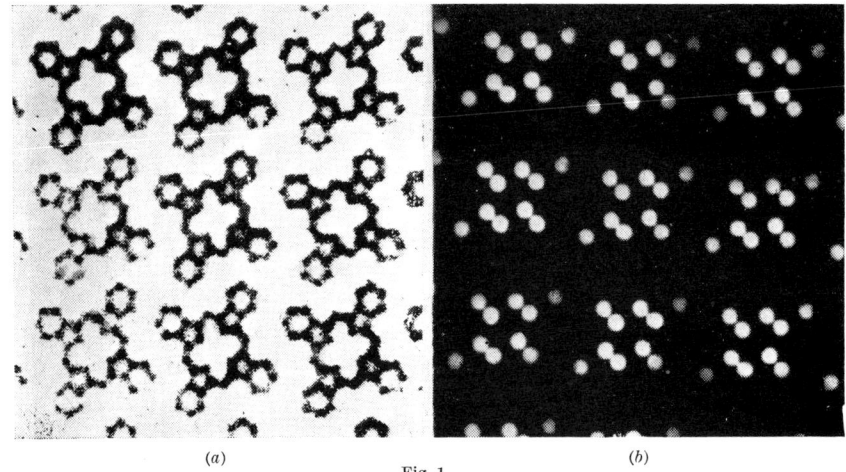

(*a*)                                                    (*b*)

Fig. 1.

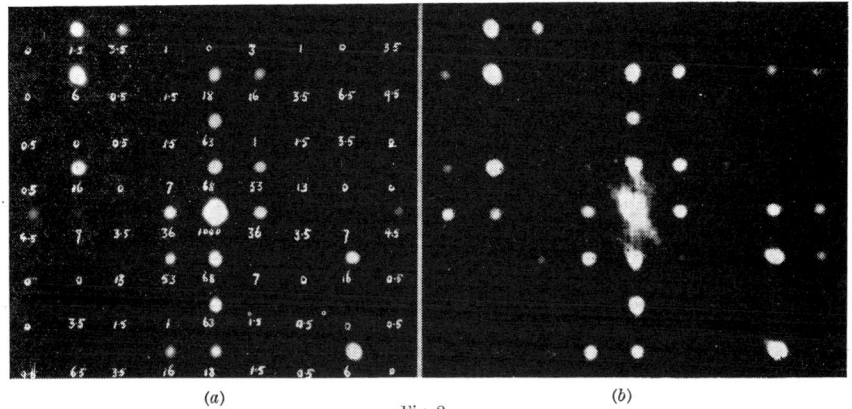

(a)        (b)

Fig. 2.

cause of the pinhole method and the grain of the photographic plate, and they are unequal in intensity because the minute pinholes are liable to be blocked by specks of dust.

The new type of 'fly's eye' described here gives much better cross-gratings. The pinholes are replaced by small lenses embossed on the surface of a 'Perspex' sheet. These are made by pressing a steel ball at regular intervals on a soft copper block, and casting or pressing 'Perspex' on the block. The actual array used for Fig. 1b consisted of lenses 0·5 cm. in focal length, 0·06 cm. in diameter and 0·13 cm. apart. A paper mask punched with corresponding holes cut out all light except that falling on the lenses.

The array of lenses, covering a circular area of 2·5 cm. diameter, with a photographic plate in their focal plane, is exposed to an illuminated ground-glass viewing screen on which black disks are laid representing the atoms in a single unit of pattern. They appear as transparent holes in Fig. 1b, which is an enlargement of the negative used as the cross-grating. The greater sharpness and uniformity of the pattern in Fig. 1b as compared with Fig. 1a is evident. The structure is that of durene[2] projected on (010), and referred to equal axes at right angles.

The cross-grating is mounted between optical flats with cedarwood oil in the interspaces, to reduce optical imperfections of the photographic plate. It is placed before a lens 1 metre in focal length, and the spectra photographed on a plate at the focus. It is convenient to use an eyepiece for viewing them. Fig. 2$a$ shows the spectra so produced, the numbers representing the X-ray intensities recorded by Robertson. If allowance is made for the more rapid falling off of X-ray intensities with angle, due to the carbon scattering factor, it will be seen that the correspondence is good. Fig. 2$b$ shows the poorer result when the optical flats and cedarwood oil were not used.

The new method has several advantages over the former one. The cross-grating is on a larger scale, hence the grain of the plate is not troublesome. The sharpness of the images should make it possible to represent the atoms as concentric rings so as to simulate the scattering curve of atoms. A series of gratings can quickly be made with different arrangements of the disks on the viewing screen, and it is therefore a rapid trial and error method in seeking a first approximation to the structure.

It is intended to publish elsewhere a more detailed account of the production and use of the gratings.

W. L. BRAGG.
A. R. STOKES.

Cavendish Laboratory,
Cambridge.   Aug. 9.

[1] *Nature*, **154**, 69 (1944).
[2] Robertson, *Proc. Roy. Soc.*, A, **142**, 659 (1933).

Reprinted from the
*Proceedings of the Royal Society, A*, 1947, volume 190, page 474

# A dynamical model of a crystal structure

By Sir Lawrence Bragg, F.R.S. and J. F. Nye

*Cavendish Laboratory, University of Cambridge*

(*Received* 9 *January* 1947—*Read* 19 *June* 1947)

[Plates 8 to 21]

The crystal structure of a metal is represented by an assemblage of bubbles, a millimetre or less in diameter, floating on the surface of a soap solution. The bubbles are blown from a fine pipette beneath the surface with a constant air pressure, and are remarkably uniform in size. They are held together by surface tension, either in a single layer on the surface or in a three-dimensional mass. An assemblage may contain hundreds of thousands of bubbles and persists for an hour or more. The assemblages show structures which have been supposed to exist in metals, and simulate effects which have been observed, such as grain boundaries, dislocations and other types of fault, slip, recrystallization, annealing, and strains due to 'foreign' atoms.

Reprinted from *Nature*, 1950, volume 166, page 399

### Microscopy by Reconstructed Wave-fronts

THE principle of Dr. D. Gabor's interesting method
of reconstructing images of objects from photographs
of the interference patterns produced when the object
is illuminated with a coherent monochromatic wave-
train is fully explained in his paper[1]. The treatment
in this note is essentially the same, but I have ventured
to present it in a very simplified form because I have
found in discussions that difficulty is sometimes
experienced in forming a physical picture of the
reconstruction of the image, when the photographic
plate can only record intensities of light and not
phases.

The object $O$ is placed close to a point source of
light $S$. The wavelets scattered by the object inter-
fere with the main waves from $S$ over a surface such

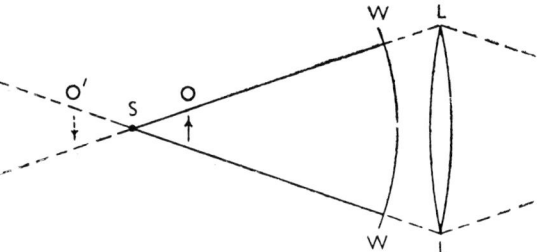

as $WW$, altering both their amplitude and their
phase. It is an essential condition for the success of
the method that the amplitude due to the scattered
waves should be small compared to that of the main
waves. A photographic plate, which for simplicity
we may suppose to coincide with a main wave surface
such as $WW$, records the intensity of the resultant
light at each point. The photograph is developed
and printed as a diapositive. The pattern is quite
unlike the object, being nearer to its Fraunhofer
diffraction pattern than to a 'shadow'. Gabor then
shows that if the diapositive is placed at $WW$, and
the light is reversed, for example, by a lens $LL$
focusing a beam at $S$, an image of $O$ is reconstructed
free from diffraction effects within, of course, the
usual limits imposed by aperture and wave-length.
Alternatively, the source $S$ may be retained, and an
eyepiece focused through the diapositive, when the
image will be seen at the position of $O$. This result
appears paradoxical because the photographic plate
has only recorded intensities, whereas the formation
of the image would seem to require that both amplitude and phase should be correctly reproduced.

The reason for the success of the method, and at
the same time its limitations, can at once be seen if
we picture wavelets scattered simultaneously by $O$
and a corresponding object $O'$ related to $O$ by a

centre of symmetry at $S$. The resultant of the wavelets from corresponding points at $O$ and $O'$ will have,
by symmetry, a phase of $0$ or $\pi$ in relation to the
main wave over the surface $WW$. Since this latter
has a much larger amplitude, the total resultant
phase is the same over $WW$ and the only variation
is in amplitude ; complete information about this
variation is recorded by the photographic plate.

When, therefore, the light is reversed through the
diapositive, its wave form is that which would have
been produced by $S$, $O$ and $O'$ (this is not strictly
accurate, but very close to the truth when the
secondary waves are small compared to the main
wave, as will be seen by comparing the vector
diagrams of amplitudes from $S$, $O$, $O'$ and $S$, $O$
alone), and all three images must be reproduced. As
Dr. Gabor has shown, this is just what is observed
when the experiment is tried. By altering the focus
of the eyepiece, one sees at first $O$ in focus against a
bright background, then the source $S$, and finally
the reversed image $O'$ on the far side of $S$. We
cannot see $O$ without at the same time seeing a
diffuse image $O'$ out of focus behind it ; this is the
price paid for being unable to record phases. If,
however, $O$ is an object such as a narrow opaque line
on a transparent background, the ideal case for the
Gabor method, the image $O'$ is almost invisible when
out of focus. The method fails when $O$ has large
opaque areas, as these do not disappear when out
of focus.

The principle of the method is identical with one
familiar in X-ray analysis of crystals. Diffracted
intensities are alone recorded, whereas to form a
Fourier representation of the crystal structure one
needs to know both amplitudes and phases. In
certain favourable cases of centro-symmetrical projections there are atoms of such high atomic numbers
at the cell-corners that all phases are zero, the other
atoms merely altering the amplitude (for example,
J. M. Robertson's analysis of platinum phthalocyanine[2]). The Fourier series can then be formed.
The heavy atom corresponds to the source $S$, and
the remaining atoms to $O$ and $O'$ in Gabor's method.

An even closer analogy is provided by the analysis
of cholesteryl iodide by C. H. Carlisle and D. Crow-
foot[3]. The crystal has no centre of symmetry. If
the Fourier series is summed with phases appropriate
to the heavy iodine atoms alone, it is equivalent to
assuming a centre of symmetry and so phases of $0$ or
$\pi$. The Fourier series, therefore, shows both the actual
molecule in the cell and its reversed image, corresponding to $O$ and $O'$ in Gabor's reconstruction.

W. L. Bragg

Cavendish Laboratory,
    Cambridge.
        July 30.

[1] *Proc. Roy. Soc.*, A, **197**, 454 (1950).
[2] *J. Chem. Soc. Trans.*, 36, (1940).
[3] *Proc. Roy. Soc.*, A, **184**, 64 (1945).

Reprinted from the
*Proceedings of the Royal Society, A*, 1952, volume 213, page 425

# The structure of haemoglobin

Sir Lawrence Bragg, F.R.S., *Cavendish Laboratory, University of Cambridge*
and M. F. Perutz, *Medical Research Council Unit for the Study of the
Molecular Structure of Biological Systems, Cavendish Laboratory,
University of Cambridge*

(*Received* 20 *February* 1952)

The paper describes the first steps in an attempt to solve the structure of a haemoglobin molecule by X-ray analysis, using a direct method. It is based on an extensive series of absolute measurements of the diffraction by various shrinkage stages of a haemoglobin crystal, and estimates based on many crystalline forms of the general dimensions of the haemoglobin molecule. The methods used are described here and applied to a direct determination of the electron density in one particular direction in the molecule. The extension of the methods to the subsequent problem of obtaining a picture of the molecule as projected on a plane will, it is hoped, form the subject of a subsequent paper.

Reprinted from
*Proceedings of the Royal Society, A,* 1954, volume 222, page 33

# The structure of haemoglobin. II

By Sir Lawrence Bragg, F.R.S. and E. R. Howells

*Cavendish Laboratory, University of Cambridge*

and M. F. Perutz

*Medical Research Council Unit for the Study of the Molecular Structure of
Biological Systems, Cavendish Laboratory, University of Cambridge*

(*Received* 24 *August* 1953)

The outer form of the haemoglobin molecule is delimited by considering the way in which
it packs into a number of crystalline forms. A simple spheroidal form of the molecule is
found to account for the lattice dimensions with a remarkable degree of consistency. The
dimensions of the spheroid are $53 \times 53 \times 71$ Å in the case of the hydrated molecule, and
$45 \times 45 \times 65$ Å in the case of the dry molecule, with an error of less than 2 Å in each direction.
The evidence of form birefringence is compatible with these conclusions. They are supported
by observed changes in diffraction effects with salt concentration.

The spheroidal shape can only be a first approximation, and the protein molecule must be
more polyhedral in shape, since in the dry form it occupies a considerably larger proportion
of the total volume than would be occupied by spheroids in close packing. The limits to its
form which are set by packing contacts are defined.

## 1. Introduction

An earlier paper with the same title, by Bragg & Perutz (1952*a*), described some
attempts at interpreting the X-ray diffraction patterns given by haemoglobin
crystals. The trial-and-error methods of analysis used for simpler crystals present
extreme difficulty because of the formidable complexity of the haemoglobin molecule. A direct method is attempted, based on the exploration of the transform of
the molecule by taking advantage of the available series of shrunk and expanded
forms of monoclinic horse met-haemoglobin. If the sign of the $F$ values over the
whole of the transform could be determined, a projection of the molecule on the
monoclinic $b$ plane could be drawn. The earlier paper indicated how the signs along
the zero layer line $h = 0$ could be established, and used to calculate the projection
of the crystal structure on a line perpendicular to the $c$ plane.

This paper reviews the evidence as to the size and shape of the molecule yielded by
the many crystalline forms of haemoglobin which have been measured. A knowledge of the outer form is important in any attempt to interpret the diffraction
data. The hydrated molecule packs as if it were approximately spheroidal in
shape with diameters $53 \times 53 \times 71$ Å. When dried it is about 7 Å less in each
dimension, owing to the removal of most or all of the bound water. The dried
molecules are very tightly packed in the available lattice space, and set close
limits to the dimensions which should be of considerable use in testing proposed
models for the molecular structure.

Reprinted from *The Times Educational Supplement*, Friday June 3, 1955

# THE ROYAL INSTITUTION

## MAINTAINING STANDARDS OF POPULAR EXPOSITION

### By Sir Lawrence Bragg

Other bodies may style themselves The Royal Institute or Institution of this or that, but " The Royal Institution " is like " The Royal Society " in appearing to regard any such explanation of its function as being quite unnecessary. Even its full title " The Royal Institution of Great Britain " accentuates this impression. In consequence many people, even those in the academic world, have a very vague idea of what takes place behind the imposing Palladian front of the building which stretches along the upper end of Albemarle Street, off Piccadilly. It was founded by Count Rumford in 1799 for the " promotion of science and the diffusion and extension of useful knowledge " and is a private society depending for its upkeep upon the subscriptions of its members, the income from its endowments, and the donations which it receives. It resembles in some ways the " philosophical societies " which were started at many centres in this country early in the nineteenth century to satisfy the growing interest in natural phenomena. It has a unique character, however, in that it has a staff of professors and a laboratory in which research can be pursued. One of the professors resides in the official flat of the institution, acts as host to its guests, and directs the laboratory.

### COUNT RUMFORD

The founder was a strange and romantic figure. Benjamin Thompson was an American who sided with the British in the War of Independence and escaped to this country in 1776. Entering the service of the Kingdom of Bavaria, he became a Count of the Holy Roman Empire and was sent as Ambassador to George III. The Government refused to receive him as he was still a British subject, and the disappointed Count Rumford turned his energies to founding the Royal Institution.

Rumford's original philanthropic scheme of a " Mechanic's Institution " was not a success. He appears to have been somewhat dictatorial and overbearing, and disagreements with the professors and managers nearly wrecked the new venture. It was saved by another very remarkable man, Humphry Davy, famous for the miner's lamp. Davy was a brilliant chemist, a brilliant lecturer, and a very attractive personality. As resident professor he gave the Royal Institution a character which it has preserved ever since. London society flocked to hear his discourses ; he made it a great social success as well as a centre of learning. And when he retired he was succeeded by Faraday, who is generally regarded as our greatest scientist since Newton.

### UNIQUE LABORATORY

To understand the part which the Royal Institution played in the first three quarters of the nineteenth century, one must remember that universities had no laboratories devoted to physical science in those days. A professor who was so eccentric as to do research had to do it at his own expense and in his own home. The Clarendon Laboratory at Oxford was built in 1870 and the Cavendish at Cambridge a year later. The laboratory in Albemarle Street was unique as a place where experiments in " Natural Philosophy " could be carried out with the resources of an institution and the inspiration of a tradition of research. Young, Davy, Faraday, Rayleigh and Tyndall were professors of the Royal Institution during this period. Davy was among the greatest chemists of his time. Faraday's experiments on electricity and magnetism were the foundation of electrical engineering. The library was a meeting place for the famous men of the time. When Davy and Faraday described their latest discoveries, Albemarle Street was thronged with the carriages of the wealthy, the learned and the curious who came to hear their discourses. Many famous men have worked in the Royal Institution since those early times. Dewar carried out his experiments on the liquefaction of gases ; the well-known " vacuum flask " was one result of his investigations. My father, Sir William Bragg, established his school of X-ray crystallography.

### HIGHEST STANDARDS

What is the function of the Royal Institution in modern times ? It is still pre-eminently a place where the highest standards of popular exposition are maintained. At the Friday Evening Discourses, which were instituted about 1825, famous men describe their recent discoveries or review some branch of learning to an audience of members and their friends. The majority of the discourses are on scientific subjects, but art, music, and literature are also represented. The members are connoisseurs who have an artistic appreciation of a good discourse ; the traditional way in which it is conducted, with lecturer and audience in evening dress, all helps to create the right atmosphere. The Christmas lectures, " adapted to a juvenile auditory " are as successful as they were in Faraday's time. Many young people have been given a bent to science owing to the inspiration they got from these lectures ; many of the best popular books on science are accounts of these lectures, and many of the best known lecture experiments were first shown on one of these occasions. But conditions are now very different from what they were in the early nineteenth century. Universities have large and flourishing laboratories thronged with research students. There are many scientific libraries, and the Royal Institution library is no longer a unique place in London where the student of science can satisfy his curiosity, nor its laboratory a unique centre for research.

In many respects the policy of the Royal Institution must be reviewed afresh, so that its peculiar assets can be used to the best advantage. These assets are its historic traditions, its very lovely and spacious setting, its lecture theatre which remains one of the finest in the world, although it was designed by Rumford so long ago, its unrivalled equipment for setting up experimental demonstrations of all kinds, and its central position, where it is easily accessible from all parts of London. One new experiment which has been tried has already shown much promise. Courses are being offered to the boys and girls in science sixth forms of schools in the London area. Each course covers some branch of physics, and consists mainly of demonstrations by experiments on a large scale which illustrate fundamental principles and historic investigations. The Royal Institution is an ideal place for such courses. Its lecture room holds 500, so it is worth while staging really spectacular experiments and also possible to call on industrial organizations or government bodies to provide demonstrations or exhibits of technical applications on a scale which would not be possible in the schools. In this way the pupils can see experiments which they would otherwise only read about in their text-books, and get the grasp of reality which is so essential in a scientific training. The experiment is being extended this term to fourth-form pupils in the hope that it will attract an increasing number of young people to a scientific or technical career. The possibility is also being explored of making the Royal Institution a place where science masters and mistresses can keep in touch with the latest developments in research, not so much by lectures, but by meeting active researchers in an informal way and seeing examples of their work. It is hoped that in these ways the Royal Institution may perhaps make a real contribution to science teaching in schools. These approaches are still tentative, and any suggestions from the schools as to what would be most useful to them are very welcome at the present time.

Reprinted from
*Royal Institution of Great Britain Procedings*, 1956, volume 36, pages 278-289

THE ROYAL INSTITUTION OF GREAT BRITAIN
# THE DISCOVERY OF
# USEFUL ELECTRICITY
*By* SIR LAWRENCE BRAGG, O.B.E., M.C., D.Sc., F.R.S.
*Fullerian Professor of Chemistry;*
*Director, Davy Faraday Research Laboratory*
Weekly Evening Meeting, Friday 9th December, 1955
STANLEY ROBSON, F.R.I.C., M.I.Chem.E., M.I.M.M.
*Secretary and Vice-President, in the Chair*

I SHOULD begin by saying something about the title of this discourse. I have chosen it because of its appropriateness to a strange
and romantic series of events which were of unique importance
in the history of science. I must gratefully acknowledge that the
title was suggested to me by the sub-title of a review called
*Galvani–Volta*, written by Bern Dibner and published in 1952
by the Burndy Library in America—though this may not be the
first occasion on which it has been used. Electrical phenomena
have been observed from very early times, and static electricity
had been a subject of study for many years before Galvani and
Volta made their experiments. The importance of their discoveries arose from their making it possible to produce a steady
electrical current, and to observe the effects of this current. This
was the start of "useful electricity", and of the many ways in
which electricity has come to play a part in our everyday lives.

Nature had kept her secret very well. There is an air of
mystery about electrical phenomena which is probably appreciated by everyone who is interested in science. The fundamental ideas of Heat, Light, Sound, and the Properties of Matter
appeal to our experience in a way which makes them come
naturally to us. The concepts of force, mass, inertia, kinetic
energy and of waves and their interactions, can all be linked to the
common experiences of our senses. But—an electric field, a
magnetic field, an electric current, electromagnetic induction—
here we are entering a new and unfamiliar world in which we can
form no ready mental picture of the things we are talking about.
Every popular lecturer is forcibly reminded of their strangeness;
he is talking about something his audience cannot see or feel,
whose existence can only be inferred, and he no longer has the
help of that common sense to which he can so readily appeal
when describing mechanical effects.

So it is not surprising that the secret was so well kept. The mechanical achievements of our technological age, the steam engines and turbines, the pumps, the textile mills, the complicated lathes and milling machines, and the triumphs of civil engineering, of vast bridges and dams and skyscrapers, all had their simpler forerunners as far back as history goes. But electricity in the service of man, as a way of sending messages, of transmitting power, of producing light, and more recently of performing almost instantaneously vastly complicated calculations, has no counterpart in the past. It is a new world, and it is really strange and romantic to realize that this new world was opened up to us by experiments on frogs' legs.

Galvani's discoveries, as so often happens in science, started from an accidental observation, and indeed one which was not made by the great man himself, but by his helpers. Galvani had been experimenting with the effect of an electrical discharge in causing contractions of a frog's legs. By chance an assistant touched the preparation with his scalpel while an electrical machine was being worked at some distance, and another assistant happened to notice that the legs were convulsed every time the machine sparked. He drew Galvani's attention to the effect, and Galvani realized its novelty and interest. He was led to a series of investigations which lasted over several years. It occurred to him to try whether the lightning discharge could produce the effect, and to this end he hung the legs on an iron trellis out-of-doors and found this was indeed the case. But sometimes the legs twitched when there was no flash, and Galvani, who thought this might be due to some form of atmospheric electricity, repeated the experiment indoors. After much patient experimentation, he traced the effect to his having hung the legs by brass hooks from the iron trellis. To summarize, he established that if a circuit was formed of two dissimilar metals in contact, one of which touched the legs and the other a point near the crural nerve, the legs were thrown into convulsions.

The long controversy between Galvani and Volta is famous. Galvani held that the effect is due to animal electricity, and that the function of the muscles is to complete a circuit in which electricity could circulate. Volta, with a more physical outlook, believed the origin of the effect to lie in the contact of the dis-

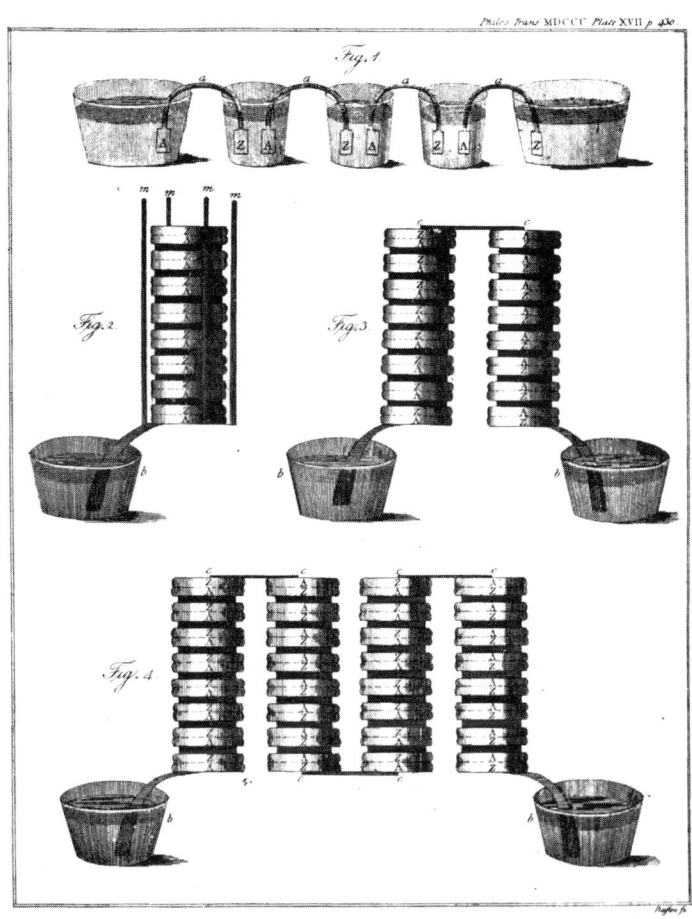

Plate I

similar metals rather than in the animal tissue, and he held that
their contact produces a driving force of the electric current
which stimulates the nerves. The controversy was a long and
bitter one, in which scientists in all countries took part and
ranged themselves on one side or the other. Volta was supported
in his view by his discovery of what we would now call "contact
potential difference", the fact that the mere contact of two dissimilar metals sufficed to charge one of them positively and the
other negatively. His establishment of this delicate and tricky
effect with his condensing electroscope was a wonderful achievement.

Volta sought to increase the driving force beyond that of a
single pair of metals. He realized that it would be of no avail to
alternate metals such as zinc and silver, because the effect at one
contact would be opposed by the effect at the subsequent one.
He therefore interposed sheets of a conducting substance of
another nature between alternate contacts, such as discs of paper
or cloth which were moistened or preferably soaked in brine
which made them better conductors. He built a "pile" of discs
in the order zinc, silver, moistened paper, zinc, silver, moistened
paper, so that the metallic contacts should all drive the current
in the same direction. He had made the first electrical battery.

Volta announced his discovery in a famous letter which he
wrote in March 1800 to Sir Joseph Banks, then President of the
Royal Society. It was read to the Society in June and appears in
the *Philosophical Transactions* for that year. The single plate in
the paper, which is reproduced in Plate I, tells the story. It is a
thrilling paper to read. Volta comes back again and again to the
two features which astonished him most. In the first place, he
had invented an electrical machine which consisted entirely of
conductors. Such bodies had hitherto been considered as 'non-
electric', as distinct from 'electric' bodies (non-conductors) on
which an electrical charge could be excited by friction. As Volta
put it: "The apparatus to which I allude, and which will no
doubt astonish you, is only the assemblage of a number of good
conductors of different kinds arranged in a certain manner."
In the second place, he could continue to get shocks indefinitely
from his pile. The shocks were not strong; he compares them to
those of a "Leyden flask weakly charged, or a torpedo in an

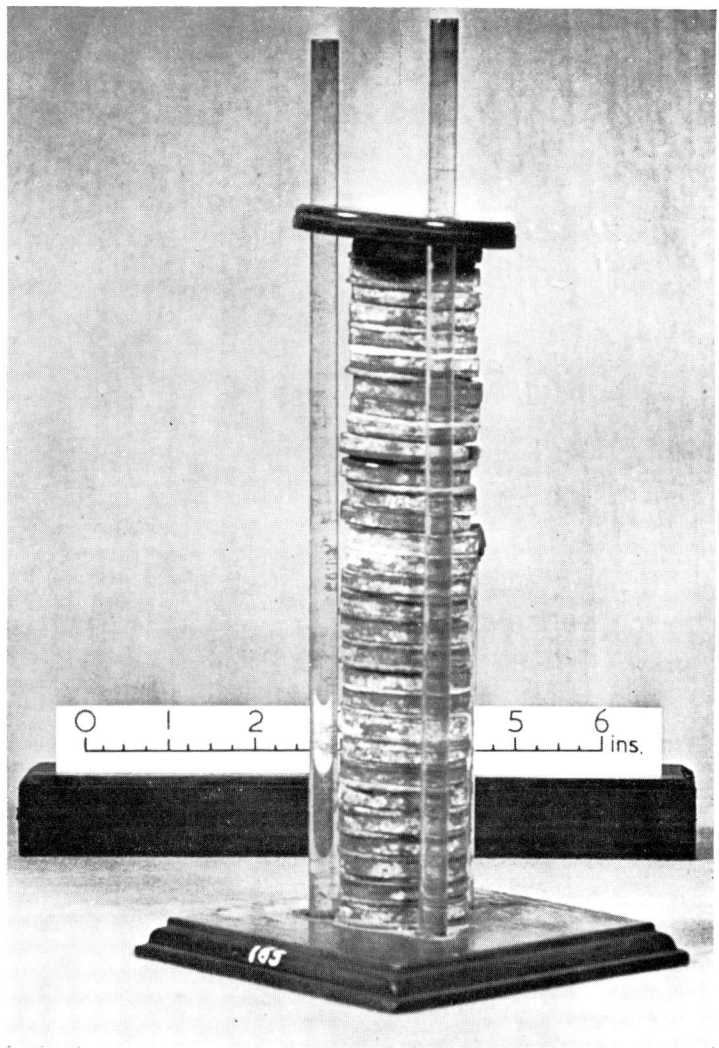

The pile which Volta presented to Faraday

PLATE II

exceedingly languishing state". But, unlike the Leyden Jar which had to be charged afresh after each discharge, his pile had "an inexhaustible charge, a perpetual action or impulse on the electric fluid". A pile which is in the museum of the Royal Institution, and which was presented to Faraday by Volta himself, is shown in Plate II.

Closely after the announcement of Volta's discovery, Nicholson and Carlisle observed the decomposition of water by the current from the pile. Cruickshank designed a battery which gave much more powerful currents than the Volta pile. Humphry Davy, following up the discovery of Nicholson and Carlisle, developed electrochemistry. He isolated potassium and sodium, and later reduced the metals calcium, magnesium, barium, and strontium from their compounds. With a large battery which he had installed at the Royal Institution, he produced a brilliant "arch of light" between charcoal points—the first form of electrical illumination. But this is not the occasion to follow the subsequent developments, made possible by means of obtaining steady electrical currents. The great secret had been discovered.

Who was right in the great controversy between Galvani and Volta, and their respective supporters? As we see it now, both had grasped some part of the truth, both were partly in error. Galvani did not realize the importance of the role played by the dissimilar metals. Volta's explanation of the driving force as arising from their mere contact gave no clue as to where the energy was coming from. The fundamental nature of the principle of the conservation of energy was not so well realized at that time. His pile, as far as he could tell, was inexhaustible. The currents drawn from it in his experiments were minute, and it was the drying of the pads between the metals, not the chemical exhaustion of the battery, which set a term to its activity. Volta made his pile last longer by surrounding it with wax. The well-known pile in the Clarendon Laboratory at Oxford has been ringing its bell for over a hundred years with no signs of running down. So it is perhaps not surprising that Volta accepted the mere contact of the metals, which he had shown to give rise to charges on them, as the driving force.

It is perhaps worth while to consider what is happening in the cell of a battery, because the student is often puzzled by an apparent paradox. In what does the "electromotive force" consist? Are the plates of a cell at the same potential when it is an open circuit, or when they are shorted by a conductor? The student feels this to be a paradox, it seems to me, because he is taught a definition of "potential difference" which is suitable for mathematical riders, but is unsound from a physical point of view. It is defined as the work done to take a unit charge from the one place to the other. No difficulty arises when the two places, between which we are measuring the potential difference, are in free space. But the definition is incomplete when we are measuring the potential difference between two conductors, except for the special case when these conductors are of identical constitution. An electrical charge has no separate existence, it is not a quantity of some kind of "electric fluid" which can be attached to matter. It is inseparable from matter, being a property of its ultimate particles. So when it is conveyed from one conductor to another, this involves the movement of matter in some form, and the work which is done depends not only on the field in the space between the conductors, but also on the energy required to detach the matter from one body and incorporate it into the other. If this is born in mind, the paradox is resolved.

The diagrammatic representation of a simple form of cell in Fig. 1 may explain this point. It is a Daniell cell, in which a plate of zinc stands in a solution of zinc sulphate, and a plate of copper in a solution of copper sulphate, the solutions being separated by a porous pot which keeps them from mixing but permits them to be in contact. The atoms in the metal plates are shown as positive ions with the negatively charged electrons as dots embodied in their structure. The metal atoms are also ions in the solution, their charge being balanced in this case by the negative sulphate ions. The upper figure represents the cell in open circuit. Suppose now that the plates be connected by a conducting wire along which electrons can run. Zinc is a more active metal chemically than copper, which implies that it requires less energy to remove an electron from a zinc atom than to remove one from a copper atom. Therefore if there is no field to drive them back, electrons will leave the zinc and embed themselves in the copper where they are more firmly held; they are, so to speak, going down hill. This is, of course, the explanation of Volta's contact potential difference. When plates of zinc and copper are in contact at one point, electrons flow from the zinc to the copper until they charge it up to such an extent that it no longer pays for

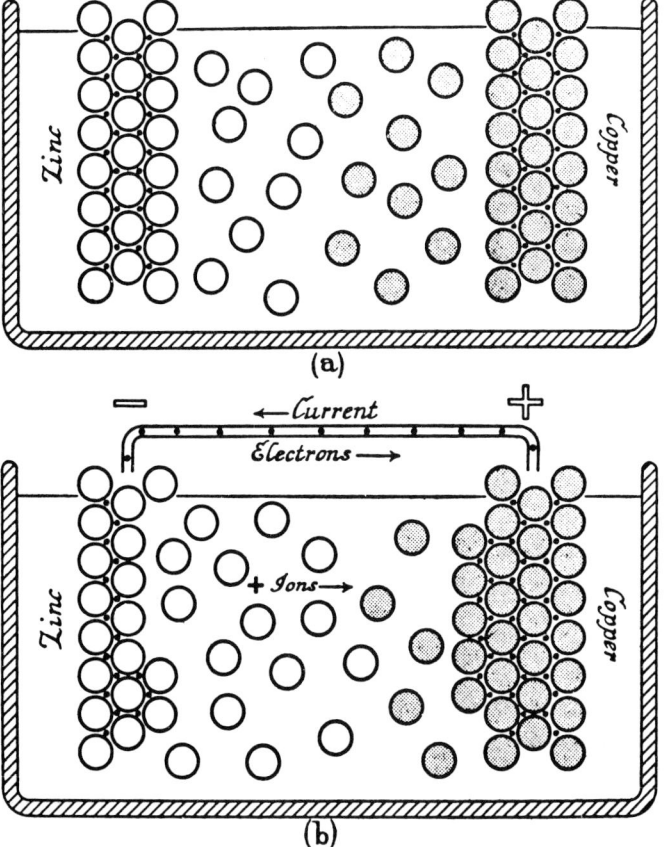

FIG 1. A diagram to show the way in which an electric cell gives a current. The circles represent positively charged metal atoms (ions) and the dots represent electrons. In the lower figure electrons are able to flow from zinc to copper.

the flow to continue. The energy gained by going from zinc to copper is just balanced by the field against which they have to move. So the current stops when the appropriate contact potential difference has been attained.

The cell is a device for allowing the flow of current to continue. As the electrons enter the copper, it is possible for more copper ions to be deposited on it from solution and the copper plate grows. On the other hand, as the zinc plate loses its electrons, zinc ions become detached from it and pass into solution. The status quo is preserved and the current continues to run until the zinc has all passed into solution. A double process is taking place in the cell. Negative electrons are going from the zinc to the copper by the upper route, and at the same time positive ions, in equivalent amount, are moving from zinc towards copper inside the cell so as to preserve the electrical balance. The electromotive force of our battery is there because when we strike an energy balance sheet, there is a gain of energy on the whole as the active zinc dissolves and the inactive copper is formed. The difference of potential between the copper and the zinc is not something we can define by the abstract idea of the work done on unit charge in going from the one to the other. The work is different according as to whether an electron takes it by the one route, or an ion by the other, and there is the answer to our paradox. Since by convention we consider a current as a passage of positive charge, we say that a current is running from the copper to the zinc and that the copper forms the positive terminal of the cell.

So Volta may be held to have been partly right and partly wrong. The driving force on the electrons comes from the contact of dissimilar metals, but this driving force has to be maintained by the chemical energy of the cell. When the dissimilar metals touch the frog's legs, it is some chemical action of the animal juices on the metals which provides the energy of the current. In Volta's pile, the moistened pads are not merely inert conductors as he supposed. They have a chemical reaction with the metals which preserves the voltage of the pile, and the pile was "running down", though to a minute extent, every time he took a shock from it.

I have been re-telling a well-known and famous story but I hope you will feel with me that no excuse is needed for refreshing our memories from time to time about the way in which the outstanding discoveries of science were made.

[W.L.B.]

Reprinted from *Discovery*, 1957, volume 18, No. 2, pages 66-67

# "SCHOOLS LECTURES" AT THE ROYAL INSTITUTION

# A NEW VENTURE

## SIR LAWRENCE BRAGG, O.B.E., M.C., F.R.S.

*Director of the Davy Faraday Research Laboratory, The Royal Institution*

The Christmas Lectures for children at the Royal Institution have long been famous. Each series consists of six talks during the fortnight after Christmas which are "adapted to a juvenile auditory". For the most part the audience is composed of young people between the ages of ten and seventeen, though there is a good sprinkling of grown-ups amongst them who have come to enjoy the demonstrations. For it is the tradition that these lectures shall be illustrated by striking experiments on a grand scale. The lecture theatre, which holds 500, is liberally serviced for setting up experiments, and behind the scenes there is a large store of equipment of all kinds. The reputation of the Christmas Lectures is such that firms and other organisations willingly help by lending, or in many cases by making, special apparatus required for the demonstrations.

The first of these series was given in 1826–7 by J. Wallis on *Astronomy*, "illustrated by transparent scenery". Faraday gave them the next year on *Chemistry*, and between then and his last series on the *Chemical History of a Candle* in 1860, he was the lecturer on nineteen occasions. The last series, by Dr H. Baines, was on *Photography*. The Christmas Lectures have now been held for a hundred and thirty years and have had a considerable influence on the progress of science in this country. Many of the experiments, first devised for the Christmas Lectures, have become the stock-in-trade of school laboratories. On over thirty occasions the lecturer has subsequently written a book based on his course and they are among the best of our popular books on science. What is perhaps most important about these lectures is that many people, whether scientists or not, confess in after life that their interest in science was first aroused by attending Christmas Lectures at the Royal Institution.

## THE "SCHOOLS LECTURES"

Encouraged by the tradition of the Christmas Lectures, we have embarked on a series of courses of similar lectures for young people from the schools in and around London, which are now given throughout the academic year. Most of the series of talks are given to pupils in their science sixth forms, others to pupils in the fourth forms, who have not necessarily all decided on a scientific career. We are helped and advised by representatives of the Science Masters' and Mistresses' Associations, and I think there can be no doubt of the success of the scheme. We show demonstrations and experiments illustrating the fundamental principles of science which are too large or costly to stage with school resources. Since

the construction and assembling of the apparatus is considerable undertaking, and much valuable equipme is generously loaned by industry, we wish to use it the best advantage. We therefore repeat each talk fo times and issue 2000 tickets for it. The tickets, for which no charge is made, are distributed to the scho by the Chief Education Officers in London and t Home Counties, who give us their warm co-operatic The scheme, which has now been going for three yea is still in the experimental stage, and is not on as lar a scale as might eventually be possible because it tak time and money to collect the equipment and to desi experiments which can be depended upon to "come o in the lecture room. But we are planning to issue 16,0 tickets next year, and if the talks inspire an interest science in a due proportion of the young people w come to them, their influence will be far-reaching.

## THE ROYAL INSTITUTION AND ITS AUDIENCE

Such occasions are, of course, no new idea; simi lectures to children are arranged from time to time many centres in this country. The Royal Institutic however, has certain rather special advantages. It F a central position, within a few minutes of Piccadi Circus, so that it can easily be reached from anywhe within a twenty-mile radius. Its famous lecture room ideal for the purpose and the Royal Institution buildir have an atmosphere of their own which contribu much to the success of any meeting held in them. T art of giving popular talks has long been studied he and the knowledge and equipment are available.

There is one feature about these lectures which is, my experience, unique. The boys and girls attendi each course are at the same stage in their education a so constitute an almost uniform audience. A po either goes down with all, or it misses fire complete an experiment excites everyone in the theatre, or fa flat so that we resolve to do it differently next da Normally, audiences include the clever and the slow, expert and the non-expert, and one is torn betwe trying to suit the one or the other; this audience "monochromatic" and offers a most exciting challen to the lecturer.

The impression I have got from the lectures, and fro our quite considerable and very encouraging fan-mail, that these experiments supply a very real need. O appreciates to the full how much the teachers do, b limitations of school resources, the exigencies of t time-table, and above all the premium set on text-bo

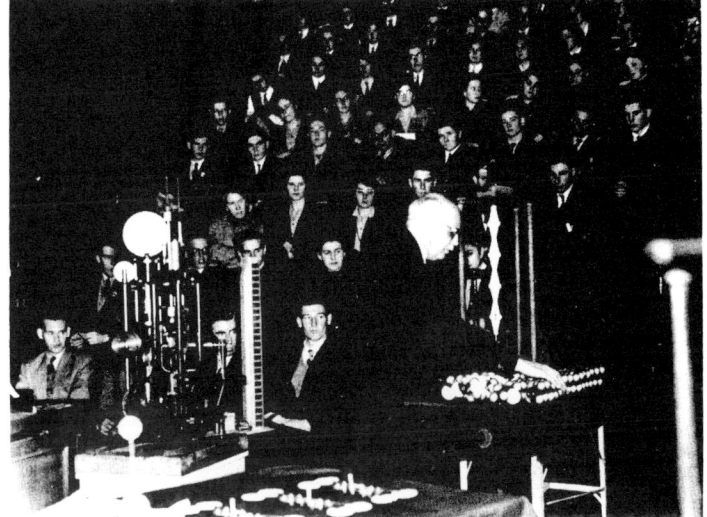

Sir Lawrence Bragg demonstrating to a typically youthful audience at one of his Christmas Lectures.

struction by the demands of examinations, make their *k* a difficult one. An experiment which is shown in a *w* minutes to a class may take as many weeks to get *o* working order. Yet science is something one learns handling matter and observing the results of experi- *nts* just as much as by reading books. The experi- *nts* the young people like best are often quite simple *es*, as long as they are done on a generous scale. *ey* are not impressed by large figures, or much im- *essed* by utilitarian considerations. It is of no use to *ow* them a spot of light travelling over a scale, or a *ter* moving, and telling them how hard it was to *ke* it do so; they like seeing the works. Most of all *ey* like an experiment which illustrates in a striking *y* some effect they can relate to everyday life, some- *ng* they have all observed without understanding the *use*. I think that here one is touching upon a rather *ndamental* feature of the British approach to science, *d* I would say of the American approach also, as con- *sted* with that of many Continental schools. We are *ppier* with the concrete than with the abstract. We *e* thinking in terms of mechanical models. We prefer *start* with particular cases, not with generalities. In *y* experience of research students from many coun- *es*, it has seemed to me that it is this practical bent *nich* enables our students to hold their own as com- *red* with the student from abroad who is often far *ore* admirably equipped as regards wealth of knowledge *d* philosophical insight. And I fear that perhaps, with *e* pressure of crowded universities and schools and *rge* classes, lecture demonstrations are fighting a losing *ttle* to the great detriment of our science teaching. *ne* lectures I remember most vividly as a student were *e* good old-fashioned ones, copiously illustrated by *illiant* experiments.

The schools lectures at the Royal Institution have led *▸* other schemes which have the same aim of assisting *ith* the problem of science teaching in the schools. We

arrange occasions when parties of science teachers meet the head of some famous research school and members of his team. The leader gives an informal talk on his projects, and for the rest of the afternoon the teachers divide into small groups and talk with the research workers, who have brought examples of their apparatus and results to show them. In this way the teachers hear something of the latest results of research and meet in a personal way the people who are doing the work. Another project we have in hand is to make the Royal Institution a centre to which the science teachers can come for help with their work. The library specialises in reference books, text-books and popular books on science, and has a wide range of periodicals. The lecture-room staff is expert in arranging demonstrations of all kinds, and can give the practical tips about details, and about getting the right materials, which save so much time and effort. We are setting up, with generous help from industry, a collection of demonstration apparatus of all kinds. Many of the sets may be too elaborate and expensive for schools, but they give ideas and show what can be done and it may prove practical to loan them on special occasions.

There is general concern at the present time about the difficulty of maintaining the standards of science teaching in schools. We hope that in these ways the Royal Institution is making an appreciable contribution towards easing the problem. It is an enlargement of its function, not a new function. The Visitors of the Royal Institution, meeting in 1827, recorded their "satisfaction at finding that the plan of juvenile lectures has been resorted to" and considered that "the system of instructing the young portion of the community is one of the most effective means which the Institution possesses for the diffusion of science". Our present aims are in complete accord with the aims of our founders, who were inspired by their love of science and their belief in its value to the nation.

Reprinted from *Nature*, 1958, volume 181 pages 807-808

# INTERPRETATION OF SCIENCE
# TO THE PUBLIC

### By Sir LAWRENCE BRAGG, O.B.E., F.R.S.

Royal Institution, London

SIR ALEXANDER FLECK'S recent address to the general assembly of the British Association, and the editorial in *Nature* of January 4, will be warmly welcomed by all who are interested in the popularization of science. The new plans for enlarging its activities which the British Association has announced focus attention on the need for presenting science in the most effective way to the general public. I am writing about this subject because the experience and traditions of the Royal Institution may afford some useful pointers in our endeavour to interest the public in science. It was founded 160 years ago for the special purpose of interpreting science to the public, and apart from the prosecution of research in its laboratories this has continued to be its primary function. The art of popular lecturing might indeed be said to be its main subject of research.

One of the oldest and most honoured traditions is that a 'Discourse' should be profusely illustrated by experiments and demonstrations. A popular talk to laymen differs in many ways from a lecture to students or an address to a learned society. To a professional scientist the description of an experiment is often quite sufficient because his own experiences in the laboratory enable him to visualize it. But a lay audience has not this advantage. To the layman the difference between the description of an experiment and the actual witnessing of it is as great as the difference between looking at a foreign country on the map and visiting it ; we grasp its geography in a far more vivid way when we have been to the place. One is struck again and again by the immense superiority, as judged by the effect on the audience, of a series of experiments and demonstrations explained by a talk over a lecture illustrated by slides. The Christmas Lectures to young people at the Royal Institution afford a good instance. It is surprising how often people in all walks of life own that their interest in science was first aroused by attending one of these courses when they were young, and in recalling their impressions they almost invariably say, not "we were told" but "we were *shown*" this or that. This impact of the witnessed experiment is all the more important because the popular talk is so dependent on emotional reactions. Students take notes, when attending a course, and colleagues listening to an account of research are alive to its bearing on their own work and see the printed account afterwards, so the context is more important to them than the manner of delivery. The final result of the popular talk is measured, however, by the extent to which the audience recalls it afterwards, and this fixation of the image is effected by arousing an emotional response of interest and thrill.

It is perennially surprising to find that it is the simpler experiments which have the warmest reception, especially if they can be done on a spectacular scale. The audience likes to see 'the works'. It is of little help to do something mysterious in a box which makes a pointer move over a scale. The simple experiment is effective because it can be grasped completely, and the members of the audience have the pleasurable feeling that it has become a part of their own experience. Again, there is an art in arranging an experiment so that it shall be æsthetically attractive. We instinctively recognize this when we say after a lecture, "That was a pretty experiment he showed". These may seem small points ; but they are important. They may make the difference between a pleased and responsive audience, and one which is bored. If the listeners go away feeling that they have really understood what the lecturer was trying to explain, then they will come again for more. Non-scientists must not be left to feel that all science is too difficult to understand, otherwise they will shut their minds and think that science is for scientists only.

The other guiding principle of the popular lecture is that of starting with something with which the audience is thoroughly familiar in every-day life, and leading them further with that as a basis. The survey of the new country must be tied on to fixed points which are already in their minds. This is one of the most difficult tasks facing the popular lecturer. He may be honestly trying to avoid technical language ; but it goes further than that. He has to put himself in the place of the intelligent layman and realize that ideas and experiences so familiar to him are unexplored country to his listener. This may seem to be a stressing of the obvious ; but I venture to stress it because I have rather special opportunities to assess the effect of popular scientific talks, and they often pass completely over the heads of the audience because an otherwise excellent talk does not establish an initial *rapport* with the listeners' knowledge and experience.

There is nothing novel in these views, they are merely a recapitulation of the principles which have been preached and practised by all the great exponents of popular lecturing from Faraday onwards. It seems to me, however, that they have an important bearing in planning our strategy for a wider interpretation of science to the public. Merely talking and writing about the wonders of science can be very ineffective because the public is nowadays so bombarded with talks and articles on subjects of all kinds through so many channels. If our message is to be heard above the general noise-level, we must use the most powerful aid we have. The primary way to interest the public in art or music is to show pictures or arrange concerts, and lectures on art or music can only be appreciated when they are related to such first-hand impressions. The primary way to interest the general public in science is to show experiments and demonstrations, and so let them share in the thrill of understanding how things work, which is after all a good popular definition of science.

The staging of a demonstration lecture requires much organization. A simple experiment which takes a few minutes to show in the theatre may demand as many weeks of preparation. There must be a supporting background of technical staff, workshop, and demonstration apparatus of all kinds as well as a suitably fitted theatre, and if a worth-while proportion of the public is to be covered, it means a whole-time use of these facilities which is costly. The Royal Institution is now running a series of demonstration talks for boys and girls throughout the school year, in collaboration with the science teachers, at which large-scale experiments are shown which cannot easily be staged with school resources. An approximate estimate of the cost, based on the proportion of overhead charges allocated to the scheme, is £5,000 a year, which is defrayed by the generous assistance of industrial firms and other bodies which are interested in the venture. Some 16,000 tickets are issued annually. The young people come from an area which includes about one-quarter of the schools in England, and their keenness indicates that this is a very repaying way of using the resources. Some half-dozen such centres operating on a similar whole-time basis would cover most of Great Britain. Certain famous annual lectures sponsored by various bodies are by tradition the occasion for numerous carefully prepared experiments, and these lectures draw enthusiastic audiences. Television can, of course, be a powerful means of transmission ; but the laboratory resources must still be there behind the scenes for providing the programmes. My contention, therefore, is that merely increasing the number of talks and articles about science will not get us very far in interesting the general public, that on the other hand one gets the most rewarding response if one stages shows of experiments for them, and that if their interest is first so aroused, they will be much more able to appreciate the talks and articles.

Reprinted from
*The Times*, July 19, 1960, page xiv

# VII—What Constitutes Life?

## By Sir Lawrence Bragg, O.B.E., F.R.S.
### *Fullerian Professor of Chemistry, Royal Institution*

I MAY perhaps begin by explaining what the formidable looking expression molecular biology means. It represents a new approach to the problem of trying to understand how living matter works; recent achievements of science have made it possible to get detailed knowledge of its structure on a much finer scale than hitherto, in fact right down to the scale when we are beginning to see how its atoms are arranged.

There have been two main ways of studying the structure of the living body, by the microscope and by chemical analysis. The microscope makes it possible to see details some thousands of times finer than can be discerned by the naked eye. The smallest lump of matter that can be seen under a microscope, however, is still some thousands of atoms across, and so contains thousands of millions of atoms. The microscope is a very long way from telling us how the atoms are arranged; it is as if it only gave us a map of England showing where the towns are,

while we want to find out something about the people who live in them. Chemistry tells us of what kinds of chemical compounds the body is built. The atoms are for the most part carbon, oxygen, nitrogen and hydrogen, with a small proportion of other elements such as sulphur and phosphorus that have a key part in the structures, and a minute proportion of " trace elements " that are needed only for certain special purposes but are still essential for life. Chemistry can break down the substances of living matter into recognizable fragments of groups of atoms or molecules, and deduce how they are joined together by chemical bonds. It can isolate large molecules that take part in the chemical processes of the body and get some idea of their function.

The new advances have resulted from the development of two new techniques. The electron microscope, which uses a beam of electrons instead of light, has immensely increased the power of seeing fine details. It is as much more powerful

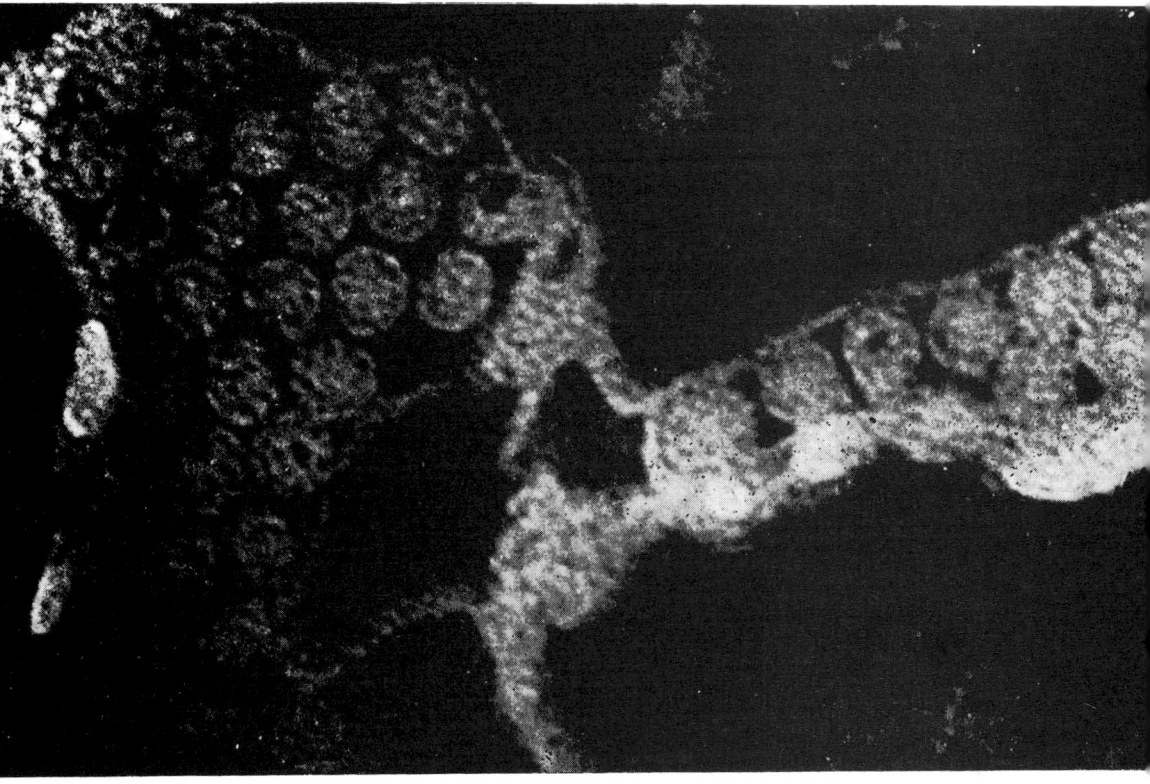

Particles of a poliomyelitis virus in a stage of assembly, magnified 400,000 times.    From a paper by R. W. Horne
and J. Naginton in the *Journal of Molecular Biology.*

than the light microscope as the latter is compared with the unaided eye.   One can distinguish elements of structure only some tens of atoms across and so containing merely thousands of atoms.   X-ray analysis studies the arrangements of atoms in bodies by observing the way they scatter X-rays.   The many different kinds of chemical compound are built of molecules, the molecules of each kind of compound being small groups of atoms joined in a definite way.   X-ray analysis started 50 years ago to find out the exact positions of atoms in molecules, at first in the very simplest kinds with only a few atoms.   As the techniques improved, it has become more and more powerful, successfully analysing molecules like penicillin with 100 or so atoms in them.   Quite recently it has succeeded in analysing all the atomic positions in large molecules containing thousands of atoms.

The exciting and very important stage has thus been reached when there is a completed bridge between the techniques. The electron microscope has attained such a resolution that one can " see " (in photographs) details of structures containing thousands of atoms;  and X-ray analysis, approaching the problem from t  other end, has reached a stage when we c..n learn from it how the atoms are arranged in bits of structure of this size. For the first time we are beginning to be able to read the whole story, from the atoms upwards.

It is only possible here to give the briefest indication of the kind of new knowledge that is being gained. We have already learnt much more about the most important constituents of living matter. All living matter consists of cells; the simplest organisms are just one cell, more complicated ones are masses of cells of different kinds which have different functions in the body. The cell, inside its envelope, is mainly composed of protein, large molecules of many different kinds containing thousands of atoms, each of which has a definite function in the chemical processes taking place in the living cell. Inside this mass of protein is the nucleus, which appears to be the seat of the hereditary character. It is, as it were, a little book of instructions inside the cell telling it how it should be made up. Growth takes place by cells dividing into two, and when this happens the nucleus of the mother cell somehow prints off copies of this book of instructions, one going to each daughter cell. The atomic arrangement in the nucleic acid, the long chain compound that contains this code of instructions, was deduced a few years ago by Crick and Watson at Cambridge, and the fascinating feature of their solution is that it gives a hint how the

one code is turned into two, that is, how heredity is handed on. The nucleic acid is made of two intertwined chains of atoms of a complementary kind, like the wards of a key and of the lock into which it fits. In duplication the chains come apart, and as it were each key picks up the right bits to form another lock, and each lock to form another key, so that we have two sets of instructions in place of one

Recently, Perutz and Kendrew, with their collaborators, have succeeded in making the first analysis of one type of protein molecule and many more kinds will no doubt follow. On the one hand we have a blueprint of the molecule to help in explaining how it performs its chemical tasks; on the other it may be hoped that it will explain how the nucleic acid acts as a template to make protein molecules. The elements of the code mechanism are quite simple, but in a higher form of life like a mammal there are thousands of millions of them in the tiny nucleus; if they were letters of books they would fill a large library.

It is not possible to mention in so short an article the names of the many workers who have made these new advances; our own country has played a large part in exploring this fascinating new field of science.

Reprinted from
*Science, New York*, 1965, volume 150, pages 1420-1423

# The Schools Lectures at the Royal Institution

The Institution provides a "repertory theater" of
scientific experiments to be shown to young people.

Lawrence Bragg

The Royal Institution has a long and famous history. It was founded in 1799 by Count Rumford (Benjamin Thompson) at a time when there was a growing interest in Natural Philosophy and when "Literary and Philosophical Societies" were being formed in many centers. The founder, however, designed for it a structure more ambitious than that of other institutions, and although he failed to realize all his aims, his originality and foresight gave the Institution a unique character which it has retained. Not only was it to be a place where the intelligentsia would meet each other, hear discourses about science, and consult a library of scientific books and periodicals, it was also to include what we would now call a research center and a technical college. It was to have professors who, as well as informing the members of advances in science, were to do original work in the Institution's laboratories. It was to have classes for mechanics, because Rumford was convinced that they would do their work more efficiently and with greater interest if they knew something of the scientific basis of craftsmanship. One of Rumford's great interests was the application of scientific principles to objects of everyday use—grates, stoves, chimneys, ventilation systems, cooking utensils, clothing—and many of the things we take for granted nowadays—for example, the kitchen range, the pressure cooker, the coffee percolator, and the double-walled saucepan—are Rumford's inventions. His plans for training mechanics failed; he was before his time and was defeated by apathy and misunderstanding. On the other hand, his plan for combining the popular exposition of science with original research was gloriously successful, and these two functions have set the pattern for the Royal Institution for more than 150 years. For the first three-quarters of the 19th century, in the great days of Humphry Davy, Faraday, and their successors, it was the "center" for the physical sciences in Great Britain.

I have given this brief account of the history of the Royal Institution in order to sketch in the background for my description of the Institution's Schools Lectures. The Royal Institution is a private body, supported by its members' subscriptions, its endowments, and donations given by industrial and other bodies in recognition of its educational work. Being a private body, it is free to make experiments on its own initiative and to start new ventures.

Sir Lawrence Bragg is director of the Royal Institution, 21 Albemarle Street, London, W.1, England.

## The Christmas Lectures

One such venture, which has since become famous, was started in the year 1826. It was a course of six lectures "adapted for a Juvenile Auditory," given in the fortnight after Christmas. The Christmas Lectures have been held every year since then, except when interrupted by the two world wars. They are planned for young people between 12 and 17, though in the "Juvenile Auditory" all ages from 8 to 80 are often represented. By tradition these lectures are the great occasion for devising thrilling and novel experiments on a grand scale. Everyone knows about the Christmas Lectures and is willing to help. In particular, industrial firms will go to immense pains to provide something really exciting for the occasion. The lecturer gives his talks on some theme in the physical sciences, biology, or engineering and illustrates it with his demonstrations, though, it must be confessed, in choosing experiments their thrillingness is often given rather more weight than their precise appropriateness to the subject.

There have been two interesting features of these Christmas Lectures. The first is the number of people, in all walks of life, who say that their first realization of the interest of science came from their attending, as children, a Christmas Lecture at the Royal Institution. And invariably they say, not "He told us so and so" but "He showed us so and so." It is the experiment that creates the vivid and lasting impression. The second is the number of popular scientific books which have been based on the Christmas Lectures. The lecturer is generally invited afterwards to put his lectures into book form, and many—some 40 in all— of the best popular science books in Great Britain have originated in this way.

## The Start of the Lectures

About 10 years ago the tradition of the Christmas Lectures suggested the idea of giving similar lectures to school pupils all year round. The Royal Institution has certain advantages in such a scheme. It has a lecture room that is very convenient for showing experimental demonstrations to a large audience. As so often happens, this advantage is as much the result of accident as of design. Rumford's idea was to have a theater with a lower auditorium to be occupied by the nobility and gentry and an upper gallery for his mechanics. The gallery had a separate exit to the street, so that the general herd should never meet the gentry and cause embarrassment on both sides. The result is an ideal semicircular auditorium, holding an audience of up to 500, in which every one has a clear and near view of the experiments conducted on the lecture bench and the large area of floor space around it. Again, the Institution is situated right in the center of London and so is easily accessible. Since England is a small country and the population around London is especially dense, about one quarter of the schools in England can conveniently send their boys and girls to an afternoon occasion at the Royal Institution.

The scheme was started in a small way at first, in collaboration with the science teachers of some of the London schools. They were invited to send their 6th-form science pupils (aged about 17) to lectures on quite general subjects such as electricity, magnetism, waves, and properties of matter. As the schools got to know about the lectures, there was a pressing demand for tickets and the attendance rapidly increased. At present about 22,000 tickets are issued annually. They are free and are distributed to the schools by

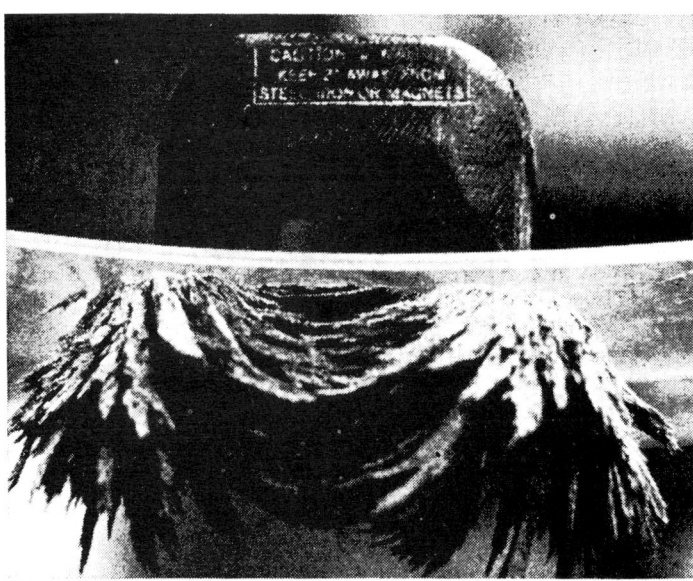

Two demonstrations used in the Schools Lectures. (Left) Lines of force in three dimensions, shown by iron filings in the neighborhood of a strong permanent magnet. This demonstration, which is shown on closed-circuit television, has an advantage over the ordinary demonstration in which iron filings on a card are used, in that it shows the lines of force in all three dimensions.

The Ewing model of a ferromagnetic material. The atoms are represented by a large number of very small compass needles; this illustration shows domains in the absence of a magnetic field. A number of experiments can be done with the model. If it is given a knock or otherwise agitated, the magnets set themselves in the direction of the earth's field; magnetization can be illustrated by stroking a magnet over the model; the agitation due to an irregularly moving magnet can be made to explain the Curie point.

the educational authorities in the different areas. Most of them go to pupils in the top science forms of the grammar schools, which teach science at a high level. Some go to younger pupils in the 14-to-15 age group, and recently the preparatory schools (up to 13 years) have asked for simple lectures suitable for these young people who are only starting their scientific training.

There are between 400 and 500 schools of grammar-school standing in the Greater London area, which extends into the adjacent counties, so each school can get some 40 tickets annually to give to its most promising and keen pupils. Although at present it is only the classes specializing in science which are served, there is just as great a need to serve the schools in which pupils are getting a general education, and it is hoped that the number of places can be doubled in the near future; the limiting factor is not the demand for tickets, but the physical limitation on the number of experimental lectures which can be staged in the theater.

As I mentioned above, no charge is made to the schools for the tickets. The expense of organizing the talks is helped by contributions from industrial firms, which recognize the value of interesting young people in science.

**The Nature of the Lectures**

The object of the course is to show the boys and girls experiments which they read about in their textbooks or hear about in class but which they cannot be shown in a school with its limited resources. The talks are in no sense in competition with the teaching of the science masters and mistresses. Great care is taken to avoid any possibility of overlap; in fact, the courses have been planned in collaboration with a small group of science teachers who advise on their nature. We

concentrate on the fundamental phenomena of science. Applications of science, recent researches, and topical events are brought in only when they serve to illustrate the fundamental laws.

It is obvious that the number of opportunities any one pupil has to come to a lecture are very restricted. Each school, getting some 40 tickets a year, can give one ticket to a large proportion of the pupils in the senior class, or can give tickets for a group of lectures to a smaller number. In any event, each pupil (during the 2 or 3 years he spends in the top form) can come on only a few occasions. But I believe that the influence of the Royal Institution lectures is out of all proportion to their number. They supply something which supplements what the pupils get at school in a very important way, just as a small quantity of a vitamin makes a vital difference to the functioning of the body. There is a vast difference between reading about some crucial scientific experiment in a textbook and seeing that experiment performed in an impressive way. It is like the difference between looking at a map of a country and paying a visit to it; one's whole outlook is altered, and the country becomes real. It is not necessary, in order to get this new viewpoint, to visit every country on the map; to travel abroad somewhere effects the psychological change. In just the same way the young people get a new and more living interest in science by seeing the great experiments performed with all the art one can muster to make them impressive.

**A "Repertory Theater"**

I have so far described the Royal Institution lectures without any reference to the many other centers which now arrange talks for young people.

These are organized by scientific institutions, by universities, by museums, and by industry. Although the Royal Institution, with its Christmas Lectures beginning in 1826, was very early in the movement, it is now only one of many bodies which cater to this recognized need. The justification for the present account must be certain unique features which I believe the Royal Institution's lectures to have.

I have used the description "repertory theater" because the lectures for the young people are like a set of plays, which the actors and assistants are trained to perform as part of a repertory. Each lecture has a "run" during which it is given a number of times. The properties for it are stored and brought out again for another run, generally in a 3-year cycle because in that time the school population changes. In the interval between the runs, any new experiments which suggest themselves can be tried out and developed, and new equipment can be acquired.

At present there are about 30 standard lectures in the repertory, including three on electricity, one on magnetism, three on properties of matter, three on waves and vibrations, and corresponding series in chemistry and biology. These lectures are given by the full-time and part-time members of the Royal Institution staff. In addition, special talks are given from time to time by lecturers from other institutions.

There are advantages in the repertory scheme which make it a very efficient one. The development of a demonstration experiment is often a lengthy affair. Even when it appears to be simple, it is surprising how many snags one encounters, and how many tricks of technique have to be learned. An experiment which takes a minute or two to show in the lecture room may take weeks or months of patient investigation before it runs smoothly. To rig up all the experiments from scratch for a new lecture is a formidable task. Experience shows that it can easily demand experts' time measured in many months. On the other hand, once an experiment has been thrashed out, the essential gear can be stored, with notes on how to set it up and with detailed "tips" on how to make it work. It is well worth while to put time and money into a demonstration when it is used again and again.

In the second place, it is a great saving to repeat the lecture a number of times consecutively as in a short run of a play, of course to a different audience each time. The one setting up of the apparatus serves for the whole series. One point has particularly impressed me about such a run. It might be thought that it would be tedious for the lecturer to repeat the same talk day after day, but my experience has been exactly the reverse. How often, after one has given a lecture, does one profoundly wish for a chance to give it all over again with corrections of one's mistakes? A series provides this opportunity for both the lecturer and the assistants. Weak features of the experiments can be put right, one can eliminate parts of the talk which clearly went across badly and dwell longer on the parts which went well, the drill can be perfected, and above all one can improve the timing. I have often felt I am being a showman when I take advantage of my experience as to what stirs interest or arouses pleasure. But I think it is fair to use such knowledge to the full, because the purpose is to make a lasting impression on the audience by holding its attention.

There is another point about these series of lectures which has much impressed me. When lecturing to a group of pupils such as the 6th-form science classes, the audience is homogeneous, and this is an unusual situation for the lecturer. Generally an audience is composed of old and young, scientific and nonscientific, clever and less clever. The lecturer has to make a compromise in trying to give everyone something. It is most dramatic to lecture to an audience in which all the members are the same age, all are about equally clever, and all have had the same background of school teaching. A point either is made with complete success or it falls completely flat, and one soon finds out which. The talk can be tailored in a way which is impossible with a mixed audience.

The lecture technician and his staff of assistants have the setting up of the experiments as their main duty; this experience makes them very clever in this art, and at using the lecture room equipment such as closed-circuit television, magnetic blackboards, overhead projection, matched lanterns for double projection, and motion-picture projection. They must be backed by a good preparation room, ample store rooms, and the services of a workshop.

To sum up, the more one concentrates on an organization whose main function is to present a continuous series of lectures to young people, rather than an occasional series undertaken as an extra to other activities, the more one can streamline the organization with a great increase in efficiency and improvement in quality. The less also is the strain on the lecturer. If a highly specialized staff prepares the demonstrations for him and can be counted on to see that all goes smoothly in the lecture, his work is much lighter. He is like a surgeon entering an operating theater when skilled assistants have made all ready for him

and he can concentrate on his expert task.

The simplifying of the lecturer's task is very important. Outstandingly good lecturers are generally busy people and reluctant to take on anything which makes large demands on their time. The really good ones with a gift for talking to young people are few, and every possible aid must be given them in order to secure their help. They are people who can project themselves into the minds of the audience, who can in fact be at the same time both audience and speaker and sense the effect on their listeners of what they are saying. They have to be able to ask themselves "How did I think when I was 17 years old, what points puzzled me, what explanation satisfied me?" It is astonishing how many great scientists are unable to project themselves in this way and quite fail to give a good talk to the young. On the other hand, by search and trial one can find the gifted few who possess the art.

**Science Centers**

I am convinced that organizations of this kind, devoted to giving scientific talks to young people and specially planned for that purpose, would be of the very greatest benefit in increasing the scientific potential of a country. They can only function in places where there is a concentration of population sufficient to give them continuous use, but this concentration need not be very great, because the school population is so large. The main part is that the more such organizations are planned for the special function the greater is their efficiency, and the more continuously they can be used the less is the cost in time and money needed for creating one more enthusiastic devotee of science.

Reprinted from
*Contemporary Physics*, 1966, volume 7, pages 358-361

## The Royal Institution Lectures in Science for members of the Administrative Class of the Civil Service

by Sir Lawrence Bragg

Director of the Royal Institution

It was announced in the House of Commons by the Chief Secretary to the Treasury on 5th May 1964 that " a course of lectures and seminars in scientific subjects for members of the administrative class is being arranged at the Royal Institution of Great Britain. The aim of these lectures is to give administrators an introduction to the fundamental laws of science and some idea of scientific methodology."

The idea of having such a course was first proposed by Mr. J. Goldsmith, one of the Managers of the Royal Institution, and it was sympathetically received by Sir Laurence Helsby, Permanent Secretary of H.M. Treasury, who warmly encouraged the venture. The classes were to consist of administrators of the rank of Principal and Assistant Principal, from all Departments, who had no scientific training or at most had taken science up to ' O ' level. As it turned out, some members of the class had received more advanced training, but in planning the courses no previous knowledge was assumed.

The first course, for a class of 150, began in October 1964, and continued with breaks until June 1965. The course comprised six lectures covering the fundamental problems and conceptions of physics, chemistry and biology, which were attended by all the members. Each lecture was followed by a fortnight of seminars for which the audience was divided into three smaller groups of 50 so that they could be more informal. Four of the periods were assigned to physics, one to chemistry, and one to biology. They were given by Professor King, Professor Boyd, Professor Harrison, Professor Porter and myself. The subjects were:

> ' The Properties of Matter ', ' Electricity and Magnetism ', ' Waves ', ' The Atomic Nucleus and Fundamental Particles ', ' Chemical Compounds and Chemical Reactions ' and ' Cells, Fundamental Units in Biology '.

A number of mistakes in this first year's course were revealed by letters from the class and by a questionnaire which was circulated at its end.

(a) The content was not quite right. I think we were influenced too much by experience with the ' Schools Lectures ', the course for top 6th science forms of London schools which are held in the Royal Institution throughout every year. These lectures are planned to illustrate the fundamental laws of science by means of a number of experiments, particularly those which are too complex or on too large a scale to be shown with school resources. They aim to supplement the very thorough and quite advanced scientific training which the young people get in the sixth form. Though every effort is made to make them lively and entertaining, they are essentially didactic, and this was not the right fare for the administrators. It was both too simple and elementary as regards concepts, and too advanced in requiring previous knowledge. The graphic experiments designed to bring home the fundamental laws to the school pupils must often have seemed a waste of time in the Civil Service lectures. I suppose we ought to have realized this in planning the course, but it is experience which drives such points home.

(*b*) The seminars with groups of 50 were a mistake. They were arrived at as a compromise. The Treasury was particularly keen that the class should be divided into smaller groups so that contact between teacher and class in question time would be more informal. To have divided the class into really small groups of 10 or so would have meant a large number of seminars which would have imposed far too heavy a load on the Royal Institution staff. So as a compromise it was decided to have three groups of 50, and to hold the seminars in each week between lectures. However, a group of 50 proved to be too large for informal questions, and the scheme degenerated into each seminar being in fact a further lecture which might just as well have been delivered to the whole class.

(*c*) The times of meeting were unfortunate. Members of the class often found it difficult to get away at 5 o'clock in the afternoon, or when they could they were tired at the end of the day. In consequence, we experienced a large drop in the number of attendances as the session progressed.

The arrangements for the second session have, I believe, been much more satisfactory. The whole course was held in the autumn term, and was designed for Assistant Principals who entered the service in 1963/64; the class included 100 members. The sessions extended over nine Thursday mornings and consisted of 18 lectures, after each of which the members withdrew into ' syndicates ' of about 12 to consider questions which they subsequently put to the lecturer. Syndicate members took it in turn to act as the chairman who summarized the questions. The meetings then took the following pattern.

|  |  |
|---|---|
| 9.30–10.15 | First lecture. |
| 10.15–10.40 | Syndicates consider questions. |
| 10.40–11.10 | Question time in lecture hall. |
| 11.10–11.25 | Coffee break. |
| 11.25–12.10 | Second lecture. |
| 12.10–12.30 | Syndicates consider questions. |
| 12.30– 1.00 | Lecturer takes second question session. |

The ' question ' times went much better when arranged in this way. The questioners had time to plan what they wanted to ask, and the fact that the questions were put by the chairmen helped. The questions were very much to the point and most interesting. Everyone was fresh in the morning, and as our lectures were part of a wider plan of training we had no falling off in attendance. The plan could of course be improved further, but we felt much more satisfied with it this time. The content of the course was modified as the result of previous experience. The methodological, historical and philosophic aspects were stressed much more, as against the attempt to ' teach ' the basic facts of science, and I think we had a much more appreciative response from our audience. But it is not easy to cover the whole of science in nine mornings, and it is a challenge to the lecturers to plan how they can best use this time. A very careful selection of the main topics had to be made. As far as possible each was designed as an artistic whole, to illustrate some one main facet of scientific knowledge. The nine groups of lectures were: two on ' Electricity and Magnetism ', two on ' The Properties of Matter ', ' Waves and Vibrations ' and ' Waves, Conveyors of Energy and Information ', two on ' The Interaction between Radiation and Matter ', ' The Atomic Nucleus ' and ' Atomic Energy ', ' The Elements and their Compounds ' and ' Molecules in Motion ', ' Thermo-dynamics and Chemical Change ' and ' Biochemistry ', two on ' Cells and Reproduction ', two on ' Communication Mechanism in Biology '. As a finale, separate lectures were given by Professor Boyd on ' Space Science ' and by Sir Peter Medawar on ' Fact and Fiction about " The Scientific Method " '.

The subject for the first morning was ' Electricity and Magnetism '. The main idea in planning the morning was to describe the break-through, when a whole new world of science was opened up by the experiments of Galvani and Volta a century and a half ago. Galvani's experiment offered an excellent example of the scientific spirit of curiosity, the desire to understand more about nature without any thought of the uses to which that knowledge can be put. Volta's interpretation of Galvani's results, imperfect though it was, led to the pile as a first way of getting a steady electric current. Galvani's experiments with frogs' legs were demonstrated, and a Volta pile was constructed in order to bring home the nature of the observations which have so entirely altered all scientific thought, and transformed the ways in which power and information can be sent from one place to another. Electricity and magnetism were chosen as subjects for the initial lecture, because the concepts are essential to the subsequent lectures. The importance of the concept of electric and magnetic fields was stressed. Faraday's discovery of electro-magnetic induction was described as the break-through into a way of producing currents without chemical batteries. The discovery of the electron revealed that the electric charge is atomic, which was brought out in a number of ways in subsequent lectures. It was possible to go on to outline the great advances in practical application, with telegraph, telephone, radio, and radar as means of getting or conveying information, and with the motor and dynamo as a way of sending power to a distant point. These last afford a good example of the principle that energy is constant in total amount, though it changes in form.

The second section was on ' The Properties of Matter '. It was based on the theme that, in order to think intelligently about the properties of matter in bulk, one must have some understanding of the nature of an atom, and of how science has gained this understanding. Dalton's ideas are the starting point. Experiments were shown which brought home the reality of the existence of atoms (for instance, Brownian movement was demonstrated to the class).

The atomic structure and the nature of the forces which bind atoms together were considered in a very simple way, involving little more than ideas about number and symmetry as explaining the origin of the Periodic Table.

From this one could go on to play a kind of ' Animal, Vegetable or Mineral ' game in seeing how to explain the very different properties of inorganic com-pounds such as salts and minerals, the vast organic world with its complex living structures and its artifacts such as synthetic rubbers and plastics, and the metallic world with again its very different characteristics.

The third subject was ' Waves and Vibrations '. The two forms of physical reality are matter and waves, and the nature of a wave is a very important conception. Starting with simple vibrations, and their importance in time measurement, examples were given of longitudinal and transverse waves. This led to electromagnetic waves. The history of the particle-wave controversy brings in the principle of interference, and that of resolution.

Waves transfer energy from point to point without the transfer of matter, and this transfer is capable of communicating information. Speech, sight, radio, radar, and radio-astronomy are examples of applications.

One could now combine the study of the properties of matter, and that of waves, into an examination of the interaction between waves and matter. Energy associated with matter can naturally be transformed into wave energy and vice versa. But when one examines the transfer more closely, it is seen that it is far from a simple matter, and the need for the quantum theory becomes apparent. A new 'Quantum Mechanics' must be created for elementary processes on the atomic scale. The wave-particle duality is a fruitful field to discuss, and helps to illustrate to the non-scientist the thrill of exploring new scientific conceptions. The 'Uncertainty Principle' and 'Determinism' are fascinating subjects.

Many of the most important physical properties of materials can only be explained satisfactorily in terms of quantum-mechanical ideas, such as electrical conductivity, semi-conductors, fluorescence and phosphorescence and the behaviour of transistors and lasers.

Session five was given to the atomic nucleus and atomic energy. It was shown how the study of radioactivity provided the first clues to nuclear constitution, that the nucleus was in itself a composite structure and that the nuclei of some atoms are unstable and spontaneously break up. This was continued by an account of the harnessing of nuclear energy and of high-energy particles both artificial and cosmic.

The lectures on chemistry and biology have been listed above. There was a close cross-linking between the talks. For instance, Professor Porter in his chemical sessions started with 'The Elements and their Compounds' and dealt also with the way the properties of atoms could be explained in terms of the inner structure, but more from the chemical point of view. In his last lecture he linked with biology by describing the complex molecular structure of the molecules in living bodies. Professor Harrison's first lecture on cells led on to a discussion of reproductive patterns and control of populations, eugenics, ageing processes; blood transfusion; preservation, transplantation and replacement of tissues. His second, on 'Communication Mechanisms', led to practical applications of the knowledge to enable man to deal with his environment.

After each course the Treasury has circulated a questionnaire to those who have taken part in it. The answers are frank, revealing, and in some cases devastating, but others are very warm. The course has had a better response this year than last, but it is clear that much exploration remains to be done. I believe a main trouble is that of trying to concentrate the whole of science into nine mornings, with a class that on the whole has no scientific background. If there had been such a basis on which to build, our efforts to explore the new scientific concepts in nine sessions would have had much greater impact. But on the whole there is a sufficient number of favourable responses to the questionnaire to give considerable encouragement; and it has been decided that the course shall be held again this year so there will be an opportunity of improving it further. It has been a fascinating experiment, and though the course is still imperfect it may still be the start of something much better to come.

Reprinted from
*Royal Institution of Great Britain Proceedings,* 1966, volume 41, pages 92-100

THE ROYAL INSTITUTION OF GREAT BRITAIN

# REMINISCENCES OF FIFTY YEARS' RESEARCH

*By* SIR LAWRENCE BRAGG, O.B.E., M.C., D.Sc., F.R.S.

*Director and Fullerian Professor of Chemistry*

Weekly Evening Meeting, Friday 11th March, 1966

Lord Fleck, of Saltcoats, K.B.E., D.Sc., LL.D., F.R.S.,
*President, in the Chair*

I expect that all scientists, when looking back at the years they have spent on research, remember vividly certain moments of the greatest excitement when some turning point occurred. The new idea, or check of some important point, or experimental discovery, may not be one of great importance in the final structure of the research of which it forms part. It may be some quite minor point, but it is one which, the researcher intuitively feels, shows that he is thinking on the right lines. Personally I remember these occasions so vividly that I can recall just when and where and how they happened.

I first tasted blood as a young researcher in 1912 when I was poring over the pictures obtained by von Laue and his colleagues, which appeared to prove that X-rays were diffracted by crystals. Laue had applied to their explanation the same reasoning as for diffraction by a line grating, but extended in this case to three dimensions. The direction of a diffracted beam must be such that there is a whole number of wavelengths in path difference for waves scattered by corresponding points in the pattern along all three axial directions in the crystal. In a line grating we speak of an $n^{th}$ order for a given wavelength, meaning that there are n waves in path difference between one line and the next for that particular diffracted beam. Since a crystal is a pattern in three-dimensions, one must speak of the order (hkl), h wave lengths between two neighbouring points along the a axis, k for the b axis, l for the c axis. Laue's most significant photograph had been obtained with a crystal of zinc blende. With this "order" formulation, Laue explained the spots in his photograph by assigning a spectrum of five definite wavelengths to the X-rays, and accounting for each spot as one of the orders of one or other of these wavelengths.

It seemed to me to be a complicated explanation and I tried to think of a simpler alternative. Now we had lectures by J. J. Thomson in which he explained X-rays as pulses due to the sudden stoppage of the electrons when they hit the anti-cathode in an X-ray tube. He pictured these pulses as "whip-cracks" in the lines of force attached to the suddenly arrested electron. Also, I had attended C. T. R. Wilson's brilliant lectures on optics, the very best of material presented in the very worst delivery of any lectures I know. He had analysed the production of a spectrum of white light by a line grating. It can be considered that all colours of light are present in the white light. The red is diffracted through a large angle because of its greater wavelength, the green through an intermediate angle, and the blue least—hence the rainbow sequence of the spectrum.

There is another way of looking at the phenomenon. White light can be considered as a series of quite formless pulses, a "noise" of light. When one of these pulses falls on the grating, wavelets spread from each line. In the direct line of transmission these wavelets remain in step, but in an inclined direction they arrive as a regular train of equally spaced copies of the pulse—in fact as coloured light. The greater the angle of inclination, the further apart are the pulses, and so the redder the light. In other words, instead of lights of different colours in the white light being analysed by the grating, the grating is fabricating colours from formless white light.

This is how my brainwave came. Suppose X-rays were formless pulses, sweeping through the crystal, they would be reflected by the sheets of atoms in regularly spaced planes which are a consequence of the crystal structure. The reflected wavelengths from each plane would lie behind each other at regular intervals, just like the pulses from the lines in a grating. There were not special wavelengths in the X-rays; the crystal was "making" special wavelengths from "white" X-rays.

Then of course came the checks. Were Laue's diffracted beams in directions corresponding to reflections from crystal planes? They were. If Laue was right, a tilt of the crystal would spoil the conditions for diffraction and the spots would disappear. If I was right, they would remain, for other directions of reflection. Laue had tried this experiment, and the spots had remained. Did a very flaky crystal like mica reflect X-rays like a mirror? I tried it and it did. I remember so well taking my terribly crude picture of reflection to show to J. J. Thomson. He betrayed his excitement in a characteristically J. J. way by thrusting his spectacles up on his forehead, ruffling his hair violently, and making a peculiar mixture of grin and chuckle. It was a great moment. I read my first paper to the Cambridge Philosophical Society in November 1912 and published the structures of the alkaline halides next year.

Yet the reflection was not a really novel idea. It was only Laue's analysis expressed in a different way. Treating the diffracted beam as a reflection in crystal planes satisfied two conditions for phase relationship, and the third was satisfied by the law $n\lambda = 2d\sin\theta$ (Bragg's law) which was based on the spacing of the reflected pulses. Further, the Laue method remained a very complex way of analysing crystals. I was right in saying that the Laue spots were due to "white" X-rays, but it was my father's discovery that there were discrete wavelengths characteristic of the anticathode which made crystal analysis so powerful a tool. I should have gone a very short way had I not been able to join forces with him for our later researches together. I was fortunate in that Professor Pope, my kind counsellor at Cambridge, inspired me to try the Laue method on the crystalline structures of the alkali halides, which proved to be so simple that I was successful in determining the atomic arrangement.

The First World War put an end to our researches in 1914. I was first posted to a Territorial Horse Artillery battery training in England, where I was very much a fish out of water. My fellow officers were all Leicestershire hunting folk, extremely knowledgeable about the horses, of which there was such an abundance in these batteries. The relief on the side of the battery was as great as, if not greater than, it was on mine when after a year I was summoned to the War Office and told that I was to proceed to France to start experiments on a method of determining the positions of enemy guns by sound which had been developed in the French Army. The French were trying several methods, all based on the same principle that if one could measure the time intervals between the arrival of the sound at a series of microphones spaced along a base some thousands of yards long, one could place the origin of the sound. One system had a recorder in which the signals from the carbon granule microphones were registered on smoked paper (this became the standard French method). In another, the carbon microphones were replaced by ones which had coils moving in magnetic fields. There was still another which had been designed by Lucien Bull, of the Institut Marey in Paris, and this was the one the British had decided to test. It was distinguished by the elegance of its recording system. The recorder was a six-string Einthoven galvanometer in which the currents from the microphones displaced the corresponding fine wires in a strong magnetic field. The movements of the wires were registered by throwing their shadows on a moving cinematograph film, and interrupting the light one hundred times a second with a toothed wheel governed by a tuning fork. The system had the disadvantage of the rather tiresome necessity to develop and fix the film before it could be read. This was far more than compensated, however, by its great accuracy in timing and the faithful way in which the galvanometer strings recorded the currents without imposing their own characteristics. The timing was so accurate, indeed, that later in the war the same recorder with a speeded-up film was used quite successfully to time the interval between a shell passing through two wire screens some 100 feet apart in calibrating guns.

Another young scientist, Robinson (later Professor at Queen Mary College), and I set up our gear at the front just south of Ypres. At first it was an almost complete failure. This failure was in no way the fault of Bull's recording apparatus, which worked perfectly; it was due to the nature of our microphones. They were carbon granule microphones used for long-distance telephoning on the continent. They were extremely efficient at recording rifle-fire, passing transport, people talking, dogs barking, and in particular the loud crack which comes from a high-velocity shell going through the air faster than sound. This crack is now familiar to us as the noise made by aeroplanes which have passed through the sound barrier. Our microphones turned an almost completely deaf ear to the low pitched "Wumph" which is the actual report of the gun, and of course the noise on which we wished to range.

We knew one thing about the gun report. Although barely audible when coming from the other side of the front line, it produced quite large pressure changes which rattled windows. We were aware of the pressure changes in another way. We were living in tarred felt huts in bitterly cold weather at the time, and we noticed that whereas the "shell wave" was a deafening crack, the faint gun wave blew jets of very cold air through the readily available holes in the sides of our hut. Now I had in my unit a certain Corporal Tucker, who in peace time was a lecturer at Imperial College and who had made experiments on the cooling of heated fine platinum wires by currents of air. The joint brain-wave came to us, I think mainly to him, that we could use this effect. We sent to England for a supply of the thin wire. We scrounged some ammunition boxes, bored a hole in each, and stretched the wire across the hole. We incorporated this in one arm of a Wheatstone Bridge, with a sufficient current to heat it to a dull red, the Einthoven wire of course being in the usual galvanometer position in the bridge. The idea was that the high-pitched noises which were so troublesome would have such rapid fluctuations that they would hardly displace the shell of warm air around the wire, whereas the low-pitched gun wave would blow a blast of air through the hole, sweep the warm air away, cool the wire, and so reduce its assistance, upset the bridge, and make the galvanometer record a current.

It worked like a charm. I shall never forget the evening when we first rigged up a local circuit with our ammunition box microphone. A German field battery obliged by firing towards us. The piercing shell wave hardly disturbed our string; the faint "Wumph" from the gun produced a large displacement of characteristic form. Eureka! It was the complete answer. From this time Sound Ranging became a powerful and trusted method of locating the enemy's artillery in both world wars. The hot-wave microphone has since found many uses as an ideal instrument for registering low-frequency change of pressure or of air movements generally. It was born that evening on Kemmel Hill; a great moment.

After the war, when I was appointed to the Physics Chair at Manchester, R. W. James and I set ourselves the task of making X-ray analysis a quantitative science. Until then, it had been sufficient, for the simple crystals so far analysed, to note whether diffracted beams were "strong", "medium", "weak" or "very weak". We started making "absolute" measurements, in which the strength of the diffracted beam was expressed in terms of the strength of the beam incident on the crystal. The result was that we could tackle far more complex crystals with confidence. I must admit that at first this confidence was not shared by X-ray crystallographers abroad. A measure of the complexity of the crystal is the number of what have come to be known as "parameters" which define the structure. For instance in rocksalt all the atoms lie precisely at centres of symmetry, so the number of parameters is zero. In calcite, on the other hand, the oxygen atoms lie on twofold axes away from which they cannot move, but their position along the axis is not defined by symmetry and must be fixed by the X-ray measurements. The structure has one parameter. So far the only crystal structures which had been determined had one, or at most two, parameters, and it was widely doubted whether it would ever be possible to venture further. We started to tackle crystals with ten or twenty parameters, being able to do so because the quantitative measurements restricted possibilities and led much more rapidly to the right answer.

This led us to examine the silicates as good examples of complex patterns, with the most unexpected reward that the whole scheme of their structures fell into order. They form the greater part of the earth's crust, and one could say with some justification that the earth's crust could be explained on the back of an envelope.

The full explanation only dawned slowly, but I can remember certain exciting moments. The crust is mainly composed of silicon and oxygen. Oxygen is the space-filling material; the other atoms can be thought of as tucked between the interstices of a fabric composed of packed oxygen ions. In certain simple cases we had found that the oxygen atoms were in one of the forms of closest packing on either the face-centred cubic lattice or a hexagonal lattice. These lattices have certain characteristic axial dimensions, determined by the dimensions of the oxygen ion. If a silicate structure is based on a close packing of oxygen atoms, then the axial dimensions of its pattern must be related in some way to the simpler oxygen framework, just as the dimension of a pattern in a sampler is related to the pattern of the fabric on which it is woven. Now we were examining the structure of a silicate called kyanite, Al$_2$SiO$_5$, which is triclinic, that is to say its axes and the angles between these are unequal, the lowest form of symmetry a crystal can have. The number of oxygen atoms per unit volume indicated that they were in close packing, yet it seemed most mysterious how a triclinic crystal could be based on, for instance, cubic-closest packing, or indeed how a multiple of five oxygen atoms could be accommodated in any cubic or hexagonal block. The particular moment of excitement which I am recalling came when the answer to this problem suddenly "tumbled out". It is shown in Figure 1. It will be seen that the triclinic axes correspond to lines joining oxygen atoms

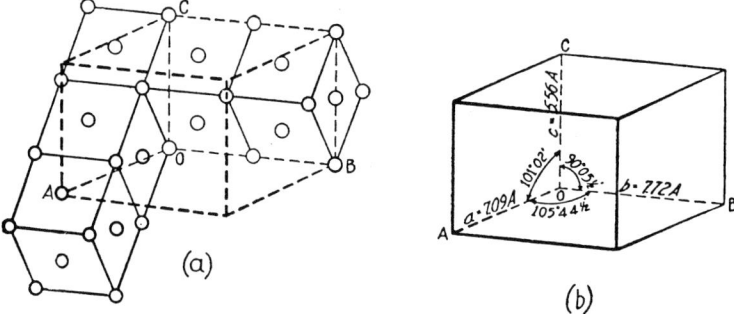

Fig. 1. The foundation of the kyanite structure upon a basis of oxygen atoms in close packing. (*a*) The face-centred cubic arrangement of oxygen atoms. The atom A is at the centre of the upper face of the nearest cube. (*b*) The corresponding unit cell of kyanite.

in a cubic structure. This may seem a small point, but it played a key role in showing that the idea of the oxygen atoms controlling the dimensions was essentially right.

I might quote a number of other examples, but I will pass on to the most recent experience which to me has been the greatest of all, although this time I was an onlooker on the side lines rather than an active participator in the game. For very many years I had been deeply interested in the investigation by Perutz into X-ray diffraction by proteins. I first came in contact with their investigations when I went to Cambridge in 1938, and Perutz showed me the very detailed and perfect photograph of X-ray diffraction by haemoglobin. We worked on this together after the war, and got scraps of information which sufficed to keep up our interest, while still being an almost infinite distance from making a solution of the structure of these vastly complex molecules possible. Kendrew had joined the team and was working on myoglobin. A brilliant piece of work by Perutz showed the way to further progress. He found that heavy atoms or complexes containing heavy atoms could be attached to the molecules in a protein crystal without disturbance of the crystal structure. Further he found that the differences in intensity of diffraction, when the heavy atoms were added to the protein, could be measured. In principle, this discovery made a direct solution of the protein structure possible, though the calculations were extremely long and complex. A first measure of success in the form of a two-dimensional solution was obtained which showed the projection of the haemoglobin molecule on a plane, though this told us little or nothing about its structure, because so many atoms are inextricably superimposed in the projection. It was a moot point whether the solution could be extended to three dimensions. Could the position of the heavy atoms in three dimensions be fixed and could the diffraction changes be measured with sufficient accuracy to enable the "phases" characteristic of each diffracted spot to be determined? It proved at this stage to be too difficult in the case of haemoglobin, but Kendrew's myoglobin presented a more favourable outlook. Kendrew lent me a number of his measurements to mull over, and my great moment came when I convinced myself that the answer to both the above questions was "yes". My calculations had no influence on the steady march of Kendrew's analysis; they were like the "colours" in a pan which show a miner that he has struck gold, but they proved that the answer to protein structure which we had sought for twenty-five years had at last been achieved. I could not resist testing one diffraction after another, seeing the answer come out in each case, till I worked myself to a complete mental standstill. It still seems to me miraculous that X-ray analysis, which started with such simple structures, can now determine the position of thousands of atoms in a protein molecule, and do it with such precision. It has come as a wonderful climax to fifty years of research in this field.

Reprinted from
*Marine Technology,* 1967, volume 4, pages 258-261

# The Art of Talking about Science

I propose to analyze "Talking about Science." How is it best done? Why is it that a subject presented by A is a thrilling account which leaves a deep impression, whereas the very same material presented by B is dull and boring and produces no impression whatever? How should we present our branch of science to fellow scientists who work in quite another field? How can we present science to those who have little or no scientific background, as is often the case with men of high ability who are important in affairs of state? How can we make the nonscientist understand why its study means so much to us, a passion they sometimes find very difficult to understand? The gap between C. P. Snow's two cultures is not so much due to a lack of understanding as to a lack of desire to understand. There are philistines as regards science as well as regards the arts.

These problems have been brought vividly home to me in a number of ways. I was for many years president of the Physics Solvay Conference. It must be one of the most exclusive of international science gatherings, because only some 20 participants are invited to discuss the subject chosen for the meetings which are held every 3

years. I have listened for 12 years to all the Friday evening discourses at the Royal Institution, where a broad review of some branch of science is given, and the speakers are both well known in their fields and artists in framing their talks. I talk to many thousands of school pupils every year, and find the nature of their response to be a fascinating study. Recently we have been framing courses for men and women who are new entrants to the Civil Service, and who have had no scientific training. I cannot help but be interested in the basic principles which apply to all talks of this kind.

What is the basic character of a "talk"? I think it can be expressed by saying that its primary object is to create a state of mind, or point of view, not to convey information. I can perhaps illustrate what I mean by dwelling on the vast difference between the spoken and written account. Under the heading "talk," I am not including a course of lectures where students take notes and the lectures follow each other as a composite whole. Nor do I include the "get together" of two or three experts in the same line of research, for which no rules are necessary. I am considering the hour's talk to an audience whose attention one has to retain and whose interest one has to arouse. The written account can also aim at creating a viewpoint, but its main function is to be a storehouse of information. The argument can be meaty and condensed. It can be packed with tables, graphs, and mathematical equations. This is possible because the reader can always pause and digest it at his leisure, going back over parts which he finds to be difficult. The written account has a quality also which I find hard to define. It is as if the writer were giving evidence on oath, and had to justify the accuracy of every word. He must be careful to give references and all due acknowledgements. I do not mean to imply that one can be irresponsible in a talk, but one need not cross all the "t's" and dot all the "i's." In fact, the talk would be spoiled by an attempt to do so.

A talk is therefore different altogether from a "paper." To my mind the governing factor which determines its art form is this: The success of the way in which the subject has been presented is measured by the extent to which the average member of the audience remembers it next day.

This may seem an obvious statement, but if we use this principle as a yardstick to assess a lecture we have listened to, or in planning a lecture of our own, it creates a very significant viewpoint. The value of a lecture is not to be measured by how much one manages to cram into an hour, how much important information has been referred to, or how completely it covers the ground. It is to be measured by how much a listener can tell his wife about it at breakfast next morning, or, if she is not interested, a friend in the morning train. If we honestly put this question to ourselves and think how little we can remember of talks we have heard, it gives us a sense of proportion and of values in planning a lecture and

makes us realize that what we say will go over the heads of the audience if we set our sights too high. I would like now to list what I believe to be some of the considerations which apply in planning a talk.

For instance, suppose we ask how many main points can we hope to "get over" in an hour? I think the answer should be "one." If the average member of the audience can remember with interest and enthusiasm one main theme, the lecture has been a great success. I like to compare the composition of a lecture to that of a picture. Of course this is dangerous ground on which to venture, because art experts differ so much among themselves. But in simple terms, is it not held that a picture should have one main centre of interest? It may have numerous subsidiary features, but the composition is so cunningly arranged that when the eye falls on these and follows their placing it is subtly led back to the main centre of interest and does not fall out of the picture frame. A lecture should be like that. There should be one main theme, and all the subsidiary interesting points, experiments, or demonstrations should be such that they remind the hearer of the theme. As in a picture, so in a lecture, the force of the impression depends upon a ruthless sacrifice of unnecessary detail. I do not mean that a lecture should be like some modern pictures, consisting of an otherwise blank canvas with one button or other object sewn on it at a place which I suppose has enormous aesthetic significance. It can, on the other hand, be richly endowed with exciting details, but they must be of such a kind that the recollection of them inevitably brings the main theme back to mind. In other words, the lecture must "compose" in the sense of having a pattern because it is this pattern which helps so much to impress it on one's memory.

**Reading**

I feel so strongly about the wrongness of reading a lecture that my language may seem immoderate. I think it is a dreadful thing to do, something quite out of keeping with all that a lecture should mean. The spoken word and the written word are quite different arts. Though the reader can pause and go back to a passage he has found difficult, the listener cannot do so and may lose the thread of the argument. It is boring in a written account to be repetitious; it is right in a spoken account to put a key idea in several ways to make sure the audience has grasped the point. When a man writes out his lecture he inevitably writes it as if it were to be read, not heard. The ideas follow each other too fast. It is, of course, far easier for the lecturer to read than for him to "think on his feet" by constructing his sentences on the spot, because he can frame his sentences at his leisure. I realize that many lecturers read their material from a feeling of modesty, thinking they will give a poor rendering if they have no script. While appreciating their reluctance, I am sure they are wrong. I feel that to collect an audience and then read one's material is like inviting a friend to go for a walk and asking him not to mind if you go alongside him in your car. It is easy for the lecturer to deliver well-considered rounded phrases, but the audience has to follow and to think. If someone says, "I dare not talk. I must write it out," I am tempted to ask, "Then why lecture? Why not send a written account to your friends and let them read it comfortably at home, instead of dragging them all out to a lecture hall to listen to your reading the very same thing?"

We come back, it seems to me, to the essential feature of a lecture which justifies bringing the lecturer and his audience together. It is the emotional contact between lecturer and audience.

If a lecturer has to find his words as he speaks, he will be automatically restrained from going too fast because he is thinking along with his audience. Every lecturer knows the trick of watching a few sympathetic faces in the audience and of judging (by noting their response) whether he has been successful in making his points or whether he must put things another way. A lecturer who reads is earthbound to his script, but the lecturer who talks can enjoy a wonderful feeling of being airborne and in complete accord with his audience. It is the greatest reward of lecturing.

Just as the troops used to say "The worst billet is better than the best bivouac," so one is tempted to say in a similarly approximate way "The worst spoken lecture is better than the best read one." But there are exceptions to all rules. Some very fine lecturers read their lectures, and I have tried to analyze the peculiar quality which makes their performance possible. I think they are the people who so refine and weigh every word and sentence that their beautiful prose almost becomes poetry—it is like a poet reading his verse. Eddington read his lectures marvelously, and on the arts side I have heard most moving read lectures delivered with great dramatic effect. But I think one ought not to venture to read a lecture unless one has these considerable poetic gifts.

**The First Ten Minutes**

A lecture is made or marred in the first 10 minutes. This is the time to establish the foundations, to remind the audience of things they half know already, and to define terms that will be used. Again this seems obvious, but I have listened to so much splendid material lost to the audience because the lecturer failed to realize that it did not know what he was talking about, whereas, if the precious first 10 minutes had been spent on preparation, he would have carried his listeners with him for the rest of the talk.

## Slides

Lecturers love slides, and in a game of associations the word "lecture" would almost always evoke the reply "slide." But I think we ought to apply to slides the same test, "What will the audience remember?" Some information can only be conveyed as slides, photographs, or records of actual events, such as the movement of a recording instrument, for instance, a seismograph. But slides of graphs or tables of figures are in general out of place in a lecture, or, at any rate, should be used most sparingly, just because the audience has not time to absorb them. If the lecturer wishes to illustrate a point with a graph, it is much better to draw it, or perhaps clamp the component parts on a magnetic board or employ some device of that kind. I remember well the first time I was impressed by this latter device, during a lecture on airflow through turbine blades. The lecturer altered the angle of incidence and the air arrows by shifting the parts on the board. It was far better than a series of slides. It is again a question of tempo—the audience can follow at about the rate one can draw; one is forced to be simple, and the slight expertise of the drawing holds attention. One must constantly think of what will be retained in the audience's memory, not of what can be crammed into the lecture.

## Experiments

Faraday had much to say about experiments that was very wise. The best experiments are simple and on a large scale, and their workings are obvious to the audience. The worst experiment is the one in which something happens inside a box, and the audience is told that if a pointer moves the lecturer has very cleverly produced a marvelous effect. Audiences love simple experiments and, strangely enough, it is often the advanced scientist who is most delighted by them. There are tricks too about demonstration. The wrong way is to do the experiment, ask the audience if they noticed this or that, and then explain what this or that meant. The right way is to start by explaining the significance of the effect you are aiming at producing, tell the audience what to look for, and then, after a pause to make sure you have their attention, to bring it off. These tricks are important because they are all part of fixing your message in the minds of the audience; they have the humble but necessary function of the hypo in fixing a photographic exposure.

## The Arousing of Interest

Here a most important principle comes in which I think of as the "detective story" principle. It is a matter of order. How dull a detective story would be if the writer told you who did it in the first chapter and then gave you the clues. Yet how many lectures do exactly this. One wishes to give the audience the esthetic pleasure of seeing how puzzling phenomena become crystal clear when one has the clue and thinks about them in the right way. So make sure the audience is first puzzled. A friend of mine, a barrister, told me that, when presenting a case to a judge, if he could appear to be fumbling toward a solution and could entice the judge to say "But, Mr. X, isn't the point you are trying to make this or that?" he had as good as won the case. One wants to get the audience into this frame of mind, when they are coaxed to guess for themselves what the answer is. Again I fear I am saying the trite and obvious, but I can assure you I have often sat and groaned at hearing a lecturer murder the most exciting story just by putting things in the wrong order.

We all know the tendency to go to sleep in lectures; how often have I felt ashamed at doing so myself. Though the best lecturer can never entirely escape from producing this effect, there is much that can be done to minimize it. A continuous even delivery is fatal. There is something hypnotic about it which induces sleep (this is another reason why it is so bad to read). Pauses and changes of tempo are essential. Above all, jokes have a marked and enduring effect. The science lecturer is of course greatly helped by his experiments and demonstrations which make useful breaks.

### Timing

Some try to get the timing of a lecture right by, as they say, "running over it beforehand" and seeing how long it takes. I am doubtful of the usefulness of this exercise when applied to the lecture as a whole. I prefer to divide it into some half dozen portions, and allocate about 10 minutes to each, marking this timing in the margin of my rough notes. One can sometimes fall into a dreadful trap with a subject in which one is a specialist. One thinks "that point will only take a minute or so to explain" and realizes to one's horror in the actual lecture that, having to start from scratch, it takes ten times as long. Of course the way in which each 10-minute section is to be put has to be carefully thought out and its timing roughly estimated. The advantage of dividing the time up in this way is that the pace can be adjusted during the lecture when it is clear that it is going to be too long or (rarely) too short.

If time is running short, the part to shorten is the middle where it will be little noticed. The beginning or the end must not be hurried. It is rather like fitting a patterned carpet in a room which is too small for it. If this heroic measure must be adopted, it is much better to cut a strip from the middle of the pattern rather than to cut off an edge. An hour is as much as an audience can stand, and it is most unfortunate when a lecturer has to race through his material at the end and even then runs over the hour.

### Kindness to Lecturers

A lecture is a tour de force and a good and conscientious lecturer is both nervous beforehand and prostrate afterwards. I think there is a great deal to be said for the tradition at the Royal Institution that the lecturer should be immured in a small private room termed "The Lecturer's Room" for at least half an hour before the lecture starts. Tradition has it that this was originally laid down because once a lecturer (actually Wheatstone of Bridge fame) ran away from nervousness just before the lecture started, and so a guard has been placed over the room ever since. In fact, the guard is there not to keep the lecturer in but to keep intruders out. Most if not all lecturers value this quiet time to have a last run over their material and get their minds into the right mood. In particular, if members of the press realized the state of mind of one about to give a lecture, which is much like that of an athlete about to run a race, I am sure they would refrain from tackling him just before the lecture starts, to get, for instance, his views on the atomic bomb. After the lecture he should be at their service and oblige them in any way he can, because he is free to switch his mind off his lecture.

I have emphasized the difference between the spoken and written word. To prepare a talk, and to write an account of it, are two separate tasks and the latter may be much the heavier. I think, therefore, that, when a man is invited to speak, it should be made clear at the same time whether he is to write as well. I know to my cost what a difficult position one is placed in if one discovers, after agreeing to talk, that the heavy labor of writing up the material is also expected. I am sure the task is often imposed unwittingly, under the idea that if a man is talking he will have written what he wants to say, but you will have realized from my remarks about reading that I feel this ought not to be assumed. The most embarrassing thing is to be told that a tape recording will be made, and asked if one would please correct it. It is embarrassing to see a verbatim report with all the remarks recorded literally, and it is generally far less trouble to write it from the beginning than to try to patch the record.

In conclusion, I hope you will realize that the last thing I want is to seem to lay down the law about lecturing. I have spoken so feelingly about the pitfalls because I have so often fallen into them myself. One has to be constantly watchful if they are to be avoided, and even then one does not escape. It is most dangerous to be complacent about a lecture, to think that it will be all right because one knows the stuff and has given a similar talk elsewhere. Every lecture must be approached as if it were a new problem. No pains are too great in the attempt to make a talk a success, and I believe that, given the right treatment, any subject can be made fascinating to any audience.

The author retired this year from the directorship of the Royal Institution, London. This article is adapted from an address delivered 28 December 1966 at the AAAS meeting in Washington, D.C.

Reprinted from
*Proceedings of the Royal Society, B,* 1967, volume 167, page 349

# Introduction

By Sir Lawrence Bragg, F.R.S.

*The Royal Institution,* 21 *Albemarle Street, London, W.*1

On behalf of the Royal Institution, I wish to express our pleasure that this discussion on 'The structure and function of lysozyme' is being held in its theatre this afternoon. Dr Phillips and his team have been investigating the structure of lysozyme in the Davy Faraday Laboratory for some years, and have recently been able to analyse that structure in considerable detail. They have also been able to mark down the sites on the molecule to which inhibitors of its action attach themselves. It is a great day for the Laboratory to take part in a meeting at which experts in this country and abroad have gathered to discuss the significance of the new knowledge about structure; and our warm thanks are due to Dr Perutz for organizing the present conference on behalf of the Royal Society.

The initiation of a project to study a selected protein structure requires very careful consideration; it is rather like a decision as to which new type of aeroplane to build. The cost in manpower, time and money is considerable, and if the structure proves to be obdurate this expenditure shows little return. Lysozyme, which Dr Poljak had already studied when he joined the Davy Faraday team in 1960, proved to be a fortunate choice. It is the third protein structure to be successfully analysed, and the first enzyme.

I have been forced to eat my words in two ways. I estimated not long ago that the analysis of a protein required fifty man-years of first-rate researchers' time, and a quarter of a million pounds. The cost for lysozyme has been about one half in each respect. Then again, at the end of a paper read to the Institute of Physics and the Physical Society two years ago, in talking about Kendrew's successful analysis of myoglobin, I wrote,

'It will be very interesting to see how long it will be before any other laboratory produces a molecular model of a protein with the wealth of detail now firmly established for myoglobin. My guess, though admittedly a dangerous one, is that it will be between five and ten years before this summit of precision is reached by another party of investigators.'
My own laboratory has proved me to be wrong, which is perhaps the most pleasant way in which it could have happened.

I must end by acknowledging the debt this Institution owes to Dr Perutz and Dr Kendrew for their help. The Davy Faraday Laboratory team, who carried out the work, is an offshoot of the Medical Research Council's team for Molecular Biology in Cambridge and without this assistance it could hardly have been started on its career.

Reprinted from
*Punch*, September 11, 1968, volume 255, pages 352-354

# MARGINS OF SCIENCE

Science and technology are more and more a part of our lives. What forces are at work behind, and perhaps ahead of, the men in white coats?

## The White-Coated Worker

by Sir Lawrence Bragg

THE qualities which make for success in research are very elusive. Applied research, which seeks to use scientific knowledge for practical ends, demands judgment and the courage to follow it, a knowledge of economics and affairs and an organising ability, which are not required to anything like the same extent by the fundamental scientist whose aim is the gaining of a deeper knowledge about Nature. Like most scientists, I have had some experience of applied research in war-time, but except for this my work has all been in fundamental research. I will confine myself to this side, taking my illustrations from my own subject of physics though equally good ones could have been chosen from other sciences.

Although it is the art and skill of the engineer in using science for practical ends which has made such a vast difference in the way we live in this technological age, practically all great advances in scientific knowledge have been made without any idea whatever of putting them to practical use. Electricity is a supreme example. Its many applications make it the mightiest technological advance of all. Yet its secrets, which Nature had so jealously hidden, only began to be revealed some hundred and fifty years ago when Galvani noticed that legs dissected from a frog kicked in the presence of an electric spark, and Volta, dissatisfied with Galvani's explanation, was led to invent the Voltaic Pile, the original battery, which provided for the first time a steady electric current. They were both inspired by pure curiosity. By a strange paradox, as long as knowledge was only sought for practical ends, technical advance was very slow. When it came to be sought for its own sake, an understanding of Nature grew so rapidly that it resulted in the technological revolution.

The men who make the great scientific advances are of very different types. The greatest are those who teach us to think in a new way. Wordsworth said of Newton's statue

"*The marble index of a mind for ever Voyaging through strange seas of thought alone.*"

In modern times we recognise Bohr as our greatest theoretical physicist, because he developed a new mechanics to explain the properties of atoms. He realised that although large-scale objects made of atoms obeyed Newton's laws, it did not follow that atoms could be explained as little machines. How obvious! and yet his ideas at first seemed entirely contrary to common-sense, just as Galileo's did to his contemporaries. It is just this "common-sense" which the Great by-pass.

Scientists like Röntgen who discovered X-rays and Bequerel who discovered radioactivity are in another class. They were not looking for what they found; in the course of a quite un-related investigation they noticed a strange phenomenon which did not fit into the accepted pattern of science and they had the wit to realise its great importance. In general, such people make just this one great contribution. They are like Novae, new stars which blaze suddenly into brilliance and then fade into ordinary objects in the heavens —but they have opened a path to new realms of scientific exploration.

Then there are the inventors of some new type of apparatus for getting information about Nature. A striking example is the "Wilson Cloud Chamber." Before its invention the behaviour of small particles like atoms and electrons could only be inferred from large-scale effects. C. T. R. Wilson showed that such particles, when darting through moist air, pro-duced cloud trails much like the vapour trails which aircraft sometimes make, so that one could see precisely how one individual atom or electron had behaved. The Cloud Chamber has become the vital means for studying the ultimate particles of matter, and is responsible for a major part of modern physics.

Michael Faraday, whom we count as our greatest scientist since Newton, sought for truth like a hunter exploring every brake and thicket for his game. His diary records a patient trying of this and that with an intuition which guided him to find new relationships between natural phenomena. A famous German scientist said of him:

"*Er riecht die Wahrheit.*" "He smells out the truth."

Scientists are sharply divided into lone workers and heads of teams.

Faraday was one of the former, he had no pupils. The lone worker makes his own observations and does not have to trust to the eyes of his juniors to see opportunities, which they may well miss. On the other hand, the head of a re-search team spreads his influence widely and has the fascination of seeing clever young pupils develop and do brilliant original work, but he almost in-evitably pays the price of losing direct touch with experiment.

What qualities have successful re-searchers in common? I would put in the first place "enthusiasm." Research demands great patience; for most of the time one is exploring alleys which turn out to be blind. My father used to say that if one looked back at the end of a year, one could see that all its research could have been done in a week. A young man once asked Faraday how to do research and Faraday replied, "Start it, carry on with it, and finish it," which was very wise and to the point. There must be the determination to see it through to the end.

Another essential quality is the open mind, in the form of a readiness to scrap preconceived ideas when Nature indicates quite different ones. It is perhaps because preconceived ideas have not yet gained a mastery that most original scientific achievements are made in such early years. Popular imagination may picture a scientist as a grey-beard, but actually almost with-out exception famous men such as Newton, Einstein, Rutherford and Bohr made their outstanding contributions in their twenties. They expand them in later years, but they have sunk so much capital of experience and reputation in their first line of work that it is very hard to cut losses and start a new line. In war-time many scientists were jolted out of their ruts by the demands of a war problem, and it was interesting to note that they often took up a quite new line after the war; it was as if they had a second flowering season.

The quality of which I have so far made no mention is "cleverness" in the sense of the brains which, for instance, make a good showing in examinations. It is hard to assess the importance of cleverness. Some ventures in physics demand abstruse mathematics, or more often an ingenuity in finding a suitable mathematical tool, but this ability is not essential. Rutherford discovered the nucleus of the atom by observing the scattering of $\alpha$ particles from radium by matter, a classic experiment with enormously important consequences. Yet the late Professor H. Robinson, who was a research student in Rutherford's laboratory at the time, once told me that he and other members of the team had to labour for over a month to make Rutherford understand the equation for the path of one particle repelled by another, a piece of mathematics within the grasp of a clever sixth-form schoolboy. Bohr's revolutionary ideas were based on the simplest algebra. Faraday had no mathematical training whatever. It is the same with manipulative skill. Some great researchers have depended on ability to design apparatus and use it. But J. J. Thomson, who by discovering the electron opened the door to modern physics, was unhandy with apparatus, and I have been told on good authority that Rutherford's students tried to keep him away from their experiments because disaster so often followed if he intervened. There is a something about the great man in comparison with which cleverness is of quite secondary importance.

While it is difficult to lay down the conditions which lead to success in research, it is easy to say what makes it impossible. The fatal enemy of research is a full engagement book. The Muse of Science cannot be commanded and is capricious in her visits, but of one thing one can be certain, she flees from the busy man. Looking back, I recall that the precious occasions on which I have started a good idea have all been times when for some reason I was free from engagements—it may even have been the gift of a free day because a meeting had been cancelled. Of course, once the idea has secured its grip everything else is thrown to the winds; it is the start which is so easily prevented. The traditional scientific vagueness is a defence mechanism against distraction. Newton must be allowed to boil his watch and put the egg in his pocket, or he would not be Newton. Withdrawal is essential if Nature is to tell her secrets. And when, after the long search, some new fragment of truth has been captured, it comes not as something discovered but as something revealed. The answer is so unexpected, and yet so simple and aesthetically satisfying, that it carries instant conviction, and that wonderful never-to-be forgotten moment comes when one says to oneself "Of course that's it."

Reprinted from
*Royal Institution of Great Britain Proceedings*, 1969, volume 42, pages 397-410

# WHAT MAKES A SCIENTIST?

*By* SIR LAWRENCE BRAGG, C.H., O.B.E., M.C.,
D.Sc., F.R.S.

*Professor Emeritus of the Royal Institution*

Lecture for Civil Servants, Wednesday 11th December, 1968

THE qualities which characterise a scientist are very elusive. Before I try to deal with them, I would like to clear the air by touching on two points.

The first is the very real difference between fundamental and applied science, the first being 'knowledge orientated' and the second 'project orientated'. I want to emphasise right away how strongly I dissent from the view that the one is in any way finer or more inspiring than the other.

The 'project orientated' problems cover a much wider range than those which face 'knowledge orientated' scientists like myself. Social habits, politics, economics, all enter into them. The time factor is often vitally important. Bold decisions must be made on insufficient evidence. The scientific requirement in their schemes is often the least formidable one to meet. I remember Sir John Baker, the head of the Engineering Department in Cambridge, giving one of the schools lectures at the Royal Institution; his subject was the Morrison shelter in the last war as an example of the many problems which have to be mastered before such a scheme can be launched. The scientific idea behind it was ingenious and sound. The shelter had to provide a reasonably comfortable retreat inside a house, because one could not expect people to sleep in damp, cold dugouts. It therefore had to withstand a bombed house falling down on top of it. Masonry and rubble falling on a brittle structure, even though it is strong, will crack it. Baker realised that this could be avoided by constructing the shelter of yielding steel, so that the energy of the falling building was absorbed as work done in deforming the roof of the shelter. Calculation showed that it could be so made that, though it would yield considerably, its top would still stay well above the sleeper under its cover. So far so good. But authorities

had to be convinced of the soundness of the plan, priority obtained for the necessary steel, manufacturing and distribution
had to be arranged, all a far more arduous task than just having
the good idea. Professor Baker had chosen a telling instance to
show the young people how much more than just science was
involved in an engineer's career.

Like other fundamental scientists, I have had a taste of
applied science in two world wars, when we were drawn into the
war effort, and although our problems were simpler because the
making of a profit was not a consideration, this experience gave
us all, I think, a proper and healthy respect for the applied
scientist.

I stress this difference because it seems to me that the word
'science' is often loosely used to describe two quite distinct forms
of human endeavour. There is first the search for more knowledge
about nature, a movement which can be traced far back but
which really only started in strength in the seventeenth century.
This search has built up a body of knowledge and concepts which
is continually being extended by scientific research. Then, there
is the use of that knowledge for technical ends backed up by an
intensive industrial research directed towards the particular
project in hand. Man has always exercised his ingenuity in trying
new ways of achieving practical ends, but the discoveries of
science have, comparatively recently, immensely amplified his
powers of invention. For instance, the scientists' discovery of the
fundamental laws of electricity and magnetism, at the beginning
of the nineteenth century, opened a new world to technology by
starting electrical engineering. However, the really widespread
application of science to industry is mainly a phenomenon of the
present century. So when people talk about all the new and
marvellous achievements of technology, they often loosely call
them 'science', bracketing them with the pursuit of fundamental
knowledge. The achievements are possible because the engineer
can draw on the body of knowledge which the scientist has
created, but they are the product of many social forces to which
science may only make a minor contribution.

The second point is that although the knowledge and skill of
the engineer, drawing on the body of scientific knowledge for
assistance, has brought about the great extension of technical

achievement which we call the scientific revolution, yet the scientific advances which have so increased technical powers have been almost entirely made without any thought of their possible practical use. One can put this more strongly—they would never have been made if their practical application had been regarded as a necessary condition for doing them. I confess that when I was preparing this talk and consulted the early history of the Royal Society, I wondered if I had been too positive in making the above statement. The early Fellows were assiduous in their protestations that their enquiries would be of great importance to the economy of their country. But on reflection I still believe it to be true of the discoveries in those early days. One cannot help suspecting a certain element of propaganda by the members of the Royal Society which was struggling to establish itself and gain support. When Charles II was moved to such mirth by the spectacle of the Fellows studying the weighing of the air, I do not think they were pursuing this research with an industrial end in view.

No better example can be taken than the start of 'useful electricity'. It is fun to play the game of imagining that one were able to talk with a distinguished man of the past, and thinking how one would explain modern technical achievements to him. I would feel fairly sure of being able to explain a steam engine to a Roman engineer. Though the Romans had not arrived at such an engine, the mechanical principles would appeal to him as natural and familiar. But—a radio set— or even how one could light a room by pressing a knob! I remember that when my father was Director of the Royal Institution, the American Electrical Engineers, who had built a new headquarters in New York, invited my father to participate in the opening ceremony. He was to strike a match and light a candle in Faraday's candlestick in his study at the Royal Institution, and this act was to switch on all the lights in the new home of the Engineers. Now any sixth form schoolboy could guess how this was done—a photoelectric cell activitating a relay and switch, a radio signal crossing the Atlantic, which in turn activated a relay and closed the main switch in the building. How simple, yet how magical it would appear to our Roman that lighting a candle in Britain would light a building two thousand miles away.

How did it start? The ancients knew practically nothing about electricity, except for a few electrified toys. Then around the start of the nineteenth century Galvani discovered that the contact with two dissimilar metals made a frogs legs twitch. Volta, dissatisfied with Galvani's explanation in terms of animal electricity, seized on the fact that dissimilar metals seemed essential to build his 'pile'—the first battery, and the first time man had at his command the power to study a continuous electric current. Galvani and Volta's names are part of our common language. Every householder knows about volts. It is strange to think that when, for instance, a letter to *The Times* says that this Government department or that needs to be galvanised into action, it literally means that the hind legs of its members should be made to kick by the application of an electric shock.

The availability of an electric current led twenty years later to the discovery that a current produced a magnetic field, and this in due course gave an entirely new power to mankind, that of practically instantaneous communication all over the world. This power was based on the fact that some bodies conduct the current almost infinitely better than others. One only has to remember that an electric current, fed into the copper conductor of a cable, prefers to run from one side of the Atlantic to the other rather than to jump across an inch or so of insulation to the surrounding sea. Thirty years later Faraday discovered that a current could be created by moving a magnet, and this in due course led to dynamos and the efficient transmission of power over wide areas with all the changes it has brought about. Yet none of these consequences could possibly have been foreseen when Galvani and Volta, excited by mere curiosity, discovered the existence of a new world by a series of experiments which at the time seemed completely remote from any practical application.

Like all who give talks about new scientific discoveries, I am often asked "To what use can this discovery be put", and I always give the same answer "Come back in fifty years time and I will tell you". There was a story current in Cambridge that shortly before he died, Lord Rutherford, who was the outstanding figure in radioactivity and had discovered the nucleus, explained at great length to a visitor (I think the American

Dr. Conant) why it was physically impossible ever to tap the vast stores of energy in the nucleus—this only a few years before the atomic bomb and the atomic power station. Scientists are sometimes adjured only to find out knowledge which can be used for good purposes, and to eschew research which could be put to bad purposes. Such an attitude can only come from a complete ignorance of how science works. There is no difference between good and bad knowledge; all the knowledge goes into a central store from which the technologist draws the many bits of information he wants for some particular scheme. There is rarely a one-to-one correspondence between a discovery and utilization—in general each exploitation depends on the work of many scientists in many fields. The scientist cannot foresee and be responsible for the use of his discovery, not because he lives in an ivory castle, but because the future holds so many surprises.

In this broad survey I shall divide scientists into four categories. If I draw my examples mainly from the field of physics, you will realise that this is because it is the field most familiar to me.

First, there are the thinkers, those who establish some new way of regarding the phenomena we observe. Newton is a supreme example in that, following the start made by Galileo, he conceived the earth and heaven as obeying the same fundamental laws. At the time of the Newton tercentenary, the late King paid a visit to Trinity College in Cambridge and various fellows were detailed to say something to the King about Trinity's greatest son. I had to 'do' gravity. I remember the King saying "What's all this about an apple? Had not many people seen an apple fall before?" "Your Majesty, the point was that Newton realised that the law which governed the fall of the apple to the earth also governed the continual falling of the moon towards the earth." "The moon falling towards the earth—that's the first I ever heard of it" and the King passed on leaving me discomfited at the inaptness of my explanation.

Then, in our own times, there is the advance made by the great Danish physicist Niels Bohr, and here I would like to pause and examine in some detail what he did, taking as it were a sounding in depth whereas so far I have been skimming over the surface, because Bohr's work is such a wonderful example of what a new way of thinking can mean.

J. J. Thomson discovered that electrons were constituents of all atoms; Rutherford discovered the heavy positive nucleus at the centre of the atom whose attraction binds the negative electrons in the atomic structure. Models of the structure of the atom built on this basis at once came up against an insuperable difficulty. An electron rotating around the nucleus like a planet going round the sun should give out light, and hence energy, and eventually fall into the nucleus just as an artificial satellite falls to earth when it experiences the resistance of our atmosphere. It does not do so, the atomic structure lasts indefinitely. Again, as it approaches the nucleus it should circulate faster and faster, raising the frequency of the light it emits. But on the contrary, when the atom emits light it is of one pure frequency. As I once heard it put at a Solvay Conference by the Dutch physicist Ehrenfest: "Ze problem—vy ze atom a pure tone geef, and not a noise like ze leet cat make".

Bohr cut the Gordian knot. He saw that the difficulty arose not because the right model had not been found but because new assumptions must be made about the mechanical laws which governed it. Because a steam engine, obeying Newtonian mechanics, is made of atoms, it had been tacitly assumed that an atom obeyed Newtonian mechanics like a very small steam-engine. Bohr formulated new laws, and in them a certain constant 'h' reappeared, which related frequency to a quantum or parcel of energy, and which Planck had postulated to explain the properties of radiation. As atomic mechanisms were explored further, the same constant 'h' turned up in other guises. To cut a long story short, it appeared that light, the wave nature of which had appeared to be so firmly established by Young and Fresnel's analysis of interference, had other properties which pointed equally clearly to light being a stream of projectiles, with an energy related to the wave frequency by Planck's constant. And then, to crown it all, Davisson and Germer and G. P. Thomson showed that electrons, whose particle nature no one doubted, showed interference effects as though they were waves with a wave length given by Planck's constant. As my father summed up the situation, one had to believe they were waves on Monday, Wednesday and Friday, particles on Tuesday, Thursday and Saturday, and have a rest on Sunday. As time went on, a deeper synthesis became possible. The character of a particle is that it is something at a definite point in space. The character of a wave is that it extends throughout space, though it may have a much greater amplitude in one place than another (some places may be stormy and others quiet). We can sum up the position by saying that if we are given a definite set of conditions (a cause) and want to calculate what will happen (its effect) we must cast our prediction in the form of a distribution of probabilities and, waves in simple cases are a convenient way to describe probability. All we can say is it is much more likely the effect will be this, much less likely it will be that. But when the event has happened, whether it is a light quantum hitting a particular silver grain on a photographic plate, or an electron making a track through a cloud chamber, it is a history of particles. The moment 'now' is like a sieve passing steadily through time. In front of it is a probability future, a 'wavy' future if you like, in which we can only predict how likely some result is to happen. As time streams through our sieve, it coagulates this wavy future into a particle past, where the precise history of events is recorded.

Why should predictions of the future inevitably have this probability character? Let me take an analogy. Suppose a doctor were so clever that by making a thorough examination of a patient for a life insurance company, he could say exactly when that patient was going to die. The very examination, however, gives the patient such a shock that he now will not die at the calculated time. One can only tell exactly what the shock has done by making a further examination, and this in its turn upsets calculation by administering a further shock. This is what happens when we examine nature. We say "we will find out the present state of affairs, and by doing so be able to predict the future". But "finding out the present state of affairs" means asking the atoms to give signals as to what they are doing. Sending out a light signal is a shattering event to an atom, entirely altering its nature. The observer cannot be separated from the observed. If we try to find out what a given system is going to do, the questions we ask it force it to do something which causes it to behave in future in a way quite different from what it would have done if we had not asked it what it was going to do. I hope I make myself clear!

This means, as you will realise, that Determinism in the sense of a one-to-one relationship between cause and effect, has no place in the physical world. Metaphysicians may talk about it if they like, and science cannot deny its possible existence, but the nature of the physical world is such that it can never establish such an idea.

Such revolutions in thought are the stuff of which science is made. Science is sometimes said to be a collection of facts. In a sense this is true, but the relationship of facts to science is like the relationship of a painter's palette of colours to his picture—there is more to a Rembrandt than flake-white and yellow ochre. The greatest scientists are those who present us with new ways of thinking.

My next category is that of the Discoverers. Röntgen's discovery of x-rays, Becquerel's discovery of radioactivity, or as an earlier instance Oersted's discovery of the effect of a current on a compass, are examples. Such discoveries are immensely important events in the history of science, because they open up new worlds. There is a curious feature about most of them, however. The men who make them are justly famous but they seldom go on to further scientific achievements. They are like the novae in the heavens, stars which burst into extreme brilliance for a few days or weeks and then dwindle into ordinary stars. This is not to belittle their discoveries. As well as being helped by the fortunate chance which came their way when they were looking for something else, they had the wit to realise the immense importance of the strange effect they noticed.

Next, there are the designers who have produced some new form of apparatus which has opened up quite a new range of scientific research. An outstanding example is C. T. R. Wilson's development of the Cloud Chamber which has been the vital tool in the study of the ultimate particles of matter. It can tell us the history of a single one of these minute particles, which leaves a trail in the cloud chamber like that left in the upper air by an aeroplane under certain meteorological conditions. Another example is Lawrence's cyclotron for accelerating particles to high energies and studying their reactions. The cyclotron is the parent of all the 'atom smashing' machines. Such machines, costing perhaps a thousand million pounds and covering a square mile, are able to produce in a space the size of a pin's head conditions which resemble those in the interior of a star. The energies of the reactions are astronomically great compared with those of the gentle chemical reactions of coal or dynamite. Like Prometheus, we have stolen this star-fire from the heavens and now we are wondering if the gods will destroy us to punish us for our boldness.

Finally there is a class, containing some of the most famous names, which I can only describe as 'The Hunters'. You will know how a smart dog which we are taking for a walk will look into every bush, smell every hole, examine behind every log in the hope of finding something exciting. Faraday was a hunter; one can see from his notebooks how he explored every possible variation of conditions in the search for some new scientific relationship, guided of course by a wonderful intuition as to what would be a profitable hunting ground. A famous German scientist once said of him "Er riecht die Wahrheit", he smells the truth. Rutherford, in the field of radioactivity where he reigned, was also a hunter though he went about it in a far more boisterous way than Faraday. "There's a big man with a gun, and he's having lots of fun", to quote a well-known pop song, reminds us of Rutherford rather than Faraday.

I next come to another classification which applies to all these types. Scientists are rather sharply divided into heads of teams and lone workers. The lone worker is embarrassed by disciples, and he continues to make his own experiments and draw his own conclusions from them. Names that occur to one are C. T. R. Wilson, Aston who established the isotopes, Lord Rayleigh who touched on every aspect of classical physics and adorned everything he touched, and to a large extent G. I. Taylor. Such men tend to maintain their originality all their lives. There is a story of G. I. Taylor attending a meeting in London during the war, to which he was called as a consultant because our ships of war appeared to be breaking up disconcertingly readily when attacked by a mine. G. I. Taylor is said to have worked out the cause of the constructional weakness on the back of an envelope returning from Liverpool Street to Cambridge. It is one of those stories which, if it is not true, ought to be true because it is so typical of the man.

In contrast the leader of a team spreads his influence over a number of disciples, but he can easily lose his direct touch with nature. He inevitably has cares of administration and direction, and must largely abandon direct experimentation. His pupils may miss some clue, the importance of which he would have realised. It has seemed to me that the maximum number of other brains with which the leader can be in direct contact is about five. If the 'school' is larger, each of these may have another five under him, making twenty-five in all. Schools of 125 are not uncommon, but I have never heard of the work of one leader involving 625.

What makes a scientist? What qualities have the great in common? This is a difficult question to answer and the first quality which comes to my mind may seem a surprising one.

It is enthusiasm, which is very necessary. Research is extraordinarily inefficient. It was a saying of my father's that if one looked back over a year's research, one could see that it could all have been done in a week. This is of course not always true, since a long time must often be spent in a series of measurements. He was referring, however, to all the explored alleys which had blind ends, to all the upturned stones which had nothing beneath them. Faraday was once asked how to do research and his reply was "Start it, carry on with it, and finish it". The tempo of research is slow; the unit of time is five years. Thinking back on the young men I have had in my group who have had a brilliant career, I see in them all a sort of bulldog spirit. If you hang on to a problem long enough, it seems to get exhausted and yield up its secret—provided of course that some-one else does not get there before you. Enthusiasm and optimism are vital factors in keeping up the morale of a research team.

I find it hard to name the next essential quality. It is partly described as being 'The Open Mind', a readiness to scrap previous ideas and start on quite new lines. Another ingredient is imagination, and originality comes into it. When some genius makes the break-through, the answer seems so obvious that one could kick oneself for not having spotted it. What stopped one doing so? It is something to do with its being so hard to take a fresh look. I notice that when I have settled down to the after-dinner crossword, and am absolutely stuck trying to interpret a clue, if I drop off into a short nap as one is apt to do on such occasions, I see the answer at once when I wake up. I do not think this is because my subconscious mind has been at work, I believe it is because I have forgotten the ways I was trying to solve it before. It is for this reason, perhaps, that most great scientists have produced their major contribution while they are young and their minds are fresh. Scientists are often pictured in the popular press as grey-beards looking down microscopes. This is the reverse of truth; such people as Rutherford, Bohr, and Einstein were in their twenties when they produced the work which made them famous. It is difficult for them in later life to break away from the line they started on when young, scrapping its capital and experience and starting afresh. I remember when my wife and I went to Sweden in early days and were entertained by the famous Arrhenius, my wife asked a Swedish friend what Arrhenius had done. He replied "When he was a young man he made a very famous theory; since then he has gone round the world accepting honorary degrees". It is interesting, too, to note the effect of war work. Many scientists, switched off their habitual lines by having to do something quite different for the war effort, had a kind of second flowering and were brilliant again in quite a new way. It is a fascinating thought that it would probably contribute greatly to our scientific potential if we could take all our scientists at the age of thirty-five and make them drink the waters of Lethe, so that they forgot all they had studied in the past and started again.

You may have remarked that in listing the qualities for greatness I have said nothing about 'cleverness' in the sense of the mental ability which, for instance, leads to success in examinations. It is hard to assess its importance, and it is certainly not an essential. Rutherford discovered the nucleus of the atom by noting that $\alpha$ rays were turned back on their tracks. Yet I remember the late Professor Robinson, who was a research student in Rutherford's laboratory at the time, telling me that he and Charles Darwin had to struggle for a month to explain to Rutherford the equation of the orbit of one body repelled by another, an equation which a clever schoolboy could solve. In Bohr's epoch-making first papers, the algebra is of the simplest kind. Faraday had no mathematical training whatever, and he never used '$x$' and '$y$', yet he was probably the greatest scientist since Newton. One might think that lack of mathematical ability was compensated for by manipulative skill but again we draw a blank. J. J. Thomson had no great manipulative skill, and I have heard that Rutherford's students prayed he would not come near their apparatus because the results could be so disastrous. The greatness of these men is due to some quality which transcends cleverness.

There was a tradition when I was a student at Cambridge that one must excel in mathematics in order to do physics. I think this was partly because the tradition of Newton was still so strong. The Mathematical Tripos drew largely on the natural sciences for its exercises, and if the laws of science were not convenient for mathematical treatment, they were suitably modified. In the Tripos they took on a form which bore the same relation to nature that a gymnastic climbing frame does to a mountain. The mathematical exercises on which we spent our time and energy have nearly all disappeared from physics courses nowadays.

If it is hard to define the qualities which lead to greatness, it is easy to say what stops research. It is a full engagement book. The muse of science is capricious in her visits and we can never count on her breathing inspiration on us, but we can be quite sure that she will flee from the busy man. When one is trying to work out some knotty problem a process goes on in one's head like the Titans piling Pelion on Olympus and Ossa on Pelion in their attempt to scale the heavens. The structure tumbles down each time it is disturbed and has to be started again. There is a story about Newton that he was once discovered boiling his watch with the egg in his waistcoat pocket. True or not, he would not have been Newton if he had not been capable of such feats of complete abstraction. Scientists, when they feel that possibly some light may be going to dawn, are apt to reply by grunts—scientists wives have a dull life at such times. It is regrettable that when a man has achieved fame, there seems to be a conspiracy to see that he does no more by demanding that he should become a man of affairs.

Curiosity-prompted research, as Professor Blackett has termed it, has great rewards to offer. Part of the thrill comes, I think, from the fact that one is judged, not by one's fellow men, but by nature herself. When some fragment of truth has been discovered,

the answer seems so simple and natural and aesthetically satisfying that it almost always carries conviction. In any case it soon
becomes clear whether one is right or wrong from the way the
answer fits into the general pattern of increasing knowledge.
I have now reached an age when the days of original research are
long past, but recently a researcher consulted me about his
work and asked for suggestions. In mulling over his results I
experienced once more that wonderful feeling that one grudged
having to break away in the evening and could hardly wait till
next morning to go on with the hunt. One feels that one is an eye,
allowed to see something universal in which man is merely an
insignificant incident. The students, I think, catch something of
this vision. University unrest is not a phenomenon associated
with the science side. I was very interested recently when a
young researcher said to me how extraordinary it was that he was
actually paid to do something which he enjoyed so much. Here,
perhaps, a point might be made—in return for his privileges I
think a researcher ought to put all the energy he can into studying
the art of good teaching, and passing on his expertise to the next
generation. A due amount of teaching is good for a researcher
and does not detract from his research. The association of teaching with research in our universities is, I am sure, right.

In conclusion, I would like to deal with two points. The first
concerns the relation of fundamental science to industry. The
industrialists often say that fundamental research is attracting
too many of the best men, stressing quite rightly that the life of
the country depends upon the high technical level of our indus-
tries. As I have heard it put, the worst brain drain in this country
is to the universities. I think the answer, however, is not to blame
the universities for making pure science too attractive; it is to
increase the attractiveness of a scientific career in industry. Is
there not perhaps still too great a gap between management on
the one hand and research and development on the other? A
director must know enough about science to know what kind of
questions science can answer. If this is not so the scientist cannot
be inspired to give of his best.

My second point concerns the relation between scientists and
the community, the place of scientists in society. They are sometimes accused of living in ivory towers, and of shirking the

responsibility for the possibly disastrous consequences of the discoveries they make. They indeed have a responsibility, not only for suggesting "How to do it" but also for foreseeing as well as they can the dangers of rash exploitation of man's great powers. I think it can be fairly claimed that they do feel the latter responsibility, and are amongst the first to canvass against thoughtless elimination of wild life, careless cultivation leading to erosion, irrigation leading to ruining of the soil, poisoning of our streets by the traffic and of our food by additives, and social habits which lead to diseases. It is unfair, however, to reproach them for discovering knowledge about nature which could be turned to bad ends as well as to good ends. Though the scientist must be ready to explain what science can do, the choice of what shall be done is surely a moral responsibility which we all share equally.

# Bragg's Second Law

## JOHN M. THOMAS, FRS

The uniqueness of Bragg's law of diffraction (see pages 15 and 150-156) is so widely acknowledged that any suggestion that there exists a second law bearing the same eponym inevitably stimulates curiosity. During the final stages of the editing of this book, an old friend, Jack Dunitz, whose mythopoetical insights into the folklore of crystallography adds an extra vitality to his conversation, phoned me to ask if I was aware of Bragg's Second Law. On confessing my ignorance, I was promptly regaled with an outline of incidents that occurred in the USA in 1933 and in the UK in 1934. Full details of the story were published by the prime witness of the enunciation of the 'Second Law', the late E.W. Hughes (EWH)[1], in a book entitled *Patterson and Pattersons* (edited by Jenny P. Glusker, Betty K. Patterson and Miriam Rossi) and published by the International Union of Crystallography and Oxford University Press in 1987[2].

Each year, the Department of Chemistry, Cornell University, Ithaca, New York, invites a world famous scientist to present the so–called George Fisher Baker Lectures. The aim of this extended series is to highlight important advances in aspects of science of vital interest to chemists. The invites speaker takes up residence as Visiting Professor for a semester or more in the Baker Laboratory of the University, and is normally provided with a dynamic young assistant from the research or junior teaching staff of the Department.

In the late winter of 1933, WLB was the Baker Lecturer and EWH his assistant. One weekend WLB went to visit A.L. Patterson at the Massachusetts Institute of Technology, and there he learned, prior to publication, about the Patterson method[3,4]. EWH takes up the story.

"He arrived back at Ithaca early on a very bad winter's day; it had sleeted all night, then frozen and snowed slightly and the streets were sheets of ice. He arrived at the laboratory safely by taxi and asked if I could deliver him to a local appointment. My Model A Ford had sat out all night in a nearby parking lot and would not start. I suggested that he get in and steer while I pushed it down a nearby hill. He objected that he was not familiar with American cars and insisted that I operate it while he pushed. Fortunately it started and we set off south on East Avenue. The University B & G trucks had spread ashes on the east side of our road but not yet on our side."

"He then started enthusiastically to tell me about the Patterson method, which he pronounced to be the most important advance since his father, Sir William Bragg, had introduced the use of the Fourier series. He used the fingers of one hand to represent atomic position vectors and those of the other hand to represent their differences, and I soon forgot all about the ice. Until suddenly, approaching Central Avenue, I became aware of a red traffic light and a heavy truck rushing west on Central to make his green light. Ashes had been spread on both sides of Central. We skidded about badly but by pure good luck lurched to the left onto the ashes at the last instant and scrunched to a halt, well into the intersection. The truck managed to swerve and miss us by about a foot. Our light turned green and I continued, very cautiously. Through all this Bragg continued to wave his hands and lecture on Patterson's vectors, but to a deaf audience! When he had finished there was a brief pause and he suddenly said, 'I say! we skidded a bit back there, didn't we?' Later, in the security or his office I got a repeat of the Lecture."

"The following year I was in England with proofs for the figures in his Baker monograph. Once, when we were driving (in his car) to his office we passed the scene of a recent bad road accident, which reminded me of what could have happened in Ithaca. I asked him if he remembered the incident and when he said that indeed he did, I remarked upon how impressed I had been by his calm nonchalance in the face of very real danger. He then stated what I have come to call *Bragg's Second Law*."

"'When travelling in a foreign country I make it a point of personal honour not to show fear, anger, or mirth, or surprise at any happening that does not seem to be unusual to the natives.'"

"'And', he added, 'you didn't seem to be frightened so I was jolly well determined not to be frightened either.'"

EWH ended his personal reminiscence of WLB by saying that he considered this "Law" to be excellent advice and "...have tried to follow it, but one thing is clear; on that winter morning in Ithaca he was not very good at estimating the reaction of the native".

## Notes

1 E.W. Hughes received his research training at the Baker Laboratory, Cornell University. Apart from assisting WLB in preparing for publication the *Atomic Structure of Minerals* (Ithaca, 1937), he also assisted another Baker Lectures, Linus Pauling, in the production for press of *The Nature of the Chemical Bond* (Ithaca, 1939). He left Cornell in the late 1930s to become Research Fellow in Chemistry at the California Institute of Technology, where he spent the rest of his working life. He passed away on December 25th, 1987, aged 83. His crystallographic achievements were considerable. He was the first to introduce, in 1941, the use of the 'least squares' fitting of crystallographic data. In 1946 he and his graduate student W.N. Lipscomb, who later won the Nobel Prize, further pursued the method of least squares to crystal structure refinement.

2 This book constitutes the proceedings of a symposium held at the Institute of Cancer Research, the Fox Chase Cancer Center, Philadelphia, USA, November, 1984.

3 The X-ray methods used by WLB to solve the structure of rock salt and diamond, and by Bernal and Kathleen Lonsdale to solve graphite and hexamethylbenzene respectively, involved trial and error. A major step forward in the feasibility of determining crystal structures by X–ray methods was provided by A.L. Patterson (see page 34 of Sir David's "Memoir" in this book[4].)

4 In essence, Patterson's contribution was to show that from the intensities of the various diffractions it is possible to construct a 'vector map' that gives the distances between pairs of atoms. We may describe a 'vector map', following Judson[5], using the analogy of a party. Everyone has their shoes nailed to the floor and everyone wants to meet everyone else! The vectors are the directions each person has to turn to shake the hand of another guest and how far that person has to extend his or her arms. The strength of the handshake is analogous to the atomic numbers of the two atoms at the end of the guests at the party. It is as if the only information one possesses about the party is the distance and angle of the handshake of each person when he or she met everyone else. Equipped with this complicated knowledge, it should then be possible to find where everyone stood in the room relative to each other.

5 Judson, H.F. 1979. *The Eighth Day of Creation: Makers of the Revolution in Biology*. Simon and Schuster, New York.

# Acknowledgements

We are most grateful to the following publishers for permission to use extracts from Sir Lawrence Bragg's publications:

Cambridge Philosophical Society
IOP Publishing Ltd
Macmillan Journals Ltd
New York Academy of Sciences
Punch Publications Ltd
Taylor and Francis Ltd, London
The Royal Society
Times Newspapers Ltd
Verlag von Wilhelm Engelmann
Weidenfeld and Nicolson